THE POWERS
OF THE HOLY

DAVID AERS *and*
LYNN STALEY

The Powers
of the Holy

RELIGION, POLITICS,
AND
GENDER IN LATE MEDIEVAL
ENGLISH CULTURE

The Pennsylvania State University Press
University Park, Pennsylvania

Library of Congress Cataloging-in-Publication Data

Aers, David.
    The Powers of the Holy : religion, politics, and gender in late
medieval English culture / David Aers and Lynn Staley.
        p.   cm.
    Includes bibliographical references and index.
    ISBN 0-271-01541-1 (cloth : alk. paper)
    ISBN 0-271-01542-X (pbk. : alk. paper)
    1. England—Church history—1066–1485. 2. English literature
—Middle English, 1100–1500—History and criticism. 3. England
—Religious life and customs. 4. England—Intellectual
life—1066–1485. I. Staley, Lynn, 1947– . II. Title.
BR750.A35   1996
274.2′05—dc20   95-25309
                                                         CIP

It is the policy of The Pennsylvania State University Press to use acid-free
paper for the first printing of all clothbound books. Publications on uncoated
stock satisfy the minimum requirements of American National Standard for
Information Sciences—Permanence of Paper for Printed Library Materials,
ANSI Z39.48-1992.

Contents

Introduction

DAVID AERS AND LYNN STALEY

> Could one *address oneself in general* if already some ghost did
> not come back? If he loves justice at least, the "scholar" of the
> future, the "intellectual" of tomorrow should learn it and from
> the ghost. He should learn to live by learning not how to make
> conversation with the ghost but how to talk with him, with
> her, how to let them speak or how to give them back speech,
> even if it is in oneself, in the other, in the other in oneself.
> —Jacques Derrida, *Specters of Marx*

This book explores certain configurations of holiness, especially representations of Christ's humanity, and certain configurations of gender, especially
as they are used in some of Chaucer's explorations of contemporary political conflicts. It addresses some of the ways in which different groups and
individuals drew upon the resources of Christian traditions (plural), selected, revised, reinvented, forgot and remembered; sometimes, for some
people, this proved to be a dangerous memory. We describe the deployment
of powerful religious symbols, narratives and vocabularies even as we analyze just what the selections and deployments, the forgetting and remember-
ing meant within the particular networks of social relations where they
were made and received. In this society words were certainly deeds.[1] This
was harrowingly illustrated in July 1381: in a Cambridge pub, or tavern,
John Shirle had said that "the stewards of the lord the king as well as the
justices and many other officers and ministers of the king were more deserv-
ing to be drawn and hanged and to suffer other lawful pains and torments

---

1. This allusion is to a famous paragraph in Wittgenstein's *Philosophical Investigations*,
546; see Wittgenstein (1958), 146.

than John Balle." Indeed, Shirle had declared that Ball "had been condemned to death falsely, unjustly and for envy by the said ministers with
the king's assent, because he was a true and worthy man, prophesying
things useful to the commons of the kingdom and telling of wrongs and
oppressions done to the people by the king and the aforesaid ministers."[2]
John Shirle's sentiments were shared by thousands of English women and
men who had put words into memorable deeds in June 1381, and Hugh
de la Zouche and his fellow justices had no hesitation in immediately killing
this Nottinghamshire laborer, hanging him into silence, meeting dissident
word with death-dealing act enwrapped in the juridical language of the
society's legal apparatus in which it survived in the medieval ruling
classes' archive.

Harrowing as this is, we should not only see it for another example of
one of Walter Benjamin's most cited "theses on the philosophy of history":
"cultural treasures," he writes, "owe their existence not only to the efforts
of the great minds and talents who have created them, but also to the
anonymous toil of their contemporaries. There is no document of civiliza-
tion which is not at the same time a document of barbarism."[3] We should
certainly see it as that, a haunting reminder of the realities of dominion
and subjection, a reminder that disciplines whose major focus of attention
tends to be textuality and theatricality are time and again in danger of
occluding. But we should also see it as an example of the way that "any
act of communication always constitutes the taking up of some determinate
position in relation to some pre-existing conversation or argument." From
which, as Quentin Skinner continues, it follows that "if we wish to understand what has been said, we shall have to be able to identify what exact
position has been taken up."[4] Perhaps Shirle's words in the Bridge Street
tavern in summer 1381 are an unusually explicit example of Skinner's
arguments, but they are equally relevant to far more complicated and
oblique utterances—like Chaucer's, or perhaps more surprisingly given the
frameworks within which she is habitually celebrated, Julian of Norwich.
Those exploring the language and images of a sanctity so often apparently
"conventional" and embedded in "tradition" may need constantly to recollect Skinner's observation that "even if we find that a given philosopher is
merely reaffirming an established line of argument, we still need to be able

---

2. Translated from Public Records Office documents in Dobson (1986), xxviii–ix; quoted
in full in Aers (1988a), 1–2, and discussed in Aers (1996); also discussed in Hanna (1992).
3. See Benjamin (1969), 255–66.
4. Skinner (1988), 274–75; see esp. 29–67 and 231–41.

to grasp what he or she was doing in reaffirming it if we wish to understand the argument itself."[5] Or if we wish to understand the image, or meditation or poem, . . . Skinner's comment has broad ramifications.

The symbols of Christian sanctity held immense power in the culture we study even as they were themselves bound up with all the sources of social power: gender, class, status, military, legal, literary—the political in its broadest sense. They were essential components of the paradigms through which human beings formed their specific identities and lived out their specific lives. Through them people sought to understand and shape the massive dislocations, shifts, possibilities, and conflicts in the half-century following the great plague. These complex shifts, together with the different opportunities, conflicts, and anxieties they entailed, had implications for the relations between women and men, in all dimensions, those around the divisions of work, those around the divisions of sexuality, and those around the construing of gendered identities.[6] This time included the great schism in the church, included sharpened struggles between agriculturalists of all kinds and the taxing, law-forming, rent-extracting classes, included struggles between magnates and crown (culminating in the deposition and murder of the anointed king, a usurpation only made secure by the uncompromising support and sacralization given by Archbishop Arundel). It also witnessed the first challenge the church in England had received to its hegemonic claims, its claims to be the one true ark outside of which there could be no salvation. In fact people in these years were living through, making, and resisting, major disruptions in the political orders and in the credibility of received legitimations of authority. As Sarah Beckwith has recently noted in her outstanding study of Christ's body, identity, and culture in late medieval writings, symbols "give body to divergent notions, claims and practices," encouraging "the creative attribution of multiple meanings to themselves" as they become the "subject of political and social contestation."[7] The religious language of the period was both powerful and extraordinarily flexible, because of its enmeshment in the social and political networks of conflicting communities and interests, which were encountering a very specific, unprecedented, and thoroughly contingent set of problems. It comprised a rich resource for *thinking*, for

---

5. Skinner (1988), 283.

6. For recent work on these issues, see esp. Howell (1986 and 1988) and Goldberg (1992); for Margery Kempe in some of these contexts, see Aers (1988a), chap. 2 and Staley (1994).

7. Beckwith (1993), 3–4.

exploring, for addressing a wide range of seemingly intractable conflicts. These resources could certainly be used in most unsubtle and aggressively polemical ways (whether in defense of the established blocs of power or against their various elements); but they could also be used with great complexity, with self-reflexive criticism and with the kind of nuances that will be noticed only by those who seek to discover the relation of the writing or action in question to the particular range of discourses and practices it assumes. Of course, any complex text will often be designed to do a wide range of things, and we appreciate that many of these will be beyond our abilities to register. On this matter our views are close to Quentin Skinner's:

> I have always insisted that . . . we inevitably approach the past in the light of contemporary paradigms and presuppositions, the influence of which may easily serve to mislead us at every turn. I have also conceded that the enterprise of recovering the kinds of intentions in which I am interested requires a level of historical awareness and sheer erudition that few of us can aspire to reach. I have further conceded that, even when we feel confident about our ascriptions of intentionality, such ascriptions are of course nothing more than inferences from the best evidence available to us, and as such are defeasible at any time. My precepts, in short, are only claims about how best to proceed; they are not claims about how to guarantee success.[8]

Defeasible as our analyses may be, undoubtedly replete with limitations as our erudition in the face of our tasks and favored methodologies undoubtedly is, the period we consider is one in which the terms, images, rituals, and ideas of holiness became the object of unprecedently *public* and *vernacular* contestation in England. This is definitely not only a matter of a struggle between orthodox writers and heterodox or heretical ones. What we encounter is far more complicated, as will emerge in our studies of three writers who could not, at the time they wrote, be classified as "heretical" or "heterodox."

To put the matter as succinctly as possible, we are engaged with a period in which we can follow the making, the (re)invention of "orthodoxy" and "orthopraxis" in dialogue with a range of challenging voices—and events.

---

8. Skinner (1988), 281.

What was to *become* the "traditional religion" of fifteenth- and early sixteenth-century orthodoxy was currently in the process of being formed but was not (not yet) the formation that emerged around and after the general publication of Arundel's Constitutions in 1409.[9] Nor was it yet that which emerged from the Leicester parliament of 1414, a parliament that gave the secular power the kind of control over Christianity deployed more famously by Henry VIII. Let us, for a moment, recall item 7 of that 1414 parliament, against the "secte de heresie appelle Lollardrie." The decision is that chancellor, treasurer, justices, justices of the peace, sheriffs, mayor, bailiffs of cities and towns and all other officers having governance of the people must take an oath on accepting office "to put their whole power and diligence to put out and do to be put out, cease and destroy all manner of heresies and errors, commonly called Lollardries." Perhaps most remarkably of all, justices of the king's bench, justices of the peace and justices of assize were to have full power ("pleine poair") to inquire into all those who hold any errors or heresies, such as Lollards and all who sustain them by any means, including writings, sermons, schools, conventicles, congregations, and confederacies. Justices of the peace are to issue a *capias* and the sheriff is bound to arrest the person suspected of error. He or she is then to be handed to ecclesiastical judges within ten days.[10] As Jeremy Catto noted in his study of religious change under Henry V, the king now maintained "that the service of religion was a matter for his government," a position totally supported by the leaders of the church. The hierarchy, Catto shows, silenced "the anxious and confused debates which had racked the previous generation . . . and in their place we can see a confident, coherent religious leadership emerging, consistent in the forms of public cult it wished to impose, and systematic in its attempt to control opinion," a control focussed on the "suppression of the Lollards." Crown and church leaders produced "the integration of religious and secular authority" such that religious ritual was made "a division of propaganda" in the service of royal policy, royal warmongering, and the royal sacralization of crown power. Catto illustrates how Henry V intervened directly in making forms of holiness and worship especially well suited to these projects.[11]

---

9. For a massive work that occludes these processes of tradition-forming and their politics in the late fourteenth and fifteenth centuries, see Duffy (1992); for reflections on this peculiarly dehistoricized and idealized history, see Aers (1994c). On the fifteenth century and the counter-reformation initiated by Arundel we have learned much from Watson (1995).

10. *Statutes of the Realm* (1816), 181–83.

11. Catto (1985b), 106–11, quotations from 98 and 106–7; see also Beckwith (1993), 72–77; Powell (1989), chap. 6; Patterson (1993a).

It is one of the ironies of history that in embracing royal power to strengthen the rule of the church of Rome in England the ecclesiastical leadership was forging the spades and shovels with which their royal successors and supporting clerics would dig the grave of that church in England during the next century.

But the constitution and crystallization of "orthodoxy" and "tradition" under Henry V lay in the future and will not skew our responses to the last forty years of the fourteenth century. For what we see then is the processes, the doubts, the conflicts, the arguments—the often contradictory and shifting, unstable groupings in which "orthodoxy" and "tradition" was being put in question, forced to revise, to remake itself.[12] However different their forms of writing, their religious and political visions, Langland, Chaucer, and Julian of Norwich were intensely aware of many interlocking, clashing lines of force that had dislocated received models of authority, of holiness, and of order in the diverse communities of late medieval England. These writers explored some of the clashes and dislocations, imagined new possibilities (devotional, doctrinal, political), sometimes thoroughly bleak ones, sometimes utopian, while showing how the configuration "orthodoxy" and "tradition," remained, for them, an open question. Of course, what is a moment of creative possibility and enhanced expectation for some social groups and individuals is a moment of fear and wrath for others, the openness of the questions we have outlined an anarchic threat to their customary authority and privilege. Such a stance is well represented by Gower's response in *Vox Clamantis* to the struggles of wage laborers to raise their standards of living above the subsistence level (and less) of the pre-plague century, or by Walsingham's similar response to the political and economic action of agriculturalists and townspeople in Bury Saint Edmunds or Saint Albans.[13] And similarly, one could say that for the later Wyclif, in his massive polemics against the Roman church, while the configurations that might emerge could not be known (although the worst had to be expected) not too many questions seemed to have remained open. We, however, have not chosen to write a survey; we have not sought to "cover" the period (whatever "cover" could mean). Our aim has been, as we outlined in the opening paragraph of this introduction, to investigate some configurations of holiness, devotion, gender, and politics in the pe-

---

12. Brian Stock has some extremely pertinent remarks on such modernizations of tradition in Stock (1990), chap. 8.

13. Gower, *Vox Clamantis,* book 5.10 (see book 1, passim) in Gower (1962); Walsingham in Dobson (1970), 269–77, 244–48, 256–61.

riod, and in relation to issues and texts that have fascinated us. In doing so we have been enabled by some outstanding recent work on forms of medieval Christianity, particularly to the studies of Wyclif and Lollardy by Margaret Aston and Anne Hudson, work on the eucharist and Christ's body by Miri Rubin and Sarah Beckwith, and the magnificent editorial work on Lollard texts by Anne Hudson and Pamela Gradon. We have also been greatly stimulated by the books of Caroline Bynum and her attention to issues of gender in many kinds of religious texts and devotional practices. We hope that our own book illuminates aspects of Christianity and politics in the period, offers some worthwhile readings of the writing on which we have concentrated and pursues critical practices that may facilitate further investigation of other late medieval religious writings.

At this point it might seem appropriate to offer a definition of the term *power,* one given prominence in our title and in many areas of the book. We have decided against any such move here. We are analyzing some extremely diverse relations of power and resistances to power, of domination, subordination and rebellion in thoroughly different, if related, domains of life; thus, in our book the term *power* will develop a range of inflections as we respond to different materials and questions. Connections, contrasts, and articulations of the polysemous aspects of power emerge in an accumulative manner, not appropriately dealt with by formal definition. We offer a brief example of how this inductive procedure might evolve. When the first part of the book engages with figurations of Christ's body, the need is for a model of power that will enable us to follow the processes that are congealed and occluded in certain commonplace reifications (both medieval and modern). The reifications at issue have constrained thought; an appropriate model of power will enable us to ask questions about who was doing what to Christ's body, and with what effects, linking these questions with ones concerning gender and the putative "empowerment" of women in relation to the body of Christ on the cross. Not surprisingly, the turn here is to the genealogical historian who studied some of the ways in which the body is "involved in a political field":

> power relations have an immediate hold upon it; they invest it, mark it, train it, torture it, force it to carry out tasks, to perform ceremonies to emit signs. This political investment of the body is bound up in accordance with complex reciprocal relations, with its economic use; it is largely as a force of production that the body is invested with relations of power and domination; but, on the other hand, its

constitution as labour power is possible only if it is caught up in a system of subjection.[14]

Foucault's *Discipline and Punish (Surveiller et punir: Naissance de la prison)* concentrates on changes in regimes of discipline, punishment, education, exploitation of the laboring body and the institutions of surveillance in the eighteenth and nineteenth centuries, particularly in France. Yet insights such as those quoted above have proved invaluable in parts of our work on an earlier period, one strand in our own conceptualization of power, its exercise and effects. However, we certainly do not describe our overall model as Foucaultian (nor as anti-Foucaultian). First of all there is obviously not one Foucaultian model of power, any more than there is just one relationship between Foucault and Marxist traditions. With Foucault's earlier structuralist-functionalist work our approaches have no affinities, while we find no good evidence for, and in fact reject, components of his later discussions of power in the first volume of his *History of Sexuality.* Examples of what we see no good reason to accept in that work are the following: claims that power always comes from below (an assertion that remains very vague in this text; there is actually one sense it could be given that would be congruent with either Marxist or Freudian traditions, precisely the targets of Foucault's criticism here; claims that there is no overall opposition between dominant classes and subordinate ones (we can make absolutely no sense of 1381 and the history of taxation, labor legislation and working people's varied resistances in such terms, nor can we believe that people who talk as Foucault does here have reflected carefully on cases like John Shirle's—a man hung by the justices of the ruling classes in July 1381); claims that power relations are intentional but without subjective agents (a position congruent with both functionalist Marxism and the earlier Foucault, of course); and universalizing claims that the pluralities of resistance to power are *never* other than one of the strategies of that power.[15] As our references to class, the English rising of 1381 and the case of John Shirle indicate, we have seen no reason to cultivate a paradigm that makes it implausible to talk about the flow of power in close relation to the structures of classes and the divisions of labor, resources, and military forces in a specific social formation. On the contrary, however complex the twists and turns of power, we cultivate models that allow us to identify exploita-

---

14. Foucault (1979), 25–26; see 24–30 passim.
15. Foucault (1981), 92–102; here drawing on 94–96.

tion, to identify those who had the power to expropriate the resources of others' bodies and labors, the power to tax, to make laws, to hold courts, to hang people, to organize and make war, the power to command what should be spoken from the country's pulpits, the power to determine who should be classified as a heretic and the power to make that determination have consequences—on human bodies and in actual communities. We have also needed terms that allow us to address the culture's constitutions of gender, the sources of a massive range of power, controls, and exploitations but ones that were of little concern in Foucault's work. So while we have drawn on certain strands of this work, our models of power necessarily include concepts whose sources are elsewhere. For example, Judith Butler's studies provided great help in showing how concepts of reification in Marx and Lukács could be fruitfully developed in areas that were relevant to the present book. At the same time she helped clarify the responses to Caroline Bynum's works that are articulated in Chapter 1.[16] As *The Powers of the Holy* moves on, from Langland to Wyclif and Wycliffites, to Julian of Norwich and Chaucer, the conceptualizations of power are adapted to the subjects being explored even as they simultaneously enable these explorations. In the end, so we think, this way of proceeding offers a richly articulated model of powers and resistances to powers, one in excess of any formal definition, one that would be misrepresented by any such definition. It is eclectic, but necessarily so, an eclecticism whose composition has been accompanied by sustained theoretical reflections and informed by choices that have been self-consciously ethical and political.

One final word about our methods of writing this book. Although most of the chapters can be read independently of one another, they have been written and organized so that they contribute to an overall account of relations between devotion and politics in the period, offering modes of analysis congruent to the extraordinary heterogeneity of Christianity's resources, conflicts, and potentials in the moments on which we have concentrated. We wrote this book out of numerous discussions and commentaries on emerging work, in a long conversation from which we have both learned a great deal, perhaps especially in and through our differences, differences we have enjoyed interrogating and made no attempt to disguise when they remained after such explorations.

---

16. Butler (1990); the uses made of this work have been helped by some clarifications in Butler (1993).

Our debts are manifold and no list of acknowledgments can begin to convey our recognition of those who have made this book possible, or our gratitude. In our footnotes we have, of course, recorded the works on which we are conscious of drawing. Beyond that, however, David Aers thanks those who have discussed with him ideas and materials that have been relevant to writing the following chapters. Among these, especially, he thanks Sarah Beckwith and Derek Pearsall (both for help extending over many years), Anne Hudson, Allen Frantzen, Lee Patterson, Karma Lochrie, Nicholas Watson, and the person who is most certainly one of the spirits with whom much of this work has been a communing, a teacher, brilliant scholar, and friend whose influence on his work has been immeasurable: Elizabeth Salter. He also thanks Allen Frantzen for an invitation to discuss aspects of this work at a conference held at Loyola University in the spring of 1994. And he thanks the graduate students at Duke University who have been such marvelous, exuberant participants in discussions of medieval literature, religion, and politics. Finally, however bizarre in this context, he would like to thank his wife Christine Derham for the way she combines critical perspectives on the forms of life intrinsic to academic work with quite extraordinary generosity, kindness, and support.

Lynn Staley thanks Colgate University for its ongoing support of her research and its students for their willingness to explore new territory with her. Thanks also go to C. David Benson, to the Program Committee of the Medieval Feminist Newsletter, to Glending Olson, to Daniel Donoghue, and to David Aers, for offering chances to read papers on both Julian of Norwich and Chaucer at conferences sponsored by the International Congress on Medieval Studies, the Modern Language Association, the Harvard Medieval Doctoral Conference, and the New Chaucer Society. Earlier versions of portions of Chapter 5 were published as two separate essays in *Studies in Philology*. Sarah Beckwith offered a remarkable reading of Chapter 5 at a crucial stage. Gordon Kipling was kind enough to share his work on pageantry, and H. Ansgar Kelly supplied points of information about late medieval liturgical practices. Lynn Staley also expresses her gratitude for the generous flood of letters and essays from Michael Wilks and Nicholas Watson that provided important information and new perspectives. Both Theresa Coletti and Derek Pearsall provided us with readers' reports of extraordinary lucidity; their sensitivity to our arguments, their diligence, and their intelligent responses are truly exemplary. Lynn Staley also expresses special thanks to Derek Pearsall, who over the years has provided her with friendly, sharp, and helpful readings, with conversation about matters medieval, and, in the truest sense, with a sense of academic fellowship. Finally we mark our great debt to Philip Winsor, senior editor of Penn State Press, whose command of his resources and whose far-reaching vision distinguish him among his peers. We thank him for his early interest in this book and for his commitment to seeing it through with such grace, speed, and good humor as only he can summon.

At last, and truly last, this book constitutes an extended conversation between two scholars of frequently different habits of thought. As young scholars we began in very different places, and we do not always finish (though we hope we are not finished) in the same place. We have traded letters and arguments, points of interest and moments of illumination in letters and phone calls since January 1993. Although our work is individual, it is so only in the most formalistic sense; it is doubtful that either of us would have written alone what we have written together. This conversation is a testament to how much we scholars need to speak openly with one another; it has brought home the true value of creating scholarly communities, held together by something we can only follow Cicero in calling a friendship of common goals. We shall remain thankful for the opportunity to help write this book.

PART
I

The Humanity of Christ: Reflections on Orthodox Late Medieval Representations

DAVID AERS

He went round the whole of Galilee teaching in their synagogues, proclaiming the Good News of the kingdom and curing all kinds of diseases and sickness among the people.
　　　　　　　　　　　　　　　—Matthew 4:23[1]

Even if we did once know Christ in the flesh, that is not how we know him now.
　　　　　　　　　　　　　　　—2 Corinthians 5:16

Once we take as seriously as medieval people did the idea that on the altar God becomes food (torn and bleeding meat), we can see as never before how much of such piety was literally imitatio Christi.
　　—Caroline W. Bynum, *Holy Feast and Holy Fast*[2]

This chapter opens our reflections on certain aspects of the ways in which Christ's humanity was represented in the later Middle Ages, reflections that will lead into the book's focus on late fourteenth- and early fifteenth-century England. Here the aim is to ask some questions about the political,

---

1. Quotations from the Bible are from *The Jerusalem Bible* unless particularities of the vulgate text seems relevant: then I use *Biblia Sacra* and the Douai-Rheims English translation as cited in our bibliography.

2. Bynum (1987), 274; hereafter cited in text as *HF,* followed by page number.

ethical, and social implications of some central religious iconography and its theological support. Exploring such questions will, we hope, contribute to our understanding of late medieval English Christianity, culture, and especially the texts on which the most detailed analysis is concentrated. This kind of exploration is especially appropriate in studying a culture where, as Janet Coleman has observed, "politics and theology" were "viewed as inseparable" and where "the more political and ecclesiastical ramifications of modern theology could be heard in sermons delivered at Paul's Cross."[3] In the domains addressed in this and the next two chapters recent studies by Sarah Beckwith, Miri Rubin, and Peter McNiven have shown particularly well just how thoroughly, and complexly, Christian sacraments, doctrine, and iconography were enmeshed in the deployment and daily legitimations of power, as well as in resistances to that power.[4] It did not take the English Reformation and Tudor state to make what the church classified as "heresy" into "sedition" and "sedition" into "heresy."[5]

The starting point here is the familiar transformation in the representation of Christ from the late eleventh century. It is usually described in terms such as those found in Richard Kieckhefer's study of fourteenth-century piety:

> Throughout the high and late Middle Ages there was increasing attention and devotion to the humanity of Jesus, particularly to those moments in his life that aroused sentiments of love and compassion: his infancy and his passion. With major stimulus from the writing of Bernard of Clairvaux, and with strong support from Francis of Assisi, the humanity of Jesus became central in medieval spirituality.[6]

This offers a good summary of the transformation, one that has been exceptionally well documented by numerous scholars in diverse disciplines of research.[7] In art, for example, James Marrow traces how from the twelfth

---

3. Coleman (1981a), 232, 244.
4. Beckwith (1993); Rubin (1991); McNiven (1987); see also Aston (1994) and Justice (1994b), chap. 4.
5. Aston (1984), chap. 1; McNiven (1987); Aers (1994c).
6. Kieckhefer (1984), 90. For examples of early opposition, see Camille (1992), 212.
7. Consult Beckwith (1993); Belting (1990); Bynum (1982), 16–19, 129–46, 151–54; Bynum (1987); Kieckhefer (1984), chap. 4; Lane (1984); Macy (1984), 41, 86–93; Marrow (1979); Ringbom (1965); Rubin (1991); Schiller (1972); L. Steinberg (1984); Woolf (1968), chap. 2.

to the sixteenth century "Christ's humanity and passion became focal points of the new piety," the aim being "to approach the Divine through intimate knowledge and empathic experience of Christ's humanity and the human ordeal of His passion."[8] Likewise, in studying late medieval religious lyrics, Rosemary Woolf showed how in the thirteenth and fourteenth centuries the "dominant theme" became the visualization of "Christ in His humanity," represented through the Passion and infancy. This, she noted, was a "completely new" focus in Christian devotion, one "quite alien" to earlier forms of Christian engagements with Christ and the doctrine of the Incarnation. In the latter she found no focus on the Christ child and "no intense stress upon the suffering of Christ," whereas in the lyrics of the later Middle Ages, meditation on the Passion becomes "a devotional exercise complete in itself," while "the figure of Christ is isolated from the historical sequence of the Passion." She describes the lyrics as representations of "Christ in His humanity," and exemplifies their focus on "details of the number of Christ's wounds, the wrenching off of His skin with His clothes, the pulling of his arms to reach the holes already bored in the wood, the violent dropping of the Cross in its socket, and the mourning of the Blessed Virgin."[9] It is, as Sarah Beckwith notes, "a commonplace of late medieval histories of spirituality that the late Middle Ages witness a new and extraordinary focus on the passion of Christ."[10] The humiliated, tortured, whipped, nailed-down, pierced, dying but life-giving body of Christ, the very body literally present in the eucharist—this body became the dominant icon of the late medieval church and the devotion it cultivated and authorized. This is the body at the heart of the "commonplace" on which this part of our book is a meditation. That bleeding, dying body had, as Miri Rubin recently demonstrated, come to be identified "as the essence of Christ's humanity."[11]

So successful was this identification that it set down deep roots and survived the supersession of the culture in which it was made. It became so dominant that it was reproduced in modern scholarship—reproduced rather than approached as a topic for interrogation. This convention has already been illustrated in the quotations from Richard Kieckhefer, James Marrow, and Rosemary Woolf. Without any qualifying analysis, the commonplace at issue is described as "devotion to the humanity of Jesus"

---

8. Marrow (1979), 204, 1, 8, 44; see also his examples on 109–10, 53.

9. Woolf (1968), 24–25, 26, 184–85, 231.

10. Beckwith (1993), chap. 1.

11. Rubin (1991), 303; see esp. 302–16, but chaps. 3–5 passim.

(Kieckhefer), "empathic experience of Christ's humanity" (Marrow) and "Christ in His humanity" (Woolf). It has been described by Robert Frank as "a complete incarnational poetic" that made Christ "unmistakably human," "a human figure."[12] Such descriptions and the perceptual framework to which they belong may seem inevitable in a scholarship that is committedly historical, a responsible reflection of dominant iconography and ideas in the earlier culture, a veritable sign that the modern writer has successfully avoided the solipsistic sin of "presentism" and all traces of "anachronism." And yet this form of historicism may become an impediment to critical reflection on late medieval figurations of Christ, an impediment that will necessarily affect our attempts to understand the devotion to which such figurations belonged and their relations to contemporary sources of power. How could this happen? It could happen very easily and in a very unostentatious manner, as the consequence of an admirable enough historical commitment. The attempt to reproduce the terms of the past culture of discourse, including the terms in which Christ was imaged, can very easily naturalize that discourse, so familiarize it as to make it seem inevitable. In this way a historically contingent constitution of the "humanity" of Christ becomes "the humanity of Christ," *the* humanity of Christ that, at last, was grasped for that which it was, is and shall be, grasped from the late eleventh-century onward. The contingent acts, performances, and doctrinal shifts that made the dominant late medieval representation of Christ's humanity dominant as well as those contingent acts, performances, and ideas that may, perhaps, have been in some kind of opposition to the dominant are occluded. So, ironically enough, the historical ambition to describe in its own terms the "commonplace" well summarized by Sarah Beckwith comes to bestow an unhistorical ontological solidity on what was a historically contingent *version* of Christ's humanity. Such is the way of all reifications: to occlude their own constitution in specific networks of power and contingent historical forces, to turn processes and complex (sometimes contradictory) effects into essence, verbs into nouns. In my view the historian's task is not to reproduce such reifications, whether they became dominant in a medieval or in a twentieth-century culture, not to collude with them in their self-representations. On the contrary, the task is to understand the processes and forces at work in their formation, in their achievement of dominance, in their naturalization and in their appearance of inevitability,

---

12. Frank (1990), 41, 44, 43; see similarly G. Gibson (1989), 14, and passim.

of transcendent essentiality.[13] So here I shall seek to step back from the framework assumed by the dominant late medieval tradition and its forceful imagery, aiming to make this "incarnational poetic," its version of Incarnation and Christ's humanity topics for critical historical reflection. What did it mean, after all, to cultivate a version of the Incarnation in which, as Miri Rubin has shown, "Christ's wounds were hailed as the essence of Christ's humanity?"[14]

Before offering some answers to this question, a question that threads through this and the next two chapters, it may be helpful to recall some examples of the dominant representations of Christ's humanity in late medieval culture. Such recollections can be brief because the relevant materials have been well exemplified by numerous historians, including those already referred to in this chapter;[15] their role here is as a reference point. A characteristic example of the composition of Christ's humanity through an almost exclusive focus on passion and crucifixion can be taken from the immensely influential work of Richard Rolle:[16]

> A, Lord þi sorwe, why were it not my deth? Now þei lede þe forthe nakyd os a worm, þe turmentoures abowtyn þe, and armede knyʒtes; þe prees of þe peple was wonderly strong, þei hurled þe and haryed þe so schamefully, þei spurned þe with here feet, os þou hadde been a dogge. I se in my soule how reufully þou gost: þi body is so blody, so rowed and so bledderyd; þi crowne is so kene, pat sytteth on þi hed; þi heere mevyth with þe wynde, clemyd with þe blood; þi lovely face so wan and so bolnyd with bofetynge and with betynge, with spyttynge, with spowtynge; þe blood ran þerewith, þat grysyth in my syʒt; so lothly and so wlatsome þe Jues han þe mad, þat a mysel art þou lyckere þan a clene man. Þe cros is so hevy, so hye and so stark, þat þei hangyd on þi bare bac trossyd so harde.
>
> A, Lord, þe gronyng þat þou made, so sore and so harde it sat to

---

13. The ideas about reification here owe much to Marxist traditions, especially Marx (1970), chap. 1, sect. 4 and Lukács (1971). Especially influential has been their rethinking and application in Butler (1990); also relevant are Butler (1993) and Brennen (1993).

14. Rubin (1991), 303; see also Rubin (1994), 113–14; also Dugmore (1958), 62, 78; and Bynum (1991), 129–34; contrast the late scholastic treatment especially represented by Gabriel Biel in Oberman (1963), chap. 8, sects. 1 and 2.

15. Besides work cited in note 7, see also Bennett (1982); Gillespie, (1987); and Pezzini (1990).

16. Rolle (1963), 21. On Rolle's work, see Watson (1991).

þe bon. Þi body is so seek, so febyl and so wery, what with gret fastynge before þat þou were take, and al nyȝt wooke withowten ony reste, with betynge, with bofetynge so fer ovurtake, þat al stow-pynge þou gost, and grym is þi chere. Þe flesch, þere þe cros sytteth, is al rowed; þe bleynes and þe bledderys are wanne and bloo; þe peyne of þat byrden sytteth þe so sore, þat iche foot þat þou gost it styngyth to þin herte.

As we find so copiously illustrated in James Marrow's discussion of north-ern European art, here we meet the stress on physical vulnerability, humili-ation, and details of parts of the body under torture (the hair clotted with blood and blowing in the wind is typical, as is the swollen face, bare back and pulverized body). The mode is of course encapsulated in that great storehouse of late medieval devotion, the *Meditationes Vitae Christi* and we can see how it was conventionally used in this early fourteenth-century English meditation:

> Whan he to caluarye mounte was broȝt,
> Beholde what werkmen þere wykkedly wroȝt:
> Some dyggen, sum deluyn, sum erþe oute kast,
> Some pycchen þe cros yn þe erþe fast;
> On euery syde sum laddres vpp sette,
> Sum renne aftyr hamers, some nayles fette;
> Some dyspoyle hym oute dyspetusly,
> Hys cloþys cleuyn on hys swete body;
> Þey rente hem of as þey were wode:
> Hys body aȝen ran alle on blode.
> A! with what sorrow hys modyr was fedde.
> Whan she say hym so naked and alle bled!
> Fyrþer more, þan gan she to seche,
> And say þat þey had left hym no breche.
> She ran þan þurgh hem, and hastyly hyde,
> And with here kercheues hys hepys she wryde.[17]

The clothes clinging to the body through dried blood, then being violently stripped off, the mother's haste to cover his naked "hepys," the manic

---

17. *Meditations* (1985), lines 609–24; see lines 425–706. See also Marrow (1979), 53, 95, 109–10, and Lane (1984).

energies of the "werkmen" applied to the minute particulars of their job—the accumulation of such details is sustained at great length as we read of the body being beaten up, tortured, pierced, stretched, and pulled about on the cross. This is the context in which a cult of Christ's wounds emerged. Indeed, so marked is the fixation of the body of Jesus that even when it is dead we find Mary kissing an arm, embracing it to her breast and seeking to prevent its burial, or to be buried with it, putting the dead head in her lap, gazing at the way, "hyt was ybroke, / Prykket, and broysed wyþ many a stroke," shaved, rent with thorns and all red with blood.[18] The text thus directs the meditant to go over, once more, the bodily mutilation and pain she or he has just imagined, now identifying with the mother holding the dead body. This is the tradition favored by those who compiled the urban plays produced by late medieval guildsmen, brilliantly presented in York in the plays for the Shearmen and the Pinners. A long, powerful sequence enacting the Crucifixion concentrates on minute physical particulars in the torturing and killing of Jesus, while the cycle as a whole certainly lays most stress on the sequences centered on Christ's birth and his Passion.[19]

This tradition is exemplified in the "Privity of the Passion," one of the English renderings of the passion sequence from the *Meditationes Vitae Christi*.[20] The laconic statement of Christ's scourging in the Gospels (Matthew 27:26, Mark 15:15, John 19:1; cf. Luke 23:22) becomes the following:

> Thene þey dispoylede owre lorde dispitousely withowttene any pete & made hym nakyde, & bande hys handis by-hynde hyme and feste hym till a pelere; & bett hym withe scharpe knotty schourges, a longe whyle. And as some doctours says, one euery knott was a scharpe hok of Iryne, þat with euery stroke þey rofe his tendyr flesche. He stode naked be-fore theme a faire ȝonge mane schamefull in schapp, and speciouse in bewte passande all erthely mene: he

---

18. *Meditations* (1985), lines 901–62.

19. Beadle (1982); see Shearmen, lines 310–32, and Pinners, lines 157–252; on Nicholas Love, see Salter (1974), 52–53 and chaps. 4 and 5. On the "greatest emphasis" on nativity and passion, see Beadle and King (1988), 98; for even more marked emphasis on this direction in the Towneley (Wakefield) cycle, see Lepow (1990), 97. Some contrasts with the Chester cycle are argued for by Ashley (1978) and Travis (1982), chap. 5: I remain unpersuaded by these arguments and their theological claims. I cannot pursue this unpersuasion here, but hope to explain it in the future.

20. Horstmann (1895–96), vol. 1, 198–218: page references in my text are to this edition; on the work in relation to Nicholas Love, see Salter (1974), 103.

> sufferde þis harde paynefull betyng of these wikkede mene in his
> tendireste flesche & clenneste. . . . He es betyne and betyne agayne,
> blester appone blester, and wonde appone wonde, to bothe þe beters
> & þe be-holders were wery. (203)

This elaboration of physical details (from the design of the scourges to the
exhaustion of the beaters) is a constant feature of the work as it concentrates on figuring forth a lacerated body and eliciting affective responses
in the reader. After describing the Crucifixion's violent abuse of the body
in familiar details the text comments:

> And whene he was thus sprede o-brode one þe crosse more straite
> þan any parchemyne-skyne es sprede one þe harowe, so þat mene
> myghte tel all þe blyssede bones of his body: thane rane fro hym
> one euery syde stremes of blode owt of his blessede wondes. (206)

Such details, so familiar in verbal and visual performances, are crucial to
the dominant version of Christ's humanity and its intense concentration
on Passion and Crucifixion, on a tortured, suffering sacrifice out of whose
"stremes of blode" comes humanity's salvation. True enough, this tradition
also bestows much attention on Christ's infancy, as Kieckhefer and many
others have observed.[21] And yet here too what Leo Steinberg called "the
humanation of God" was repeatedly defined in terms of his Passion, Crucifixion and death, with a marked focus on the child's blood-shedding at
his circumcision, both prefiguring the Crucifixion and demonstrating his
"humanity."[22]

What kind of imitation might this dominant model encourage among the
devout? Addressing this will constitute a major part of this chapter and,
by implication, the next, but here I shall give a couple of examples in late
medieval English. In a rendering of Jacques de Vitry's life of the holy
woman, Mary d'Oignies, so important to Margery Kempe, we encounter
one characteristic response.[23] Here we read how Mary had such profound

---

21. Kieckhefer (1984), 90.

22. Steinberg (1984), esp. 10ff., 28ff., 65ff., 82ff., 107–8; Sinanoglou (1973); Lepow
(1990), 80–83, 87. For Caroline Bynum's criticism of Steinberg, see Bynum (1991), chap. 3;
she does not, however, contradict Steinberg's discussion of the area I have outlined here.

23. The edition used here is Horstmann (1885): the life of Mary of Oignies is on 134–86,
quoted here from 139–40; the Latin text is in *Acta Sanctorum ivnii*, vol. 5 of 25, 547–72;
here see book 1, sect. 22. There is a modern English translation by Margot King (Jacques de
Vitry 1994).

spiritual awareness that "alle flesely delyte was to hir vnsauery." So much
so, apparently, that when sickness forced her to eat a little flesh and drink
a little wine her revulsion was so great at this "abomynacyone" that

> she punyshed hir-selfe and hadde no rest in spirite, vnto she hadde
> made a-seth, wonderly turmentynge hir fleshe for þos delytes before,
> siche as was. For with feruour of spirite she, loþinge hir fleshe, cutte
> awey grete gobettis and for shame hidde hem in þe erþe. . . . And
> whan hir body shudde be washen after she was deed, wymmen fonde
> þe places of woundes, and hadde mykele maruaile; but þey þat knew
> hir confessyone [i.e., the author], wiste what it was (I. 7, 139–40)

The model of Christ and his humanity, the model for as literal, as fleshy
an imitation as possible, is made almost exclusively out of the Passion and
Crucifixion as we have seen it represented in the later Middle Ages. We
find a similar outlook in the English version of "Cristyne þe meruelous"
who chose to enter, so we read, hot ovens:

> hoote—brennynge ouenes, redy to bake brede in: and she was tur-
> mented wiþ brennynges and heet as oon of vs, so þat sche cryed
> hidously for angwysche; neþeles, whan she come oute, þere was no
> soor nor hurt seen outwarde in hir body. And when she hadde no
> fourneys nor ouenes, thanne she keste hirselfe in to houge fyres and
> grete in mennes houses, or allonly putte in hir feet and handys, and
> helde hem þere so longe, vnto, but if hit hadde be myrakelle of
> god, þey myghte be brente to askes. Also oþer-while she wente into
> cauderons, fulle of hoot-boylynge watir, to þe breste or ellis to þe
> lendys. . . . Also she wente to þe galous and hengyd hir-selfe vp wiþ
> a gnare [= noose] amonge honged þeues, and þere she henge a daye
> or to.[24]

We can see how the dominant model of Christ's humanity encourages quite
specific forms of imitation. They seem characterized by the freely chosen
infliction of bodily pain, miraculously sustained by God so that the holy
person can go on and on performing such activities, reiterations that themselves confirm and sacrilize the model that informs them. But these performances take us, of course, into areas of medieval devotion explored by

---

24. Horstmann (1885), 122–23.

Caroline Bynum, and given that some of her main theses are considered below I will, for the moment, leave these devout imitations of the late medieval Christ.

Given this version of Christ's humanity, so centered on Christ's bloody sacrifice, it can be no surprise that it was systemically reproduced, and hence decisively reinforced, at the heart of the eucharist, with its official and ferociously enforced dogma of transubstantiation. As Eamon Duffy remarks in his lovingly idealized and charmingly depoliticized account of late medieval religion:

> Christ himself, immolated on the altar of the cross, became present on the altar of the parish church, body and soul and divinity, and his blood flowed once again, to nourish and renew Church and world. As kneeling congregations raised their eyes to see the Host held high above the priest's head at the sacring, they were transported to Calvary itself.[25]

Christ's humanity, the eucharist, and the dogma of transubstantiation were inextricably bound together, performed by the priest not only on every altar but in processions through towns and villages, celebrated in the iconography of churches, books of hours, paintings, innumerable exempla and particularly focused upon at the festival of Corpus Christi.[26] This doctrinal, iconographic, and social history has been extensively described in Miri Rubin's *Corpus Christi* while in her recent *Christ's Body* Sarah Beckwith explores, with great subtlety, the complex political, psychological, and social forces shaping, and shaped by, this symbol, so central in late medieval culture and the formation of identities.[27] I do not intend to go over the work they have done on the eucharist, the feast of Corpus Christi, and the Host as a site of conflict in which ideological boundaries, inclusions, and exclusions, were struggled over, established, and struggled over. All I do

---

25. Duffy (1992), 91; see chap. 3, "The Mass." On Duffy's idealizations and his systematic occlusions of political powers in late medieval religion, see Aers (1994c). For a nice contrast with Duffy's pious image, compare William Thorpe's experience in early fifteenth-century Shrewsbury (Thorpe [1993], 52).

26. See esp. Rubin (1991); Beckwith (1993); Lane (1984); and Sinanoglou (1973). For oppositional potentials completely occluded by Duffy, see, for example, Aston (1994); Justice (1994), chap. 4; and James (1983).

27. Rubin (1991; 1992); Beckwith (1993; 1992; and 1986). Much that Duffy's approach conceals is discussed in the works of Aston, Justice, Rubin, and Beckwith; see also McNiven (1987).

here is recollect the standard representation of Christ's humanity in the eucharist of the late medieval church, recollection that, once more, will serve as a reference point in ensuing discussion.

Nicholas Love's *Mirror of the Blessed Life of Jesus Christ,* an English version of the *Meditationes Vitae Christe,* was an immensely popular work throughout the fifteenth century.[28] As Michael Sargent notes in the introduction to his critical edition of the *Mirror,* Love suppressed "a good deal of the *Meditationes Vitae Christi,*" choosing to substitute material "directed toward the theological concerns of his own day," concerns that were explicitly and very emphatically part of the church's "campaign against Lollardy" led by Archbishop Arundel.[29] He approved Love's work and saw it as part of the "confutation of heretics or lollards [ad . . . heriticorum siue lollardorum confutacionem]," a perception, as Sargent stresses, shared by its author.[30] From this important and characteristic work of late medieval English orthodoxy I shall take an example of the habitual construction of Christ's humanity in the eucharist. This comes from the "Treatise on the Sacrament," which was part of Love's conception of his *Mirror,* as Sargent demonstrates, and was always attached to it (liii–lviii). Love recounts how a woman in Rome used to offer St. Gregory loaves of bread "whereof was made goddes body." One day, on hearing the words "þe body of oure lorde Jesu criste kepe þe in to euerlastyng life" she burst out laughing, in "dissolute lawhtere." Being asked why she laughed she replies, "by cause þat þou clepedest goddus body þe brede þat I made wiþ myn handes." The priest prays for the woman's "misbyleue" and at once finds the real presence of Christ's humanity demonstrated: "he fonde þe sacrament turnede in to þe likenes of a fynger in flesh & blode," enough to turn the woman "in to þe trewe byleue" (232–33). In John Mirk's version of this familiar exemplary tale, "þe ost turnet into raw flessch bledyng" which the priest "toke and schowet þis woman." At once she recognizes in the raw, bleeding flesh the identity of God in his humanity: "now I beleue þat þou art Crist."[31] The same version of Christ's humanity is affirmed when a priest sees "þe blod drop doun from þe ost fast into þe chalice" and some doubting clerks see

---

28. Nicholas Love's *Mirror* is read in the critical edition by Sargent (1992); still invaluable is Salter (1974); see also Beckwith (1993), 63–70, and Hudson (1988), 437–40.

29. Quotations here from Love (1992) xxix and xliv: see xxviii–xxxv and xliv–lviii.

30. Sargent's translation of the memorandum is on lxv, the Latin on 7; see the numerous annotations "contra lollardos," exemplified by Sargent, for example, on xlvii, xlviii, xlix.

31. Erbe (1905), 173; on this sermon, see Rubin (1991), 222–24. On Mirk and Lollardy, see Fletcher (1987).

his "fyngurys blody and blod rane of Cristis body into þe chalis." They at
once bless the priest "þat has þis grace þus to handul Cristis body" and
become "good men and perfyte alway aftyr in þe beleue."[32] The dominant
version of representing Christ's humanity in the late medieval church is thus
confirmed by the eucharist even as the latter is confirmed by the presence of
this "humanity." Love's collection of eucharistic miracles are designed to
encourage "wirchipyng of þat sacrament" and include "opune prefe" of its
power. Indeed, so overwhelming is the "auctorite" of his "merueiles &
myracles" that nobody could speak against their force unless "he be worse
þan a Jewe or a payneme"; that is, worse than the excluded, scapegoated
others against which orthodoxy constituted itself.[33]

Nor should we overlook the stupendous utilities the presence of Christ's
human body, whether as dismembered infant or wounded adult, brought
the faithful in the present world. Let us recall some of these as they were
so frequently reiterated:

> als ofte as a man or a woman cometh into þe chirch to here masse,
> God ȝeueþ hym seuen ȝeftis; and þo ben þes: That day hym schal
> wonte no bodely fode; idul speche þat day is forȝeuen hym; his idul
> lyȝt oþes ben forȝeton; he schal not þat day lese his siȝth; he schal
> not þat day dey no sodeyne deth; and as longe as þe masse lesteþ
> he schal not wax olde; and his angele telleþ eche paas þat he goþ
> to þe chirch in gret worschip to hym.[34]

Mirk's itemization of the utilities that flow from seeing the transubstanti-
ated Host, Christ's body, are utterly conventional.[35] John Lydgate's poetry
bears witness to this, confirming Mirk's list but characteristically enlarging
it even further. Not only will it work "Vs to susteyne in bodyly gladnesse,"
but it pays attention to the particular needs of our worldly occupations
and needs. For example:

> Masse herde aforne, the wynde ys nat contrary
>   To Maryneres that day in theyr saylyng,

---

32. Erbe (1905), 170–71.

33. Here we are on ground admirably explored in Rubin (1991) and Beckwith (1993). On
the virulent anti-Judaism of orthodox eucharist materials, see Biddick (1993), 401–12, and
Beckwith (1992); a typical example of this aspect can be found in Erbe (1905), 251–52.

34. Erbe (1905), 169–70.

35. For examples of this commonplace, see Simmons (1879), 131–32, 367–73; and Duffy
(1992), 100–101.

And all thyng that ys necessary,
> God sent to porayle that day to theyr fedyng;
> Women also that goon on trauaylyng,
Folk well expert haue thereof founde a prefe,
> That herde masse in the mornyng
Were delyueryd and felt no myschefe.[36]

In such ways the dominant version of Christ's humanity, bodily present in the eucharist, brings markedly worldly benefits that enmesh it in the material particularities and hopes of the faithful. Not that its powers are confined to this world, of course: Lydgate observes that each mass "ys egall to Crystes passion" in helping "sowlys out of purgatory," a belief that underpinned the whole apparatus of masses for the dead so prominent in the late medieval church and in social relations.[37] There can be no doubt that Eamon Duffy is right to maintain, along with all modern historians of the subject, that "preoccupation with the moment of Christ's death, and with his sufferings" dominated late medieval orthodoxy and the devotion it fostered and was fostered by, extending to conventional grants of "enormous indulgences (up to 32,755 years of pardon) for those who devoutly repeated before the image [of Christ suffering] five Paters, five Aves, and a Creed."[38]

Perhaps the materials we have been considering can be read in ways that may return theological formulations, iconography, and received terminology to the contingent historical processes from which they emerged. Asking what it meant to cultivate a version of the Incarnation in which "Christ's wounds were hailed as the essence of Christ's humanity" can perhaps best be answered by identifying reiterated performances in regulative but thoroughly contingent networks of customs, institutions, and social powers. Certainly scholars have given reasons for the distinctive turn in Christianity that led to the discovery of this "humanity" of Christ over a thousand years after his death. It has been explained as a response to Anselmian soteriology (stressing the death of Christ as a propitiatory sacrifice to a dishonored feudal ruler whom no fallen human could appease) and as a part of a general shift in Western European economies and cultures that entailed an increasing interest in the natural world, in human embodiment,

---

36. Lydgate (1911), 1:87–115; quotations here from line 622 and lines 633–40.

37. See Lydgate (1911), p. 114, lines 641–48; on the apparatus in question, see LeGoff (1984); Rubin (1991), 153; Duffy (1992), 142–43 and chaps. 9–10.

38. Duffy (1992), 241–42, 239; here, see 234–56.

particularities of human emotion and the "individual." Such a shift, we learn, encouraged the "humanization" of the Pantocrator who had ruled from the Cross in sublime power and apparent impassibility.[39] Plausible as such accounts of early medieval cultural transformation may be, their effects in the present field of study may be less than helpful. These macrohistorical narratives tend to take for granted the term which is here the *explanandum*, the "humanity" of Christ. Encouraging us to assume that we know what it is, in all its familiarity, they suggest that what we need is an account of macrohistorical changes that made its emergence natural, inevitable. This effect has been strengthened by a tendency to reproduce Christ's "humanity" as it is found in the discourses of late medieval culture, as I have noted, thus congealing and naturalizing the very reifications that need to be broken down into the actions, performative networks, and social struggles they occlude.

The work that needs doing here has been well exemplified in recent books by Sarah Beckwith and Miri Rubin, books that have greatly helped my own inquiries.[40] But here I turn to another historian whose work has certainly neither naturalized nor rendered comfortably familiar late medieval representations of Christ's "humanity": Caroline Bynum. I select her work for a number of reasons. It centers on figurations of Christ's humanity; it is immensely influential, outside as well as within medieval studies; it is documented with most unusual abundance; it strives for a hermeneutic that respects the "otherness" of the past even as it seeks to avoid what Bynum calls "presentism"; and yet, especially important to my own concerns, it has addressed issues sidelined in scholarship on this topic.[41] Bynum has, that is, explored late medieval devotion to Christ with unprecedented attention to the constitutions of gender, sexual differentiations, and human bodies in that culture. The fascinating work she published in the 1980s involved a major shift in historical paradigms. This shift enabled the study of power where that had seemed irrelevant in the received scholarship on "Corpus Christi," on Christ's body and his humanity. Whatever the force of Kathleen Biddick's critique of Bynum's work, and however critical the ensuing

---

39. Influential works here include Southern (1953); Chenu (1968); Morris (1972; 1980); Murray (1978); Bynum (1982), 82–109; Benson and Constable (1982); Stock (1983; 1990). Of especial interest to the present project is Moore (1987).

40. Rubin (1991) and Beckwith (1993).

41. Bynum (1982); *HF*; Bynum (1991; referred to in text as *FR* followed by page number); for the history of the resurrected body, promised in *FR*, see Bynum (1995), a work of wonderful, astounding erudition in the genre of intellectual history, but not much interested in the specificities of historical institutions, and the politics of theological discourses.

comments in this chapter, I cannot imagine anyone now writing on the topics I address without owing a great deal to Caroline Bynum.[42] Her work, an always searching, profound companion, has certainly stimulated and guided my own explorations.

Both *Holy Feast and Holy Fast* and *Fragmentation and Redemption* concentrate on the devotion and ascetism of women, "female imagery," the "female body," and the relations of women's religious practices to the "body" and "humanity" of Christ.[43] Bynum is "fully aware that most of the women" she selects for study are "exceptional," and yet she maintains that she is "explaining the women by their context and the context by the women," (*HF* 7). Through their devotional experience she believes she can disclose the "religious experience" of "medieval people," can gain access to those she calls "Pious folk in the later Middle Ages."[44] And she will gain it, we recall, within a paradigm that will generate research not undertaken by traditional accounts of "the humanity of Christ," research into its relations to forms of power and gender mediated through the symbolism of Christ's body.

Yet, despite the admirable innovations in her paradigms of inquiry, it turns out that Bynum's attention to gender, bodies and Christ remains, at one decisive point, within the conventional historical approach I have illustrated. She habitually *identifies* conventional representations of the tortured body of Jesus (exemplified earlier in this chapter) with "Christ's humanity."[45] As she follows the attempts of certain women to imitate the dominant figuration of "Christ's suffering humanity," Bynum maintains that the "self-inflicted suffering" through which they "were becoming more wonderfully and horribly the body on the cross" comprised "a profound expression of the doctrine of the Incarnation: the doctrine that Christ, by becoming human, saves *all* that the human being is."[46] Furthermore, it is within the familiar framework of this identification that she develops a major thesis: that imitating the dominant figuration of Christ empowered women, especially, one supposes, the women on whose ascetic practices she

---

42. Biddick (1993).

43. The phrases in quotation marks are chapter titles in *FR* and represent Bynum's major concerns.

44. See *seriatim*: *FR* 182, 184, 185, and *HF* 300. The term "medieval people" is frequent in these pages and elsewhere: it is used as a homogenizing term often contrasted with the equally homogenizing "modern people" (*HF* 300) or "modern sensibilities" (*FR* 182).

45. This identification pervades Bynum's work, but see, for example, *HF* 294, 246, 252, 263, 264, 274.

46. Quotations here, *seriatim*, *HF* 26, 296, and 294 (italics in original).

concentrates. For, so the argument goes, as Christ's suffering humanity saved the world so suffering women, subjected by their culture in numerous ways, became the most powerful representatives of the powerless, bleeding, suffering but salvific Christ. I shall present some objections to this thesis, to its allegedly historical underpinnings and to its assumptions about the political implications of the way Christ's humanity was predominantly figured through the wounded, bleeding, and nurturing body on the cross. I shall also, in this and the next two chapters, consider some late medieval sources occluded by Bynum's work but relevant to the inquiries she has initiated.

I will begin my consideration of Bynum's treatment of "Christ's humanity" by recollecting her arguments about food. These arguments are foundational ones in *Holy Feast and Holy Fast,* directly pertinent to its version of Christ's humanity and its interpretations of medieval materials. She maintains that food was "particularly a woman-controlled resource," and that "To prepare food is to control food." In fact, she asserts, "by means of food women controlled themselves and their world."[47] Summing up her claims, she writes, "In short, women had many ways of manipulating and controlling self and environment through food-related behavior, for food formed the context and shape of women's world" (*HF* 208). Bynum's position characteristically dissolves the realities and consequences of the political and social organizations of the means and modes of production, including the production of food. At all social levels these organizations were under the control of men: in villages, in towns, in ecclesiastical corporations, in castles and courts.[48] What women prepared in kitchens (and what men working in employers' kitchens prepared) was itself the product of systems of production, extraction of resources and distribution determined by struggles between conflicting social groups with conflicting economic and political interests. Bynum's claims that to prepare food is to control food and that to cook food is to control the environment and world one lives in fails to acknowledge how the kitchen, its resources, and the work done there existed within networks of power, chains of command, and financial resources dominated by men. She fails to see that in these social contexts "power" and "control" in cooking is contained, structured,

47. *HF* 189, 191, 193; see chaps. 3–6.
48. The kind of work that needs to be consulted as a corrective to Bynum's approach to this subject can be exemplified by the following: Bennett (1987; 1992); Dyer (1989); Hanawalt (1986a); Hilton (1975; esp. chaps. 1–3); Hilton (1985a), chaps. 15–20; Howell (1986); Swanson (1989).

and ordered within institutions, customs and ideologies under male domination, structures and forces that remain when the direct employer happened to be a woman. There can be no adequate understanding of social
relations in kitchens and around the preparation of food if we abstract
these from the social networks and sources of power within which they
exist and have their being. What Bynum calls "women's world" was never
an autonomous domain.[49]

From her assertion that food was a concern of women rather than men
she argues that this made food a religious symbol of more importance to
women than to men. Not only did women prepare food but, Bynum argues,
"They fed others with their own bodies, which, as milk or oil, became
food" (HF 114). So while, as we shall see, she emphasizes that women's
"imitation of the cross" included physical practices that made them into
"the macerated body of the Savior, the bleeding meat they often saw in
eucharistic visions," women's bodies were always already food, always
already, therefore, an imitation of Christ in his "humanity." She traces
"medieval assumptions" that "associated female and flesh and the body of
God" (FR 215): "Women's bodies, in the acts of lactation and of giving
birth, were analogous both to ordinary food and to the body of Christ, as
it died on the cross and gave birth to salvation" (HF 30). Or, in another
typical formulation: "Since Christ's body was a body that nursed the hungry, both men and women naturally assimilated the ordinary female body
to it" (HF 272). This is a very strong claim about how "men and women
naturally" viewed "the ordinary female body" and whether it could with-
stand exposure to a wide range of medieval writings and close attention to
the culture's misogyny seems doubtful to me,[50] although I do not address
the issue here.

Bynum herself has no such doubts and stresses that "women" gained
"power" through this constitution of their bodies in medieval discourses
and the corresponding convergence with Christ's humanity.[51] She provides
copious exemplification of the convergence through images of Christ's

---

49. Bynum's homogenization of "women" has been rightly criticized by Biddick (1993),
391–96.

50. For examples of Bynum's own awareness of medieval misogyny, see HF 22–23, 86,
261–63; FR 195, 200–205; also her earlier work, Bynum (1982), 14–16, 143–44, 244–46.
Bynum's later work should be set alongside Dronke's excellent but all too brief comments on
some of the Montaillou women persecuted by the inquisition and Marguerite Porete in the
final chapter of Dronke (1984).

51. See, for example, HF 208, 275; FR 195. To the sources for studying medical discourses
cited by Bynum should now be added the invaluable work of Cadden (1993).

wounds as a breast "exuding wine or blood into chalices or even into hungry mouths," reiterating that "identifying woman with flesh and Christ's flesh with the female" was "widespread in the culture."[52] As Christ's "own flesh did womanly things, it bled food and gave birth to new life," so "women" allegedly found that "their flesh could do what his could do: bleed, feed, die and give life to others" (FR 215, 222). In such ways Christ became "female" and "women" thus always nearer than men could ever be to a "literal, bodily *imitatio Christi*," nearer to God and his "humanity" than the men who ruled church and world. Whereas men had to cross-dress, as it were, women were already "there," "naturally." Thus, so the argument goes, were women empowered in and through the dominant forms in which Christ's humanity was represented. And the empowerment was, apparently, extremely substantial. It enabled "women" to gain "control" over "their bodies and their world," "to gain power and to give meaning" through which they "controlled and manipulated their environment."[53] Through their "food practices" and related identification with the humanity of Christ as it was figured forth in the late medieval church, women "controlled their religious circumstances as well as their domestic ones," finding here a way of "controlling those in authority" (HF 237, 243). To gain control over patriarchal forces, institutions, and "those in authority" (presumably in ecclesiastic, political, legal, military, and domestic authority) must, indeed, have been a monumental subversion of traditional structures of power and their diverse legitimations.[54] And, irony of ironies, it was apparently one sponsored by the church, its male rulers, and admiring confessors who wrote the *vitae* on which Bynum draws so heavily.[55]

But what exactly was the imitation of Christ that the dominant figuration of Christ's humanity shaped? The focus of the *imitatio Christi* practiced by the women Bynum studies was the Passion and Crucifixion as represented in the conventional materials illustrated earlier in this chapter. Their

---

52. The quotation is from FR 206; see also 205–222, and HF 268–78, chap. 9 and plates 4, 12, 18, 19, 25–30. Biddick (1993) includes important criticism of Bynum's use of visual materials.

53. Quotations from HF 189, 208, 218; see also 220–22 and chaps. 6–7.

54. For an interesting example of a medievalist seeking to fuse Bynum's materials and account of empowerment with work by Kristeva, Clément, and Cixous, see Lochrie (1991b), 3, 33–46, and Lochrie (1991a), 128–39; also Petroff (1991), 92–94, 105–108, 111–13; and Finke (1992), chap. 3, esp. 94–95.

55. See FR 195; she is very clear on the strengthening of patriarchal authority in Bynum (1982), 15–19, 31, and chap. 4.

attempt was to achieve, if that is the right word, "a fusion with Christ's agony on the cross" (*HF* 211–12). Bynum's treasury of such imitations seems endless, as one of her own summaries of her central materials nicely suggests:

> Deliberate and systematic physical punishment was part of the daily routine for many religious women. . . . Alda of Sienna, for example . . . whipped herself with chains, wore a crown of thorns. . . . Dorothy of Montau put herself through a pantomime of the Crucifixion that involved praying with her arms extended in the form of a cross and later, in imitation of Christ's burial, lying prostrate with the entire weight of her body supported only by toes, nose, and forehead. Jane Mary of Maillé stuck a thorn into her head in remembrance of Christ's crown of thorns. Reading the lives of fourteenth- and fifteenth-century women saints greatly expands one's knowledge of Latin synonyms for whip, thong, flail, chain, etc. Ascetic practices commonly reported in these *vitae* include wearing hair shirts, binding the flesh tightly with twisted ropes, rubbing lice into self-inflicted wounds . . . thrusting nettles into one's breasts. . . . Rolling in broken glass, jumping into ovens, hanging from a gibbet . . . lacerating their bodies until the blood flows, with all kinds of whips. (*HF* 209–210)

Following the same models of *imitatio Christi*, Angela of Foligno drank water that "came from washing the sores of lepers," exulting when one of the scabs stuck in her throat, and Catherine of Genoa ate scabs and burned herself (*HF* 144–45, 182). Catherine of Siena told her biographer, the Dominican Raymond of Capua, that she had drunk the pus from the putrefying breast of a dying woman. She commented: "Never in my life have I tasted any food and drink sweeter or more exquisite [than this pus]" (*HF* 171–72). As for her marriage with Christ, Catherine saw this as enacted, "with the ring of Christ's foreskin, given in the Circumcision and accompanied by pain and the shedding of blood," her distinctive image of putting on Christ (*HF* 175). Bynum acknowledges that Catherine of Siena "abhorred her own flesh," and yet because of this saw the body as uniting her to God's "humanity," a "humanity" symbolized by the cut-off foreskin, a union "by suffering" (*HF* 175). Catherine herself wrote, "we must attach ourselves to the breast of the crucified Christ. . . . For it is Christ's humanity that suffered . . . and, without suffering, we cannot nourish ourselves with this milk" (*HF* 176). Not surprisingly, Rudolph Bell's *Holy Anorexia* provides many similar examples, such as Eustochia of Messini wearing a pigskin undergarment to gouge out her flesh, whipping herself, melting candlewax over her head, burning her face, and using ropes "to stretch her arms in the form of a cross."[56] All these practices allegedly exemplify what Bynum describes as "a profound expression of the doctrine of the Incarnation" (*HF* 294), a culturally normative, if exuberant, understanding of the dominant figuration of Christ's humanity. This, then, is the combination of model and imitation that *empowered* the subordinate, that *subverted* the logic and religion of a patriarchal and profoundly mysoginistic culture.

I confess that I remain unconvinced by Bynum's "empowerment" thesis, and unconvinced by her interpretation of the conventional representations of Christ from which this chapter set out, at least insofar as that interpretation relates to power in late medieval society. And perhaps she herself may yet come to be equally unconvinced, for in an essay first published in 1989 she made the following observation in relation to "women's mysticism as a form of female empowerment":

> This argument must also recognize that the clergy themselves encouraged such female behavior both because female asceticism, eucharistic devotion and mystical trances brought women more closely under the supervision of spiritual directors and because women's visions functioned for males, too. . . . Moreover, theologians and prelates found women's experiential piety useful in the thirteenth-century fight against heresy . . . against Cathar dualism. (*FR* 195)

However, this important comment is still not allowed to move from the margins to the center of her inquiries, not allowed to unravel her own "empowerment" thesis. Yet in my view it should actually guide our attempts to understand the constitution of the humanity and the body of the late medieval Christ. Taken seriously, brought in from the margins, it will lead us to networks of force that are very relevant to our inquiries.

Basic to the shift in perspective here will be the acknowledgment that the dominant figurations of Christ's body, *including its alleged "feminization,"* were *made* dominant, *constituted* as dominant, *maintained* as dominant. So we will now approach the appearance of Christ's body in the late medieval church with the understanding that human bodies are produced

---

56. Bell (1985), 143.

within specific discursive regimes with specific technologies of power. Denise Riley has observed, "'The body' is not, for all its corporeality, an originating point nor yet a terminus; it is a result or an effect." It only "becomes visible *as* a body," she argues, "under some particular gaze—including that of politics."[57] As Foucault's study of surveillance and punishment exemplified:

> the body is also directly involved in a political field; power relations have an immediate hold upon it; they invest it, mark it, train it, torture it, force it to carry out tasks, to perform ceremonies, to emit signs. This political investment of the body is bound up, in accordance with complex reciprocal relations, with its economic use; it is largely as a force of production that the body is invested with relations of power and domination; but, on the other hand, its constitution as labour power is possible only if it is caught up in a system of subjection (in which need is also a political instrument meticulously prepared, calculated and used); the body becomes a useful force only if it is both a productive body and a subjected body.[58]

It seems to me that such reflections as those of Riley and Foucault on "the body," production, and power are an immense help in carrying out the task of breaking down the reifications, past and present, discussed earlier in this chapter. They encourage us not to collude in any fetishization of categories such as "the body" or "the humanity of Christ," but to explore the processes, performative acts, and powers in and through which they became fixed, normative, seemingly inevitable. So we will be both encouraged and enabled to ask whether "feminizing" the tortured body of Christ as material, for instance, may not actually reinforce some basic premises and fantasies in traditional patriarchal constitutions of "women." This in turn will lead us to ask whether particular late medieval "feminizations" of Christ may not contribute to the divinization of maternity as the essence of "woman."[59] This would hardly be the subversive and challenging innovation Bynum and others have seen in these "feminizations."

---

57. Riley (1988), 102 and 106. This study seems a particularly good corrective to Bynum's rather uncritical deployment of the term "women."

58. Foucault (1979), 25–26; in my view there are aspects of Foucault's treatment of power, production, and the body in *Discipline and Punish* (and elsewhere) that are not at all incompatible with attempts to explore these relationships within Marxist traditions, particularly from the Frankfurt School.

59. Especially relevant here is the critical commentary on Kristeva's work in Butler (1990), 88–91; also Biddick (1993), 397–401.

In pursuing these critical inquiries it is necessary to bear in mind that pleasures and desires, including pleasures that are viewed as transgressive, even "delicious groveling" (*HF* 290), may be produced by current relations of power as a move in the perpetuation of those relations of power. As Foucault remarked in an interview with the editors of *Quel Corps* in 1975, "power is strong . . . because, as we are beginning to realise, it produces effects at the level of desire."[60] This insight, part of Foucault's critique of "the repressive hypothesis,"[61] should be particularly fruitful here. It suggests that the practices and symbols celebrated by Bynum as subverting the logic of patriarchy need to be explored as possibly being among the very effects of the ecclesiastical and normative powers that she thinks were being circumvented by making "women" the body on the Cross, and the body on the Cross "feminine." The abjections that she explicates as subversive might be better viewed, to put the issue starkly, as themselves a product of modes of piety designed to make their practitioners objects of control— albeit, perhaps, sometimes, or often, ecstatic ones. Judith Butler's critical analysis of Kristeva's "body politics" identifies the issues I have in mind here. She argues that "Kristeva fails to understand the paternal mechanisms by which affectivity itself is generated," while the very vocabulary of affect renders the relevant and productive paternal law invisible."[62] Indeed, this vocabulary, together with Kristeva's theories about "a pre-paternal causality," the disruptive potential of the semiotic and maternity, are now seen "as a *paternal* causality under the guise of a natural or distinctively maternal causality." Butler observes that "whereas Kristeva posits a maternal body prior to discourse that exerts its own causal force in the structure of drives, Foucault would doubtless argue that the discursive production of the maternal body as prediscursive is a tactic in the self-amplification and concealment of those specific power relations by which the trope of the maternal body is produced."[63] This observation certainly encourages a far more critical and cautious use both of Kristeva and Bynum than are found in some recent attempts to argue for the subversive and empowering forces

---

60. Foucault (1980), 59; see similarly Butler (1990), 90.

61. See Foucault (1981) and Butler (1990), chap. 3; for a characteristically independent and lively attempt to deploy both Foucault and Freud, see Dollimore (1991), chaps. 8, 11, 12, 14 and the comments on this at 105–6, 175–90.

62. Butler (1990), 91; contrast the use of Kristeva in Lochrie (1991a; 1991b).

63. Butler (1990), 90–92; see also her comments on "the law's uncanny capacity to produce only those rebellions that it can guarantee will—out of fidelity—defeat themselves and those subjects who, utterly subjected, have no choice but to reiterate the law of their genesis."

of late medieval devotion centered on imitations of the dominant figuration of Christ's body and humanity.

The perspectives elaborated upon here by Foucault, Riley, and Butler encourage a question that is slightly different from those shaping traditional research in this field and from Bynum's. The question can be formulated as follows: To what technologies of power was Christ's body being subjected, and with what consequences? When I have summarized some possible responses, I shall ask another question: Did anyone in late medieval England resist what was being done to this humanity? Did anyone seek to circumvent the dominant figurations of the tortured, bleeding body on the Cross? And if anyone did, can we discover the reasons and consequences?

In considering what the late medieval church did to Christ's humanity we can recollect James Marrow's observation that "the Man of Sorrows, or suffering Christ, does not really appear in the Gospels," nor does a focus on "the physical distress" of Christ.[64] This is true not only of the very "high" Christology of Saint John's Gospel but of the synoptic accounts too. Characteristic of their vision of Jesus of Nazareth are descriptions such as the following:

> And Jesus went about all Galilee, teaching in their synagogues and preaching the gospel of the kingdom and healing all manner of sickness and every infirmity among the people. (Matthew 4:23)

> And Jesus making answer said to them: Go and relate to John what you have heard and seen. The blind see, the lame walk, the lepers are cleansed, the deaf hear, the dead rise again, the poor have the gospel preached to them. (Matthew 11:4–5)[65]

The Gospels' Jesus is what his disciples recollect on the road to Emmaus: "a prophet, mighty in work and word before God and all the people" (Luke 24:19). Mobile, articulate, teaching, healing, he is a layman with a public and prophetic set of practices. Time and again the Gospels show his life and words as an unacceptable challenge to dominant institutions and traditions: "Why do thy disciples transgress the tradition of the ancients?" (Matthew 15:2). For this reason he can be classified as one who threatens the survival of true religion, a diabolic subverter of divine tradition and

---

64. Marrow (1979), 44.

65. For similar descriptions of Jesus's practice, see Mark 1:14–14, 32–33, 40–42; Matthew 9:35; Luke 4:16–22.

the customs of his people (for example: Matthew 9:10–14, 34; Matthew 12:22–24 and 26:1–5; Luke 8:43–48 and 11:14–15; John 8:1–11, and 11:45–50). Nor did he hold back in his own response to those who "occupy the chair of Moses" (Matthew 23:1–36),[66] or in his challenges to key components of devotional norms (for example, Matthew 12:1–8; John 2:13–20; Luke 6:6–11).

Here it may be helpful, given Bynum's concentration on food practices and food symbolism in the late medieval "imitation of Christ," to recall the Gospels' own concerns in this domain. Such recollection can help us focus on the specific and thoroughly contingent nature of late medieval accounts. "The Son of man came eating and drinking" (Matthew 11:19), says Jesus, and the Gospels' emphasis here is on communal meals, table-fellowship and its symbolism. Typical of the practice and its symbolism is the following:

> as he was sitting at meat in the house, behold many publicans and sinners came and sat down with Jesus and his disciples. And the Pharisees seeing it, said to his disciples: Why doth your master eat with publicans and sinners? (Matthew 9:10–11; for similar examples see Luke 7:36–50 and 19:1–10).

Jesus's response to this orthodox attack is to redirect attention toward the needs of the excluded, toward love and mercy (Matthew 9:12–13). Such conflicts around table-fellowship in the Gospels are, as Marcus Borg has shown, "about the shape of the community whose life truly manifests loyalty to Yahweh."[67] The Pharisees' meal symbolized the construction of "a holy community," one demanding exclusion of the unreformed, the impure, the ritually unclean, the outcasts—"sinners." Jesus' feeding, his "table-fellowship," was a public, and profoundly political challenge to this model: "table-fellowship with the unacceptable or outcasts was part of the restorative healing process."[68] It was a performative and alternative image of community, of inclusiveness.

Comparison with the Gospels brings out how the "holy" fasting and feasting Bynum collects was strikingly separatist and, most important, under the confessorial direction and narrative authority of the official cleri-

---

66. For a characteristic Wycliffite commentary on Matthew 23, see Hudson and Gradon (1988–90), 3:88–91; and esp. Wyclif's own "Exposicio" in Wyclif (1913), 313–53.

67. Borg (1984), 81.

68. Borg (1984), chaps. 4–5, 9; on food and its symbolism, see also Crossan (1991), 341–44, 360–67. On "table community," see also Schussler-Fiorenza (1983), 344–46.

cal elite. Here were a set of practices presented as an *imitatio Christi* and now, we have seen, uncritically described as such by historians. But such description occludes the way they were an *imitatio* of the dominant and officially produced body of Christ, while official body, *imitatio,* and modern descriptions all occlude the fact that according to the Gospels it was the official unacceptability of Jesus' public teaching and style of life that led to his trial and horrible death. As the Dominican theologian Edward Schillebeeckx has pointed out, "Jesus did not seek his own death, and he did not even want his passion—Gethsemane is a radical contradiction of that."[69] Once the occlusion I have just noted has taken place, it becomes easier to transform "Christ's humanity" into his tortured, bleeding body and set up that body as the dominant figure of Christ in late medieval devotion, an icon to be adored and a model to be imitated. Furthermore, as illustrated earlier, the "imitation" of this officially produced body was accompanied by narratives of miracles that vindicated this "imitation," vindicated the official model of Christ's body on which the "imitation" was grounded and, in relationship to the eucharist and eucharist miracles, vindicated the presence of this very body in the eucharist "Corpus Christi," the "corpus verum et proprium," the body that only the institution's male officials could make. Juxtaposing the body of Christ figured in the late medieval church with the Gospels' Jesus can bring out an aspect of the later construction that seems not to be much discussed in current literary and historical work. It is, however, lucidly articulated by Edward Schillebeeckx in some observations on orthodox late medieval devotion:

> Cradle and cross were an initiation into the "suffering Jesus": a helpless child between ox and ass and a Jesus who goes staggering up to Golgotha. . . . However authentic this experience may be, here the Christian interpretation of suffering enters a phase in which the symbol of the cross becomes a disguised legitimation of social abuses, albeit to begin with still unconsciously. . . . "Suffering in itself," no longer suffering through and for others, took on a mystical and positive significance so that instead of having a critical power it really acquired a reactionary significance. Suffering in itself became a "symbol."[70]

---

69. Schillebeeckx (1990), 794; see also Schillebeeckx (1979), 179–87; see similarly McCabe (1991), 92–94.

70. Schillebeeckx (1990), 699.

This is an extremely important insight, whatever qualifications it invites, because it raises as a topic for reflection the flow of power, of official institutional power in the making of the late medieval body of Christ, and in the incitements to "imitate" that body. Schillebeeckx maintains that Christ's suffering became isolated "from the historical events which made it a suffering through and for others because of his critical preaching."[71] In this way, he notes elsewhere, the dominant tradition sidelined the active preacher of the kingdom, the one demanding "unconditional and liberating sovereign love . . . a new relationship of human beings to God, with as its tangible and visible side a new type of liberating relationship between men and women," a society "where master-servant relationships no longer prevail, quite different from life under Roman occupation."[72] Undoubtedly true of later medieval orthodoxy in the English church, a fact to which we shall return in a moment, Schillebeeckx's history could be related to aspects of liberation theology in Central and Latin America from the 1960s, while this could in turn stimulate further research into the political implications of late medieval representations of Christ's humanity, in theology as well as in devotional practices, sermons, and iconography. For liberation theologians have been acutely self-reflexive about their own church's relationships to existing social and political forms of domination, attentive to all aspects of their church's traditions and a God who called an enslaved people to freedom, transformed but preserved that call in the life of Christ, and continues to demand its practical elaboration in present circumstances. Juan L. Segundo writes in his monumental study of Jesus:

> there is no divine revelation that does not take its course through preferences and concrete realizations on the plane of interpersonal relations, education, economics, politics, and societal life. The revelation of Jesus does not constitute an exception. . . . On the basis of divine revelation he was destroying the foundation of an authority structure that was political in the name of an idolatrous conception of God, that was conveying a false image of God.[73]

Like other liberation theologians Segundo's biblical exegesis works to bring out how readily religious forms sacralize oppression while his model of

---

71. Schillebeeckx (1990), 700.
72. Schillebeeckx (1987), 19–20.
73. Segundo (1985), 85, and see chaps. 5–7.

conversion is a movement from "oppressive security" to "liberating insecurity."[74] As David McLellan has noted, "liberation theology sees the message of Exodus as ultimately fulfilled through the ministry of Christ the Liberator. The key texts here are the Beatitudes, the preaching of the kingdom by Jesus, and the separation of the sheep from the goats in Matthew 25."[75] The contrasts between late medieval orthodoxies and these exegetical, iconographic, and theological orientations around the Gospels and the "humanity" of Christ are sharp. In fact McLellan makes an observation that goes to the heart of such contrasts and illuminates my present concerns: in liberation theology, he writes, "there is more emphasis on the Resurrection than the Crucifixion."[76] And the implications of such an emphasis, the choices involved, are perfectly clear to Segundo as he reflects on the traditions of his church:

> We cannot minimize the fact that the shadow of the cross, which his disciples must carry "daily," has caused us to forget something just as important: Jesus was, and wanted to be, a sign of *joy* for the masses in Israel. . . . Jesus himself defines the proclamation as an announcement of joy to sinners and the poor. And he goes even further than that. He says that his parables (his main preaching instructions) are not designed to convert adversaries of the kingdom; he states that in fact the parables are purposely designated to make conversion difficult. Such a purpose is hardly believable in terms of any standpoint except a political one, which essentially entails bringing real conflicts out into the open and accentuating them.[77]

If late medieval orthodoxy in England did not "forget" the Jesus who Segundo finds in the Gospels, a Jesus who had been perfectly familiar to Saint Francis, it certainly sidelined that Jesus through its intense concentration on Passion, crucifixion, and the tortured body we have discussed and exemplified. But does this turn to liberation theology make me guilty of what Bynum calls "presentism"? Does it mean that I have abandoned this

---

74. Segundo (1985), 131, and see chap. 8.

75. McLellan (1993), 57.

76. McLellan (1993), 63; the differences between the emphasis on "the Resurrection" in this context and the emphasis in Bynum (1995) are fascinating and should be a fruitful topic of inquiry.

77. Segundo (1985), 146–47, 148; see also Schillebeeckx (1979), 179–87, and Schillebeeckx (1987).

book's commitment to the analysis of late medieval England and its forms of Christianity? Is the exegetical perspective and the version of Christ's humanity we find in Juan Segundo or Edward Schillebeeckx utterly alien to anyone in the later Middle Ages, the outcome of incommensurable traditions? Did the dominant representations of Christ's humanity on which we have concentrated, including both its form in the eucharist and its role as privileged model for pious imitation, achieve an absolute hegemony in late medieval English culture?

All these questions must be answered in the negative. The projects of many late medieval Christians included a response to the Gospels, and to current orthodoxies, quite congruent with aspects of commentary by Segundo and Schillebeeckx. It is to oppositional traditions in late fourteenth- and early fifteenth-century England that we now turn, focusing only on those aspects that are most relevant to this inquiry into representations of Christ's humanity, imitations of Christ, and the political dimensions of orthodox figurations, doctrine, and devotion in this domain.

CHAPTER TWO

The Humanity of Christ: Representations in Wycliffite Texts and *Piers Plowman*

DAVID AERS

But, as Austyn notiþ heere, þis maystir made his cros as a
chayer, and tauȝte hangynge on þe cros, for he hatiþ ydelnese.
—*English Wycliffite Sermons*, "In Die Parasceues"[1]

That on þe friday folwynge for mankyndes sake
Iusted in Iherusalem, a ioye to vs alle.
—*Piers Plowman*, B version, 18.162–63[2]

In the first part of this chapter I consider how Christ's humanity was
represented in Lollard or Wycliffite Christianity.[3] Reflection on this opposi-

---

1. Hudson and Gradon (1988–90), 3:183; references to this volume hereafter in my text.

2. *Piers Plowman: B version* (Langland 1988); references to passus and lines hereafter in my text. When reference is made to C version, edition is *Piers Plowman: the C-text* (Langland 1979).

3. On the term *lollard*, see Scase (1989), 125–60, and Hudson (1988), 2–3; reasons for using the terms "Wycliffite" and "Lollard" as synonyms given in Hudson (1988), 2–4.

tional tradition can contribute to understanding the figurations of Christ in the orthodox religion of the period and reminds us that these were not inevitable, not uncontested, not politically neutral and not part of a homogeneous "traditional religion" in a homogeneous world.[4] Lollards can exemplify some of the ways in which late medieval culture came to include conflicts over what constituted appropriate forms of Christian discipleship, over access to the Scriptures, over hermeneutic authority, over many aspects of ecclesiastical organization, including its economic and political power, over the legitimate sources of religious authority and over such fundamental symbols of Christian unity and salvation as the body of Christ, including the form and effects of its presence in the eucharist.[5] The figuration of Christ in his humanity, together with the call to practice imitation of that figuration, was as important to Lollard Christianity as to orthodoxy. But, as we shall see, the constitution of that humanity was markedly different.

Before addressing some examples of Christ's humanity in early Wycliffite writings in English it seems appropriate to give a brief indication of the master's own approach toward the end of his life. He stressed that "Christ, our God, head of the universal church, was during the time of this pilgrimage, the poorest man."[6] Christ's humanity was not only a model of poverty, but of pacifism, of freedom from attachment to place (however sacred), of a thoroughly mobile preaching ministry that involved a commitment to challenge established authorities—as befits the greatest of prophets, Wyclif remarked.[7] Once upon a time the friars had grasped the implications of the Gospels' figuration of Christ but that was a long time ago and today the

---

4. For a monumental and recent attempt to defend such a picture of "traditional religion in England," see Duffy (1992); on this attempt, see Aers (1994c) and on the ideological tradition to which it belongs Aers (1988a); relevant to the issues here is Patterson (1987), part 1.

5. The relevant literature here is formidable, but see particularly the following: Aston (1984; 1993); Beckwith (1993), chaps. 1–3; Cameron (1984), chap. 6; Hudson (1988); Ladurie (1978); Leff (1967); McNiven (1987); Moore (1987); Rubin (1991), chap. 5; Thomson (1965).

6. "Christus, Deus noster, caput universalis ecclesiae, fuit pro tempore huius peregracionis homo pauperimus," *Opera Minora* (Wyclif 1913), 19. See too *De Ecclesia* (Wyclif 1886), 169–80, 187–90; *Dialogus Sive Speculum Ecclesie Militantis* (Wyclif 1876), 11–16, 35–36, 68–69, 83–84; *Tractatus de blasphemia* (Wyclif 1893), 69. For a stimulating attempt to think again about the relations between Wyclif's teaching and the English rising of 1381, see Hudson (1988), 66–70; and, from very different perspectives, Justice (1994), chap. 2.

7. See, sequentially, Wyclif (1887), 277–78, 266–68; Wyclif (1876), 42–43, 59; Wyclif (1913), 76–77; Wyclif (1876), 56–58; and Wyclif (1893), 196–98. On Christ as prophet, for example, see *Sermo 3* in *Sermones* (Wyclif 1888), 1:18–19.

mendicant orders would be sadly unrecognizable to their founders.[8] In Langland's terms, evangelical charity was once found "in a freres frokke" but that was "fern and fele yeer in Frraunceis tyme; / In þat secte siþþe to selde haþ he ben knowe" (15.230–32). Both Wyclif and Langland recall and, in different ways, relate to their own circumstances earlier struggles between radical Franciscans and the hierarchical church over the constitution of the model of evangelical perfection together with its implications for contemporary pursuits of holiness. The struggles in question culminated in Pope John XXII ruling that the renunciation of dominion and lordship was irrelevant to the pursuit of evangelical perfection. The church's lordship and worldly power could not possibly be a problem for Christians.[9] Wyclif found this ruling, and the realities it sanctified, a sign that not Christ but Antichrist was now lord of the church, a perspective that shares more than a little with the representation of the church's situation at the end of *Piers Plowman*.[10]

Wyclif thus sponsored an *imitatio Christi* that depended on having read the Gospels in a manner that extricated them from their conventional meditations, ones so influentially turned into English by Nicholas Love.[11] The imitation of Christ was to involve social engagement, an attempt by laity as well as clerics to reform not only the inner self but the church, through mobile preaching, through teaching and through making the Scriptures accessible to all in the vernacular. Such an imitation of Christ would encourage challenges to the authority and power of the church in many domains: legal, political, economic, military, and theological. In Wyclif's own case these included a clearly articulated policy of ecclesiastical disendowment

---

8. See, for example, Wyclif (1893), chaps. 14–15, and note the use of FitzRalph invoking Saint Francis against modern friars on 232–38.

9. For a summary of this controversy and the pope's attack in the 1320s, see Aers (1988a), 22–25, and notes 14–16 on 186.

10. On the modern church as being under the rule of Antichrist, see exemplification in Leff (1967), 2:536–41; *Piers Plowman*, 20.53–379 (with which compare Wyclif (1887), 258). On Langland's representation of the church and apocalypticism, see Aers (1980), chaps. 2 and 3; Emmerson (1994), which includes important comments on Kerby-Fulton (1990), which attempts to sideline the specificities of post–Black Death England, of Wycliffism, and of much in *Piers Plowman* in order to assimilate it to a Joachite apocalypticism.

11. Nicholas Love explicitly presents the *Mirror* as a substitute for the Gospels, one allegedly more "pleyne" and more suitable "to comun vndirstondyng" of "symple creatures," the laity not fit for the "sadde mete of grete clargye," whose monopoly of direct access to the Gospels must be preserved; see Love (1992), 10. On the Wakefield cycle of plays and Love treating Christ's ministry "almost perfunctorily," see Lepow (1990), 97. For comments on Wyclif's Christ, see Justice (1994b), 83, 85, and 101.

ment to force the church toward forms of life in accord with the version of Christ's humanity Wyclif found in his readings of the Gospels.[12] A Wycliffite imitation of Christ would have encouraged energetic agency, both individual *and* collective, agency that would have revolutionized the organizations of power in the church and transformed the sources and forms of authority.

Not that he forgot the conclusion of Christ's earthly pilgrimage. He maintained that if Christ were to visit Wyclif's world as an unknown priest to preach and practice as he had done during his earthly life, he would be excommunicated by the Roman curia and unless he recanted the truth he taught he would be condemned and burned as a heretic and blasphemer. This is certain, he writes, because we can see how Christians who show a spark of Christ's discourse and seek to imitate his way are persecuted by the modern church.[13] So Wyclif's representation of Christ's humanity does not negate the Crucifixion nor occlude his suffering. What it does do is refuse to split these off from Christ's prophetic ministry, its transgressions of existing powers and its political, communitarian dimensions. It becomes very difficult to abstract cross and suffering from contingent particularities of human power, authority, justice and self-legitimating ideologies. The imperative "to perform an *imitatio Christi,* to become what Wyclif termed a *Christicola,* a dweller in Christ in whom Christ himself is to be found" might well lead to persecution under the present church.[14] The preacher "was not to govern people but to direct by word and deed into the ways of love" and his activities might well lead to suffering, including death like Christ's.[15] Such suffering would involve sacrifice, representative sacrifice of the self for the community, for the "salvation of the kingdom as a *populus Dei.*" If this happens, the situation recapitulates that in which the Old Testament prophets were stoned; and stoned by the same "Ecclesia hereticorum."[16] Suffering, pain, and death are certainly not the aims at all. The aims are the reformation of England, "reformatio regni et ecclesiae," one

---

12. Wyclif's insistence on disendowment of the church is pervasive and one of the earlier strands in his development of radical reformist positions: see, for example, *De Ecclesia* (Wyclif 1886), chaps. 8, 9, 12, 14, 15, 16; *De blasphemia* (Wyclif 1893), 32–36, 81–84 and chap. 17 (esp. 267–69), *Dialogus* (Wyclif 1876), chap. 36; see Leff (1967), 2:541–43.

13. Wyclif (1893), 62; see also 72 and Wyclif (1876), 22. On this whole topic, see Wilks (1994).

14. Wilks (1994), 53: this paragraph draws heavily on Lynn Staley's perceptions of the relevance of Wilks's essay to our own project.

15. Wilks (1994), 53–57 (quotation from 53, 56, 57).

16. Wilks (1994), 59, 56.

that in Wyclif's view depended on Caesar, on the lay ruling classes and, particularly, the monarch.[17] Such a rhetoric of suffering, and an enactment of the fate it anticipates, has virtually nothing in common with the self-tortures, individualistic abjections, and bodily imitations of a "feminized" Christ that Caroline Bynum has illustrated, imitations considered in the previous chapter. Indeed, in that context it is worth noting that Wyclif does not characterize either this suffering or Christ, its model, with images and stereotypes of the "feminine."

Wyclif's opposition to the dogma of transubstantiation in his last years is well known and it is only recalled here to round off this brief consideration of his representation of Christ's humanity. He maintained Christ's real presence in the eucharist but not in the literal and bodily manner affirmed and so vividly illustrated by the orthodox, as exemplified in the previous chapter. Christ's real presence was in spiritual power; his body present figuratively; and the reception of Christ spiritual, in faith. The priest's words did not annihilate the substance of bread or the substance of wine any more than they produced the actual body that was tortured, bled, and died on the cross, the body produced by the orthodox church.[18] Wyclif's position was thoroughly Augustinian.[19] But however Augustinian such views they could not be heard with sympathy in the late medieval church, as the burning of Sawtry and Badby would soon show.[20] This was because the orthodox version of Christ's body, so literally and so efficaciously present after the priest's words of consecration, had become invested with immense power, immense utilities, and had also become a stupendous guarantor of ecclesiastical and clerical power, in just the ways Sarah Beckwith has recently described.[21] As Gordon Leff remarked many years ago, Wyclif's theology of the eucharist had "directly ecclesiological consequences":

> By locating the change to the host in the spiritual coming of Christ,
> rather than the physical disappearances of the bread, the role of the

---

17. Wilks (1994), 61; see Aers (1980), chap. 2.

18. For examples of Wyclif's teaching on the eucharist in his later years, see Wyclif (1893), 20–31; (1876), 54; (1888), 2:453–63 (a sermon on Corpus Christi day); good accounts of this teaching can be found in Leff (1967), 2:549–57 and in Hudson (1988), 281–83.

19. For Augustine on John 6, see his *Homilies on the Gospel of John* (*In Joannis Evangelium Tractatus*), tractate 24–27, English translation in Augustine (1986). This work is explicitly used by Wyclif in the sermon cited in note 18 (Wyclif 1888, 2:456).

20. On the burning of William Sawtry and John Badby, see McNiven (1987).

21. Beckwith (1993); also Zika (1988).

priest was correspondingly altered. Where previously his words of consecration had made the bread and wine into Christ's body, these now became the occasion, the efficacious sign (as he called it), of Christ's hidden presence.[22]

Nor was the priest's role, and the church's role, merely "altered." As the defenders of the orthodox version of the humanity of Christ and its presence in the eucharistic sacrifice understood, within the lines of a Wycliffite approach the priest's role could come to seem irrelevant, a role that could certainly be taken by devout laypeople, men *and* women. They could discern the potential effects of the shape they saw stalking onto their domains, the doctrine of the priesthood of all believers, men *and* women, effects soon to be detected among East Anglian laypeople: "every man and every woman beyng in good lyf oute of synne is as good prest and hath as muche poar of God in al thynges as ony prest ordred, be he pope or bisshop." So Hawisia Moone of Loddon maintained, a view supported by many other Norfolk and Suffolk people forced to abjure and do public penance, including public floggings, in that particular purge which saw the burning of William White, William Waddon, and Hugh Pye in Norwich, in 1428.[23]

People like these, finding much to commend, follow, and develop in Wyclif's teaching, tended to represent Christ's humanity and its imitation in ways similar to those just ascribed to Wyclif.[24] They aimed at radical transformation of a wide range of Christian practices and doctrines, from the eucharist to marriage, from pilgrimages to the nature of the priesthood, from the place of Scripture to the current mandatory penitential systems, from the role of images to the range of activities open to women. In this multifaceted challenge to the most powerful and wealthy institution in Europe it is hardly surprising that their vision of Christ should focus on his prophetic ministry and lifestyle or that they should have had no interest in isolating the tortured bleeding/nurturing body of Christ produced by the late medieval church as the central object of devotion. In their paradigm, like Wyclif's, imitation of Christ would not concentrate on this body or

---

22. Leff (1967), 2:557; see also Rubin (1991), 325–26 and McNiven (1987), 23–29, 38–40.

23. See the text edited by N. P. Tanner, 142; similar examples are on 49, 52, 60–61, 67, 81, 140, 147, 163, 166, 179; see Hudson (1988), 276, 325–27. On the role of women in Lollardy, see esp. Cross (1978) and Aston (1984), chap. 2. For the city to which these East Anglian Lollards were summoned, see Tanner (1984). For a rather different but not contradictory approach to these Norfolk and Suffolk Lollards, see Justice (1994b).

24. *English Works of Wyclif* (Matthew 1902), 451 and 377; similarly, 368–72, 376–82.

entail self-inflicted sufferings. If violent suffering came to Wycliffite Christians, it was to be the result of confronting powerful human organizations with teachings and practices Lollards found entailed by the representations of Christ in the Gospels, but which their orthodox opponents found subversive, anarchic, and demonic.[25] They had, it seems, recaptured what a modern Catholic theologian calls "the dangerous and subversive memory of Jesus."[26]

How this "dangerous and subversive memory of Jesus" could work in early fifteenth-century England can be exemplified by considering the Lollard account of William Thorpe's interrogation by Archbishop Arundel in 1407.[27] Near the opening of the testimony Thorpe aligns "Cristis gospel" with the term "freedom." He goes on to argue that the cause of the Incarnation is to be understood in relation to this term: "for which fredom Crist bicam man and schedde oute his hert blood" (25). For Thorpe to mean freedom from sin would be conventional enough. Any yet while this meaning may doubtless be assumed it turns out not to be the one that concerns Thorpe. Nor does he choose, here or later, to concentrate his imagistic or analytic attentions on the shedding of blood he mentions here. Where then does he go with Christ's humanity? And what model for the *imitatio Christi* does he compose?

The "fredom" for which Christ became human is here part of a model of Christ centered on the mobile and prophetic preacher committed to bringing the "gospel," and its "fredom," to all people (25, 44–47, 49, 59). The model is not the twisted, pulverized, tortured, bleeding body that had become the dominant version of Christ's humanity in late medieval devotion. Nor, consequently, does it sponsor a call to imagine and dwell on such a body. Still less, it follows, was it a summons to *identify* with this figure, whether in the immensely influential forms cultivated in the *Meditationes Vitae Christi* (just about to become a major vernacular text in the church's attempt to eliminate Lollardy), or in the more embodied forms celebrated by Caroline Bynum in *Holy Feast and Holy Fast.*

The model and its imitation is exemplified in the account of Thorpe's

---

25. For characteristic orthodox response to Lollardy, in the vernacular, see Hoccleve's poem to Oldcastle, Hoccleve (1970), 8–24; see Hudson (1988), chap. 9. On the place of the Gospels, see Matthew (1880), 371, 381–82.

26. Tracy (1981), 427.

27. *The Testimony of William Thorpe* is cited here in the text from Anne Hudson's edition as listed under Thorpe (1993). There is some discussion of Thorpe's "play" and his "imitatio" of Christ in Kendall (1986), 61–63.

activity in Shrewsbury, the place of his arrest. The archbishop charges
Thorpe with having "troublid þe comounte of Schrovesbirie" with his
teaching (44–45; see also 43). Thorpe does not seek to deny this accusation. On the contrary, he claims to have been pursing an *imitatio Christi*.
He reminds his superior how "alle þe comountee of þe citee of Ierusalem
was troublid wiþ þe techynge of Cristis owne persone." In the divine humanity, Thorpe emphasizes, is found, "þe moost prudente prechour þat
evere was or schal be" (45). As for the trouble in the church, so memorably
related later in the testimony (52), Thorpe evokes his model: "al þe synagoge of Nazareth was so moved aȝens Crist, and so fulfillid wiþ wraþþe
towardis him for his prechinge aȝens þat þe men of þe synagoge rison vp,
and þei þresten Crist out of her citee, and þei ledden him vp unto þe heiȝþe
of a mounteyne for to have þrowen him doun þere heedlyngis" (45). The
model invoked here comes from Luke's gospel. It recounts how Jesus read
from the scroll of the prophet Isaiah, choosing these words: "The spirit of
the Lord is on me, for he has annointed me to bring the good news to the
afflicted. He has sent me to proclaim liberty to captives, sight to the blind,
to let the oppressed go free, to proclaim a year of favour from the Lord."
Jesus then tells those present that the text is now being fulfilled. But he
accompanies this proclamation of emancipation with disturbing warnings
and memories: "no prophet is ever accepted in his own country;" nor could
Elijah and Elisha save all those suffering (Luke 4:16–27). Here all become
"enraged" and take him out of the town, "intending to throw him off the
cliff" (Luke 4:28–29). The model is of a prophetic preacher bringing a
gospel of freedom to captives, a gospel of healing; but also a gospel that
will incense those whose form of life seems threatened by such a proclamation. And those threatened may be not only the leaders of the established
religious institutions but those Arundel describes as "þe bailies and þe
comouns" of Shrewsbury who, so he tells Thorpe, want the troublesome
preacher executed (43). It is important to notice that while imitating this
model of Christ's humanity may lead to physical violation and execution
it will only do so contingently. That is, the purpose and focus of the imitation does not make bodily suffering the goal. On the contrary, just as Christ
in this instance escaped those who wished to kill him (Luke 4:30) so Lollards were notoriously prepared to do what they could to escape the
church's punitive aims. Their model taught them that imitating Christ
meant a prophetic, vernacular and mobile proclamation of the gospel and
its "fredom": persecution and, finally, violent death might be the outcome
but the tortured, suffering body was not the icon shaping the project.

The memory of the troublesome Christ, let alone an imitation modeled on such a figure, was hardly prominent in orthodox devotion and the archbishop is unimpressed with Thorpe's typology. For him the issue is clear: Thorpe preaches without episcopal licence and assumes a calling that sidelines ecclesiastic authority: "ȝe doon wiþouten autorite of any bischop. For ȝe presumen þat þe Lord haþ chosen ȝou oonli for to preche as feiþful dissciplis and special suers of Crist" (45). Thorpe's response is that his priestly office gives him an especially sharp obligation to follow the "ensaumple of his [Christ's] moost holi lyuyage," which means "to preche bisili; frely and treuli þe word of God" (45). As for the "autorite" here, Thorpe maintaines it is in the gospels, "Goddis word" (46). The archbishop treats this as grossly irrelevant: "Lewed losel! . . . I sent þe neuere to preche" (46). He and his subordinate not only hold different understandings of "autorite." They also assume different models, different images of Christ's humanity and, it follows, of what would constitute imitating Christ in the contemporary world. Thorpe's relationship to the sources of his model in the gospels was plainly mediated by his chosen teacher, "maistir Ioon Wiclef," a teacher Thorpe describes as "þe moost vertuous and goodlich wise man þat I herde of owhere eiþer knew" (40–41). Time and again he returns to Christ's humanity as the model for his own troublesome and oppositional practices, "in prechinge and in techinge" (50), a model that sidelines the role of the priest as bestower of the sacraments, especially of the eucharist (49–52, 69–71). Indeed, as this teaching should lead people "inward," lead them to close off their "outward wittis" and their habitual attention to "vtward seeing and heeringe," so he emphasizes that Thomas's concentration on the holes made by nails driven into Christ's body and by the lance in his side was a symptom of lack of faith rather than an orientation encouraged by Christ (59; see John 20:24–29): "siþ Crist blessiþ hem þat seen him neuere bodili and have bileued feiþfulli into him, it sufficiþ þane to alle men þoruz heerynge and knowinge of Goddis worde, and in doinge þeraftir, for to bileuen into God þouȝ þei seeȝen neuere ymage maad wiþ mannes hond" (59; see also 79). The church's Christ, Thorpe maintains, is a version of his humanity which works "to make men þralle" whereas, he reiterates, Christ's Incarnation and death was "to make man fre," a freedom that includes freedom from many ecclesiastic "obseruaunces and ordynaunces" that are not found in "þe lyvynge ne þe techinge of Crist" (85).

Thorpe's views on the eucharist are interrogated (52–56). Like Wyclif, Thorpe turns to Saint Augustine to explain his understanding of the real presence and the role of faith in the reception of Christ (54).[28] The body of Christ produced by the church is thus negated and with that its power and authority. Again, the words ascribed to Arundel justly reflect the hierarchy's perceptions and treatment of the issues here: "I purpose to make þee to obeie þe to þe determynacioun of holi chirche" (55).[29] For Lollards such a purpose showed that what passed for truth and knowledge was an effect of the power they sought to resist. The representation of Christ's humanity was enmeshed in what Sarah Beckwith has analysed as the mobilizations of "symbolic meanings in the service of power."[30]

At this point it seems worth asking what a Wycliffite sermon on Good Friday would do. Here, if anywhere, we might expect a convergence with orthodox representations of Christ's humanity and with orthodox devotional forms around the cross. In the Wycliffite sermon cycles so superbly edited by Anne Hudson and Pamela Gradon we find a sermon for the day on which "men shulen speke of Cristis passioun, and se in what forme he sufferide."[31] And yet, even here, no such convergence emerges. This seems surprising enough to invite a brief account of how the writer treats the Passion and Crucifixion in John 18 and 19. The mode of proceeding is typified by the reading of Christ's arrest. John's text, the preacher notes, teaches us that "Crist louyde not for to fi3te" and this becomes an "ensaumple" directed against the contemporary church which, while claiming to be Christ's mystical body organizes, legitimizes, and glorifies a range of wars (173–74). Yet Christ's own nonviolence, the writer observes, involved an active and sustained opposition to established power, one that showed exemplary "hardynesse" (175). Even when it comes to the gospel's brief account of the scourging and crowning with thorns, and even though the day is Good Friday, the sermon offers absolutely no focus on Christ's body, none of the traditional late medieval elaborations of the scene and its violence (179). Instead of these, it examines the nature of Pilate's injustice and moves on to consider Christ's trial as a trial for "heresye" (180). The Passion and Crucifixion thus figure forth the constitution of "heresye" in late medieval England and its persecution not only by church, by

28. See Hudson's citations of Augustine on 118, n. 1008 (Thorpe 1993); see also note 19 above.

29. For an excellent account of the processes of such making, see McNiven (1987); also Catto (1985b).

30. Beckwith (1993), 115, and Rubin (1991), 319–34; see similarly in William Taylor's Paul's Cross sermon of 1406, edited with Thorpe's testimony by Hudson, in W. Taylor (1993), 5–13, 18–19.

31. Hudson (1988–90), 3:172–87, page references in my text.

"bischops," but also by the secular powers Wyclif had hoped to involve in his projects of reformation, "seculer iugis" (181). The writer addresses the way pope and cardinals "brennen men as heretikes" for refusing to obey ecclesiastical laws that are human inventions "not groundide on Goddis lawe" (181). In this way meditation on Good Friday, Passion and cross sustain both the model of Christ's humanity we have identified as Wycliffite and also its imitations in contemporary communities. To the very end of his life, on the cross itself, Christ continues his prophetic, teaching, and preaching ministry: "þis maystir made his cros a chayer, and tauȝte hangynge on þe cros" (183).[32] This striking and strangely revealing image is then followed by the writer turning the seven last sayings of Christ into a sermon on the seven sins which includes critical observations on aspects of the modern church (183–84). Even when he comes to the blood and water flowing from Christ's pierced side, such a major focus in late medieval devotion, the preacher offers none of the familiar images of breast or milk or womb or vulva, no hints of "feminization" of Christ's body, no depictions of nurturing blood flowing into open mouths or chalices—in fact none of the commonplace figurations addressed in Chapter 1. He finds it sufficient to comment that the blood and water miraculously flowing from the dead Christ "bitokeneþ ful biggyng of man, and ful waysshyng of his synne" (186). This sharp contrast with dominant late medieval traditions of devotion continues in the sermon's treatment of the deposition. Instead of the Virgin Mary lamenting, swooning, and clinging to the dead body we read reflections on the need to defend Christ's teaching against orthodox priests, the successors of priests who killed Christ, and the need for the help of secular powers to help in this defence (186).[33]

Given this approach to Christ's humanity on Good Friday itself, and given Wycliffite opposition to the dogma of transubstantiation and its battery of supporting eucharist miracles, it is not surprising that a Lollard sermon for Corpus Christi day will stand in sharp opposition to conven-

---

32. Wendy Scase, examining the complex history of the term *lollard* quotes from "a tract on biblical translation" in which "Christ on the cross was "þe most blessed loller þat euer was or euer schal be . . . for our synnes lollynge on þe rode tree" (Scase 1989, 154). For the preacher of the Good Friday sermon I am discussing here, "lollynge" would not convey a sufficiently active, focused teaching and control, a control he finds in Christ even on the cross. There is much in common here with Saint John's representations of the Passion and Crucifixion; see Ashton (1991), chap. 13.

33. For characteristic representation of the Virgin Mary here, see *Meditations* (1985), 25–26, 29–30.

tional ones.[34] But because the eucharist was a crucial place for the production and reinforcement of the orthodox figuration of Christ's humanity, I mention it here, very briefly. As in Wyclif's thought about the eucharist, Saint Augustine's homily on John 6 is a guide and the writer explicitly invokes this (248).[35] The real presence is "goostly," the reception of Christ "spiritual" and enabled by "good loue" and faith—"and herfore seiþ Austyn 'Bileue wel, and þou hast etyn.'" The priests words neither annihilate any substance nor introduce Christ's humanity in the "bodily" manner orthodoxy maintained, "necke and bac, hed and foot," a manner vividly illustrated by John Mirk, Nicholas Love, and many others, as we noted in Chapter 1. Christ's presence is real and sacramental, "sacramentaliche Goddis body," so that if the Host happens to be eaten by the mouse, the mouse "etiþ not Cristis body, al ȝif he ete þis sacrament, for þe mous fayliþ gostly witt to chewe in hym þis bileue" (247–48). This is all extremely close to Augustine's insistence that the sacrament is for one who eats "within, not without; who eateth in his heart, not who presses with his teeth."[36] Yet however Augustinian the approach may be in the sermons I have discussed or in the vision of Thorpe, or Wyclif, it is not hard to see how an orthodox late medieval Christian might feel that Wycliffite Christians not only subverted "þe sacramentis seven," together with the divinely sanctioned and exclusive mediations for the "grauntyng of grace," but that "Cristis bitter passioun, ȝe sette not at an hawe."[37] Yet however understandable, this judgment involved not only a misrecognition of Wycliffite understanding of Christ's death and their forms of devotion. It also involved a misrecognition of just why Wycliffite approaches to Christ's Passion should seem so impious. For their revisions here contributed to a perception that central aspects of contemporary doctrine, ritual, and iconography were not, as the church maintained, transcendentally warranted but the thoroughly contingent productions of identifiable human agents whose reiterated performances were both the effects and guarantors of powers whose beneficiaries they were. The vernacular propagation of a gospel that included such perceptions could hardly be welcomed by the church.

34. See Hudson (1988–89) 3:247–48; and for a good example of conventional orthodox materials here, Erbe (1905), 222–24.

35. For Augustine on John 6, see note 19; the quotation below from "Austyn" is from tractate 26.1, p. 168.

36. Augustine (1986), 26.12, 172.

37. Friar Daw's Reply in Heyworth (1968), lines 95–98; on this text, Hudson (1988) 188–90.

Conflicts over the representation of Christ's humanity and the appropriate focus on the Passion, Crucifixion, and earthly body of Christ were issues of very immediate experience in late medieval England. A couple of examples from Susan Brigden's work on London and the reformation conveys something of this:

> Crosses were everywhere in Tudor London as a remembrance of Christ's sacrifice, but Lollards despised such reminders. Why should the cross be worshipped, asked George Browne, when it was but "a hurt and pain unto our Saviour Christ in the time of his passion?" As the crucifix was carried to the Lollard Thomas Blake as he lay on his death-bed, Joan Baker protested to their parish priest in St Mary Magdalen Milk Street that "the crucifix was not to give confidence nor trust in but as a false god."[38]

Joan Baker and George Brown uttered these views in the early sixteenth century but we can now see out of what a long tradition they spoke, a tradition that had challenged orthodox figurations of Christ's humanity and the devotions centred on them, identifying the dominant symbols of the holy as productions of human power that lacked the divine foundations it claimed. In her book *Christ's Body* Sarah Beckwith includes a chapter on "crucifixion piety," during which she considers the trial of the Wycliffite peer, Sir John Oldcastle in 1413, before Archbishop Arundel. She quotes a Lollard account of Sir John's response to one of his clerical interrogators who was demanding if he would "worship . . . the cross of our Lord Jesus Christ": Sir John "spread his arms abroad" and replied, "this is a very cross."[39] Out of context, the gesture itself could be taken as yet another orthodox "imitatio" of the officially produced body of Christ: perhaps like Eustochia of Messini using ropes "to stretch her arms in the form of a cross"; or perhaps like Margery Kempe's, in Jerusalem:

> whan þei cam vp on-to þe Mownt of Caluarye, she fel down þat sche mygth not stondyn ne knelyn but walwyd & wrestyd wyth hir body, spredying hir armys a-brode, & cryed wyth a lowde voys.[40]

---

38. Bridgen (1989), 95.

39. Beckwith (1993), chap. 3; on Oldcastle, 70–76; quotation here is on 72.

40. See, respectively, Bell (1985), 143, and Meech and Allen (1940), 68; see similarly 70 and 140.

But Margery is being helped by friars, as befits one whose approach to the body of Christ whether in the liturgy, in visions, or in the eucharist confirms official doctrine and iconography. However often she was interrogated her orthodoxy was always vindicated—hence her charming encounter with Archbishop Arundel, in which "her dalyawns contynuyd tyl sterrys apperyd in þe fyrmament," an encounter utterly different to Oldcastle's.[41] As for Oldcastle, Beckwith quotes the following: "being asked what honour he would do to the image of Christ on that Cross, he expressly replied that he would only do it the honour to clean it and put it in good custody."[42] Oldcastle's reply involves a striking rejection of the dominant production of the body of Christ and the devotion organized around it. His subversion was recognized as such, with the full consequences.

We can find a similar understanding, though often expressed more fiercely, in the surviving ecclesiastical records of those Norfolk women and men rounded up by the church in 1428–31.[43] Here are some characteristic views:

> . . . no more reverence oweth be do unto the ymages of the crosse than oweth be doon to the galwes whiche men be hanged on. (148)

> . . . the signe of the crosse is the signe of Antecrist, and no more worship ne reverence oweth be do to the crosse than oweth be do to the galwes whiche men be hanged on. (154)

> . . . every suche crosse is the signe and the tokene of Antecrist. (166)

To these people the cross itself had become "the signe" of institutional power: the language they used was an attempt to disenchant (in their terms) the cross, presenting it once more as the mark of actually existing power, "the galwes." Nor were they always satisfied with talk. In the record of John Burrell, servant ("famulus") to Thomas Moone of Loddon in a household devoted to Lollardy, we find that as he and Edmund Archer were walking to Loddon, at vespers, they saw a certain old cross placed near the gate of Loddon Hall. John Burrell struck through it ("percuciebat") with

---

41. Meech and Allen (1940), 37; see Aers (1988a) 108–16, Beckwith (1993), chap. 4; Staley (1994).

42. Beckwith (1993), 72; see also the Ely group discussed in Hudson (1988), 142 and n. 152.

43. N. P. Tanner (1977), references to this edition of the record of these proceedings follow in my own text.

a "fagothook" he had been carrying (76).[44] In an action related both to this and to Oldcastle's gesture at his trial, Margery Baxter of Martham supported her argument against the orthodox use of images, including crucifixes, by stretching out her arms and saying, "this is the true cross of Christ, and you ought and can see and adore that cross every day in your own house" (44). Little could bring home more sharply what was at stake (all too literally) in late medieval figurations of the body of Christ. As Sarah Beckwith demonstrates, "images such as Christ's wounds were not simply subject to an intensely affective devotion of private religion—they were also symbols of political power."[45] This was certainly the understanding of Wycliffites, one seemingly shared in many ways by the church hierarchy in its attempt to exterminate Lollardy and pertinacious Lollards. The humanity of Christ that these people sought to imitate was particularly threatening because it called women and men to develop collective forms of resistance to the powers of the church, resistance to the institutionally guaranteed body of Christ, which in turn guaranteed the sanctity of the institution's power. Contrary to oft-repeated modern assertions, it was not a model of Christ and holiness which fostered an individualism and privatization of piety in opposition to communitarian practices and aspirations.[46] Persecution and the need to go "underground" will always tend to isolate an endangered group from communities in which the majority of people either support the established powers or, if they do not positively support them, restrict their opposition to private or occasional acts of noncooperation and resistance. Nevertheless, as Anne Hudson has shown, Lollards strongly opposed religious forms that necessarily set people apart from their fellow Christians involved in the daily practices on which the preservation of their communities depended, practices that had traditionally been classified as "lay," as worldly or secular. This will to integrate Christianity in the daily life and daily groupings of the working community can be seen in the traces

---

44. Asked by John Wardon's son why he had struck the cross with the fagothook, John Burrell replied that even if he'd struck it more fiercely and with a sharper weapon, that cross would never bleed (N. P. Tanner 1977, 76). He seems to be contrasting his action with the church's punishment of the living images of God (for example, see Margery Baxter in N. P. Tanner 1977, 44). At the same time he is suggesting that the church has, in effect, produced such devotional images to reify and control the humanity of Christ through the Cross as institutional icon, a reification his action symbolically undoes.

45. Beckwith (1993), 75.

46. Invaluable here is Anne Hudson's "Lollard Society" in Hudson (1988), chap. 3; for corrections to clichés about the Protestant invention of and practice of "individualism," see Collinson (1982).

of Lollard practices found in the records edited by Norman Tanner as *Norwich Heresy Trials*.[47] There we find early fifteenth-century Norfolk women and men organizing the study of the Scriptures and their forms of devotion within their homes, trade networks and villages, striving to develop communities of worship, resources (material and spiritual), and human solidarity in which orthodox boundaries between laity and clergy, secular and sacred spaces, secular and sacred people, secular (vernacular) and sacred (Latin) language were dissolved. The Lollard "school" and the Lollard preacher/minister belonged within the "lay" community. From this perspective the urgency of the Lollards' radical reformation of the sacraments, the priesthood, and the place of women in Christianity becomes perfectly cogent. Their challenge to the patriarchal structures sanctified by the male elites who ruled the church, ones reinforced even in standing arrangements for divine worship, is especially noteworthy given current claims for the allegedly "subversive" nature of the practices described by Caroline Bynum, which we considered in Chapter 1. In the contexts of such current scholarship it seems reasonable to note that the project to dissolve the sacralized hierarchy of the church, of divisions between priesthood and laity, women and men, did not come from any "feminization" of Christ's humanity, nor from the dominant figuration of Christ's humanity and the conventional affective languages of suffering, abjection, and pathos. This will be no cause for surprise once we have acknowledged that the conventional, suffering body, together with its "imitation" was one of the effects of power, of an identifiable historical power. The resources for a collective, radical challenge to this power lay elsewhere. This the Wycliffites of late medieval England knew.

And so did the author of *Piers Plowman*. The dominant representations of Christ's humanity, together with the *imitatio Christi* these figurations sponsored, were not set aside only by Wycliffites. They were also set aside in this great and profoundly Christocentric poem. Argumentative, politically engaged, inconsistently but pervasively reformist, it generated some extremely radical positions on the church and its authority while remaining within the framework of orthodoxy as this was constituted in the period between the coming of the Black Death and the burning of John Badby.[48]

---

47. N. P. Tanner (1977); on the courtbook Tanner edits, see Hudson, (1988), 33–36.

48. For editions of *Piers Plowman* used here, see note 2. On the reformist politics of *Piers Plowman*, and their elusive, shifting relations to a shifting orthodoxy that was in a process of making, see Hudson (1988), 398–408; Gradon (1980); Aers (1990); Middleton (1990); Justice (1994b).

I shall now examine the ways in which Langland represents Christ's humanity, establish what a Langlandian *imitatio Christi* might entail and—bearing
in mind the devotional, doctrinal, and cultural contexts followed in this
and Chapter 1—address the political and theological implications of his
choices. I especially want to suggest just why this poet should have found
the dominant representations of Christ's humanity incompatible with his
own Christian project and what his choices may tell us about the figuration
of Christ in late medieval English culture.

The poem opens with a vision of England as a society in which, as
Holy Church remarks, most people's energies are fully absorbed in gaining
material goods and status: "Of oother heuene þan heere holde þei no tale"
(Prologue; 1.7–9). There is a brief reference to those who resist this form
of life through "preieres and penaunce," resistance exemplified by anchors
and hermits. While the poet does not specify what kind of penitential life
he considers an appropriate way of pursuing "loue of oure lord," there
is no hint that this would involve self-inflicted suffering and "abjection"
cultivated by specialized and ecstatic ascetics whose *imitatio Christi* was
modelled on the crucified body of Christ (Pr. 25–30).[49] Certainly by the
time we reach Passus 15 we will know that the love most valued by this
poet is simply not closely bound up with specialized religious vocations
(15.149–250). But we do not have to move far into the poem to meet an
account of *imitatio Christi*. Holy Church promises that, if followed, it will
lead the disciple toward an identification with Christ in which she or he
will become "a god by þe gospel" and "ylik to oure lord" (1.85–91).[50]
What does this entail? Becoming "ylik to oure lord" is being "trewe" of
tongue, doing "þe werkes þerwip" and willing ill to nobody (1.87–91).
Furthermore, the truth Holy Church presents as leading people toward
God's likeness, an imitation of Christ, is based in the maintenance of justice
in the community (1.94–97). The emphasis here on a socially embodied
and collective imitation of Christ, grounded in justice, proves to be characteristic not only of this guide but of the whole poem.[51] From a compressed,

---

49. Attention to the role of hermits in the poem is given by Godden (1984) and Hanna
(1994). I am unpersuaded by James Simpson's view that the poem seeks to discredit Holy
Church and her mode of construction. It seems that he is forced to propound this claim by
his wider thesis about the relations between authoritarianism and fraternal discourse in the
poem; see Simpson (1990b), 24–37.

50. Langland cites Luke but as Pearsall notes in his edition of the C version, the "basic
gospel text here is John 10.34" (Langland 1978, 46). On the idea of becoming gods, see
Augustine (1986), tractate 48.9, p. 269.

51. For diverse studies on the role of justice in the poem, see Bloomfield (1961), chap. 5;
Stokes (1984); Simpson (1990b); and Aers (1994b); on the poem's relations to biblical prophets, see T. L. Steinberg (1991) and Kuczynski (1995), chap. 6.

allusive sequence of images focused on the redemptive forces which divine activity releases in human hearts (1.142–74), she moves to make a prophetic challenge to the rich and mighty in contemporary communities: for them love entails giving to the poor goods that are from God (1.175–84). The sequence joins together creation, Christology, and pneumatology in a quest for justice and charity in contemporary social relations, especially for prophetic justice for "þe pouere." It is revealing and appropriate that Holy Church invokes the epistle of James at this point, directing us to its stress on practical love of one's neighbour and the deadliness of faith without works (1.185–87; James 2:14–26).[52] Her oration contains no implication that imitation of Christ would involve any of the virtuoso feats of "abjection" that could come from a commitment to dominant representation of Christ's humanity. On the contrary, love of neighbor in social practice is given a Christological basis and given as the way humans may move toward God, an ethical disposition which becomes the path of salvation.[53] In this perspective it would make no sense to isolate the individual's pursuit of salvation from the individual's complex and practical relations with neighbors.

Passus 2 begins with the dreamer mentioning "þe blissed barn þat bouʒte vs on þe Rode" (2.3). But instead of a traditional meditation on the passion this introduces a long exploration of social relations pervaded by forces the poet personifies in the female figure he calls Mede.[54] The problems of establishing just relations in the community are not seen as some extraneous "superstructure" to the "real," which is spiritual. On the contrary, reforming Reason preaches "wiþ a cros" while his "sermon" stresses that the quest for a life which "may saue yow alle" is bound up with issues of work, the education of children, the organization of family relations, the practices of "prelates and preestes," and the forms of power in the community (5.9–59). This outlook is affirmed in the collective repentance which follows, sin being presented, traditionally enough, as embedded in specifiable social occupations and relations.[55] This leads to the moving prayer made by Repentance, for mercy and grace to live out the intended conversions. While

---

52. This is at the heart of the teaching offered by Christ in Passus 17.

53. For reflections by a modern theologian that I have found helpful when thinking about these aspects of *Piers Plowman*, see Rahner (1974), chap. 16, esp. 234–35, 242–44.

54. On this figure Yunck (1963), is still indispensable; for recent attempts to consider the role of gender in its making and political function see Aers (1994a) and Lees (1994).

55. For an example of a manual showing this orientation clearly, see Thomas of Chobham (1968). On sin and confession in this context, Tentler (1977).

this Christocentric prayer recollects the death of Christ on "good fryday for mennes sake," the poet gives no attention to the standard focus on the physical tortures and sufferings of Jesus. Instead, he integrates Crucifixion with creation, harrowing of hell, and the power displayed in and through the resurrection. The emphasis is on the way divine power, through the Incarnation, is identified with the cause of humankind (5.477–505).[56] This is the knowledge that gives the community "hope" and the desire to pursue the quest for Truth, calling on Christ and his mother (5.506–12).

However obscure the "way" turns out to be, nothing could be further from this scene's call to pursue this "way" than an imitation of Christ conceived as self-inflicted "abjection" or an asceticism that isolated the individual from ordinary secular life by concentrating on a freely chosen wounding of the body. When the lost but penitential community stumble across a guide who will later, much later, figure forth God's *humana natura* and emerge as the ideal mediator of the divine grace, he is seen as a Christian *layman* engaged in the collective action on which the perpetuation of earthly life depended (5.537–629).[57] He seeks to embody the two commandments on which "hang the whole Law, and the Prophets also" (Matthew 22:37–39; see 5.561–65 and C7.205–12), while acknowledging the need for grace and the sacrament of penance to recover the long lost vision of truth and charity (5.595–608). It is characteristic of this poet's work that discovery of God, the goal of the pilgrimage, within the individual, is the outcome of a way that is emphatically communal and ethical.[58]

However basic this integration is to the poet's Christianity, its realization is fraught with immense difficulties—both collective and individual. Because I have written about the political and ethical problems the poet seeks to confront, and its slant toward employers' interests and ideology, I will not discuss the ploughing of the half-acre and its relations to social conflicts after the Black Death.[59] What does need remarking on here, however, is

---

56. For a tradition of late medieval Christology that seems to have affinities with Langland's, see Oberman (1963), 185–248, 251–78, 330–60, esp. 261–70. The most sustained attempt to relate *Piers Plowman* closely to the "moderni" in late medieval universities remains Coleman (1981b).

57. On the figurative modes here Aers (1975), 109–23, moving to consideration of political dimensions, quite specific to the 1360s, 1370s, and 1380s, Aers (1980), 12–24, and Aers (1988a), 40–53; also Justice (1994b), chap. 3, for a different but historically engaged perspective.

58. On the discovery of truth and charity within the searching individual, see esp. Zeeman (1958) and Salter (1962), chap. 3; also Wittig (1972).

59. Aers (1988a), chap. 1; also Clopper (1992) and Justice (1994b), chap. 3.

that Piers's own alignment with the employers' "statut" (6.320; see 166–70, 316–20) does not occlude a vision of Christ as one whose life sets his followers a model from which they know that even those who resist one's most cherished social projects are to be seen as fellow creatures, "my blody breþeren for god bouȝte vs alle" (6.207). So any *imitatio Christi* necessitates a practice directed toward one's neighbors. Even Hunger confirms that "cristes loue" must be the model not only for meeting the unthreatening needy but also those judged to have "doon yuele": "Loue hem and lakke hem noȝt; lat god take þe vengeaunce" (6.220–28). Once more, an imitation of Christ is manifested not in acts of ascetic control over the individual body but in a practical movement toward the other which, Langland makes clear enough, goes against the grain. Already we are given an image of how the poem's Christ calls for impossibly inventive resolutions of what Piers, with his maker, experiences as a contradiction between a divinely sanctioned justice (the so-called "wasters" are judged not to be rendering what they owe to others) and that nonjudgmental love so often demanded by Christ.[60]

Piers hopes he has solved this contradiction by receiving what seems to him a "pardoun *a pena & a culpa*" from Truth (7.1–106). However, his public claims to authority unintentionally affront a priest, just as they most certainly would have done in the world the poet inhabited. Piers shows the priest the text that has been so confidently expounded. The result is stunning. The priest points out that this long explication is gloss on two lines from the Athanasian creed, lines that in this isolation can hold no comfort to human beings who are aware of their failures to "do wel" (7.107–118). Neither Piers nor narrator challenges the priest's observations about the actual contents of the text. Instead, he makes a move that has inevitably sponsored a large and very divided critical literature, and which Langland deleted in rewriting the poem.[61] Piers pulls the text asunder and proclaims a shift of orientation which has the intensity one associates with a conversion (7.119–35). The rupture here is with the immediate past in which Piers sought to impose the employers' "statut" on wage laborers who did not accept its justice. Piers now gives up the attempt to control others, a control that had involved the invocation of the gentry's law-enforcement powers

---

60. On the profound problems, ethical as well as political, in Piers's version of justice (and the poet's), see Aers (1988a), chap. 1, and Aers (1994b).

61. For the pardon, see esp. Frank (1951); Burrow (1965); Middleton (1982b), a characteristically brilliant essay on the poem's form which includes commentary on the pardon scene; Harwood (1992), 31–32, 99–101, 152–56.

(unsuccessfully, 6.152–70) and the punitive wish for a shortage of food to make laborers accept their rulers' version of a fair wage (6.171–201). Indeed, Piers's new renunciation of governance goes with a decision that he will "cessen" from his "sowyng" (7.122). In terms of the "lawes" and "statut" he has been imposing, this could make his own position seem like that of those classified as "wasters," or like that of the vagrant poet so reluctant to perform manual labour and so trenchantly challenged by Reason and Conscience in C5.1–108.[62] Furthermore and also transgressing officially policed boundaries between laity and priests, Piers quotes, in public, from the Old Testament and from Christ's words "in þe gospel" to vindicate his decision (7.120–35). It is precisely to this aspect of Piers's performance that the priest responds, for Piers had made no personal attack on him nor any direct challenge to the priesthood:

> "Were þow a preest, Piers", quod he, "þow myȝtest preche whan þee liked
> As diuinour in diuinite, wiþ *Dixit insipiens* to þi teme."
>
> (7.140–41)

To this aggressive response, the layman replies fiercely, making a direct appeal to Scripture against the priest: "litel lokestow on þe bible" (7.142–43). Here the poet raises increasingly pressing issues about authority, access to the Scriptures, the right to public discourse concerning salvation, issues that far transcend any questions about the limitations of this particular priest. He is a representative of a potentially embattled group, and Piers's appeal to "þe bible" could hardly seem reassuring (7.141–44).[63] After all, the priest stands for an order which had an exclusive monopoly over the circulation and interpretation of the Bible, including, of course, the authority to keep it in Latin and make those who defied its authority here (or elsewhere) into "heretics." The scene in which the "preest and Perkyn apposeden eiþer ooþer" is a gripping one, replete with meanings which would be unfolded in the next century and a half of western European history. It also contains a Langlandian *imitatio Christi*. This, significantly, focuses on the mission, message, and lifestyle that, for Langland, constitute the "humanity" of Christ. Piers lays claim to a personal intimacy with God

---

62. On C5.1–108, see esp. Middleton (1990); see also Clopper (1992) and Justice (1994b), 240–50.

63. On the battle here, see Hudson (1988), 375–82, 196–97, and chap. 5.

and like the layman Jesus of Nazareth draws on a trust grounded in this intimacy to direct Scripture against the religious establishment which mediates it to the people (for example, compare Luke 4:17–23). But in the medieval church such claims and such access to Scripture by pious laypeople seemed a witness not to the gifts of the Spirit but to demonic anarchy. No wonder, then, that the dreamer finds the scene opaque (7.148–53). After all, Piers himself is perfectly orthodox in intention: not only is he an obedient payer of tithes, but he also insists that nobody should preach without the bishop's licence (6.91–95, 149). Yet here his stance, grounded in appeals to Christ's teaching and authority, pushes him toward a prophetic role which could prove more dangerous to ecclesiastical authority than any conventional *imitatio Christi* fostering "abjection" and the choice of self-inflicted injuries. Indeed, Passus 7 shows how Piers's stance draws the spectator to question the role of official pardons, triennials, the buying of "þe popes bulles" and the general authority of the contemporary church (7.143–86). This in turn inspires an imitation of Piers's prophetic voice: Christians, especially powerful Christians, are challenged in a way that again puts in question the authority that sustains the orthodox circulation of indulgences and pardons (7.187–200). Whether the voice is Will's or the poet's more direct intervention, it recalls the "dangerous memory" of one whose life could readily be seen as demanding an "imitation" which is active, verbal, and public. This, as we have seen, was how many Lollards understood it, seeing an *imitatio Christi* as entailing activity such as vernacular preaching, organizing communities of study, worship, and biblical readings.

Yet in *Piers Plowman* the puzzled Will has to continue his search for the sources of salvation without either the newly converted Piers or his earlier teacher, Holy Church (8.1–8). This quest includes a number of brief allusions to Christ, but I shall focus on those that indicate how the poet imagines the humanity of Christ and what *imitatio Christi* that would encourage. Passus 9 stresses the obligation of all Christians to accept that the goods of the world are "cristes good," which must be used to foster kindness and solidarity in communities (9.82–94). This emphasis recurs in those passus that scholars tend to treat primarily in terms of Will's "inward journey."[64] Any *imitatio Christi* within this framework demands an attempt to reproduce Christ's solidarity with those classified by dominant groups and their course as outcasts, to understand our "kynde" in ways that com-

---

64. Still immensely influential is the rich study by Wittig (1972).

pel us to resist pressures of the market and to acknowledge, in practice,
how inseparable is the "loue of oure lord" from love of "þe peple."[65] All
encounters with the poor take place in an eschatological perspective (Matthew 25:32–46): imitating Christ's humanity calls not for self-inflicted abjection but for an identification with his practices toward the poor and an
internalization of his egalitarianism (11.185–211, 232–47). Indeed "cristes
blood" itself becomes a sacrament of fraternal unity in which social divisions are washed away (11.199–204, 208–211). The poet is, inevitably,
aware of conventional iconography and doctrine here: Christ ordered all,
"souke for synne saufte at his breste" (11.119–22). But this is never elaborated or treated as a cue for a meditation on the Passion and Crucifixion
in which Christ's side-wound is identified with a woman's breast from
which men and women drink blood/milk, identifications copiously illustrated by Caroline Bynum and well represented in *The Prickynge of Love*
and *A Talking of the Loue of God*.[66] Instead of such figurations the poet's
emphasis is on the universal inclusiveness of Christ's merciful call, a call to
an "vs" without exclusion (11.119–20, 137–39; see 18.365–399). The image of the wound/breast is simply not elaborated and the poem moves to
Trajan's forceful entry where the emphasis is on salvation through "loue
and leautie," "laweful domes," "sooþnesse" in "werkes" and "lyuynge in
trupe" (11.140–66).[67] Nothing could have less to do with the focus of
conventional figurations of sucking at the wound/breast than this image of
salvation through practical reason, justice, and God's generosity "wiþouten
syngynge of masses" (11.151). There is thus no invitation to detach Christ's
Passion from his prophetic life or to detach readers from their communities
and the pursuit of justice. On the contrary, the "inward journey" constantly
returns to the present communities and problems of Langland's England,
displaying the concerns of a reformer drawn to the idiom of the canonical
prophets (for example, 10.311–18).[68] In this refusal to elaborate detailed
meditations on the wounds of Jesus, even when a conventional image is
introduced, as in the refusal to encourage individualistic, private devotions
centered on such imagery and the Passion, the poet and the Lollards were

---

65. Marriage is shown as being immersed in market relations, thoroughly commodified:
9.159–68 (contrasting 9.119–20); for love of the people, 11.175 and the challenging manifestations of Christ here, 11.185–99, 232–42.

66. See Bynum (1987), 270–76; for *The Prickynge of Love*, Beckwith (1993), 57–60, and
for this and *A Talking of the loue of God*, Gillespie (1987), 128–29.

67. On Trajan, see Vitto (1989), 64–72; Whatley (1984); Simpson (1990b), 126–28.

68. On the "inward journey," see Wittig (1972); on Christ and the Old Testament prophets,
T. L. Steinberg (1991), 29, and Kuczynski (1995).

fellow travelers. Scripture herself directs the confused Will to the resurrection of Christ, invoking Saint Paul's letter to the Colossians:

> whoso wolde and wilneþ wiþ crist to arise,
> *Si cum christo surrexistis &c,*
> He sholde louye and lene and þe lawe fulfille.
>
> (10.358–60)

Saint Paul tells his readers, "if you be risen with Christ, seek the things that are above, where Christ is sitting at the right hand of God. Mind the things that are above, not the things that are upon the earth" (Colossians 3:1–2). Scripture insists that the consequences of such demands involve daily practice of love within the ordinary worlds of actual communities (10.359–76). Understandably Will does not want to hear such instruction (10.377–78), but it is not one the poet will abandon. It returns even in a figure whose teachings sometimes tend toward an allegorical mode in which the problems of actual communities, mediated in the poem itself, can be occluded, even dissolved.[69] But this figure, Patient Poverty, also traces a movement *"Per passionem domini"* to the renunciation of pomp and pride embodied in a social practice that would make all "in commune riche, noon coueitous for hymselue" (14.189–201). The vision of Christ sponsored by this authoritative neo-Franciscan figure[70] certainly involves abandonment of worldly power and wealth in imitation of the Christ who "bereþ þe signe of pouerte" (14.258–59). But there is no idea of the physical "abjection," which, as we have seen, could come from conventional representations of Christ's humanity and poverty as the tortured, bleeding body on the cross. And once again there is no cultivation of any asceticism whose practices sharply differentiate the disciple of Christ from the community, no signs of a spirituality which would isolate or detach the individual from the daily concerns of her or his neighbors. On the contrary, this figure of Poverty actually opposes extremes of poverty in society as the product of human *vnkyndenesse*, the result of certain groups' determination to live in a manner which both isolates them from their fellow creatures and causes scarcity. This, we are plainly told, involves a direct rejection of Christ's words (14.71–75, 140–48, 171–80).

---

69. On this, Aers (1980), 28–29.

70. On neo-Franciscanism and its relations to the poem's explorations of poverty, see Aers (1988a), chap. 1; and, in general, Bourquin (1978).

The emphasis here recalls an earlier vision of Jesus pursuing us in the form of the contemporary poor, looking on us "To knowen vs by oure kynde herte and castynge of oure eiȝen" (11.185–96). The test is whether we can develop a "kynde herte" that will turn our faces, our recognition, toward those with no power or status, or whether we prove to "loue þe lordes here bifore þe lord of blisse" who appears as the dispossessed. The responses called for here, kindness and recognition, themselves constitute an *imitatio Christi*, one to which Christ himself "exciteþ vs by þe Eu-aungelie." Given my earlier observations on the symbolism of meals in the Gospels, symbolism strikingly different to the food symbolism and practices traced by Caroline Bynum, it is worth noting that here the kindness and recognition called for is evoked by the table open to "þe croked and þe pouere" in Christ's teaching at Luke 14:12–14 (*Piers Plowman* 11.190–96). The emphasis is on an "imitation" of Christ that requires no specialized or spectacular forms of bodily asceticism and, an interesting contrast with Bynum's subjects or Margery Kempe, no special clerical services and affir-mation (whether as admiring confessors, hagiographers, or makers of the eucharist.) "Alter alterius onera portate," he quotes from Saint Paul (Gala-tians 6:3), bear one another's burdens, and he comments on this: "be we noȝt vnkynde of oure catel, ne of oure konnyng neiþer" (11.209–13). The model and imitation of Christ contributes forcefully to the poet's refusal to separate the spiritual from the social, the individual pursuit of the virtu-ous life, of salvation, from the pursuit of justice in communities where even what might count as justice seems far from clear.[71] It is a model of Christ's humanity that readily sanctioned a prophetic and reforming voice, a mem-ory that the late medieval hierarchy certainly found a dangerous one.

Passus 15 contributes to our understanding of how this should be so. There the poet pursues core questions about charity and its manifestations in the modern world (15.98, 15.148). Will's instructor, *Anima,* focuses on the contemporary church and presents it in such a way that the mere mem-ory of Christ's form of life becomes a radical challenge to its authority and material resources (15.92–148, 417–573): "Allas, ye lewed men, muche lese ye on preestes" (15.128). The poet draws attention to the subversiveness of this critique by observing that the heads of holy church who live off the labors of others, "wol be wrooþ for I write þus" (15.488–69) and ex-

---

71. The poem's refusal to split the spiritual from the social emerges well in Simpson (1990b); on some of the intractable problems the poet's conceptions of justice encounter, see Aers (1994b).

claiming, "I dar noȝt telle þe soþe" (15.549). Yet the passus certainly overcomes any anxieties its writer may have felt at the "wrooþ" of the hierarchy. For the memory of Christ's life becomes a summons to an imitation that would demand public proclamation against the assimilation of the church in contemporary networks of worldly power, military and economic (15.489–91, 539–73). In this way the memory of Christ threatens a reformation that would utterly transform the existing church: "Takeþ hire landes, ye lordes, and leteþ hem lyue by dymes" (15.564). Ecclesiastic possessions and power are a poison, disendowment a remedial medicine to be administered by a reforming laity (15.553–69). This radicalism, with its appeal to the "parfit prophete" of Palestine (15.588), is one that sponsors collective, and explicitly collective agency, agency that brings out the political theology in conventional representations of the "humanity" of Christ as the tortured body in the Passion, on the cross and in the eucharist. It is also, of course, one of the most overt convergences between *Piers Plowman* and Wycliffite versions of the radical reformation needed in the church.

But the vagrant Will is far from belonging to groups in which such agency might become a reality and he continues asking for further exemplification of "what charite is to mene" (16.3). This is fortunate, since it leads into the sublime and extraordinarily subtle writing of Passus 16–18. Here the poet answers his core questions about charity through visions of Christ. Once more the poet shows no interest in elaborating the conventionally dominant figurations of Christ's humanity: no interest in the popular infancy narratives or the holy nuclear family and its domestic relations; no interest in the familiar details of the tortured body in the Passion and on the cross; no interest in the body of Christ in the eucharistic sacrifice. The focus is on the power of Jesus, spiritual and material. The prophetic figure who was ready to have "yfouȝte wiþ þe fend" as a child (16.101–2) is ready to use an element of force in the attempt to reform the "chirche" of his day (16.127–29)—the "corde" with which he "knokked" on those in his challenge to temple practices is emphatically not an instrument of self-flagellation or self-"abjection." It is an instrument and symbol of an active challenge to the profitable relations of the "chirche" to existing economic and political networks. Langland makes it clear that it is no cult of suffering and pain that leads Jesus to his cruel death but the organized opposition of identifiable human agents challenged by his lifestyle and teaching (16.127–66). The Passion and the Crucifixion in the *vita Christi* of Passus 16 receive just five lines. And in these five lines there are no images of

torture or mutilation, no details of physical suffering, no images of the
passive, infinitely suffering and bleeding body:

> [Jesus] on þe friday folwynge for mankyndes sake
> Iusted in Iherusalem, a ioye to vs alle.
> On cros vpon Caluarie crist took þe bataille
> Ayeins deeþ and þe deuel; destruyed hir boþeres myӡtes,
> Deide and deeþ fordide, and day of nyӡt made.
>
> (16.162–66)

Even on the cross, Christ, in his humanity, takes the battle to the forces of
evil, in a "joust" whose consideration is inseparable from the resurrection,
a "ioye to vs alle." In the contexts of late medieval piety, as Malcolm
Godden has recently observed, this is a "highly unusual presentation of the
Redemption." However, it seems mistaken to think, as Godden does, that
this fact demonstrates a lack of interest in "the humanity of Christ."[72] The
scholar seems to assume that the dominant late medieval versions of "the
humanity of Christ" are the only conceivable ones, assuming that if we do
not find these there simply can be no interest in "the humanity of Christ."
This is an example of modern literary historicism contributing to the reification of past concepts and images in a way that uncritically reproduces
medieval strategies which were also strategies of orthodoxy and the powers
this sustained. Langland refuses to think of the Incarnation in terms which
isolate the Passion from creation, from the prophetic ministry, from the
resurrection and from salvation history. The great visions of Passus 16 have
been mediated by a transformed Piers and it is for him, *"Petrus id est
Christus"* (15.212), that Will now seeks (16.167–68). This quest involves
another dazzling recapitulation of salvation history, a quest with Abraham
and Moses, in faith and hope, for the subject most fully revealed in the
Incarnation, the only answer to Will's questions about salvation, charity,
and the good life (16.167–17.356).

In Passus 17 Christ appears as the good Samaritan, now riding to joust
in Jerusalem. Once again Christ *in his humanity* is represented as an immensely active force, jouster and healer (17.51–82). Even the direct reference to eucharistic food (17.100) is given none of the fleshy and bloody

---

72. Godden (1990), 127 and 129; also Harbert (1990), 65 and 67. It is significant that the
narrative sequence from Passus 15 is "the most sustained of the entire poem," as Anne Middleton (1990) noted, 46.

elaborations so commonplace in the poet's culture and, as we have illustrated, in the church's exempla and imagery for propagating the doctrine
of transubstantiation. The emphasis is on the liberating, empowering, and
healing effects of Christ's life, death, and resurrection (17.109–26), while
any "imitation" will necessarily concentrate on the practices of loving *kyn-
denesse* within the community (17.136–37), something Christ himself ex-
pounds with great care in some exceptionally beautiful passages
(17.215–92, 347–54). The one sin that cannot be forgiven becomes *vnkyndenesse* (17.252–264).[73] This is seen as a final denial of one's own *kynde,*
one's inalienable connections with others (see 11.199–204) and with the
kynde who is both Creator and "creatour weex creature" (16.215).[74]

The Samaritan reaches Jerusalem and the poet again approaches "cristes
passion and penaunce" (17.8). Christ is now seen as "semblable to þe
Samaritan and somdeel to Piers þe Plowman," riding on an ass's back,
without spur or spear, but hurrying to the joust where he will be dubbed
and win his gold spurs (17.9–14). Once more Langland chooses to treat
the Passion and Crucifixion in a mode that sets aside the dominant imagery
and affective practices of his culture. This has been thoroughly explicated
in relation to Passus 18 by scholars who have identified the iconographic
traditions on which he drew (especially that of Christ as knight) and their
theological orientations.[75] We are given a twenty-four-line narrative of the
Passion and Crucifixion that seems not at all designed to invite, let alone
stimulate, any affective identifications with a suffering Jesus (18.36–59).
Godden comments on this sequence in terms especially relevant to the present chapter:

> As an account of the Passion Langland's vision is strikingly different
> from the treatment given in most Middle English writings. There is
> no long description of the trials and scourging such as we find in
> the mystery plays or *The Northern Passion,* and no emotional ac-
> count of Christ's sufferings on the cross and the lamentations of his
> followers, such as we find in the lyrics and art. Instead, Langland
> presents the Passion as a triumphant battle fought by God with
> death and the devil. The central debate is represented not by the
> familiar trial scenes, in which Pilate, Herod and the Jews condemn

---

73. On this sequence, see White (1988), 101–11; on received allegorical readings of the
samaritan parable, see Smith (1966), chap. 4.

74. On this, see Aers (1975), 107–9.

75. See Gaffney (1931) and Waldron (1986).

Christ, but by the Harrowing of Hell in which Christ condemns the devils. The dominant character is the dramatic celebration of the power and divinity of Christ, not his suffering humanity.[76]

Likewise J. A. W. Bennett had written some years earlier that even in his treatments of the Passion, "of Christ's sufferings he says nothing, noting only that he swoons piteously and grows pale." And as soon as the poet's reserved account of Passion and Crucifixion is completed, "We move back once more to the jouster of heroic temper" in lines that are "knightly" (18.75–86).[77] Here it is also noteworthy that the wound made in the side of the body is presented in the chivalric idiom of jousting (19.75–90). Instead of the familiar concentration on the physical wound and the life-giving eucharistic blood flowing from the side, the poet punningly takes note of the way in which the blood "sprong doun by þe spere and vnspered" the eyes of the blind knight Longeus (see 18.78–91).[78]

From here the poet moves to the celebration of Christ's liberating power, figured forth through Will's descent into the prisonhouse of hell to witness its harrowing, a joyful emancipation (18.110–424). Critics have admired the poetic energies in Langland's version of the harrowing of hell while they have also explicated its relevance to the poem's theological perspectives, stressing particularly its celebration of the power displayed by God in redeeming humankind.[79] Yet this celebration should not occlude Langland's continuing engagement with the Incarnation and his own model of Christ's "humanity." The power that overwhelms the ruler of this world *("princeps huius mundi")*, the "Dukes of þis dymme place" and their fortifications (18.316–25), only becomes an emancipatory one through its embodiment in specific human form. Christ's humanity remains the key. Taking up an earlier strand (16.215, 100–110) the poet depicts God's Incarnation as a process of divine learning about the grimmer realities of human experience (18.212–15), an existential exploration of "alle wo" by the being that is source of "alle ioye" (18.221–25).[80] Christ chose a form of life that set

---

76. Godden (1990), 139; similar emphasis in Bloomfield (1961), 64, 100, 125, 128–30; Allen (1988), 55.

77. J. A. W. Bennett (1982), 107, 108.

78. See Weldon (1989), 53–55; J. A. W. Bennett (1982), 109; Waldron (1986).

79. See esp. Godden (1990), chap. 8 (and 200–201 on the C version); Simpson (1990b), 209–17; Bloomfield (1961), 123–29. Once again it seems worth noting possible affinities with Oberman's account of Gabriel Biel and what he called "nominalist" Christology. See Oberman (1963), 185–248, 251–78, 330–60; see particularly the comments on Biel at 233–35, 273–74.

80. These powerful paradoxes were discussed in Aers (1975), 106–9, 128.

aside dominion and "taking the form of a servant" took on the risks of unmerited, unjust suffering (Philippians 2.6–11). Out of this choice comes a solidarity with humans and the grounds for the Christian fraternalism repeatedly affirmed in the poem (as at 11.171–213, 14.174–82, 17.254–60). The emancipatory force displayed in the harrowing of hell is inextricably bound up with this emphasis on the Incarnation and Christ's human existence, God's strange but decisive identification with the very *kynde* of humanity. So Passus 18 suggests how Christ acts out, makes good, his teaching in the previous passus, in the form of the Samaritan, on kindness, on the powerful love that makes neighbors out of strangers and turns out to be the model for salvation. Anticipating his role at the final judgment he promises that his own "kynde" obliges him "to be merciable to man," recognizing that "we beþ breþeren of blood, ac noȝt in baptisme alle": "I were an vnkynde kyng but I my kynde helpe" (18.375–99). This vision of immense emancipatory power and forgiveness ends with church bells ringing on Easter morning and Will calling his wife and daughter to reverence "goddes resurexion" by creeping to the cross (a ritual normally enacted on Good Friday) and kissing it "for a Iuwel" that now "afereþ þe fend" (18.421–31). Here, as elsewhere in *Piers Plowman,* there is no separation of cross from resurrection and the liberating force of Christ's acts, the cross seen as a powerful jewel that, in the words of J. A. W. Bennett, "vanquished the power of darkness."[81]

Passus 19 opens with Will getting dressed for church, to hear mass and to receive communion (19.1–3). We might now expect some focus on the eucharist, some display of conventional eucharistic visions around the body of Christ and the orthodox doctrine of transubstantiation. But the writer falls asleep in the middle of the mass (19.4–5). True enough, he then dreams of a bloody figure and this might suggest the poet is representing the doctrine of transubstantiation and the Host, that he is about to fulfil conventional expectations like those affirmed in Nicholas Love's work on the eucharist, illustrated in Chapter 1 (19.5–8). However what we get in this vision bears no resemblance to such materials, either in the modes of writing or in the doctrinal orientations. The poet emphasizes the ambiguity in the vision ("Is þis Iesus þe Iustere. . . . Or is it Piers þe Plowman"). In this

---

81. J. A. W. Bennett (1982), 111; Harbert (1990), 68 notes that "it is a cross that he goes to kiss, not a crucifix." If this distinction is indeed intended (yes, intended) by the poet at line 428, it would certainly accord with the poem's overall distancing from the dominant ways of figuring Christ's humanity. On creeping to the cross, see Skeat (1968), 2:265 (nn. 475 and 478).

way he suggests the disciples' immense difficulties in recognizing the risen Christ (Luke 24:13–32; John 20:14–16; John 21:4) and that we are confronting something more enigmatic than a familiar devotional image from which we can read off familiar doctrinal propositions. A relatively authoritative interpreter emerges to decipher the figuration:

> Quod Conscience and kneled þo, 'þise arn Piers armes,
> Hise colours and his cote Armure; ac he þat comeþ so blody
> Is crist wiþ his cros, conqueror of cristene.'
>
> (19.12–14)

The decipherment itself recalls the earlier allegorical gloss in the representation of Christ as a jouster, "semblable to þe Samaritan and somdeel to Piers þe Plowman," who jousts "in Piers armes . . . *humana natura*" (18.1–35). The allegorical mode, with its complex theological implications, calls for a strenuous exegetical activity which stimulates further questioning and explication (19.15–68). In doing so it once again rejects all elaborations of the conventional figuration of Christ's humanity as the tortured, bleeding body, whipped and nailed to the cross, or as the man of sorrows, or as the figure in the pietà. The rejection is both of a literary mode and of a series of commonplace devotional images with their affective strategies. Instead the poet's allegorical vision focuses on the term "conquerour" (19.14), selecting this for sustained meditation in response to the dreamer's request for the reasons why Jesus is named Christ by Conscience and known by the title "conquerour" (19.15–198). It is worth reflecting on this long sequence in Passus 19.

Conscience's teachings about Christ and the title "conquerour" concentrate on the conquest of forces of pain and death achieved in his life, death, and resurrection envisaged as a dialectical unity (19.42–198). Commenting on the dreamer's vision of Christ as Piers "peynted al blody" coming in "wiþ a cros" (19.5–7), Conscience maintains that "þe cause þat he comeþ þus wiþ cros of his passion" is to teach us "to fiȝte" against temptations and "fenden vs fro fallynge into synne" (19.63–65). As befits the poet's striking selection of chivalric images to represent the Crucifixion, even the vision of the "blody" Christ during mass has as its "cause" the encouragement of moral struggles envisaged as a perpetual battle. The emphasis throughout this passus, as earlier in the poem, is that Christ, even on the cross, is a model for strenuous ethical activity, for a daily practice which demands a reiteration of the struggles and generous love of human enemies disclosed by the "conqueror noble" (19.110–14; see 11.163–84).

Toward the end of Conscience's recapitulation of Christ's works we meet the wound in Christ's side. This, as we noted in Chapter 1, was a focal image in the dominant late medieval figurations of Christ's humanity and the "feminization" of his body.[82] The poet recounts Thomas doubting the resurrection and Christ's resolution of this unbelief when he invites Thomas "to grope / And feele wiþ hise fyngres his flesshliche herte" (19.170–71). But instead of responding to his culture's elaborations of meditations around and in this wound, instead of inviting the reader to identify with Thomas's touching fingers and affectivity, Langland follows the emphasis he found in John's gospel. Thomas is blessed, but blessed are those who have not seen and have believed, "I loue hem and blesse hem" (19.177–81: John 20:27–29). It is not without interest that in his version of the scene Nicholas Love actually deletes the gospel's emphasis here together with the words ascribed to Christ and quoted by Langland, "Beati qui non viderunt & crediderunt [blessed are they that have not seen and have believed]." Instead he substitutes comments on Christ's goodness in that he allowed "for oure profite, to þe more opun preue & certeyntye of his verrey Resurrexion" together with an explanation of why Christ "reserued in his gloriouse body þe steppus [marks] of his wondes."[83] The orientation in *Piers Plowman* here is not only nearer John, it also has more affinities with the Lollard Christ (who, we recall, turned the cross into place of energetic teaching).[84]

Out of the conquests and teachings Conscience relates, Christ founds the church, giving Piers power "to assoille of alle manere synnes," to reproduce Christ's own kindness to "alle maner men" (19.182–85; recall 18.371–76, 182–87). Not that salvation is unconditional: humans must do all they can to act justly, to render what they owe to others and to God (19.186–98). Here the poet's model of Christ leads into a strongly ethical and communitarian understanding of what the pursuit of holiness entails, an understanding reinforced by his treatment of Pentecost (19.199–257, 274–394). Grace

---

82. For characteristic examples, see Beckwith (1993), 57–62; Bynum (1987), 271–72. It is striking, and as far as I am aware a comparison and topic not yet explored, that Langland figures Christ's *humana natura* through a plowman, masculine, whereas in the traditions Bynum traces it seems not unusual to represent Mary as "the *tunica humanitatis*, the clothing of humanity, that Christ puts on" (Bynum 1987, 265; see also 266–67, 270).

83. Love (1992), 208–9.

84. Hudson and Gradon (1988–90), 3:183.

is poured out to "þe comune," both collectively and individually (19.227), as the poet seeks to imagine what would constitute imitating his Christ in the complex historical mazes with which the poem has engaged.

Christ's demands that humans act without "vnkyndenesse," the sin against the Holy Spirit according to Langland's Christ (17.204–34, 248–60) and seek to live justly *("redde quod debes")* prove unacceptable. Indeed, to people whom Langland shows as shaped by market relations Christ's demands seem quite incomprehensible. The "laws" of the market govern conscience and dictate what is considered natural, the fulfillment of the species, our "kynde" (19.386–423, 223–24). No longer can conscience make what the poet considers traditional and just distinctions between social exchanges that are "right" and those that are "wrong," even when the latter are usurous (19.348–50).[85] In this context Langland confirms the grim vision of the church presented in Passus 15, one that has sidelined the ethical teaching and lifestyle of the founder it claims to mediate and represent. Here, once more, and finally, we see how the poem's visions of Christ's humanity, with the correlative version of what might constitute an *imitatio Christi,* could become a memorial with dangerous force in the present.

Will (presumably here like his maker) has every wish to see the church fulfilling its own self-descriptions, to find it an oasis in the desert, the sole saving ark in the watery wilderness (20.212–216). But the vision of reality proves far otherwise. Once again Langland presents the church, its priesthood and spirituality assimilated to the structures of Mede (20.218–31, 304–79). It is now that the memory of Christ and his representative Piers will become a "dangerous memory," for it drives Conscience, however reluctantly, *outside* the actually existing Church (20.375–86). That is, in response to the poem's vision of Christ and what might constitute a worthwhile attempt to "imitate" him, Conscience is now compelled to break unity, to make a choice against the actually existing medieval church and to set out on a renewed quest for Piers the Plowman and Grace outside the official mediators and agencies offered by that church as the exclusive and sole way to salvation. If Conscience, Will, and the poet were to pursue such a quest, in such a manner, and in the vernacular, at some point in the near future they would find themselves classified by the hierarchy and imminent Lancastrian state as heretics, as Lollards.[86]

---

85. On the issues here, see Aers (1994b).

86. See Hudson (1988), 408; Bowers (1992), 10–30; Aston (1984), chap. 1; and McNiven (1987).

This perspective helps us remember, once more, that representations of Christ are made in determinate contexts, contexts that are ecclesiastic, political, and economic. It helps us remember that representations of Christ hold political consequences, offering as they do vital models for the *imitatio Christi* to which all Christians are, in some sense, committed. From a particular model of Christ's life and teaching flowed implications which were theological *and* political, theoretical *and* practical, ethical *and* sacramental, individual *and* collective. The great diversity of models within Christian traditions meant that choices were made in establishing the model of Christ's humanity that dominated late medieval piety. The fact that the dominant model was not favored by Lollards or by *Piers Plowman* needs to be studied within the framework suggested here: one that seeks to return reifications, past or present, to the social and cultural processes they represent and occlude; one that encourages analysis that does not stop at the description of iconographical changes but encourages us to address the political, ecclesiastical, and ethical dimensions of such a choice against the dominant forms; one that can contribute to the understanding of the historical relations between gender and power in the so-called feminization of Jesus even as it illuminates the reasons why groups of radically critical, reformist women and men should have rejected such "feminization" of Christ's humanity in their own culture.

CHAPTER THREE

The Humanity of Christ: Reflections on Julian of Norwich's *Revelation of Love*

DAVID AERS

I beheld with reverent drede, and hyghly mervelyng in the syght and in feelyng of the swete accorde that oure reson is in god, vnderstandyng that it is þe hyghest gyfte that we haue receyvyd, and it is growndyd in kynd.

—Julian of Norwich

In many respects it might seem reasonable to read Julian of Norwich as a contemplative whose visions of Christ belong unequivocally to the conventional and dominant late medieval representation of Christ's humanity as a tortured, bleeding, and dying body. It might also seem reasonable to treat her work as part of the traditions of women's mysticism so copiously illustrated by Caroline Bynum in *Holy Feast and Holy Fast*. After all, Julian's "reuelacion of loue" begins with a move that is part of the dominant late medieval tradition of representing and meditating on Christ's humanity, the one decisively shaped by the pseudo-Bonaventuran *Meditationes Vitae Christi*.[1] She recalls her initial desire to have "mynd of the passion," and to experience it as if she had been "that tyme with Magdaleyne and with other that were Christus louers, that I might have seen bodilie the passion that our lord suffered for me" (2/285). This seems bound up with thoroughly conventional versions of imitation and affective response. She reports the wish to have "suffered with him," reflecting the familiar form of identification fostered by the *Meditationes Vitae Christi* and its traditions. And she stresses how she assumed that her wish entailed a focus on the tortured body. This assumption too is one she would have assimilated from a culture of discourse dominated by the tortured body on the cross and she herself emphasizes the focus of her desire on this body: "And therfore I desyred a bodely sight, wher in I might have more knowledge of the bodily paynes of our sauior, and of the compassion of our lady" (2/286). On top of these apparent convergences there is her work's currently well known and widely celebrated representation of Christ as "mother," a representation that might seem precisely the kind of "feminization" of Christ which Caroline Bynum has illustrated so thoroughly and which has stimulated much interest among feminist medievalists working on English writings.[2]

An account of Julian's work along just these lines has recently been published in a collection of essays entitled *Feminist Approaches to the Body in Medieval Literature* (see E. Robertson 1993).[3] There Elizabeth Robert-

---

1. The edition of Julian used here is Colledge and Walsh (1978); references in my text are to chapter followed by page: all references are to the revised long text unless preceded by "Sh"; here quotation is on 281. The traditions represented and shaped by the *Meditationes Vitae Christi* were discussed in Chapter 1; their relevance here is noted by Glasscoe (1993), 215–16.

2. Bynum (1987) discussed in Chapter 1; Bynum (1982) is also relevant. It seems that the earlier book emphasizes the masculine engenderment of such language and iconography while this is much diminished in *Holy Feast and Holy Fast;* see Bynum (1982), 111–46, 161–62, 185, 246, and especially the comments on 111–12, 143–45. As the previous chapters have suggested, I think the earlier emphasis more astute about the effects of power than the later.

3. In Lomperis and Stanbury (1993), 142–67, references to pages follow in text. It is worth noting that E. Robertson's (1993) dependence on Jacquart and Thomasset and on Laqueur for "medieval medical views of women" may need some revision in the light of work by Joan Cadden (1993): for example, compare Robertson on "feminization" of Christ and "menstruation" in Julian's work (E. Robertson 1993, 154–55) with Cadden (1993), 173–76, esp. 173 ("even those who held that menses in women were homologous to semen in men nevertheless set menstruation apart as a female idiosyncrasy"). Cadden's work should also encourage more caution than literary historians currently show in their application of Laqueur's (1990) "one sex" model in pre-eighteenth-century Europe. Medievalists studying "the body" may also gain much from Paster (1993), esp. 16–17, chaps. 2 and 4.

son maintains that "running throughout the text is the idea that her body is redeemed through the body of Christ, who is figured in feminine terms" (153).[4] The "feminine" body she finds in Julian's work is a thoroughly conventional one. It is constituted, in Robertson's own account and through the standard "medieval medical views" in which she situates this, as flesh, as physicality. From this foundation it is possible for the woman contemplative to identify with the "feminine" body of Christ in a move made familiar by the subjects Bynum has studied so memorably: "Like her, Christ as God incarnate, is dominated by physicality" (154). Thus Julian identifies with a Christ whose "feminine" figuration confirms her own apparently conventional identification as "feminine," her "sense of herself as rooted in the body" (154).

Guided by Bynum, aided by Jacquart and Thomasset's (1988) *Sexuality and Medicine in the Middle Ages*, Robertson focuses on the role of blood in Julian's text. She finds that "her revelations are permeated with images of blood" (154). It is worth following the quotations on which this statement rests. They come from visions of the Crucifixion in chapters 3, 4, and 7 in the long text and from chapter 8 in the Short Text. Put together the complete quotations read as follows (154–55):

> (1) "I saw the reed bloud rynnyng downe from under the garlande, hote and freyshely, plentuously and lively, right as it was in the tyme that the garland of thornes was pressed on his blessed head."
>
> (2) "And in the comyng ouʒte they were browne rede, for the blode was full thycke; and in the spredyng abrode they were bryght rede."
>
> (3) "The bledyng contynued" [this quotation, from chapter 7 of the long text is then spliced into one from chapter 8 of the short text, number 4]

---

4. The fact that Julian's desire for "a bodely sight" and for "more knowledge of the bodily paynes of our sauiour" are confessed as long past, apparently well before her visions and certainly very many years before the meditations we have in the Long Text is not considered. This seems an error, as my own discussion will suggest. The most thorough and persuasive recent scrutiny of the dates of the short text is in Nicholas Watson (1993). His interesting attempts to push the date of the long text into the reign of Henry V seem unpersuasive to both Lynn Staley and myself: in our view, Julian's often radical vernacular theology is most unlikely to have been possible after Arundel's Constitutions of 1407/9; see Lynn Staley's chapter on Julian in this volume. For the apparent inconsequentiality for E. Robertson of Julian's own statement that these desires were long before the text that records them, see Robertson's (1993) treatment of them, 154. Whereas Julian stresses the temporal gaps, and the processes intervening, Robertson asserts that Julian's revelations "spring from experiences

(4) "this ranne so plenteouslye to my syght that me thought ȝyf itt hadde bene so in kynde, for þat tyme itt schulde hafe made the bedde alle on blode and hafe passede onn abowte."

(5) "God has made waterse plentuouse in erthe to oure seruyce and to owre bodyly ese, for tendyr love that he has to us. Botte ȝit lykes hym bettyr that we take fullye his blessede blode to wasche us with of synne; for thare ys no lykoure that es made thay hym lykes so welle to gyffe us. For it is plenteouse and of oure kynde."

On quotation 1 Robertson comments as follows: "Here Christ's blood, like menstrual blood, is purged, matching her own natural purgation of excess" (154). On quotation 2 she maintains that here "the blood is even more evocative of menstrual blood." Quotation 3 is introduced by the observation that the "bledyng" is "like menstrual blood," and it is glossed by a sentence from the Short Text (quotation 4). After the latter, and as an introduction to quotation 5, the scholar writes that "Julian's image of blood, evocative of menstrual flow, also suggests blood lost in losing virginity; the blood of Christ is even explicitly connected with her own bed. Furthermore, the fact that the age viewed menstrual blood and semen as homologous underscores the erotic implications of the image. Christ's blood is linked with all kinds of moisture, all redemptive of feminine excess" (155). All this, she observes, illustrates Julian's "idiosyncratically feminine uses of blood imagery" (155). So what we seem to have is a late fourteenth-century Englishwoman elaborating the normative representations of Christ's humanity, the bleeding, wounded, open body on the cross, in directions which are stereotypically (not at all "idiosyncratically") "feminine," according to her culture's constitution of the "feminine." Like Bynum's female subjects she is identifying with a God whose body mirrors her own conventionally gendered being. From within this paradigm no arguments need be given in defense of reading the blood from Christ's tortured head as "evocative of" and "like" menstrual blood, no arguments need be adduced in defense of the proposition that the flow of blood caused by the crown of thorns is both "evocative of menstrual flow" *and* "blood lost in virginity," an allegedly "erotic" image—erotic for Julian, one pre-

---

of the body" in these past desires. One should, besides taking temporal differences seriously, also consider the statement in chapter 3 that when she later does receive the "bodily sickness" that had been among her earlier desires, she recollects the desire that her "bodie might be fulfilled with mynd and feeling of his blessed passion": now, however, she writes that while she wanted to experience "his paynes," "in this I desyred never no bodily sight" (3/292–93).

sumes. The wounded figure of Christ is already "feminine" and the woman contemplative apparently happy to identify both Christ and herself according to dominant cultural and physiological stereotypes of the "feminine."

This case seems to be confirmed by the place of motherhood in Julian's model of salvation, "oure moder Cryst" (58/586). In considering this aspect of the work, Robertson directly invokes Bynum's "discussion of the feminized Christ," observing that "Julian often figures Christ as a mother" and adding that she further associates Christ's feminized body, "oure moder Cryst," with sensuality: "he is oure moder of mercy in oure sensualyte takyng" (Long Text, chapter 58/586). It is through the "feminized body of Christ" that "the sensual" is redeemed, "rather than leading the contemplative to a transcendence of the sensual" (156). Here Robertson connects her reading of Julian's "feminized" Christ with the "empowerment" thesis I discussed in Chapter 1 in relation to Bynum's work. She suggests that Julian was actually "a subtle strategist who sought to undo assumptions about women and to provide, in an Irigarayan sense, a new celebration of femininity through contemplation of Christ's "feminine" attributes" (161). Although the constitutions of "femininity" allegedly being deployed by Julian are conventional stereotypes, Robertson's conclusion is that they work in a manner "similar to that of Irigaray" as "celebratory" reinvention of "feminine" attributes habitually vilified in a misogynistic culture. Both reinventions, medieval and modern, so it is claimed, create a threat to "the hegemony of the male sex" (161).

I have given a fairly long summary of Robertson's recent study for two reasons. First, it reads Julian in a manner that raises many of the issues addressed in this part of our book. Second, it suggests that the ways in which Bynum's subjects represented Christ and gender can be found in late medieval England, working to empower women and to pose a "threat to the hegemony of the male sex." Because I have questioned the plausibility of that "empowerment" thesis in relation to late medieval English culture, and given the concentration of this book on the interrelations of Christian devotion, politics, and gender in that culture, it seemed right to address Robertson's work, an innovative one in studies on Julian's revelation. Both Lynn Staley and I agree with Robertson that Julian is "a subtle strategist" (161), but I shall now seek to suggest how Julian's "subtle" rhetorical, gender, and theological strategies go in directions that are not those found in Elizabeth Robertson's account.

Robertson's quotations from the first revelation certainly suggest that

Julian is reproducing a conventional version of Christ's humanity, figured through the tortured, wounded, bleeding body on the cross. But only seems. For while Julian does undoubtedly set out from the dominant commonplace of late medieval devotion with which this part of our book began, her distinctive rhetorical strategies actually resist it, unravel it, estrange us from it and, gradually but decisively, supersede it.

How she achieves this I will now illustrate, an illustration that demands rather longer quotations than are normally required. We can begin where Robertson began, with the opening of the first revelation:

> And in this sodenly I saw the reed bloud rynnyng downe from vnder the garlande, hote and freyshely, plentuously and liuely, right as it was in the tyme that the garland of thornes was pressed on his blessed head. (4/294)

Here we meet the most familiar icon of late medieval devotion, complete with concentration on physical details, the "bodely sight" and "knowledge of the bodily paynes of our sauiour" that she had prayed for. But instead of elaborating these images, she adds a section to the Short Text that does not fulfill such conventional expectations:

> And in the same shewing sodeinly the trinitie fulfilled my hart most of ioy, and so I vnderstode it shall be in heauen without end to all that shall come ther. For the trinitie is god, god is the trinitie. The trinitie is our maker, the trinitie is our keper, the trinitie is our everlasting louer, the trinitie is our endlesse ioy and our bleisse, by our Lord Jesu Christ, and in our Lord Jesu Christ. And this was shewed in the first syght and in all, for wher Jhesu appireth the blessed trinitie is vnderstand, as to my sight. And I sayd: Benedicite dominus. (4/294–96)

What happens here is that the kind of elaborations encouraged by the dominant forms of devotion of Christ's humanity and passion are not delivered. Indeed, they are positively blocked off as the familiar images are turned into theological reflections on the Trinity—already, at the beginning of the text's first revelation. Furthermore, the reflections are in a language that is ratiocinative and abstract, a language that resists the kind of physicality we had been encouraged to expect.[5] Similarly, the next chapter em-

---

5. There is an excellent analysis of this passage and its "progression towards abstraction and generalization" by Nicholas Watson in Watson (1992), 87–88; see also Gillespie (1987), here 154–55 n. 62.

phasizes that even as she saw the bleeding head she had "a gostly sight of his homely louyng" (5/299). What then did she see? She tells us that she "saw that he is to vs all thing that is good and comfortable to our helpe. He is oure clothing, that for loue wrappeth vs and wyndeth vs, halseth vs, and all becloseth vs, hangeth about vs for tender loue" (5/299). Once more this is neither an attempt to visualize the physical particularities of the crucified body nor even to encourage us to compose the crucifixion scene. We are being directed to move away from the literal, a movement maintained by the ensuing image in which Christ, from the cross, "shewed" her "a little thing, the quantitie of an hazelnott" in the palm of her hand, "as me semide" (5/299). Not, we note, that she saw a hazelnut, or anything else particularized, but "a little thing" whose "quantitie" is her focus. As she looks at this "little thing," she writes, "I looked theran with the eye of my vnderstanding" (5/300). Marion Glasscoe is surely right to remark that "far from being a visual image of the world as a hazel-nut held safely in the palm of her hand, this is a 'gostly sight.'"[6] As with her writing on the Trinity in the previous chapter, Julian's language here is analytic, rationally curious, abstract:

> I marvayled how it might laste, for me thought it might sodenly haue fallen to nawght for littlenes. And I was answered in my vnderstanding: It lasteth and ever shall, for god loueth it; and so hath all thing being by the loue of god. (5/300)

There is no incitement here for affective identification, for concentration on the body, whether "feminized" or not. Nor do the next sentences change this mode:

> In this little thing I saw iii propreties. The first is þat god made it, the secund that god loueth it, the thirde that god kepyth it. But what behyld I ther in? Verely, the maker, the keper, the louer. For till I am substantially vnyted to him I may never haue full reste ne verie bliss; þat is to say that I be so fastned to him that ther be right nought that is made betweene my god and me.
>   This little thing that is made, me thought it might haue fallen to nought for littlenes. (5/300–301)

This extensive quotation shows how Julian sustains a language that is a vernacular version of a scholastic discourse, a reasoning inquiry with care-

---

6. Glasscoe (1993), 224.

fully articulated questions and answers deploying pointedly abstract terms such as "propreties" and "substantially vnyted." We can see how the image of the bleeding head from which the first revelation started has actually been a provocation to explore metaphysical questions with her "vnderstanding, and thought."[7] We are, in fact, receiving lessons in spiritual reading. The image of the "little thing" is used to stimulate further reflections on our mistaken attempts to find stability, plenitude, completion in a realm of pervasive impermanence and necessary lack:

> For this is the cause why we be not all in ease of hart and of sowle, for we seeke heer rest in this thing that is so little, wher no reste is in, and we know not our god, that is almightie, all wise and all good, for he is verie reste. God will be knowen, and him lyketh that we rest vs in him; for all that is beneth him suffsyeth not to vs. And this is the cause why that no sowle is in reste till it is noughted of all thinges that is made. When she is wilfully noughted four loue, to haue him that is all, then is she able to receive ghostly reste. (5/301)

Thus the fragility of a little thing, its propensity to have suddenly "fallen to nawght for littlenes" is assimilated to theological reflections on the nature of desire in a language that is, again, strikingly abstract. As for the "feminine," we note that it is placed in the pronoun "she," the human "sowle," in fact, which cannot be "in reste till it is noughted of all things that is made," till "she is wilfully noughted for loue." Far from being the "feminine" as physicality, as flesh, the feminine here is the human "anima" in a discourse which encourages "the eye of my vnderstanding" to consider some extremely paradoxical and metaphysical reflections. For instance, the passage asks its readers to consider how the created universe is a "quantitie" that could be contained in the palm of Julian's hand, so tiny that it seems "it might sodenly haue fallen to nawght" were it not continually sustained by God's love; and yet, also, that unless the soul herself is "noughted of all thinges that is made," "wilfully noughted," she will never find peace, happiness. In this quest for "knowledge" Julian has superseded her culture's ideologies of gender and sexual differentiation even as she blocks out the imagery from which she begins in a strategy that would not be out of place in *The Cloud of Unknowing*.

---

7. On such use of imagery in Julian, see Gillespie (1987), 131–43.

Not that there is any inclination to suggest images must or can be decisively "noughted." For while her strategy has been to supersede the conventional image from which she started, she then goes on to observe that even as her reflections developed in her "vnderstanding," "in gostely syght," she simultaneously held "the bodely syght" that her own text has so subtly set aside (5/300, 7/311). In chapter 7 she returns to this "bodely syght":

> The grett droppes of blode felle downe fro vnder the garlonde lyke pelottes, semyng as it had comynn ouʒte of the veynes. And in the comyng ouʒte they were browne rede, for the blode was full thycke; and in the spredyng abrode they were bryght rede. (7/311)

This addition to the Short Text seems to return us to the normative figurations of devotion to Christ, to the *Meditationes Vitae Christi* and its successors. For Robertson, as we saw (this is her quotation 2) it also reproduces standard "medieval medical views of women," their version of the "feminine" and the matching "feminization" of Christ. And yet, if we continue the quotation, if we do not isolate this passage from its context, something far less straightforward seems to be happening:

> And whan it camme at the browes, ther they vanysschyd; and not wythstonding the bledyng continued tylle many thynges were sene and vnderstondyd. Nevertheles the feyerhede and the lyuelyhede continued in the same bewty and lyuelynes. (7/311–12)

First, it is less straightforward because we are told that copious bleeding both "vanysschyd" and "contynued." Second, her attention involves a spectatorially detached and strikingly aesthetic sense of the image's "bewty and lyuelynes." Third, Julian comments that this bleeding image was part of a design whose end was to encourage understanding ("tylle many thynges were sene and vnderstondyd"). Together these features make striking qualifications to a mode that was traditionally organized to produce intense affective and emotional responses followed by a redirection of the will in a manner that circumvented the analytic processes of rational exploration. Julian's continuation of this passage develops some well-known and exceptionally memorable images:

> The plentuoushede is lyke to the droppes of water that falle of the evesyng of an howse after a grete shower of reyne, that falle so

> thycke that no man may nomber them with no bodely wyt. And for
> the roundnesse they were lyke to the scale of heryng in the spredyng
> of the forhede. (7/312)

How do these images work and what is Julian doing with them? Important
to acknowledge is that *they draw attention to themselves*. In making them
do this, Julian shows that her aim is not to evoke Christ's pain on Calvary,
not to induce the affective responses we might have expected in a conventional meditation on the Crucifixion, and not to move us to any affective
imitation of a suffering, tortured body as an "imitation of Christ" we
should want to follow. On the contrary, the reader is placed in a rather
detached, speculative relationship to images which have been designed to
emphasize their constructedness, their rhetorical composition. Attention is
thus directed away from the particularities of the Crucifixion and its familiar meditational elaborations even as it is directed toward house eaves after
abundant rain and to the pattern, and texture, of herrings' scales. That this
is her purpose Julian emphasizes by reiterating the images in the following
lines (7/312, lines 27–30) and then offering this comment:

> Thys shewyng was quyck and lyuely and hidows and dredfulle and
> swete and louely; and of all the syght that I saw this was most
> comfort to me, that oure good lorde, that is so reverent and
> dredfulle, is so homely and so curteyse, and this most fulfylld me
> with lykyng and syckernes in soule. (7/313)

The vision may be "dredfulle" but its beholder is detached enough to include in her responses what can only be described as an aesthetic dimension,
one also displayed in the striking images she had just written. And now,
instead of elaborating instruments of torture, wounds, torturers, mockers,
and sympathizers, she turns away from the bodily scene to reflect on what
she calls the "homely" and "curteyse" aspect of God, reflections unfolded
in an "open example" of "a solempne kyng or a gret lorde" and "a pore
seruante" (7/313–14). The lord's gracious willingness to show the servant
"a fulle true menyng" inspires joy and love, faith and solace (7/314–15).
So what had seemed to be an elaboration of commonplace late medieval
figurations of Christ turns out to be nothing of the sort. Instead, the interac-
tions of image, exegesis, and reflection discourage any affective identifications with the crucified body, discourage any attempt to compose an

"imitatio Christi" as an imitation of a suffering, wounded, and bleeding body.

I have now re-read the passages from which Robertson quoted. It is clear that I consider her account of Julian's meditations in the first revelation as only explicable in terms of an a priori decision to construe Julian as analogous to Bynum's subjects, an English contemplative pursuing their models and imitations of Christ. It seems only possible to do this, however, by ignoring the minute particulars of Julian's own rhetorical strategies, especially her ability to invoke and then transform, or sideline, dominant representations of Christ's humanity. As for Robertson's emphasis on "menstrual blood" and "menstrual flow" (154–55) in Julian's revelation, it must be observed that there is absolutely no indication that Julian presents herself as a bleeding body or has any wish to be viewed in this way—unlike so many of the subjects Bynum has studied in research exemplified and addressed in Chapter 1. This was an available path she chose not to take.

I now wish to extend consideration of Julian's representations of the crucified Christ beyond those chapters discussed so far, beginning with the chapter that opens the second revelation.[8] It too starts from an image that seems made in the tradition of the pseudo-Bonaventuran *Meditationes* as the meditant gazes at the crucifix:

> in þe which I beheld contynually a parte of his passion: dyspyte, spyttyng, solewyng and buffetyng, and manie languryng paynes, mo than I can tell, and offten chaungyng of colour. And one tyme I saw how halfe the face, begynnyng at the ere, over ȝede with drye bloud, tyl it closyd in to the myd face, and after that the other halfe beclosyd on the same wyse; (10/324)

We would have learned from late medieval meditations on the Passion to expect certain details in the scene to be elaborated: for example, the agents who despise, spit, mock, and buffet; particulars of Christ's "languryng paynes;" and perhaps Christ's voice drawing attention to his pains to elicit our identification with him or his grieving mother and followers. But Julian's text moves on very differently and, in terms of the traditions she has so carefully evoked, surprisingly. First she draws attention not to pain,

---

8. On this, see Gillespie (1987), 135–36, and Glasscoe (1993), 229–31; Windeatt (1977), 9.

or torment, let alone tormentors, but to the very image she is composing. Half the face, beginning at the ear was covered with dry blood; the other half is similarly covered; and then the blood vanishes (10/324–25). At once Julian recalls that she wanted "mor bodely light to haue seen more clerly." But at this moment she receives no encouragement to give further attention to the image. She receives an answer, significantly enough, in her "reason": "If god will shew thee more, he shal be thy light; thou nedyth none but him." She understands the implications of this resistant response, a "grace" moving her to seek beyond the image, further: "I had hym and wantyd hym" (10/325–26). The discourse is again moved away from "bodely light" and the crucified body of Christ, a shift toward a focus on faith lured on by grace working through a lack and desire which stimulate a seeking that cannot be concluded "in this life." This shift is then disclosed in another extremely inventive image, one in which her "vnderstanding was lett down in to the sea grounde" to grasp how "solace and comfort" is inseparable from faith in God's presence, from "beleue" (10/326–27).[9] So we are being moved away from conventional compositions of the Passion and their concentration on the tortured, bleeding body of Christ as model for imitation and affective identification.

In chapters 16 to 21[10] she brings her meditations to the stage at which Christ dies, a process which can be exemplified in conventional mode from chapters 79–81 of the pseudo-Bonaventure's *Meditationes Vitae Christi* and from the York plays.[11] Julian describes the colors of his face and body, his "nose clongyn to geder" his body drying up, his thirst, and other particulars as Christ's passion drew "nere his dyeng" (16/357–58, 17/360–65). Here too, albeit fleetingly and "in parte" she sees "the compassion" of Christ's mother (18/366). In this sequence Julian's work comes close to the traditions of devotion focused on the tortured and dying body, the commonplace from which this part of our book set out. Discussing the "appalling" images here, Marion Glasscoe writes that Julian "identifies with the compassion of the disciples and Mary."[12] This is certainly a plau-

---

9. Even the "vernacle of Rome" is assimilated to this pattern: it reflects the changing colors on Christ's face but in her enlightened "vnderstanding" it becomes an emblematic representation of the search just described and of the theological virtues (10/331–35).

10. There are problems with Colledge and Walsh's (1978) treatment of their manuscript at the opening of chapter 21 and over the place where the ninth revelation begins; compare Colledge and Walsh (1978), 1:95–97, with Glasscoe (1993), 266 n. 39.

11. For the former, Peltier (1868), 509–630; see esp. 606–609; for the latter, *The York Plays* (Beadle 1982), plays 35 and 36, esp. 325–33.

12. Glasscoe (1993), 233.

sible response to Julian's figurations of the dying body, and one that accords with the affective identifications cultivated by their tradition. However, I am not convinced that it quite fits Julian's text.

What makes me think it does not quite fit is a move in chapter 17 that continues to astonish me. In the midst of descriptions of the body drying up, wounds opening out, the body sagging, hair clinging to dried up flesh, and the skin and flesh hanging as though about to fall down, she writes:

> How it was doone I saw nott, but I vnderstode that it was with the sharpe thornes and the boystours grevous syttyng on of the garlonde, not sparyng and without pytte, that alle tho brake the swet skynne with the flessch, and þe here losyd it from the boone. Wher thorow it was broken on pecys as a cloth, and saggyng downwarde, semyng as it wolde hastely haue fallen for heuynes and for lowsenes. And that was grete sorow and drede to me, for me thought that I wolde nott for my life haue seen it fall. (17/362)

It transpires that the meditant is actually trying to work out the physical causes of the unpeeling skin and flesh, "How it was doone." She could not see how it was done but she "vnderstode" the skin was being torn by thorns and goes on to invent yet more images to display this process "as a cloth, and saggyng downwarde," later presenting the hanging body itself "as men hang a cloth for to drye" (17/362, 363). True enough, she recollects feeling "grete sorow and drede." Yet these feelings here are strangely oriented—not to the sufferings of the dying person but to anxiety lest she see the skin and flesh on the dying body's head "fall." This orientation actually prevents any affective identification and works to estrange us from the traditions of composition which may have made us think we are familiar with both the scene and the meditational mode. It is an orientation that continues as she records her observation of further changes in the body: "This contynued a whyle, and after it began to chaunge; and I behelde and marveylyd how it myght be" (17/363). The curious phrase "how it myght be" is very like the earlier pondering of "how it was doone" and again works in a very different manner to rhetoric designed to stimulate affective responses and identifications. This is followed by close descriptions of new changes, colors, and shapes on the head (17/363, lines 35–37), a mode that creates the aesthetic detachment I have noted earlier: the body becomes a reified object whose colors and patterns become the focus of the gazer. At the end of chapter 17, however, she recalls that the multicolored object of meditation is Christ enduring immense "paynes" and that the vision filled her with pain, apparently the fulfillment of her previous wish to suffer with Christ in his passion (17/367; see 2/285–86). This seems to return us to the kind of meditational identification that had been blocked off. And yet the conclusion of the chapter does not quite leave us here. Instead of ending with a focus on identification and the will to imitate, it culminates in a revelation of her own love of Christ, a disclosure that she loved Christ above herself and that her suffering was that of one who sees "the louer to suffre" (17/365). So the outcome of this meditation is illumination about the nature of her profound love, a crucial contribution to that self-knowledge without which, she later argues, there can be no knowledge of God (17/365; 56/573).

But this chapter leaves Christ on the point of death, "nere his dyeng" (16/357). She expects to witness the death, "to have seen the body alle deed" (21/379),[13] an expectation fostered by received traditions of meditation and iconography. To her astonishment, and to her readers' astonishment, this is not what she next sees: "I saw him nott so" (21/379). *He does not die* and she now encounters the sudden change of his appearance and experiences overwhelming joy. This truly idiosyncratic choice disrupts the normative late medieval sequence of meditations. At this point they had taught people to expect detailed descriptions of the dead body, the difficulties in getting it off the cross, the wailing mother's desperate attachment to the corpse, its burial and, throughout all this, the incitement to identify with the mourners.[14] But Julian sees differently:

> And right in the same tyme that me thought by semyng that the lyfe myght no lenger last, and the shewyng of the ende behovyd nydes

---

13. Colledge and Walsh begin chapter 21 with the sentence from which this comes, although their manuscript starts at their line 6 ("sodenly"); see Colledge and Walsh (1978), 95 and note 10 above.

14. See, for example, *Meditationes Vitae Christi*, chaps. 80–82 (edition cited in note 11); for an English version, see *Meditations on the Supper of our Lord, and the Hours of the Passion* (1985), lines 777–1008. Not, of course, that this tradition did not include the view that the passion, as source of humanity's redemption was both "a pitevouse siht & a ioyful siht," as Nicholas Love expressed it in his version of pseudo-Bonaventure, *Mirror of the Blessed Life of Jesus Christ* (Love 1992, 181). It is the traditional sequence, modes, lamentations, and fleshy attachments that Julian disrupts: her idiosyncrasy is not, obviously not, in linking "piteouse" and "ioyful." With Julian's astonishing figuration of Christ not dying, compare Love (1992), 180 (line 33), 181 (line 11). For an account of Julian's relations to traditions of late medieval affectivity that is different but in many ways congruent with the one offered here, see D. N. Baker (1994), chaps. 1–2, esp. 21–26.

to be nye, sodenly I beholdyng in the same crosse he channgyd in blessyd fulle chere. The channgyng of hys blessyd chere channgyd myne, and I was so glad and mery as it was possible. Then brought oure lorde meryly to my mynd: Where is now any poynt of thy payne or of thy anguysse? And I was ful mery . . . (21/379)

Christ does not die; there are no mourners; there is no deposition, no burial. Instead, he brings words to her "mynd" in a sentence where the pronouns can apply to Christ (with Julian speaking from her "mynd") and to Julian (with Christ speaking to her "mynd"), joining her and her God in a grammar whose mode could hardly be further away from the imitations and identifications of Christ exemplified by Bynum.

From this extraordinary moment Julian writes a dialogue with the cheerful Christ (still on the cross). It focuses on Christ's love, a model that shows the dissolution of ego or self and develops her theology of "the blessydfulle trinytie of our saluacion" (23/391), a theology widely recognized as a pervasive, shaping presence in her revelation of love.[15] In this context we meet the wound in Christ's side, a prominent image in conventional devotion to the "humanity" of Christ as we have seen in previous chapters. Julian relates that Christ "lokyd in to hys syde and behelde with joy," leading her "vnderstandyng . . . by the same wound in to hys syd with in" (24/394). This image, we should recall, had a special place in the "feminization" of Christ studied by Caroline Bynum. In a chapter entitled "Woman as Body or as Food," she showed that "both men and women saw the female body as food and the female nature as fleshy. Both men and women described Christ's body in its suffering and generativity as a birthing and lactating mother."[16] As she observes, this emphasis was part of a growing stress on "Christ's humanity as bodiliness" and hence associated with "the female as flesh": this in turn led to "women's *imitatio Christi* through physicality" (263). "Both men and women," she again stresses, saw the body on the cross "as in some sense female" and associated "Christ's wounds with woman's body" (271). One ·common "parallelism" here was between "Christ's wound and Mary's breast" (272). The vision was of "the breast as food, parallel to the bleeding (i.e., nurturing wound)" and Bynum recalls literary accounts of Saint Bernard "choosing between the bleeding wound

---

15. See esp. Jantzen (1987), chap. 7; Pelphrey (1989), chaps. 4 and 5; Watson (1992). D. N. Baker (1994) is an important account of Julian's theology, especially strong on her dialogues with Augustine.

16. Bynum (1987), 260–61, chap. 9 passim; page referenes to this book follow in my text.

of Christ and the flowing breast of his mother" (272). Furthermore we
should remember that in these traditions, as shown, for instance, by Wolf-
gang Riehle, Christ's wound "caused by the lance of Longinus was interpreted as the gateway to his heart and as a precondition for the union with
God . . . an opening through which it is possible for the mystical lover to
enter into his beloved and thus become completely one with him." Riehle
finds that this gave rise "to a typical and quite consciously intended analogy
between this wound of Christ and the female pudendum: the *vulva,* as the
place of sexual ecstasy, has, so to speak, been transformed into the *vulnus*
of Christ as the place of mystical ecstatic union of the soul with its divine
beloved."[17] This pattern of devotion is clearly illustrated, as Riehle notes,
in the Franciscan *Stimulus Amoris,* a text which becomes the English work
known as *The Prickynge of Love.* Here, as Sarah Beckwith has commented,
the image of wound as breast "is developed with a literally appetizing
relish."[18] How, then, does Julian use this common and most "Bynumian"
of images as Christ leads her "by the same wound in to hys syd"?

My answer to this question is to notice how she does *not* use it. She sets
aside the "feminine" matrix so extensively illustrated by Bynum: she sets
aside the allegedly "eroticized" nexus of *vulnus/vulva* described by Riehle;
here she does *not* in fact, focus on the "feminization" of Christ at all; and
she does *not* present herself as a specifically "feminine" subject. Second, it
is her "vnderstandyng" that is led by Christ. Here we could contrast the
blessed Angela of Foligno with Julian:

> while I was standing in prayer, Christ on the cross appeared. . . . He
> then called me to place my mouth to the wound in his side. It seemed
> to me that I saw and drank the blood, which was freshly flowing
> from his side.[19]

Julian does not see and drink blood: instead, her Christ reveals in his side
"a feyer and delectable place, and large jnow for alle mankynde that shalle
be savyd and rest in pees and in loue" (24/394–95). After this anagogical
shewing she recollects the image of blood and water flowing out of the
dead Christ's side in John 19.34. In her culture, it would not be surprising

---

17. Riehle (1981), 46. For an example of the side-wound in contemporary vernacular
preaching, a nice contrast to Julian's version, see Ross (1940), 216–18. See also D. N. Baker
(1994), 59–60.

18. Beckwith (1993), 58; see 56–64 for illuminating commentary on this text.

19. Angela of Foligno (1993), 128; see also analogies cited on 368 n. 15.

if this elicited a response such as Angela of Foligno's. Yet it does nothing
of the sort: Christ "shewyd to my vnderstandyng in part the blyssydfulle
godhede," a revelation to strengthen, she says, "the pour soule for to vnder-
stande" the nature of uncreated and "endless loue" (24/395). The language
here is generalizing, abstract, and sets aside the conventional fleshy image
from which it began. Julian's mode then shifts again as she writes Christ's
declaration of his love for her and his bliss in her salvation, now choosing
to figure himself as brother and parent (24/396).[20]

The next chapter too contains an interesting invocation and treatment of
commonplace devotional iconography around the representation of Christ's
passion. Here it appears as though Christ is inviting her to fill out the scene
of crucifixion in rather more conventional ways. He asks her whether she
would like to see his mother in the place occupied in the standard composition of "the tyme of hys passion": "Wilt thou see her?" (25/398). Not
surprisingly, Julian answered, "ȝe good lorde, grannt mercy, ye good lorde,
yf it be thy wylle" (25/400). But having been lured to expect a much desired
sight of Mary in her familiar place, Julian's wishes are blocked: "Often
tymes I preyde this, and I went to haue seen her in bodely lykyng; but I
saw her nott so" (25/400). Instead of the image her tradition composed
around the cross, she is given not a "bodely" representation but "a goostly
syght of her . . . hygh and noble and glorious" (25/400), freed from Calvary
and the attachments to the body she displays in so many late medieval
depictions of deposition and burial.[21] Julian thus has Christ himself deploy
one of her own favored rhetorical strategies: namely, to evoke, with sympathy, dominant late medieval representations of Christ's Passion, with their
desires for "bodely" engagement, affective response, and identification;
then to frustrate these desires, displacing them with a "goostly" and "glorious" transcendence of Golgotha. With these displacements goes a rejection
of traditions that concentrate on the supposedly "feminine," whether as
the "feminized" Christ in his crucified humanity or as the contemplative
imitating that putatively "feminine" body. The next chapter shows Christ
yet "more gloryfyed" uttering the divine self-disclosure: "I it am, I it am

20. Glasscoe (1993), 238, seems wide of the mark when she asserts that Julian's writing
in this revelation is "simply an elaboration of this traditional image"; that is, of the "familiar
iconography of Christ's wounded side in both art and literature." This assertion seems especially surprising as she has just rightly noted that Julian's text gives us "what promises to be
a bodily sight but is instantly transposed to convey ghostly understanding." Such sudden
transpositions are far from "simply" an elaboration of "familiar iconography." Compare
Gillespie (1987), 141–42.

21. See note 14.

... I it am that is alle." This affirmation has actually informed her whole meditation, Christ as God, Christ as the telos of all desire and the source of the ecstatic joy Julian conveys in this revelation (26/402–3; and see 83/722). Julian is now in position to develop her profound and extremely unusual critical revision of standard teaching on sin, God's wrath and damnation, the most disturbing set of problems that so preoccupied the Short Text.[22] In Chapter 4 Lynn Staley will address this, exploring the daring of Julian's paths in these domains. Here I wish to continue my reflections on Julian's representations of Christ's humanity, by returning to the issue of the "feminized" Christ. The aspect that now concerns me is one for which Julian is currently widely known and admired, one briefly mentioned earlier in this chapter in connection with Elizabeth Robertson's reading of Julian: Christ as mother.[23] I have already expressed my views on the complex political issues here. I explained why I remain unconvinced by the thesis that late medieval "feminizations" of Christ, and the *imitatio Christi* they sponsored, were "subversive" of the received place of gender in existing structures of power (ideological, economic, political, ecclesiastic, military), unconvinced by claims that such "feminization" was "empowering" for women in late medieval communities—or even in relation to the ideologies with which the category "woman" was elaborated and circulated. With this I have argued that subversive opposition to orthodox Christian legitimations of normative constructions and habitual domination of women in actually existing forms of power came from elsewhere, an elsewhere that set aside the conventional identification of Christ's Incarnation and humanity with the Passion, Crucifixion, and tortured, suffering, dying but nurturing "feminine" body on the cross, the one reproduced in the orthodox eucharist. I have also sought to begin the task of specifying some of the relevant forms of opposition in late fourteenth- and early fifteenth-century English culture. There is obviously no intention to repeat arguments I have offered earlier in this book, but I mention them since they constitute part of the context for the remarks I shall make on Julian's version of the traditions which saw Jesus as mother.

The other part of the context these remarks assume is provided by the

---

22. See Watson (1993), 637–83, here 668–72. I have found this essay immensely helpful in my own reflections on Julian's work.

23. On the topic in general, Bynum (1982; 1987) is indispensable, as is Cadden (1993). On Julian in particular the literature is now substantial but the following may be especially useful: Jantzen (1987), 115–26; Bradley (1976; 1978); Barker (1982); Palliser (1992), esp. chap. 3; and D. N. Baker (1994), chap. 5.

preceding analysis in this chapter, which I shall now summarize. I have argued that Julian's visions of Christ on the cross invoke and set aside traditions that concentrate on making the body in the image of the "feminine" as constituted in dominant (masculine) discourses. I have also suggested that the delicate rhetorical strategies in which she effects these complex maneuvers contribute importantly to her own theological explorations and to her development of a distinctive language in which to write theology, a language that is as ratiocinative and subtly abstract as it is capable of composing memorable images, emblems and, in chapter 51, extensive polysemous allegory. What happens when she develops her own version of Christ as mother?[24]

Chapter 51, the "wonderfull example" of a lord and a servant, given "full mystely" (51/513), concluded with the harrowing of hell, the glorification of Christ in the Trinity, and joyful peace between Christ the spouse and humanity his "lovyd wyfe" (51/542–45). This completes a long, complex, allegorical chapter in which Julian consistently figured Christ in his humanity as masculine. His work as redeemer, as redemptive gardener, is also figured as masculine. He, like the allegory he inhabits, has affinities with Piers in Langland's *Piers Plowman*, a work that seems to me to have been put to brilliant use by Julian in chapter 51. Throughout this "example" he is quite as "masculine" as Piers, the plowman who is also gardener of the tree of Charity growing in the human heart, an agent who himself figures forth Christ.[25] And at the end of the chapter, contemplating Christ "in the trynyte," she elects to figure him as "goddys son" who is also the spouse of "his lovyd wyfe," redeemed humanity (51/545). All readers, at this point, are directed to construe themselves as "feminine" in relation to a "masculine" Christ, even as they are reminded that these are provisional and contingent categories drawn only from "this lyfe" (51/544–45). It is from here that Julian commences her writing of Christ as mother.

The next chapter begins with a statement about the understanding of God's relations to humanity that have been fostered by the long allegory of the lord and servant, culminating in her vision of the Trinity:

> And thus I saw that god enjoyeth that he is our fader, and god enjoyeth that he is our moder, and god enjoyeth that he is our very

---

24. In chapter 48 mercy is aligned with "moderhode," grace with "ryall lordschyppe" (48/502–4) but the exploration of Christ as mother is from chapter 52.

25. Reference here is especially to Passus 6, Passus 15.196–216, Passus 16, Passus 17, and Passus 19 of the B version of *Piers Plowman* (Langland 1988). On the figurative relations of

spouse, and our soule his lovyd wyfe. And Crist enjoyeth þat he is our broder, and Jhesu enioyeth that he is our savyour. (52/546)

This is a significant formulation, made in a mode of writing itself of consequence. The first point to make is that the idea of Christ as mother is introduced while we are still in the metaphysical realm where the previous chapter finished, "in the trynyte." The second is that the sentence states that it is "*god*" who is at once father, mother, and humanity's spouse. I italicize Julian's "god" to draw attention to the difference of focus and context between Julian's statement and the traditions described by Bynum. In the latter the key proportion is the following: Divinity:Christ's humanity :: Men/masculine/reason: Women/feminine/flesh. Or, to recall Bynum's own summary of this aspect of her research, in a quotation from Hildegard of Bingen: "man signifies the divinity of the Son of God, and woman his humanity."[26] The standard parallel was "woman-humanity-Christ" and the basic "association" was that "of Christ's flesh with woman." Indeed, we recall, "*woman* was the symbol of the flesh," while "God's dying body was female."[27] But this is markedly removed from Julian's formulation here. For her it is the glorified figure of Christ "in the trynyte" who can be seen both as spouse and mother, as noted above. Readers should observe the differences here from the traditions Bynum illustrates. Julian has not, emphatically not, confined the figure of mother to the realm of the stereotypically feminine, the flesh, the dying and nutritive body of Christ: she has exalted it into the mysterious realm of the Trinity. As Lynn Staley argues: "Julian's decision to remove references to literal femininity from the Long Text allows her to develop a trinitarian theology that incorporates the feminine into what is more often described as a masculine zone of power." Indeed, she comments on the way Julian "describes motherhood not simply in terms of nurture, but in the language of power."[28] Chapter 4 integrates this observation in an analysis of the way Julian's treatment of motherhood

---

Piers and Christ, see Aers (1975), 85–88, 91–95, 105–11, 122–28; and for hints of relations with Julian, see Salter (1962), 88–89, 102, although her interest here was more in relations between Langland's work and Hilton's *Scale;* see 82–89, 101–2.

26. Bynum (1987), 264: also used as epigraph to chapter 9, 260. I note that Bynum equates Hildegard's and Julian's position here on 264: it will be clear that I consider her to be mistaken in this. However, Bynum's account of Hildegard may be unreliable here; compare Newman (1990).

27. Bynum (1987) *seriatim,* 264, 268, 269, 285.

28. See Chapter 4.

and gender is part of her own complex and subtle strategies for creating her text and herself as authority.

I mentioned that the mode in which Julian introduces this sequence of figuring forth Christ as mother is itself not inconsequential. This mode can be characterized as imagistically sparse, a mode that is maintained as chapter 52 unfolds in a markedly analytic manner to address the way in which humans are strangely heterogeneous creatures: "We haue in vs oure lorde Jehsu Cryst vp resyn, and we haue in vs the wrechydresse and the myschef of Adams fallyng." Raised up with the risen Christ, "we be so broken in oure felyng on dyverse manner by synne and by sondry paynes" (52/547). In its carefully patterned arguments it is designed to facilitate "the ey of oure vnderstanding," to teach us to "knowe of oure selfe" and "oure evyn crysten in what wey we stonde," so that we may learn to deal with the flux of conflicting feelings, to understand their causes and to accept, without the self-punishment so strongly promoted by many aspects of late medieval and early modern Christianity, their inevitability in this life (52/547–50). Not only their inevitability, but, in the perspective of Julian's loving deity, a means to a spiritual life far exceeding the possibilities of an unfallen life (52/549–53; see chapters 27–40, 61). That God is our mother is thus introduced in a context and literary mode that seems to have remarkably little in common with traditions devoted to equating flesh with woman and woman with the humanity of Christ. Indeed, the form in which this theology develops reminds me of two comments made by Nicholas Watson: "With the exception of a few famous passages, the *Revelation of Love* is not rich in visual imagery;" "Julian's revelation has an imagistic sparseness and at least a surface fragmentariness to it that is largely untypical of the experiences of medieval women visionaries, and which must initially have been deeply confusing to its recipient."[29] Both comments apply even to Julian's treatment of motherhood, a domain that in her culture might have been expected to pull her out of this "sparseness."

But given the extent of her deployment of this figuration it is reasonable to ask whether the mode and approach of chapter 52 is renounced or, at least, seriously qualified. The answer is that it is not, and certainly it is not superseded in directions suggested by Bynum's subjects. In chapter 54 Julian's theological analysis of the way "god dwellyth in oure soule" includes the suggestion that "the depe wysdome of þe trynyte is our moder, in whom we be clossyd" (54/563). As befits the trinitarian context and the

---

29. Watson (1992), respectively, 85 n. 16 and 85.

language she uses, Julian offers no elaboration of the term "moder" along the conventional gendered and fleshy lines made so familiar by Bynum and others. The work continues its complex reflections on self-knowledge and the knowledge of God in chapter 56, then moves on to develop an account of what Julian calls "oure substance" in relation to "oure sensuall soule," and of both aspects in relation to God (chapter 57). Here she argues that in Christ all the potential risks of dualism are overcome in a love whereby both "the hyer party" and "the lower party" of humanity is "knytt" to God both in "þe makyng" and in the "flessch takyng" (57/577–78). It is within these trinitarian reflections that she explicates the place of the seven sacraments, part of a divine economy to enclose humanity in God, an enclosing in which human binaries are overcome (57/579–80). This image of enclosure leads into another allusion to the motherhood of Christ: "oure savyoure is oure very moder, in whome we be endlesly borne and nevyr shall come out of hym" (57/580). While this may look like a conventional "feminization" of Christ as mother/womb giving birth, the image is made to resist any concentration on conventional physical iconography and resonances. This is achieved by selecting the term "endlesly" to qualify "borne," by adding the statement that this is an enclosure out of which the offspring will *never emerge* and by concluding the sentence with the masculine pronoun "hym." These delicate qualifications mean that any attempt to visualize or elaborate the term *mother* down the tracks of familiar imagery will be catastrophic: Julian has, in fact, given us an example of the way theological language can turn the familiar into the strange— and, so the theologian hopes, thus become an appropriate bridge to a disclosure of the divine.

Chapters 58 to 61 and 63 sustain her attention to the theme that "god alle wysdom is oure kyndly mother" (58/582). This sequence too is part of her figuration of "the blyssful trynyte" in which "mother" continues to work with, and like, the relational terms "son" and "spouse," "spouse," that is, of his "wyfe" humanity (58/582–83). Her attention is fixed on "þe werkyng of alle the blessyd trynyte" and it encourages her to write, again, in a distinctly analytic mode: "in whych beholldyng I saw and vnderstode these thre properties: the properte of the faderhed, and the properte of the mother hed, and the properte of the lordschyppe in one god" (58/583–84). Nothing could be of less interest to Julian than cultivating images of the "feminine" as "flesh," of Christ as the kind of "maternal" body illustrated by Bynum and Robertson. Throughout these chapters Julian's "moder Cryst" retains the pronoun "he," as in "oure moder Cryst . . . he reformyth vs and restoryth, and by the vertu of his passion" (58/586). She seems perfectly content to represent the humanity of Christ as masculine, "he," "his." This grammar is pervasive but it seems not always taken seriously, despite Julian's consistent emphasis that "as god is oure fader, as verely is god oure moder" and having Christ himself proclaim, "I it am, the myght and the goodnes of faderhode. I it am, the wysdom and the kyndnes of moderhode, I it am, the lyght and the grace that is all blessyd loue; I it am, the trynyte, I it am, þe vnyte" (59/590). Even when Julian writes directly about the Incarnation, with Christ taking on "the servyce and the officie of moderhode" she still does not select those familiar images constituting the "feminine" as lactating, bleeding flesh. Instead she chooses "the officie of moderhode" as, at least ideally, a model of love in loyalty and selfless commitment (60/595–96). And even then she emphasizes the difference between Christ's "moderhede" and human "moders." The latter, she writes, necessarily "bere vs to payne and to dyeng" whereas "he" who is "oure very moder Jhesu, he alone beryth vs to joye and to endless levyng." And while the earthly "moder may geue her chylde sucke hyr mylke," the mother who is Jesus "may fede vs wyth hym selfe . . . with the blessyd sacrament, that is precyous fode of very lyfe" (60/595–97). So while the human mother "may ley hyr chylde tenderly to hyr brest," our masculinized "he"-mother may "homely lede vs in to his blessyd brest by his swet opyn syde" (60/598). Still, some readers might feel that in these images we do, at last, have an imitative convergence with the traditions traced by Bynum. But even if one discounts the careful contrasts between any imaginable human mother and "he," the celestial mother, there is good reason to deny any such uncritical convergence. What we encounter here is a markedly restrained application of Christ's own words in John's gospel, "He that eateth my flesh and drinketh my blood hath everlasting life: and I will raise him up in the last day" (6:55).[30] Just how markedly restrained is her use of these words can readily be seen by comparing the images and miracles in Nicholas Love's contemporary treatise on the "sacrament of cristes blessede body & þe merueiles þerof" appended to his version of pseudo-Bonaventure's *Meditationes* and by considering alongside this work the materials cited and exemplified in Chapter 1.[31] Julian certainly does lead

---

30. See John 6:35–70.

31. See 225–41 of Love's (1992) *Mirror;* Rubin (1991), esp. 108–47, 213–32, 302–16; Bynum (1987), chaps. 2, 4, 6; see also the essays by Rubin and Beckwith in Aers (1992), chaps. 2 and 3. In my view the responses to John 6 in Julian's revelation seem much closer to those of Saint Augustine than to those of Nicholas Love; compare Augustine (1986), tractates 25–27, pp. 160–78.

readers to Jesus's "blessyd brest by his swet opyn syde" but what they
meet there is neither conventional elaborations on the "feminine" nor the
eroticized responses of a text such as James of Milan's *Stimulus Amoris*.[32]
What they do meet is a cluster of phrases whose tendency is a disembodying
one: in his "blessed brest" Jesus shows "there in perty of the godhed and
þe joyes of hevyn, with gostely suernesse of endlesse blysse" (60/598). Not
for the first time, as we have seen, Julian has initiated what looked like
being a familiar pattern of sexually marked and distinctly physical imagery
only to subvert such expectations, perhaps following moves that are repeated time and again in John's gospel, as, for example, in its fourth chapter. There Jesus, having requested a drink, tells the Samaritan woman at
the ancient well that she could perhaps have asked *him* to give her water,
and he would have obliged with living water; she responds that this seems
unlikely since, as his initial question made clear, he had nothing with which
to draw up the water from the deep well. Jesus then presses against the
initial direction his image seemed to take and promises water that will
become an inner fountain, springing up to eternal life. Language attached
to the body, and literal forms of referentiality, has been turned against itself
to disclose a domain of the "spirit," one that is no respecter of traditional
pieties or sacred places but calls for recognition of God as "a spirit," one
to be adored "in spirit and truth" (4:3–24). The point I am making here
can be further illustrated by Augustine's comments on John's scene in his
homilies on that gospel. He sees the literal opening of the passage as already
hinting at something in a manner designed to make us eager to search for
further understanding. He describes Jesus's rhetorical strategy as one that
works gradually, by degrees. It invites an initially literal, "carnal" response
as a first stage in a process moving toward "a spiritual sense," one that is
bound up with something in the soul, which is called "understanding and
mind," becoming "enlightened by the higher light." It is part of a process
designed to disclose the relations between faith and understanding, to make
the listeners feel, "we had gone out of doors, and we are sent inward."[33]
It seems to me that this is the kind of rhetorical strategy pursued by Julian.
Carefully chosen and sustained, it casts her in the role of theologian, exegete, and teacher. As Lynn Staley will show, to effect this in the vernacular

---

32. On the latter here, see Riehle (1981), 46, 68, 118, and Beckwith (1993), 56–63.

33. Augustine (1986), tractate 15.6–25, pp. 100–105. The ideas about allegory here are
set out more explicitly in Augustine (1958); the epistemological implications of Augustine's
exegesis are illuminatingly discussed in Colish (1983), 15–54. For critical commentary on
Augustine's misogynistic assumptions here, see Bradley (1991), 122–26.

and as a woman, at the time when the church was involved in an increasingly aggressive struggle against Lollardy, was a distinctly radical challenge to authoritative norms and the now sacralized hierarchies of gender. Such a challenge is very different from the ones mounted by Lollard writers, preachers, and communities, but it too was a devotion to Christ that set aside the will to imitate the tortured, bleeding, dying body produced as the central icon in late medieval devotion. And it also set aside the "feminization" of this body as model.

These comments make an appropriate conclusion to my study of this topic, but I will briefly follow the remaining allusions to it in Julian's revelation of love. I do so, at the risk of a certain remorselessness, because the topic is central in a range of debates around gender, sexual differentiation, the body, power, and medieval Christianity; and because in such debates Julian is an important and, as I have been suggesting, critical subject. Chapter 61 continues her reflections on sin and on why "it nedyth vs to falle, and it nedyth vs to see it," an essential part both of self-knowledge and knowledge of God's love (61/602–3). In this context she takes up the model offered by a mother's relations to her children. Our mothers, she remarks, may perhaps abandon us, to perish, but "oure hevynly moder Jhesu may nevyr suffer vs þat be his chyldren to peryssch, for he is almyghty, all wysdom and all loue" (61/604–5). As Lynn Staley points out, Julian is presenting Christ's motherhood as love in *power,* a motherhood that is both unearthly, emphatically unlike "oure erthly moder" and "masculinized"— "oure hevynly moder . . . *his* chyldren . . . *he.*" In chapter 63 we find a passing reference to Christ as "oure derewurthy mother" responding to penitence by sprinkling the penitents "in his precious blode" (63/615–16). But there is no development of this image along lines pursued in Elizabeth Robertson's meditations on blood, menstruation, milk, and the feminized body of Christ. In the same sentence in which the phrase about sprinkling blood appears, Julian leaves the image to write that this mother, "he," will "heele vs fulle feyer by processe of tyme, ryght as it is most wurschype to hym and joye to vs withoute ende" (63/615–16). Once more the potential to elaborate a fleshy, physicalizing, stereotypically "feminine" from the images of mother and blood are rigorously eschewed. This eschewal is actually highlighted by Julian's choice to stay with figures at the core of Bynum's studies, figures of mother, giving birth, food, and child (63/615–17). Julian is fully aware of the imagistic traditions and options available to her, fully aware of elaborations of "feminine" around the medieval body of Christ and her own. Yet her choices, once more, are against these options.

Of Christ she writes "he bare vs to endlesse lyfe" (63/616–17). This is the sum of the image of maternal birthgiving and it recalls the contrasts she had just made in chapter 60 between the way "alle oure moders bere vs to payne and to dyeng" and the way Christ "alone beryth vs to joye" (60/595). A similarly marked refusal of familiar imaginistic potentials can be seen in the brief reference to the fact that "he fedyth vs and fordreth vs, ryht as þe hye souereyne kyndnesse of moderhed wylle, and as þe kyndly nede of chyldhed askyth" (63/617). Julian's figurations move away very swiftly from the literal, the "physical," to interpretation "in þe syght of oure soule" (63/617). From here her work moves through her momentary loss of faith in her own revelation, her confrontations with doubt and despair (chapters 66, 69–70), to further meditations on human suffering, failure, and sin (chapters 68, 71–82).

She then returns for the last time to the image of motherhood. It is a fleeting image in a chapter of especially dense concentration on the disclosures she has received concerning the Trinity (chapter 83). The language is characteristically analytic as it addresses "thre propertees of god, in whych the strenght and þe effecte of alle þe revelacion stondyth." Her longing is, most significantly, for her "reson" to be united with God, "vnderstandyng that it is þe hyghest gyfte that we haue receyvyd" (83/722–23). This union takes place in the light of faith, a light "comyng of oure endlesse day that is oure fader, god, in whych lyght oure moder, Cryst, and oure good lorde the holy gost ledyth vs in this passyng lyfe" (83/723–24). In this trinitarian image, "oure moder Cryst" is fully assimilated to Saint John's vision of Christ as the light which shines in the darkness, the light which enlightens all who come into this world, even though that world may not acknowledge the light of all life (John 1:1–14). There is nothing to direct readers' imaginations in the directions favored by Bynum's medieval subjects, ones that also fascinate those modern scholars who think they find convergences here with Kristeva's celebration of "abjection." On the contrary, Julian's image of "oure moder Cryst" inhabits a universe of discourse that has gently but most decisively set aside those versions of gender, of motherhood, of flesh, of Christ's humanity, decisively set aside voluntary imitations of the tortured, wounded, nurturing body on Calvary and in the late medieval eucharist. With the passages from John's gospel mentioned above, it would be appropriate here, thinking about Julian's work in relation to gender and figurations of Christ's body, to recollect Saint Paul's claim that for Christians, those "baptized in Christ," "there is neither male nor female" (Galatians 3:26–28). And when Christ's Passion is mentioned in her final chapters it is to stress that she is simultaneously "mornyng" and "glad and mery, for he is god" (71/657). Indeed, she insists she was shown nothing about the self-inflicted sufferings of voluntary penance: "For that pennance that man takyth vppon hym selfe, it was nott shewde me" (77/692). Her experience confirmed by her divine revelation was that this life provides more than sufficient penitential materials for most humans and that the real task is to learn how to deal with these as they emerge (77/692). She describes this earth as "pryson" and writes that "this lyfe is pennance" (77/693). Yet it is a penance not to be seen as punishment, retribution, or the product of God's wrath (a conventional notion she finds deeply mistaken; chapters 48–49), but as the source of spiritual enlightenment, a "remedy" in which people may find "oure lorde is with vs, kepyng vs and ledyng in to fulhed of joy" (77/694).

Having noted above that I was offering comments that would be appropriate as a conclusion to this chapter, I shall now write the ones that will end this reading of Julian's revelation. First, I have understood Julian's theology as uniting creation, Crucifixion and resurrection in a dialectical unity. This dialectical unity depends on her ability to resist the dominant modes in which Christ's humanity was represented, their fixation on elaborating imagined details of scenes of torture, Crucifixion, and deposition, including strands that made Jesus's mother a committed participant in the same fixations, culminating in her very bodily assumption and crowning. In resisting these modes Julian rejected the fetishization of suffering so astutely described by Schillebeeckx, quoted in Chapter 1. This in turn freed her to develop one of her most brilliant and original contributions to Christian theology: her profound revision of dominant accounts of sin and its place in a nexus constituted by God's wrath, infernal punishment, and the Crucifixion seen as a propitiatory sacrifice which drew God's infinite wrath onto his son and hence away from the humanity he had eternally damned. For Julian this orthodox matrix is not corroborated by "þe revelacion" (83/722) that was God's gift to her for all people (see especially chaps. 27–40, 45–48, 51, 81–86). Lynn Staley will analyze this major issue, focusing on Julian's subtle negotiations with ecclesiastical authority and power. For the moment it is sufficient to note that her original treatments of sin and her conflicts with her church's teaching were inextricably bound up with her representation of Christ's humanity. Here I have shown just how she sidelined traditions in which women were conflated with standard misogynistic constructions of the "feminine," Christ's body "feminized" and constituted as lactating/bleeding flesh. With this she also sidelined the self-punishing bodily imitations constructed around that model. So Julian rejected the technologies of power that both constituted the body of Christ in her culture and also controlled the way it should be imitated, gazed upon, and consumed. To reject such technologies of power, in her own specific circumstances was to pose some very sharp questions about the authority that both legitimized and was sustained by such technologies. This issue is addressed in detail in Chapter 4.

PART
II

CHAPTER FOUR

Julian of Norwich and the Late Fourteenth-Century Crisis of Authority

LYNN STALEY

"For twenty yere after the tyme of the shewyng saue thre monthys I had techyng inwardly as I shall sey."[1] So Julian of Norwich introduces her

---

1. Colledge and Walsh (1978), 520. Quotations from both the Long and Short Text of the *Showings* refer to this edition and will be cited accordingly in the text. Though Glasscoe (1989) has argued subtly for the priority of the Sloane manuscript of the Long Text, I have chosen to use the Paris text, edited by Colledge and Walsh. There are some passages in it that Sloane does not contain, as well as wording not present in Sloane. Though I do not here present a sustained argument for the Paris manuscript, there are a number of instances in

explanation of the mysterious parable of the Lord and the Servant in the fourteenth Revelation of the Long Text of the *Showings*. She thereby signs herself as a writer whose authority derives from her ability, finally, to explicate her own vision. However, in characterizing herself as the exegete of her own text, she also locates that text within a particular period of historic time. Her "twenty years . . . saue thre monthys" sends us back to the opening sentence of the Long Text where she announces a date for her spiritual experience even before she describes it, "This reuelation was made to a symple creature vnlettyrde leving in deadly flesh, the yer of our lord a thousannde and three hundered and lxxiij, the xiij daie of May" (LT 285). Received in 1373, expounded finally in 1393, Julian's work is contemporaneous with that of Chaucer, Gower, the *Gawain*-poet, and Langland. Social and political events that claimed the attention of those writers, including the decline of Edward III, the Good Parliament in 1376, the accession of the ten-year-old Richard II to the throne of England in 1377, the beginning of the papal schism in 1378, the English Rising of 1381, and the ongoing difficulties between Richard and his Commons, as well as between Richard and the older members of the nobility, culminating in the crisis of the Merciless Parliament in 1388, provided Julian with her own atmosphere of tension and ferment. Those same twenty years witnessed significant "rhetorical" events as well, events that are memorialized in the words of John Wyclif, Thomas Brinton, chronicle writers, Lollard dissenters, John Gower, William Langland, Geoffrey Chaucer, and John Ball. Each of these figures sought to provide events with a shaping language or myth and in so doing contributed to and expanded the terms of the debate about the nature of and basis for authority.

My focus in this chapter is the complicated truth inscribed within those dates that Julian carefully embeds in the Long Text of the *Showings*. In addition to 1373 and 1393, Julian notes in the final chapter, "And fro the tyme þat it was shewde, I desyerde oftyn tymes to wytt in what was oure lords menyng. And xv yere after and mor, I was answeryd" (LT 732), maintaining that only in 1388 or so did she begin to understand that the meaning of the original revelation was love. Each of these dates may, of course, be fictions. But, since they place in the foreground the process of composition, we need to inquire into her possible reasons for privileging certain dates, anchoring herself to historic time in ways, for example, she

---

which I feel it displays a more daring and/or dangerous use of language. When it is apposite, I have noted those discrepancies between the two manuscripts.

does not identify herself with a particular place. The issues submerged in Julian's dating are those that mark the work of more secular writers and underline the need to recognize that Julian and other devotional writers were also participants in the dialogues of the late fourteenth century. Like Chaucer, Julian needed to evolve a rhetorical strategy that allowed her the freedom to say what she needed to say; like him, she found it necessary to create an authorial self, or, in her case, selves. She characterizes the Short Text as an immediate and somewhat less assured work, one that she wrote before she had full understanding of her revelations, and the Long Text as the product of much contemplation and inward teaching. That she was more than capable of fictional self-fashioning is borne out by this Long Text, which her editors have described as a tribute to her knowledge of Latin, her mastery of Scripture, her command of certain key theological issues, and her skill in adapting the figures of Latin rhetoric to the medium of English. Edmund Colledge and James Walsh compare her to Chaucer, who was working on his translation of Boethius's *Consolation of Philosophy* around 1380, when Julian was likewise considering the strategies of composition. Where Chaucer was faced with the need to translate the elegance of Boethius into English, Julian needed to invent a mode of vernacular expression that would communicate the complexity of her own inner experience. She met the challenge by "translating" into English the inherited and revered conventions of Latin literary culture.[2] Though there are disagreements about the nature of Julian's education and the degree of her command of Latin culture, most students of Julian acknowledge that her professions of simplicity should not be taken at face value.[3] By describing herself as unlettered—and thus ascribing the Long Text to inward teaching and prayer—Julian deliberately fashioned a miniature of the mystic as divinely inspired writer that served as an insignia of spiritual authority.[4] Her self-characterization also had a political point, for she placed contemplation, rather than authorial strategy, in the foreground, affording herself the screen she needed to explore alternatives to contemporary views about subjectivity, about sin, and about the divine nature.

As recent studies by Jonathan Hughes and Nicholas Watson have demonstrated, we cannot afford to consider devotional writing as somehow dis-

---

2. Colledge and Walsh (1978), introduction, 47.

3. For other views on Julian's education, see Crampton (1993), introduction, 4–5; Pelphrey (1982), 28; Watson (1993), 673–74.

4. For a discussion of Langland and the practice of authorial inscription, see Middleton (1990).

tinct from its historical or social context.[5] Though mystics frequently described themselves as inhabiting a realm of purely revelatory consciousness, in order to communicate with others, they inevitably drew upon language that reflected contemporary concerns and points of view.[6] The very self a mystic presents is socially constructed, in the sense that it exists rhetorically and is compounded of current terms of self-definition and self-understanding. In her presentation of her self, Julian uses the conventions of late medieval spiritual writing, exploiting them in order to position herself squarely within the conversation about the nature of authority that preoccupied many of the key figures of the late fourteenth century. The very changes she made in the two versions of the *Showings,* which suggest her changing sense of audience and thus of vocation, provide evidence of her sensitivity to contemporary language and her intention of joining this conflict by offering a refiguration of the divine in terms of loving lordship and active maternity. In so doing, she demonstrated her uneasiness with the drift of contemporary devotional writing and with the tone of contemporary political or social rhetoric. She images herself as the untutored mystic, but the Long Text of the *Showings,* especially the matter of Revelation 14, the most lengthy and significant of her additions, suggests we refine that image and begin to think of her as profoundly and courageously polemical.

If she is polemical, she is by necessity politically aware. This awareness underlines her presentation of her self in both texts of the *Showings* and may well have inspired her to date her revelations so precisely. Recent work on Julian, in particular Nicholas Watson's essay, "The Composition of Julian's of Norwich's *Revelations of Love,*" has begun to focus increasingly on Julian's habits of composition and thus upon her sense of herself as a writer.[7] This is not to say that Julian was not also a mystic or a devout Christian, but that her sense of vocation was far more complicated than the simple rubric, "Mother Julian," allows. Although, as will be clear, I

---

5. See Hughes (1988); Watson, "The Middle English Mystics" (forthcoming). Marion Glasscoe (1983) also remarks on the need to situate Julian historically. For more general comments about the need to locate our analyses of individual experience and expression within a communal and/or historical context, see Aers (1988a), introduction; Beckwith (1993); Patterson (1987).

6. In addition, a number of mystics, among them Bridget of Sweden and Catherine of Sienna, spoke directly to contemporary moral and ecclesiastical concerns. In so doing, they availed themselves of the prophet's mantle, figuring themselves as descendants of the Old Testament visionaries who were directed by God to address popular lapses.

7. See Staley (1994), chap. 1; Watson (1993); Watson (forthcoming).

am not in agreement with Watson's dating of the two texts of the *Showings*, his work represents a crucial first step toward a reconsideration of Julian in relation to late fourteenth-century English literary culture.

Watson argues that the Short Text should be dated in the early to mid 1380s, rather than in the early 1370s, and the Long Text in the second decade of the fifteenth century. His dating of the Short Text is prompted by an early passage in which Julian manifests her orthodoxy by stressing her conventional use of images as aids to devotion:

> . . . me thought I hadde grete felynge in the passyonn of Cryste, botte ȝitte I desyrede to haue mare be the grace of god. Me thought I wolde haue bene that tyme with Mary Mawdeleyne and with oth-ere that were Crystes loverse, that I myght have sene bodylye the passionn of oure lorde that he sufferede for me, that I myght have sufferede with hym as othere dyd that lovyd hym, not withstandynge that I leevyd sadlye alle the peynes of Cryste as halye kyrke schewys and techys, and also the payntyngys of crucyfexes that er made be the grace of god aftere the techynge of haly kyrke to the lyknes of Crystes passyonn, als farfurthe as man ys witte maye reche. Nouȝt withstondynge alle this trewe be leve I desyrede a bodylye syght, whare yn y myght have more knawynge of bodelye paynes of oure lorde. (ST 201–2)

Watson sees the passage as designed to indicate Julian's orthodoxy at a time during the mid-1380s when the debate about the veneration of images was linked to suspicions of Lollardy.[8] Watson reads the passage as a pre-emptive response and, taken together with Julian's references to her own gender, as locating the Short Text of the *Showings* in a period when repri-sals against those suspected of Lollard attitudes about images and "preach-ing" women were more common than in the 1370s. On the basis of the late dating for the Short Text and what it suggests about Julian's deliberate pace as a writer and thinker, along with her remarks about further enlight-enment fifteen and then twenty years after the original revelation, Watson suggests we push the Long Text into the fifteenth century, perhaps into the second decade of that century.[9]

---

8. Watson (1993), 659–64.

9. In part Watson's late dating is influenced by the scribal remark introducing the manu-script of the Short Text that Julian is still alive (Short Text, 201). Watson feels the words indicate that the Long Text is not yet circulating.

Through his careful treatment of both texts of the *Showings* as evidence for Julian's *methods* of composition Watson provides a valuable reading of the works as issuing from someone who must be understood as both a writer and an English devotional writer. In making the decision to write an account of her spiritual experience when few Englishwomen made that decision and, then, to decide to rewrite that account in a strikingly different way, Julian steps (and I think consciously) into the world of a Langland or a Chaucer or a Gower.[10] Furthermore, Watson's insistence that the Short Text should not be seen as the spontaneous work she professes directs our attention to the craft and the strategy that underlies it. That strategy may well have been a response to the controversies of the 1380s. However, though I do not see the Short Text as something Julian dashed off soon after her original experience, I think her characterization of it as fresh has more to do with her estimation of the textual community to which it is directed.[11]

The opening statements, including the passage on the use of images cited above, seem designed to locate the Short text within a primarily affective school of piety that was frequently linked to female devotion.[12] Thus, Julian's emphasis upon her desire to have more "feeling" in the passion of Christ, to kneel with Mary Magdalene and other "lovers" of Christ, to see "bodily" the passion, and to suffer its anguish, in other words to go beyond the belief encoded in reliance upon images to immediate experience, speaks to the same impulse for fervent love that characterized late medieval affectivity from Saint Anselm well into the late fifteenth century.[13] The most important English medieval voice for affective spirituality was, of course, that of Richard Rolle, who belongs to the generation preceding Julian and whose works remained important throughout the late Middle Ages. Rolle would have been one of the authors against whose works Julian measured her own devotional prose. The scribal opening of the Short Text, which promises that the work will be comforting to "alle thaye that desires

---

10. For pertinent remarks on the relative paucity of English women writers, see Watson (1993), 642–57.

11. On medieval textual communities, see Stock (1983), especially 90–91. Watson (forthcoming) also suggests that the Short Text is directed at a female community. See also Riddy (1993), 111–17. Riddy does not make the same sort of distinctions between the envisioned audiences for the two texts. One of the most important essays on the two texts is still that of Windeatt (1977).

12. On female textual communities, see Riddy (1993).

13. On the figure of the Magdalene, see Johnson (1984), 148–61. The literature on affective piety is vast. A reader might begin with Woolf (1968).

to be Crystes looverse," and the gripping first sentence, "I desyrede thre graces be the gyfte of god," which rivets our attention upon the imperative demand for personal experience, serve as means of categorizing the work. The opening implies what the author of the *Book of Privy Counselling* overtly states, that we ought to seek more after feeling than knowing.[14] Though, as David Aers has pointed out, the Short Text of the *Showings* can hardly be described as lurid, or even as as startlingly metaphoric as some of Rolle's meditations on the Passion, it nonetheless presents itself as an account of Julian's physical experience of the Passion. Domenico Pezzini remarks that the Long Text converts experience into theology using the Passion as the center for an entire system of thought, but the Short Text describes the Passion as experience itself.[15]

More important than the details themselves, however, is the manner in which Julian filters them through her own consciousness. This is one of the differences between the two texts of the *Showings* and most firmly anchors Julian at this stage of her career to the school of Rolle, who conceived of his life as dramatizing a pattern of conversion, temptation, and spiritual growth.[16] From the moment he fled from his father's house wearing clothes donated by his sister, Rolle sought to transgress contemporary social codes as a way of staging the revolutionary outlines of the new life.[17] Moreover, his works describe the physical experience of hearing, smelling, and feeling the sweetness of God in order to present himself as an exemplar of devotion for his readers. Julian inserts herself into the Short Text in a number of important ways. She describes hearing the story of Saint Cecilia told in church (204–6); she makes several references to her own gender; she includes her mother among those watching in her bedroom. These details give ballast to the Short Text as the immediate and firsthand account of a personal experience. They enhance Julian's descriptions of her own fear or wonder or pain by anchoring what are impressions to the realm of the corporal, to a world of touchable crucifixes, actual bedrooms, filial relationships, and parish activities. What she thereby limns in is a notion of community that holds the individual Christian as surely as the love of Christ

---

14. Hodgson (1994), 171. On the balance Julian attains between the two, particularly in relation to the work of Richard Rolle, see Pezzini (1990). Watson (forthcoming) discusses the tension between *scientia* and *sapientia* in devotional prose.

15. See Pezzini (1990), 65.

16. See Watson (1992a).

17. For Rolle's life, see "The Office of St. Richard Hermit," in Allen (1927), 56. On transgressing social codes by means of gender shifting enacted through dress, see Dollimore (1991), 288.

"becloses" the soul. I would go even further and suggest that the community she adumbrates is a female one, as the reference to Saint Cecilia, a saint whose life seems to have been particularly important to female piety, implies.[18]

Where the Long Text, as I shall discuss in more detail later, expresses a tension between individual experience and the authority of the church, the Short Text evinces no real sense of conflict. Instead, it documents a series of revelations that may seem to be extraparochial but occur within the confines of the family of God and are intended to join the individual more fully to her "even cristen" within the enclosures of the church. Julian insists throughout the Short Text that she is joined to her fellow Christians (220), that she willingly submits herself to Holy Church (244), and that there is no conflict between what God teaches and is teaching her and what Holy Church teaches (243, 252, 258, 262, 267, 275). In a way that Rolle does not, Julian melds the self into the company of the faithful and thereby provides a way of understanding the relationship between personal experience and communal authority. Similarly, her assertion that, though she is a woman, she does not mean to teach, works to privatize—and to some extent to neutralize—the Short Text:

> Botte god for bede that ȝe schulde saye or take it so that I am a techere, for I meene nouȝt soo, no I mente nevere so; for I am a womann, leued, febille and freylle. Botte I wate wele, this that I saye, I hafe it of the schewynge of hym that es souerayne techare. Botte sothelye charyte styrres me to telle ȝowe it, for I wolde god ware knawenn, and mynn evynn crystene spede, as I wolde be my selfe to the mare hatynge of synne and lovynge of god. Botte for I am a womann, schulde I therfore leve that I schulde nouȝt telle ȝowe the goodenes of god, syne that I sawe in that same tyme that is his wille, that it be knawenn? (ST 222)

She here draws on the distinction between preaching (or teaching) and telling, once more locating her work within the context of communal codes. Though authorities followed Saint Paul in forbidding women to preach, they allowed them to instruct women and children in private.[19] Julian thus

---

18. Windeatt (1977) has commented extensively on the important differences between the two texts. He mentions many of the same incidents I do, including Julian's excision of the personal references. On Saint Cecilia, see Riddy (1993), 105; Watson (1995).

19. See Blamires and Marx (1993), esp. 40.

insists on her responsibility to "tell," but, by describing the act as telling rather than teaching, she feminizes it, assigns it to the "space" populated by priests bearing crucifixes who address her as "daughter," the same space where mothers watch, where feelings are finally channeled into the enveloping Holy Church. She maintains the persona of the "teller" throughout the Short Text, in the final section reiterating the outlines of her identity as a verbal witness to Christ's Passion:

> Alle the blissede techynge of oure lorde god was as schewed to me be thre partyes, as I hafe sayde before, that es to saye be the bodely sight, and be worde formed in mynn vndyrstandynge, and by gastelye syght. For the bodely sight, I haffe sayde as I sawe, als trewlye as I cann. And for the wordes fourmed, I haffe sayde thamm ryght as oure lorde schewed me thame. And for the gastely sight, I hafe sayde som dele, bot I maye neuer fully telle it; and þerfore of this gastely sight I am stirred to say more, as god wille gyfe me grace. (ST 272–73)

In this passage Julian reveals some of the artifice that went into the Short Text. A necessary part of her fiction is the distinction she draws between Christ (the teacher) and herself (the teller). Thus the verb "said" dominates the sentences; like Mary Magdalene, whose closeness to Christ she wished to emulate, she bears witness to private experience, to what is her own astonished sight of resurrection and hence of the new life. The heaviness of spirit and flesh she noted during parts of her revelations has been transformed into an affirmation of "bodily sight" and thus into an affirmation of the very flesh through which such sensory messages enter the mind.[20] In describing much of the Short Text as a record of this "bodily sight," she implicitly links it to other "feminized" accounts of spiritual experience, including those of Richard Rolle.[21] However, her protestations of affective piety serve her as an *accessus* to an entirely different type of writing, one

---

20. See G. Gibson (1989) for an extended exploration of the late medieval incarnational aesthetic. See also E. Robertson (1993). By suggesting ways in which Julian affirms our sensual (or female) natures as uniting us to Christ, Robertson attempts to relate Julian to those impulses within medieval spirituality that Bynum has articulated. Though I welcome Robertson's contextualization of Julian's thought, I agree here with David Aers that we should not assume that Julian herself was not capable of distinguishing between her aims and methods of approach and those of other, more conventional, devotional writers.

21. I do not mean to suggest that the Short Text is a record of bodily sight and the Long Text of spiritual. In both accounts, she weaves back and forth between the two ways of seeing.

that concerns her "gastely sight," about which she is "stirred" to say more. The verb is, of course, Rolleian, but, as the Short Text hints and the Long Text demonstrates, this project takes Julian from the world of private revelation to that of public theology. Julian retains both the passage and the discussion of human impatience and despair and divine patience and love that follows it in the Long Text (see chapter 73). However, in the subsequent chapter of the Long Text, Julian moves away from the fiction of the "seer," to that of the thinker or interpreter. Compare:

> Fore I saw foure maner of dredes. (*Showings*, ST 276)

> For I vnderstonde iiij manner of dredys. (*Showings*, LT 671)

Julian here changes more than her verb; she changes its tense. She thereby enlarges the very scope of her work, lifting it from an account of past vision to present—and presumably continuing—understanding.

This is not to say that the Short Text is radically different in meaning from the Long Text, but that it is presented differently. The Short Text certainly contains evidence of Julian's exposition of sin and of her remarkably unpunitive approach to human frailty that are so prominently expounded in the Long Text; it also contains hints of her treatment of God's maternity. Nonetheless, it seems designed for a different type of reader than the Long Text. Though Watson has argued that remarks about both the veneration of images and the difficulties with women "teaching" need to be seen in the context of Lollard controversies of the mid-1380s, they can also be seen as signs of Julian's own sense of an audience for this particular text and for her sense of vocation at this stage of her life. Short, seamless, without the apparatus of *compilatio* that distinguishes the Long Text, humble, and experiential, Julian seems to write for a community of female readers whose needs preoccupied so many English devotional writers— from the authors of the *Ancrene Wisse,* the Katherine group, and the Wooing group to Rolle himself, Walter Hilton, the compiler(s) of the Vernon manuscript and, in the fifteenth century, Nicholas Love. The Long Text testifies not only to Julian's growth as a writer, but to her ability to respond to a new series of cultural or ideological issues and to a newly developed sense of her own talents and vocation.

The Short Text itself contains hints of her awareness of her own ambition

---

However, because it is longer and has a manifestly theological intent, the Long Text gives primacy to interpretation, or to the mind's ability to join the realms of the flesh and the spirit or audacity. In deciding to compose an account of her spiritual experience, Julian implicitly separated herself from the very "even cristen," with whom she seeks to merge herself throughout the account. That the decision to write could be a troubling one for a medieval woman is borne out by Hildegard of Bingen's elaborate account of her own call to a literary vocation, as well as by her accounts of the illnesses she suffered if she did not write. Similarly, other women—both secular and religious—felt the need to develop elaborate "fictions" that served to authorize them as writers.[22] In a culture where "singularity" was not prized—and this is especially true in medieval religious culture—and where women in particular were not expected to push themselves forward, the Short Text can only be seen as an *act,* a deliberate and courageous move on Julian's part into a public arena where she could be held accountable for her words. That she was well aware of the relationship between writing and acting is clear from her careful handling of her own literary persona. The challenge presented by a "speaking woman" is neutralized almost immediately by the masquerade of immediacy and by the outlines of a feminine community with which she surrounds herself. She speaks as Mary Magdalene spoke to the disciples, "I have seen the Lord, and these things he said unto me."[23] In the Long Text Julian is at once even more careful and more audacious: she leaves the bedroom filled with women to enter a distinctly masculine preserve. Her role models for her move into the realms of theology would have been extraordinarily few; even Hildegard of Bingen, who was read in the fourteenth century, was revered primarily for her prophecies.[24] Where we can look back now on Hildegard and see a woman of amazing intelligence, energy, and interests, Julian would have had the example of a notable woman who "saw," who was inspired, who was "given" language, as it were. Her expansion and reorganization of the substance of Revelation 1 in the Long Text indicates her widening sense of audience or her growing sense of her own powers as a writer.

---

through interpretation.

22. On Hildegard of Bingen, see Newman (1987), chap. 1. See also Staley (1994), chap. 1.

23. As if to "tame" the implicit radicalism presented by the Magdalene and her experience in the Easter garden, the maker of a fifteenth-century alabaster panel depicting the *Noli me tangere,* juxtaposed her tiny, very feminine figure to that of a huge, very male Christ, who is holding a spade. The alabaster is an important cultural document precisely because these were mass-produced in the Midlands from about the mid-fourteenth century and exported to other parts of England as well as to many European countries; in the truest sense, they are examples of popular culture. See Cheltham (1984), pl. 212.

24. See Kerby-Fulton (1990), chap. 2; Wilks (1994), 45–46.

The version of the first revelation in the Short Text begins with vision and ends with words binding the visionary more closely to the body of the faithful. In it Julian attains a magnificent balance between what can only be described as a manifestation of individuality and affirmations of community. Throughout, the account is dominated by the verb "to see." She moves from the terse "And in this sodaynlye I sawe the rede blode trekylle downe" (ST 210), to a "ghostly" sight of his love as our clothing, to the "bodily likeness" of a hazelnut and of the Virgin. Even when she describes the process of understanding that issues from these sights, she employs the language of vision. Rhetorically, she does more here than suggest the intimate relationship between apprehension and comprehension; she maintains her status as a seer. Her continual affirmation of this status leads naturally into the closing sections of the revelation, where she insists on her lack of singularity ("Alle that I sawe of my selfe, I meene in the persone of alle myne evynn cristene, for I am lernede in the gastelye schewynge of oure lorde that he meenys so" [ST 219]), defends her right as a woman to tell what she saw, and stresses that what she describes are the details of bodily sight, that only God can provide us with "ghostly" sight. Julian concludes the account by returning us to the site of vision itself, the sickroom,

> Than sayde I to the folke that were with me: Itt es to daye domes daye with me. And this I sayde for I wenede to hafe dyed; for that daye that man or womann dyes ys he demyd as he schalle be with owtynn eende. This I sayde for y walde thaye lovyd god mare and sette the lesse pryse be the vanite of the worlde, for to make thame to hafe mynde that this lyfe es schorte, as thaye myght se in ensampille be me; for in alle þis tyme I wenede to hafe dyed. (ST 224–25)

With their emphasis upon death, judgment, and the vanity of the world, these sentences provide an at times striking revelation with a conventionally pious ending. As Watson has pointed out, the Short Text has a darker emphasis than the Long Text; the references to sin and corruption that we tend to associate with medieval piety and find so little of in the Long Text are more prevalent in the earlier version.[25] Such references suggest Julian's concern that we might forget the communal context for the vision; both the phrase "the folke that were with me" and the reminder of death join visionary and reader to the human community.

---

25. Watson (1993), 668–69.

The version of this revelation in the Long Text is not only far longer, but less timid, and organized in ways that somewhat free it from the constraints of affective prose. For example, in the Short Text she follows the sight of the "lytille thyng" (212), like a hazelnut, signifying all that is made, with a vision of Mary as a young girl. That she is adumbrating what is an ascending scale of significance is clear from her remark that, "For abovene hir ys nothynge that is made botte the blyssede manhede of Criste. This lytille thynge that es made that es benethe oure ladye saynt Marye . . . me thought it myght hafe fallene for litille" (ST 214). The account in the Long Text alters the impact of these sights by breaking vision with theological interpretation, thus forcing the reader to shift, in a sense, from heart to head. Julian also changes the ordering of the sights.[26] She places the passage about the Virgin first, rewriting the sentences I have just cited to read, "she is more then all that god made beneth her in wordines and in fullhead; for aboue her is nothing that is made but the blessed manhood of Christ, as to my sight" (LT 298). She then uses this reference to the manhood of Christ, the gift of his human mother, to describe Christ as our clothing that wraps us and encloses us for love. Julian subtly plays here with the traditional iconographic association between Mary's literal clothing (or veil) and Christ's clothing of flesh. But, rather than focus upon Mary's maternity, as the image seems to indicate she will do, she describes Christ in a way that foreshadows the description of the motherhood of God later in the text. Here, too, as David Aers has pointed out, Julian blocks off conventional devotional responses to the images she introduces and channels the reader into a more rationally organized response. She then moves to the description of the "little thing, the quantitie of an haselnott" (LT 299), and her analysis of it. The reorganization suggests a different sort of hierarchical ordering, one underpinned by an intellective rather than an affective rationale; her focus on the physical is less upon Christ's abject humanity than upon the details of our humanity that unite us to his triumphantly conceived flesh. Or, as the Athanasian Creed specifies, Christ is one being, "Not by the conversion of the Godhead into flesh, but by taking of the Manhood into God."

For example, in her efforts to describe the nature of the abundance of grace, she writes,

> A man goyth uppe ryght, and the soule of his body is sparyde as a purse fulle feyer. And whan it is tyme of his nescessery, it is openyde

---

26. Windeatt (1977), 6–8, also comments on this change.

and sparyde ayen fulle honestly. And that it is he that doyth this, it
is schewed ther wher he seyth he comyth downe to vs to the lowest
parte of oure nede. For he hath no dispite of that he made, ne he
hath no disdeyne to serue vs at the sympylest office that to oure
body longyth in kynde, for loue of the soule that he made to his
awne lycknesse. (LT 306–7)

By explaining the soul, which can be closed (*sparyde*, v. *sparren*) like a full
purse, by reference to a body closed against its own relief, Julian does more
than underline the relationship between the physical and the spiritual. She
suggests that the soul's health is built along principles that are "necessary"
or involuntary, that the soul's openness is an aspect of its privacy, or that
what is sealed is honestly and necessarily unsealed. Julian then goes on to
use the process of defecation as an analogue for both the Incarnation and
the daily operations of grace. This passage is omitted from the Sloane text
of the *Showings*. Even Colledge and Walsh have little to say about the
analogy, and, certainly, given Harry Bailey's outburst about excrement to
the Pardoner near the end of the Pardoner's performance, as well as both
the Pardoner's and the Summoner's presentations of the body, Julian's remarks seem to offer an unusually affirmative response to what are usually
considered the base, perhaps more shameful, operations of physicality. Her
decision not to fall back upon a more standard analogy like a description
of God's presence in the midst of tribulation evinces her own authorial
strategy in the composition of the Long Text. First, the analogy looks forward to her exposition of the motherhood of God: as *A Letter on Virginity*
reminded the female devotee, with children comes excrement, or "filth," a
word and an attitude that are notably absent from Julian's reference to the
body's needs here.[27] By specifying our physicality as a point of union with
the divine, Julian at once sanctifies the flesh and underlines God's maternal
love for the human child. However, the analogy also effectively prevents the
sort of emotive response that might be aroused by descriptions of Christ's
suffering or of human pain or of Mary's sorrow. Because it is at once
difficult to comprehend and startlingly unsentimental it forces on the reader

---

27. See "A Letter on Virginity," in Millett and Wogan-Browne (1990), 33. Julian continues
throughout this revelation to lay the foundations for the more overtly daring explanations of
Revelation 14. By likening God's courtesy to that of a king or lord for his poor servant (313),
she foreshadows the complex example of the Lord and the Servant that succeeds her discussion
of divine maternity.

an intellective or analytical process whose end is understanding rather than empathy.

A similar strategy underlies the ending of Revelation 1 in the Long Text. Julian puts the remark about doomsday, which she recasts into more positive language, into the penultimate section of chapter 8 and expands another passage from the Short Text as a conclusion in chapter 9. She thus shifts the focus from her own impaired physical strength to the types of meanings hidden in these showings. Compare the final sentences from Revelation 1 in the Short Text (cited above) to the following:

> But the goostely syght I can nott ne may shew it as openly ne as fully as I would. But I trust in our lord god almightie that he shall of his godnes and for iour loue make yow to take it more ghostely and more sweetly then I can or may tell it. (LT 323)

In the Short Text these lines precede the remark about doomsday and read,

> Bootte the gastelye syght I maye nought ne can nought schewe it vnto ʒowe oponlye and als fullye as I wolde; botte I trust in oure lorde god alle myghtty that he schalle of his goodnes and for ʒoure love make ʒowe to take it mare gastelye and mare swetly than I can or maye telle it ʒowe, and so motte it be, for we are alle one in loove. (ST 224)

There is a vast difference between using this passage, as she does in the Short Text, as a preamble to closing remarks about judgment and death and using it as the conclusion to a densely written chapter espousing God's private instruction of the soul and the unity of all souls in God. Rather than remind the reader of her own fears of death, she offers the reader an image of herself as intermediary between the reader, with whom she is joined in love, and God, who teaches all willing souls.

Though the Short Text is not without its own tension—else it would not be the finely spun work it is—the tension Julian expresses in it is rooted in the experience it seeks to make immediate to its readers. By means of her own skill as a writer, Julian communicates the awe, the fear, and the struggle she felt during the experience. Because her aims are different in this text, it can be described as a record of inner enlightenment and growth that any reader can use for private devotional purposes. Thus passages that

recall more familiar ones in the Long Text seem more personal when we
read them in the Short:

> He sayde nought: þou salle not be tempestyd, thowe schalle not be
> trauayled, þou schalle not be desesed: bot he sayde: þou schalle
> nouȝt be ouercommen. God wille that we take hede of his worde,
> and that we be euer myghtty in sekernesse, in wele and in waa, for
> he luffes vs and likes vs, and so wille he that we luff hym and lyke
> hym and myghtely triste in hym, and alle schalle be wele.
> And sone eftye alle was close, and I sawe na mare. (ST 269)

The difference between the two versions of this passage lies in the context.
In the Long Text Julian weaves between expository passages and descriptive
ones, using experience as the text she goes on to explicate. In the Short
Text, these sentences come as the culmination of other sights; thus the
entire section is impelled toward the self's apprehension of the punctuating
darkness, "and I sawe na mare."

In both versions of the *Showings* Julian manifests her sense of the authorial strategies a visionary might adopt. In the Short Text she suggests these
by positioning herself in relation to Richard Rolle, who had effectively
cornered the market on accounts of spiritual experience. Her frequent protestations against her singularity, her continual care for the community of
the faithful evoked by the recurring phrase, "my even cristen," and even
her calm tone throughout seem hints of her determination to write a work
that at once recalled Rolle and set its own course. She does not instruct;
she recounts, but with the intent of allowing us to participate with her in
the experience of unity. She thereby links herself to that impulse for the
"democratization of the spiritual life" that Watson has identified with
fourteenth-century English devotional authors.[28] The repetition of the
phrase "euen cristen" serves as a trope signifying her belief that English
can be used as a medium of true communication, that the experience of
one woman can become that of all. In denying her singular status, she does
more than beg her humility; she suggests her belief that spiritual sight is
not merely for the educated, for the elite few, for the Latinate, that God's
grace is not circumscribed by the world's criteria. In the Long Text, Julian
handles this trope in ways that suggest a more problematic relationship
among Holy Church, the visionary, and the community of the faithful. By

---

28. Watson (forthcoming).

building difference rather than similarity into her use of these terms, she implies that she, even in her role as the spokesperson for her fellow Christians, might arrive at truths not codified by Holy Church. Those truths are inherently experiential, in the sense that they are apprehended through a process of private meditation.

In placing the struggle between experience, which Julian defines as her experience of the Passion, and authority at the heart of the Long Text of the *Showings*, Julian carefully but decisively joined the debate about the concept of authority that has concerned us throughout this inquiry into some late fourteenth-century English writers. Chaucer's "voice" perhaps has the most lingering echo. In the Wife of Bath's Prologue, where she begins by announcing, "Experience and noon auctoritee," he dramatizes a situation of enormous significance (and tension) that he explores in more oblique ways throughout the *Canterbury Tales*. The Wife defines "authority" as a textual construct and casts herself as rejecting an entire system of reading that seeks to regulate access to and control the meaning of the inherently wayward text, presenting herself as a champion of the experiential and the subjective, which she defines in purely physical and materialist terms. By dividing two discursive practices along the lines of gender, Chaucer drew upon the conventions of late classical and medieval hermeneutics, which linked femininity to carnality or literalism. The text itself, or its literal meaning, was conceived of as female and hence as demanding an act of (male) interpretation.[29] Although the Wife has no problem in identifying herself with the corpus of the tale, she insists upon explicating that text herself and rejects the social and cultural authorities who would relegate her to a subordinate position. In rejecting male authority by shadow-boxing with husbands, clerics, and writers, she disallows any act of interpretation that would enforce meaning upon a text typically described as passive and elusive. Instead, she claims her rights as both text and exegete and seeks to assert that meaning is drawn out of experience rather than being imposed upon it. Through the Wife, whose gender, sexuality, mercantilism, and

---

29. This is a huge and hotly contested topic right now. See first Lee Patterson, whose 1983 essay, "'For the Wyves Love of Bathe': Feminine Rhetoric and Poetic Resolution in the *Roman de la Rose* and the *Canterbury Tales*, which was incorporated into chapter 6 of *Chaucer and the Subject of History* (1991), initiated discussion among Chaucerians about the relationship of gender to rhetoric. Since then, other voices have been raised and the subject has become more complicated. See Dinshaw (1989); Copeland (1994); Leicester (1990), 82–113; Hansen (1992), chap. 2.

aggression lend the trappings of verisimilitude to one of Chaucer's most "textual" creations, Chaucer raises issues fundamental to the late fourteenth-century debate about order, the individual, and the very nature of and basis for authority.[30]

However, the Wife's word is not the last. Chaucer responded to the question of subjectivity by neither condemning outright its claims nor endorsing the self at the expense of the communal body. Throughout the *Canterbury Tales* Chaucer dramatizes these claims by expanding our sense of what the relationship between experience and authority might mean. In the ways in which the pilgrims exploit and pass on the tales of other authors, in their approaches to social and ecclesiastical institutions, in their efforts to understand the relationship between the individual and the community, and in their attitudes toward change, Chaucer explores what is a complex, and unresolvable, series of demands and recognitions. His peculiar genius in capturing the problem as an ongoing and increasingly resonant conversation among speakers may be his own. But Chaucer shared his sense of complexity and irresolution with his contemporary William Langland, who presented the process of, or necessity for, self-recognition as a series of frequently unsatisfactory encounters between Will and key figures of authority. For Langland, the very inadequacy of some of those figures, while prompting questions about the basis for authority, did not obviate the need for or the realities of a society that derived its structure from the concept of authority.

Where both Chaucer and Langland used the ambiguities of a secular and primarily mercantile world to investigate the concept of authority, devotional writers of the period were more concerned with warning a reader of the dangers of a subjectivism that might threaten the spiritual authority vested in the clergy.[31] Possibly they felt doubly jeopardized. Wyclif's views on spiritual dominion, which had taken on a edge after 1378, when the "body of Christ" found itself with two heads, made worthiness a precondition of spiritual authority. Wyclif's attack on *ecclesia* was perceived as even more of a threat after the Rising of 1381 when many

---

30. No footnote (or article) can hope to do justice to the enormous amount of literature generated by the Wife of Bath. However, the following serve as guides to the way in which Chaucer uses the Wife's performance to explore the broader—and more unsettling—issue of authority: Blamires (1989); Dickson (1993); Fradenburg (1986); Hahn (1992); Hansen (1988); Schibanoff (1988); Strauss (1988). See also note 29.

31. Scase (1989) has suggested that the dominant topic in the late fourteenth century was the idea of dominion, of lordship.

clerical foundations felt themselves vulnerable in the face of the popular violence against landlords. As the popular risings seemed to indicate, if some parts of the church wished to play the world's games of power and wealth, they might be judged accordingly.[32] Wyclif's challenge to clerical dominion was explicit; but no less penetrating, if more insidious, was that posed by Richard Rolle of Hampole, whose many writings gave him a far-reaching posthumous influence.[33] As Watson describes him, Rolle was engaged in "living out" a dialogue with significant authority figures and seeking through his own experience and writings to validate the authority of experiential, affective knowledge.[34] Wyclif faulted the church for its inability to embody the precepts of Jesus and thus called into question the sacramental powers of the clergy. Rolle, on the other hand, subtly tested the clergy's control of the internal, spiritual life of its members. As different as the two figures may sometimes seem, both used experiential evidence as a means of challenging the intellective and hierarchically ordered system of ecclesiastical privilege and power.

Furthermore, Wyclif, like Rolle, came to understand the potential of the vernacular as a medium for spiritual instruction and change. The vernacular, the vulgar tongue, was conceived of as a separate and subordinate "discursive order."[35] It was thought to lack the right words for the precise expression of abstract thought and was relegated to the "feminine" realm of the literal, the carnal, the inherently wayward. Since women were less likely to be Latinate, the whole subject of literacy turned on the ability to acquire knowledge of and to function in the masculine world of dominant Latin culture. The authorities were quick to perceive the threat posed to existing structures by translation of the Scriptures into the vulgar (the "mother") tongue. A text whose very obscurity necessitated an act of interpretation was thereby made available to anyone (including women) who could read English. That reader would presumably begin to draw his or her own meanings from a text, inaugurating a succession of readings, each reflecting the idiosyncrasies of individual readers.[36] In place of the stable and externally imposed system of meaning to be found in Latin exegesis, the sacred text's embodiment in the vernacular presaged not only a world of shapeless pluralism, but implicitly threatened an ecclesiastical hierarchy

32. See, for example, Aston (1994); Faith (1984); Justice (1994a and b), chap. 2.
33. Watson (1992a), 260–61.
34. Watson (1992a), 23.
35. The phrase is Rita Copeland's; see Copeland (1994).
36. On translation as a potentially radical act, see Hanna (1990).

that had its foundation in textual interpretation. If all were to read and interpret the text, who then took precedence or could claim higher spiritual authority? Although such questions are woven into the fabric of fifteenth-century social, political, and theological history and, of course, were explicitly debated throughout the sixteenth century, they need also to be seen in the context of the late fourteenth-century concern about the basis for authority.

Here, Julian of Norwich stands in a pivotal and unique position. Though the late fourteenth century was somewhat less constrictive than the fifteenth, the penalties for dissent were nonetheless real. The two versions of the *Showings* bear this out; in the Long Text Julian presents material that might not have been acceptable some years later, but her method can hardly be described as forthright. Like Chaucer, she found it necessary to evolve techniques of indirection that she could use to explore potentially illegitimate subjects.[37] For a number of reasons, some of which are internal and will be discussed in the pages following, I am not only loath to assign the Long Text to the fifteenth century, but feel Julian's strategies and use of language are more easily juxtaposed to late fourteenth-century writers, particularly to Chaucer. My external reasons for wishing to associate the Long Text with the fourteenth century have to do with the history of dissent in England; that history is being remade continually as new manuscripts come to light. It is however fairly clear that the conditions of Lancastrian England were hostile—and increasingly so—to dissenting views on authority. Henry of Lancaster usurped the throne from Richard II in 1400. In 1401 England's first law, *de heretico comburendo,* establishing the right to arrest suspected heretics (here, read Lollards) and burn those who refused to recant was enacted.[38] Eight years later, in 1409, the archbishop of Canterbury, Thomas Arundel, published his Constitutions, which not only reaffirmed strictures against unlicensed preaching, but made it illegal for preachers to discuss the sacraments or the sins of the clergy in their sermons or for anyone to instruct others in matters of theology; limited university discussions of theology; forbade the study of Wyclif's writings; and, finally, forbade translation of the Scriptures into English, including single verses occurring in secular books.[39] Henry IV's anxiety about political dissent and

---

37. On the subject of strategies of dissent in late medieval literature, see, for example, Patterson (1992); Simpson (1990a); Spearing (1985), 89–92.

38. For a full discussion of the penalties for heretics under Henry IV, see McNiven (1984). See also the important essay by Aston (1960).

39. For a discussion of the Constitutions, see Watson (1995).

the possibility of revolt was matched by the fear of "his" English church that the English faithful might follow too closely the desires of their potentially wayward hearts.[40] Julian's decision to rewrite the Short Text of the *Showings* as a theological explication of her original set of visions seems unlikely in the context of Lancastrian England when, as Watson points out, precious little theology of any sort was, in fact, written.

This is not to say that the last decade of the fourteenth century was an easy one for the man or woman who wished to explore or express a highly idiosyncratic understanding of the meaning of the Passion. As early as the late 1370s or early 1380s Wyclif and his followers had promulgated an image of themselves as persecuted and continually under siege by the authorities of the English church.[41] Wyclif himself described poor priests as under threat of excommunication, loss of office, imprisonment, and death. He described the faithful as soldiers of Christ ready for martyrdom.[42] That no such massive persecutions ever happened during Wyclif's lifetime, or during the reign of Richard II (or even during that of Henry IV or V, for that matter) may be less important than the expectation that it *might* happen and that such fears were current throughout the reign of Richard II. I do not mean to suggest that these fears were without substance. As H. G. Richardson pointed out, the atmosphere in England changed after 1382 when heretics began to be treated differently by the courts. Rather than having to use the lengthy and frequently ineffectual process of excommunication, after 1382, prelates needed only to turn in the names of suspected unlicensed preachers in order to empower sheriffs to arrest and imprison them and their supporters until they should repent or the king and council proceed otherwise.[43] Thus, when *de heretico comburendo* was enacted in 1401, it gave greater substance to what had been threatened by existing legislation.

The evidence we have for inquiries into individuals suspected of holding dissenting views from about 1377 or 1378 to 1400 provides us with echoes of what must have been a richly complicated contestation among all sorts

40. It did not help matters that during the reign of Henry IV, the specter of Richard II was frequently raised in conjunction with lollardy; Aston (1960), 20.

41. I am indebted here to Michael Wilks's essay, "Wyclif & the Great Persecution" (Wilks 1994). Professor Wilks very kindly sent me a copy of the page proofs for the essay at a point in my own work where I badly needed the fruits of his. For a study of the rhetoric of martyrdom, see Kendall (1986). See also Aston (1960).

42. See Wilks (1994), 59–61. For remarks about sixteenth-century English Protestantism and its adoption of similar metaphors, see Johnson (1990), 158–61.

43. Richardson (1936), esp. 7–8.

of thinkers and writers.[44] As the next chapter will demonstrate, Chaucer chose to focus upon the political implications of this probe into the basis for authority and its relation to actual or imagined power. If his exploration of the terms of secular authority frequently employed the language of devotion, other, less covert, inquiries into the nature of spiritual authority aroused what were highly political responses in church officials. In addition to the pope's attempts to condemn Wyclif himself in 1377 and 1378 and that of Archbishop Courtney in 1382, there are several other accounts of inquiries into the beliefs of more humble citizens that suggest the ways in which dissent was perceived to threaten the security of church officials.[45] In addition to issues involving theology, like the doctrine of the eucharist, there is evidence of official dislike for practices that violated the same sorts of hierarchical ordering that underpinned the community itself. Thus, William Ramsbury (1389), William Swinderby (1389), and Walter Brut (1391) offended this order by preaching to or teaching others to question the very nature of priestly authority. Not only did they follow Wyclif in wishing to found authority in sanctity, rather than in power or common practice or sacral ordination, they suggested that any virtuous man (or woman?) might administer the sacraments. Henry Knighton, writing of the 1380s, complained that the Scriptures were being translated into English, thereby making what had been precious to the clergy all too available to the vulgar.[46] Such efforts thereby disturbed the order of society whereby priest topped layperson as man topped woman. The profound urge to present both Scripture and doctrine in English was seen as an attempt to level the grades of distinction between men and between men and women. At the examination of John Ashton, bachelor of divinity, in 1382, Ashton was required to answer in Latin "because of the lay people that stood about him; he, crying out in the English tongue."[47] In a similar vein, Foxe reports that in 1389

---

44. See, for example, Crompton (1968–69); Hudson (1988), esp. chap. 2; Tuck (1984); Wilkins (1737), 3:145–247.

45. For an account of proceedings against William Ramsbury before the bishop of Salisbury in 1389, see Hudson (1985). For the proceedings against William Swinderby in 1389 and Walter Brut in 1391, see Capes (1916); Wilkins (1737), 3:145–212. See also Knighton's (1965) account of these years. For Foxe's later—and fascinating—account of this period, see Foxe (1965), vols. 2 and 3.

46. Knighton (1965), 152.

47. The translation belongs to Foxe (1965) 3:35. The Latin reads, ". . . dictus tamen Johannes Asshton requisitus frequenter per dictum dominum Cantuar. quod in lingua Latina ad interrogata propter astantes laicos responderat, in lingua materna, clamando verba frivola, opprobiosa, et contumeliosa valde, et ad commovend. et excitand. populum contra eundem dominum Cantuar" (Wilkins 1737, 3:164). For a discussion of the issue of language as it pertains to Ashton, see Aston (1987), 297–98.

the anchoress Matilda was investigated for her views and met some difficulty because she was found not to answer "plainly and directly" but "so-
phistically and subtilely."[48]

Though such instances do not sound like Wyclif's wholescale persecution
of the saints, they provide evidence for a debate within the church about
authority that was going on at the same time Chaucer, Langland, and
their fellow civil servants and clerks were inventing a language for their
explorations of the same charged subject. While such conversations could
proceed without threat of burning, it was nonetheless wise not to have them
too openly as the experiences of a number of contemporaries illustrated.
Moreover, its terms seem remarkably similar, or its persistent focus upon
language itself—and upon the relationship between language and gender—
is pertinent to debates worked out in many areas and arenas of the country.
The continual rumors of Lollard women celebrating mass, as well as Walter
Brut's defense of women's ability to preach are indicators of the degree of
disorder associated with the Lollard heresy or of the revolutionary degrees
of Wycliffite thought, depending on which side of the divide one occupied.[49]
What is being opposed or propounded is a deliberate confusion of social
roles that is seen as threatening the fabric of society, hierarchically organized by means of status and gender.[50]

Furthermore, as records from proceedings against Lollards indicate,
though the church may have envisioned "schools" of Lollards, a sort of
ecclesiastical fifth column, it moved against individuals.[51] This, of course, is
the heart of the Wycliffite—or any evangelical—movement, the individual,
whose personal sense of the Gospel impels him or her along a path that
runs counter to that of established, mainstream religion. Hence, the emphasis upon literacy, upon translation of the Scriptures into English, and upon
preaching: each of these topics is a species of spiritual education whereby

48. The translation is that of Foxe (1965), 3:199. Knighton (1965) describes Matilda
"quam arguens de praedictis erroribus et opinionibus lollardinis." Wilkins's (1737) record of
the proceedings reads that she "potius sophistice respondebat" and was sent away for correction, thus deprived of her anchorhold and reintegrated into the community of the faithful
until her beliefs were judged properly orthodox. See Wilkins (1737), 3:209; for accounts
of ecclesiastical proceedings that directly concern the quality of faith in Norwich in 1383,
see 176–78.

49. On the subject of gender as it relates to dissent, see Aston (1960), 289; Aston (1984),
chap. 2; Blamires (1989).

50. The work of Paul Strohm is central to this type of analysis; in particular, see *Hochon's
Arrow* (1992).

51. The classic illustration of this is N. P. Tanner's (1977) invaluable edition of fifteenth-
century heresy trials.

the individual can be brought to understand the outlines of the Christian life. The voices of those fourteenth-century dissenters brought before ecclesiastical authorities ring out with a peculiar immediacy, despite the fairly uniform and almost catechisical nature of their *credo*'s from the fourteenth through the fifteenth centuries. Thus,

> In ye name of God, Amen. I, William Swynderby, prust unworthy, coveytyng and purposing holy wyth al my herte to be a trewe cristen man . . . makyng openly this protestacyon, clepyng God to recorde here byfore oure worschypfyl bysshoppe John . . .

Or,

> Ego Walterus Brut, peccator, laycus, agricola, cristianus, a Britonibus ex utraque parente originem habens . . .[52]

Where Swynderby spoke in English, Brut wished to record his answers in Latin. Both men identify themselves in terms that are at once classically Christian and confessional and startlingly moving and particular. In so doing, they challenge the basis for the church's authority by asserting, in Swynderby's case, the primacy of God's judgment over that of the "worshipful" bishop, and, in Brut's, the integrity of his identity as layman, farmer, Christian, and Englishman. That he should also be literate contains its own radical statement of independent thought.

Dissent operates not simply against authority, which it questions, but against power that rhetorically allies itself with authority. Julian's work suggests she was well aware of the vulnerability of her position but, at the same time, able to evolve a means by which she could, in Chaucer's terms, tell her own kind of story. Like him, she must have felt wary; she too depended for her livelihood on her standing in her own community. It is, of course, unclear when Julian entered the anchorhold. The first evidence we have is from 1393 to 1394, when a bequest of two shillings was made to "Julian, anakorite." The latest bequest to her was made in 1416.[53] As Ann K. Warren has demonstrated, anchorites performed a real social function in the medieval community and consequently were strictly regulated

---

52. Capes (1916), 237, 285. For a discussion of Brut's trial in relation to the issues of literacy and of the vernacular, see Hudson (1994).

53. Colledge and Walsh (1978), introduction, 33–34. See also Watson (1993), 673. For other biographical comments, see Sister Benedicta (Ward) (1988).

by the episcopal authorities. Since they required a large support system in order to be maintained within a town and since their presence in a town conferred status upon it, the issue of vocation was inevitably bound up with their spiritual, psychological, and moral suitability for the complicated role they were choosing to play. The oft-cited reference to Julian of Norwich in the *Book of Margery Kempe* demonstrates one aspect of this role: Kempe uses Julian as a means of validating Margery's own sense of vocation.[54] The degree of truth that the event may or may not contain is far less important than the truth implicit in the fiction; Margery's trip to Norwich and Julian's approbation of her locates her within a different sort of community than the one she inhabits in Lynn. Kempe can use Julian—or Julian's reputation for sanctity and hence her name—and in so doing suggest the intimate relationship between the community and the anchorite. Like poets, anchorites needed a form of patronage; when the anchorite was part of a town, the town or the parish effectively served as the patron. Thus Julian's need to maintain her standing was as acute as Chaucer's. She could be denied her vocation, or she could be separated from it. If she wished to write, she must therefore find a way to speak that did not win her the reward of the white crow in Chaucer's Manciple's Tale.

Both the Long Text and the Short Text of the *Showings* are designed as communal texts, in the sense that they are intended to participate in the ongoing life and debate of a particular community. But where the Short Text suggests a narrower audience and one whose interests are inevitably more private, the Long Text gives evidence not simply of a broader field, one that would include thinkers and writers as well as devotees, but a greater sense of the risks involved in taking on such a project. Though the risks are not those she would have faced in 1410—and this is partly why I hesitate to date the Long Text anytime after the *Constitutions*—the risks are still there. Examples like those of Matilda the anchoress from Leicestershire, not far from Norwich, underlined the need for care. Julian could not afford to be perceived as sophisticated or subtle, but must speak plainly and, presumably, humbly. Her voice must not ring out like that of Swynderby or of Brut. Given the relationship between Lollardy and "preaching women," it is little wonder she excised her gender from the Long Text! On

---

54. See Meech (1961), 42–43. In a paper I gave at the Medieval Academy meeting of 1995, I suggested that this incident might be intended to suggest a textual—rather than an actual—conversation.

the other hand, Julian also gives powerful evidence for wishing to join in a debate that concerned the very fiber of the devotional experience and an individual's attempt to understand that experience and incorporate it into his or her participation in the community of the faithful. Her handling of the subject of authority suggests her astute reading of the ways in which Rolle's endorsement of the affective had been answered by later devotional writers, especially by Walter Hilton. It is only when Julian is juxtaposed with roughly contemporary authors in the tradition within which she herself wrote and thought that we can understand something of her own talent for negotiating among the various expectations and concerns triggered by a certain type of writing.

Richard Rolle's endorsement of the affective, what Ann Astell characterizes as his increasing identification with the feminine principle in his own soul, certainly had important implications for the late medieval English church and its approach to the needs of the laity.[55] In works like *The Cloud of Unknowing* and *The Book of Privy Counselling,* which were written in the period between Rolle and Walter Hilton, we can detect a response to Rolle's potentially subversive claims for the primacy of affective knowledge. Even though both works speak to the claims of and needs of the self, they seek to contain those claims by the use of terms like "dome of Holy Church," or by stating that the sacramental life of the church is a remedy against "blind," or "individual feelings," or by warning the reader of the dangers of thinking to climb into the kingdom by other ways than the "door."[56] Like Rolle, the author(s) of these two works evinces a curious attitude toward the very feelings he seeks to elicit from the reader, suggesting the growing awareness of the need to balance affective spirituality with an intellective containment that is personified through Holy Church.

The issue is ultimately one of authority. In presenting himself as both representative self and as spiritual guide or censor, Rolle locates authority in himself.[57] Although it is certainly possible to read some of Rolle's more effusive works, like the *Incendium Amoris* or the *Melos Amoris,* and perceive him as licensing the emotions, the focus of his rhetoric is less anyone's nascent emotive spirituality than his own power as Christ's beloved. Many of his works, particularly those in English, were expressly written for women.[58] It is risky to attribute his frequently paternalistic and didactic

---

55. Astell (1990), 115. On these implications, see Hughes (1988), esp. 208–50.
56. See Hodgson (1994), *Cloud of Unknowing,* 6, 72, 104; *Privy Counselling,* 160.
57. Watson (1992a) categorizes these tendencies as apolegetic and didactic.
58. See, for example, Allen (1931). Parts of Rolle's psalter were written for Margaret Kyrby, as was *The Form of Living; Ego Dormio* and *The Commandment* were written for a nun.

tone so simply to his consciousness of his reader, particularly given the historical uncertainties involved in using gender as a standard for evaluating tonal nuances. Nonetheless, Rolle seems especially comfortable in his highly prescriptive role of adviser to a less spiritually adept, and therefore subordinate, reader. The opening and closing words of *The Form of Living* are instructive in this respect: "In euery synful man and womman þat is bounden in dedely syn ben þre wrechednesse, þe which bryngeth ham vnto þe deth of helle. . . . Lo, Margaret, I haue shortly seid þe fourme of lyuynge and how þou may cum to perfeccioun, and to loue hym þat þou hast taken þe to."[59] Both sentences manifest Rolle's sense of authority, but in the last sentence the nature of that authority is cast as personal, for Rolle speaks not as the exegete or the preacher but as a witness to the way to perfection. Similarly, in the *Ego Dormio,* written to a nun, he links the ability to read the work to the reader's desire to love God, "Gif al þyn entent to vndrestond þis writynge; and if þou haue set þi desyre to loue God, h[i]re [þise] þre degrees of loue, so þat þou may ry[s]e fro on to anoþer til þat þou be at þe heghest.[60]

Elsewhere Rolle's emphasis upon his own special experience serves to channel response to his words. For example, in the Prologue to *Incendium Amoris,* Rolle specifies the type of public he envisions for the work: "Qwharefore þis boke I offyr to be sene, noȝt to philisophyrs nor wyes men of þis warld, ne to grete devyens lappyd in questions infenyte, bot vnto boystus & vntaght, more besy to con lufe god þen many þinges to knawe; for treuly, not desputynge bot wyrkand it is kunde, & loffande."[61] Rolle thus distinguishes among readers, saying that he does not write for the learned but for the untaught, for those who wish to love God rather than to know many things. He ends the Prologue by reiterating this distinction between knowledge and feelings, "And sen I here to lufe styrris all maner of folk, and besy I am of lufe to schew hattist desyre & a-bowne kynde, 'byrnnyng of lufe' þis boke hys name sall bere."[62] Notwithstanding his claims that the work is intended to "stir" the unlearned to spiritual fervor, he prevents his reader from too easily identifying with his own piety by stressing the uniqueness of his position as lover and devotee. Rolle's frequent stern descriptions of the worldly, his warnings about the nature of heresy, and his emphasis upon the difficulties of the contemplative way

59. *The Form of Living,* in Ogilvie-Thomson (1988), 3, 25.
60. *Ego Dormio,* in Ogilvie-Thomson (1988), 27.
61. I quote from the fifteenth-century translation of Richard Misyn. See Harvey (1896), 3.
62. Harvey (1896), 4.

work to check any simplistic sense that our emotions can quickly lead us to God. Instead, the book places Rolle himself in sharp relief: the dazzling feats of this spiritual athlete seem only a vain aspiration in the face of our own clumsiness. We are rather invited to observe, to participate vicariously in, Rolle's ecstatic union with Christ. In establishing himself as a figure of spiritual authority, Rolle strikes a balance between the claims of the emotions and of the intellect. Rolle himself, as presented through his own rhetorical blend of passion and didacticism, is the figure who checks his apparent endorsement of subjectivity.

In *The Scale of Perfection,* written for an anchoress, Walter Hilton responds to the potential dangers of Rolle's affectivity and of the more obvious dangers of Wycliffite anticlericalism by emphasizing the authority of the sacramental church.[63] Hilton's project is to teach his reader how to achieve a contemplative life. Though *The Scale* may not achieve the flights of prose to be found in some of Rolle's works, it more truly functions as a guide. First, Hilton deliberately and strategically eschews Rolle's cult of personality and, rather than privileging himself, disparages his own spiritual achievements. Of his own spiritual progress he writes,

> I feel myself so wretched, so frail and so carnal, and so far in my real feelings from what I speak and have spoken, that I am fit to do nothing but cry for mercy, desiring as I can with hope that by his grace our Lord will bring me to this in the glory of heaven. Do the same yourself, and better, according to the grace God gives you. (89)

Hilton's admission of his own sense of imperfection does not have the effect of focusing our attention upon his exemplary humility. Instead, he decenters this paragraph by concentrating his focus upon the reader, whose own feelings of frustration can then become the ground of her prayers. The injunction to "do the same yourself, and *better,*" impels her beyond her mentor and guide. Later Hilton discusses the "fire of love," but admits that he has no experiential knowledge of such spiritual fire (98).

If Hilton refuses to assume a position of absolute spiritual authority it is because he presents himself as an obedient representative of the sacramental church. He therefore advises his reader to seek to contain her devotions within the boundaries established by the church. Although he writes for a woman who has chosen the solitary life, he insists upon her fundamental

---

63. See Walter Hilton (1991), 30–31; Hughes (1988), 228–29.

alliance with the community of the church. Not only does he counsel her not to abandon the "common prayer" established by the Church, but he stresses the need to subordinate any contrary "stirrings" of the heart to the necessities of orthodox belief. "Stirrings," is, of course a Rolleian term, and Hilton's usage of it bespeaks his own unease with the broader implications of Rolle's affective emphasis. However, Hilton does far more than warn against feelings; he seeks also to contain the equally dangerous impulse to knowledge:

> The second thing you are obliged to have is a firm belief in all articles of the faith and sacraments of holy church, believing them steadfastly with all the will of your heart . . . be steadfast and not too frightened by the feeling of such stirrings, but forsake your own intellect without disputing or investigating these things, put your faith generally in the faith of holy church, and never mind about that stirring of your heart which you find contrary to it. For the stirring that you feel is not your faith: the faith of holy church is your faith, even though you neither see it nor feel it. (94)

This is an arresting passage for a number of reasons. First, Hilton's assumption that intellective knowledge will succeed affective suggests his fear that heterodoxy may well be the inevitable result of stirrings in the "heart." He therefore seeks to control what is pluralistic and inherently chaotic by subsuming the heart within an already formulated standard of faith, "firm belief in all articles of the faith and sacraments of the church." In so doing, he categorizes belief as distinct from either type of knowledge, going so far as to urge the anchoress to ignore the temptation to investigate her feelings because her feelings are not her faith. Her faith is external to her, "the faith of holy church is your faith, even though you neither see it nor feel it." "Faith," then is that body of articles in which children are instructed and to which all Christians accede; its formulation is a matter of ecclesiastical business far removed from the shifting perceptions of the laity or the vagaries of the heart. Hilton does not employ the language of gender in his remarks, but in opposing the wayward and unreliable heart to the stable and objective articles of faith he draws upon a binary opposition that underlies that language. Writing in the vernacular to a female reader, he, as mild and humble a voice as he presents, speaks in order to direct the carnal impulse toward an acceptable end.

The passage aims to discourage the claims of subjectivity by personifying authority, not in Hilton himself, but in a being referred to throughout as "holy church." Like Rolle and other contemporary devotional writers, Hilton describes the church as composed of two castes, the company of the faithful and those entrusted with their instruction. However, whereas Rolle may sometimes seem to suggest that he himself has a separate and superior status because of the quality of his love, Hilton invests authority only in those men who embody and administer the sacramental church. They are finally responsible for the souls of the vast community of the faithful that he and others refer to as their "even Christians." Hilton indicates his sense of pastoral responsibility in the closing two chapters of *The Scale*. In the penultimate chapter he reiterates his warning against harmful "stirrings," urging the anchoress to allow herself to be shaped to the image of Jesus. He quotes Saint Paul's maternal words to the early Christians of Galatia:

> My dear children, whom I bear as a woman bears a child until Christ is again shaped in you. You have conceived Christ through faith, and he has life in you inasmuch as you have a good will and a desire to serve and please him; but he is not yet fully formed in you, nor you in him, by the fullness of charity. And therefore St. Paul bore you and me and other in the same way with travail, as a woman bears a child, until the time that Christ has his full shape in us, and we in him. (159–60)

Hilton's conceit here is complexly sexual. Sinful "stirrings" efface the gestating image of Christ. On the other hand, obedient devotion opens up the possibility of reversing the process of deformation; so Hilton stresses the creative maternity of Saint Paul, who labors to bring forth Christ's full shape in each Christian. However, the final chapter suggests that he sees himself as playing a part in the business of begetting and bringing forth that new soul. He first says that the book is intended to "stir" his own spiritual negligence and to "stir" his reader to toil more humbly in the contemplative life. He does not ascribe this effect to his own eloquence, "And so if there is any word in it that stirs or encourages you the more to the love of God, thank God, for it is his gift and not from the word" (160).

Hilton's complicated use of the verb *stirren* (indicating either spiritual or physical arousal) in the final chapter of *The Scale* is intended to hearken back to Rolle's use of the word to describe the physical symptoms of his passionate spiritual ecstasy. *Stirren* can also mean to set in motion, to turn aside, to rouse, to trouble, to exhort or coax, to inspire or prompt, and to incite. Hilton employs *stir* with an eye both to ambiguity and irony, using a verb of motion to describe his sense of what the contemplative state in fact is, or ought to be. He rules out the turbulence of false arousal as sterile, affirming instead the hortatory power of rhetoric to encourage humble labor within the confines of ecclesiastical doctrine. As an author whose words might well stir his reader, he disclaims his own force (as well as the maternity with which Saint Paul identified), presenting himself as the medium or go-between who conveys power not his own, whose exhortation prompts the orderly process of spiritual gestation. Hilton plays one set of meanings off against another, substituting labor for sensation and implying that *stirring* is but the initial stage of a catalytic process, a means toward an end, not the end itself. He therefore answers Rolle by redefining Rolle's own language in order to direct his reader toward an authority located outside the self.[64]

Julian of Norwich is frequently described as "influenced by" Walter Hilton, but the Long Text of the *Showings* is far from a simple reflection of Hilton's views. It should be seen as a complex response to a number of interrelated issues and strategies, including the implicitly (or explicitly) gendered language of contemporary devotional writers, who employed that language as a means of reinforcing social hierarchies.[65] By praising Julian for her serenity, we prevent ourselves from recognizing how well she mastered the terms of this conversation or how skilled and tough a polemic strategist she was. We also signal that our response to *The Showings* is, in part, a response to the work of a woman recluse and thereby categorize it even before we begin to read it.

That Julian herself was aware of the ways in which gender might shape the experience of reading is, as I have already suggested, evidenced by her careful neutering, or editing, of her own text. In the early sections of the Short Text, references to gender implicitly locate Julian in a dependent position. The first sentence, probably the work of a local scribe who produced copies of the Short Text on order, generically frames the work for its reader: "Here es a visionn schewed be the goodenes of god to a deuoute womann, and hir name es Julyan, that is recluse atte Norwyche and ʒitt ys onn lyfe, anno domini millesimo CCCC xiij; in the whilke visyonn er fulle many comfortabylle wordes and gretly styrrande to alle thaye that desires

---

64. See Hughes (1988), 228–29, 269–275, for discussions of Hilton's reaction to Rolle.

65. Hughes suggests this influence was direct, since John Thorpe, a disciple of Hilton's, was associated with the Stapelton family, patrons of Rolle and supporters of Julian; see Hughes (1988), 213.

to be Crystes looverse" (ST 201). In the second chapter, Julian recounts
the words of the priest who came to her in her sickness, sitting the crucifix
before her and saying, "Dowȝtter, I have brought the the ymage of thy
sauioure; loke there oponn and comforthe the þere with in reverence of
hym that dyede for the and me" (ST 208).[66] In chapter 6, in a passage she
omitted altogether from the Long Text, Julian confronts the subject of her
own gender as it relates to her authority:

> Botte god for bede that ȝe schulde saye or take it so that I am a
> techere, for I meene nouȝt soo, no I mente nevere so; for I am a
> womann, leued, febille and freylle. Botte I wate wele, this that I
> saye, I hafe it of the schewynge of hym tha(t) es souerayne tech-
> are. . . . Botte for I am a womann, schulde I therfore leve that I
> schulde nouȝt telle ȝowe the goodeness of god, syne that I sawe in
> that same tyme that is his wille, that it be knawenn? (ST 222)

In deleting references to her gender from the Long Text, Julian located
it within a different textual community; she also excised a response—and
perhaps reprisals—predicated upon gender. In the priest's "Dowȝtter" and
in her own use of the topos of the feeble and frail woman, Julian positioned
herself and her work in relation to contemporary social codes and interpretative strategies. The Short Text, including the scribal preface, presents
itself as a record of experience, the very immediacy of which is underlined
by the testimonial that Julian *is* a recluse in Norwich and *is yet* alive. Much
of the success of the Short Text rests on Julian's ability to present vision as
experience and to privilege it, thus claiming for the text the authority inherent in spiritual autobiography. The scribe links the work to the school of
Rolle in the final clause by saying that it will be "stirring" to those who
wish to be Christ's lovers. The sentence is rich with possibilities, suggesting
much about the contemporary reception of *The Showings*. Some ten years
after Julian had completed the Long Text of *The Showings*, the Short Text
was still being produced on demand and thus had not been superseded by
the "definitive edition."[67] Since the phrase "is yet alive" might apply equally

---

66. The Long Text version of this sentence reads, "I haue brought the image of thy
sauiour; looke ther vpon and comfort thee ther with" (291).

67. Regarding this passage, Watson (1993) suggests that perhaps Julian had not yet completed the Long Text, and the Short Text was all that was known of her work (680–81).
However, especially considering the example of a work like *Piers Plowman* and the simultane-
ous circulation of its various texts, it makes sense that the *Showings* was circulating in more
than one form.

well to the author of the Long Text, the shorter, earlier version must have spoken to its audience by its very experiential immediacy. Moreover, its author must have been perceived as a witness of a special order, whose words we turn to to trigger our own nascent spiritual desire. The scribe's insistence on Julian's name, gender, vocation, and geographic provenance then serves as a guarantee of veracity by assuring us that the text itself, the visible corpus of its author's spiritual experience, should be interpreted and used by the person who reads it. Any authority Julian claims for herself is subsumed into her role as lover and visionary.

In contrast, in the Long Text Julian claims for herself the authority of the exegete. She creates a different sort of "I," one that derives its authority from more than simple visionary experience. The authority Julian assumes in the Long Text rests upon her ability to meditate upon, to interpret, and to explain the experience recorded in her earlier version of the *Showings*. By deleting references to her gender from her second version, she implicitly adopted a "male" voice, one that allowed her to explain or to objectify the subjective text of the visions she originally recorded. If the Short Text resembles a diary of spiritual experience, the Long Text offers evidence of her successful search for a language that will present that experience in the most authoritative way possible.[68] Her method of presentation, as well as her translation of the figures of Latin rhetoric and her employment of themes and motifs drawn from the traditions of monastic devotional prose, combine to form a striking (and subtle) affirmation of subjectivity. Julian, in fact, applies the (male) tools of intellective authority to the (female) matter of experience and in so doing avoids the rhetorical traps laid by contemporary devotional writers. Rather than opposing intellect to experience or faith to feeling, Julian demonstrates the fundamental inadequacy of categorizing knowledge in terms of binary oppositions.

Let us return to the matter of her first revelation and to a passage that Aers has already discussed. In both versions Julian recounts the sight of the blood flowing from Christ's crown of thorns:

> And in this sodaynly I sawe the rede blode trekylle downe fro vndyr the garlande, alle hate, freschlye, plentefully and lyvelye, ryght as me thought that it was in that tyme that the garlonde of thornys was thrystede on his blessede heede. (ST 210)

---

68. This is, of course, a question with which Langland also wrestled. For studies of Langland's efforts to "authorize" himself, see Kerby-Fulton (1990) and Middleton (1990).

> And in this sodenly I saw the reed bloud rynnyng downe from
> vnder the garlande, hote and freyshely, plentuously and liuely, right
> as it was in the tyme that the garland of thornes was pressed on his
> blessed head. (LT 294)

The sentences suggest Julian's attention to style; the second is stronger and
more authoritative. "Running" more justly harmonizes with its adverbial
modifiers than does "trickle," and the phrase "ryght as it was" avoids the
hesitancy of the former version, turning supposition into declaration. But
it is in her use of this revelation that Julian truly indicates what will be her
method throughout the Long Text. In the Short Text she records her immediate and emotional response to the visible evidence of Christ's physical
suffering. She delays her account of this response in the Long Text, adding
a section on the nature of the Trinity to this revelation: "And in the same
shewing sodeinly the trinitie fulfilled my hart most of ioy, and so I vnderstode it shall be in heauen without end to all that shall come ther" (LT
294–95). Only after she explains something of the nature of the Trinity
and says that "wher Jhesu appireth the blessed trinitie is vnderstand" does
she insert the phrase "Benedicite dominus," with which she caps the sight
of the bleeding head in the Short Text. By interposing the measured and
analytic language of theology between the sight of Christ's suffering and
subjective exclamation, the passage channels a reader's response to the text.

In the Long Text, Julian's accounts of her revelations, which frequently
resemble taxonomies of experience, insist on the need to apply the techniques of analysis and classification to the raw data of history. She meticulously records whether she saw something with her spiritual sight or with
the "eye" of her understanding, thereby differentiating between two modes
of knowledge. However, she does not privilege one form of knowledge at
the expense of the other, but demonstrates the fundamental and necessary
relationship between the two. For example, in an addition she inserts into
the Long Text near the end of her account of the first revelation, she returns
to the sight of Christ's bleeding head. She provides three similes for the
plenteousness and roundness of the drops of blood flowing down Christ's
forehead, "lyke pelottes, semyng as it had comynn ouȝte of the veynes,"
"lyke to the droppes of water that falle of the evesyng of an howse after a
grete shower of reyne," and "lyke to the scale of heryng in the spredyng
of the forhede." She then recapitulates these observations: "Thes thre
thynges cam to my mynde in the tyme: pelettes for the roundhede in the
comyng ouȝte of the blode, the scale of herying for the roundhede in the

spredyng, the droppes of the evesyng of a howse for the plentuoushede vnnumerable" (LT 312–13). By reiterating and epitomizing her original observations, Julian anchors them in the memory in a way that joins our own records of experience to our rational appraisal of it. The similes are at once concrete, in the sense that we can "see" them because we know what herring scales, coursing water, and pellets look like, and purely intellective because we store them in our memories under the rubric, "blood, Christ's" and draw them out of that storehouse through a rational act of retrieval.[69]

Julian also attaches experience to intellect through her careful reliance upon classical rhetoric and Christian arguments and ideas. For example, in the first revelation she describes Christ as showing her "a little thing, the quantitie of an haselnott, lying in þe palme of my hand, as me semide, and it was as rounde as a balle" (LT 299–300). Again, she draws on a reader's experiential knowledge, choosing something as homely as a hazelnut as a means of approaching the relationship between Creator and creation. However, she moves quickly from the tactile to the abstract, relying upon rhetorical figures, biblical allusions, and references to mystical works like the spurious *Golden Epistle of Saint Bernard* to elucidate the oneness of God and creation through the triune nature of God as maker, keeper, and lover.[70] Her grounding in authority serves two purposes. First, her use of tradition helps to maintain her tone of serious inquiry into the nature of her prior experience as she carefully subjects the series of sights recorded in the Short Text to rational scrutiny. She thereby creates an authorial voice as immediate as Rolle's and as objective as Hilton's. Like Rolle, she claims special sight, but disclaims singularity, and like Hilton, aligns herself with the great company of the faithful, her "evyn cristen." Moreover, her complicated use of authority—rhetorical, theological, and social—betrays her keen sense of the tensions inherent in making original contributions to theological writing. In a move of pure genius, Julian builds this tension into the Long Text as an extended dialogue between her spiritual understanding and her belief in the teachings of Holy Church. In so doing, she transforms the reader—who might potentially be a censor or critic—into an advocate, since she places him in a position to "overhear" a dialogue as pronounced as it is unresolved.

---

69. On the use of the memory as such an intellective capacity, see Carruthers (1990).
70. See notes to Colledge and Walsh (1978), 299–301; Guillaume de St. Thierry (1973); Colledge (1975).

In fact, one of the key differences between the two versions of the *Show-ings* lies in Julian's growing sense of distinction between what she knows to be true and what she has been taught is true. Therefore, her references to Holy Church and to her "evyn cristen" in the Short Text are relatively uncomplex, since they are designed to indicate her oneness with that communal body. She insists that she writes so that her fellow Christians can "see" through her:

> And so ys my desyre that it schulde be to euery ilke manne the same profytte that I desyrede to my selfe and þerto was styrryd of god in the fyrste tyme when I sawe itte; for yt (ys) comonn and generale as we ar alle ane, and I am sekere I sawe it for the profytte of many oder. (ST 220)

Throughout the Short Text Julian maintains her identification with her fellow Christians, disclaiming any singular status for herself. Her frequent use of the phrase "evyn cristen"—which she even uses as the last two words in this version of the *Showings*—serves rhetorically to compose a community of the humble and the faithful into which she inserts herself by affirming her own obedience to the doctrines of Holy Church. By assimilating herself and her writing to an undifferentiated mass of fellow believers, she explicitly reaffirms the ultimate authority of the church as an external censor and interpreter.

In the Short Text, Julian presents her relationship to this authority as relatively unproblematic. For example, she disallows our seeing any conflict between her private visions and her externally derived faith: "Neuer the lesse Jhesu in this visionn enfourmede me of alle that me neded. I saye nought that me nedes na mare techynge, for oure lorde with the schewynge of this hase lefte me to haly kyrke, and I am hungery and thyrstye and nedy and synfulle and freele, and wilfully submyttes me to the techynge of haly kyrke with alle myne euencrysten in to the ende of my lyfe" (ST 244). In this passage Julian skillfully moves from her private communication with Jesus to the community of the church, not only implicitly denying that there might be any difference between the two sets of teachings but explicitly stating that she submits her will to the church, merging herself into the anonymous company of her "euencristen." In the Long Text, Julian retains only the outline of the first sentence, which she places in a dependent clause, and omits entirely her protestations of obedience, frailty, communal solidarity, and submissiveness. Instead, she recounts Jesus' private words to her about the relationship of sin to providential good: "But Jhesu that in this vysyon enformyd me of alle that me nedyd answeryd by thys worde and seyde: Synne is behouely, but alle shalle be wele, and alle shalle be wele, and alle maner of thynge shalle be wele" (LT 405).

The change is a striking one and illustrates her radical reevaluation of her own authorial voice; she substitutes assurance and balance for neediness and dependency. Furthermore, she allows into the Long Text hints of a conflict between her subjective knowledge and the objective teachings of the church that does not really appear in the Short Text.[71] In her earlier version, she consistently presents herself as submissive and obedient, engaged in recounting experience that she herself passes on to the reader in its raw, uninterpreted form.[72] This version invites the reader to see himself or herself as an active, shaping force and encourages the reader to assume that reading is an act of interpretation performed *upon* a text. That impression of textual passivity, like her references to her own gender, disappears in the Long Text. Let me return to the first revelation. In the Short Text, Julian concludes the account of her first revelation with a chapter stressing her lowliness, oneness with all Christians, female frailty, and general unsuitedness for teaching. She ends this string of modesty topoi with the sentence,

> I speke of thame that schalle be safe, for in this tyme god schewyd me non othere; bot in alle thynge I lyeve as haly kyrke techis, for in alle thynge, this blyssede schewynge of oure lorde, I be helde it as ane in god syght, and I vndyrstode neuer nathynge þer yn that stoneȝ me ne lettes me of the trewe techynge of halye kyrke. (ST 222–23)

The Long Text version of this passage is far more polished but also far less easy:

> I speke of them that shalle be savyd, for in this tyme god shewde me no nother. But in all thing I beleue as holy chyrch prechyth and techyth. For the feyth of holy chyrch, which I had before hand vnderstondyng, and as I hope by the grace of god wylle fully kepe it in vse and in custome, stode contynually in my syghte, wyllyng and meanyng never to receyve ony thyng that myght be contrary

---

71. Roger Ellis (1980) has also noted this tension.

72. For other comments about Holy Church in the Short Text, see Colledge and Walsh (1978), 219–23, 243, 252, 262, 275.

ther to. And with this intent and with this meanyng I beheld the
shewyng with all my dyligence, for in all thys blessed shewyng I
behelde it as in gods menyng. (LT 323)

She carefully distinguishes here between the faith of the church, which has
been previously taught her, and the experience of revelation. Though she
affirms here her absolute belief in the teachings of the church, she nonetheless does not relinquish her right either to see or to seek to understand (and
hence explain) what she is seeing. The passage might well go unremarked
if it did not anticipate more obvious conflicts that preoccupy her throughout
her efforts to affirm the validity of her own experience.

The most important of these conflicts concerns the relationship between
human sin and the divine nature. In sharp contrast to her contemporaries,
Julian is more interested in seeking to understand God's mercy than she is
in explicating his justice. Even the briefest pass through the sermons and
the penitential and devotional literature of the late fourteenth century emphasizes what seems to be an inordinate amount of attention devoted to
analyzing, warning about, and providing remedies for the many different
ways in which men and women can fall into sin. Here, Chaucer's Parson's
Tale provides a reference point; the glimpse in the final paragraphs we are
allowed of our future perfection in grace can seem an inordinately delayed
reward for the many pages reminding us of our foulness and imperfection.
Those clean and lovely bodies we will inhabit gleam elusively beyond the
barrier of the flesh the Parson calls up for judgment. Although the Parson
and Julian are obviously not telling the same type of tale, we can find a
similar disdain for the corporal realm in the works of Rolle, whose ecstatic
spirituality might lead us to expect a more positive approach to the things
of this world.[73]

I shall postpone Julian's idiosyncratic treatment of sin and judgment and
focus for now on her manipulation of the figure of Holy Church in a topos
that she uses to preface some of her less conventional views. For example,
in Revelation 13 of the Long Text, she prefaces her remarks about sin with
a paragraph affirming the oneness between God and his church ("he it is,
holy chyrch"): "He is the grounde, he is the substannce, he is the techyng,
he is the techer." She then goes on, "Alle thys that I haue now seyde, and
more as I shalle sey aftyr, is comfortyng ageynst synne; for in the thyrde

---

73. For a discussion of late medieval literature on sin, see Patterson (1991), 374–86; and
Patterson (1978). See also Wenzel (1989).

shewyng, what I saw that god doyth all that is done, I saw nott synn, and than saw I that alle is welle. But when god shewyde me for synne, than sayde he: Alle schalle be wele" (LT 431). Although there is nothing heterodox about this statement, it is subtly biased toward subjectivity in ways that might make figures like Hilton or Arundel uneasy. But Julian contains those implications by first stating that God is the church. She then defines God in conventional terms as the ground of being and as both the teacher and the teaching. However, that process of education is going on not in a dialogue between a priestly teacher and a pupil, but in the mind of the pupil herself. Moreover, she is receiving images and teachings that encourage her to focus upon the merciful nature of God, our mother, rather than upon the judicial figure of paternal wrath who plays so prominent a role in the sermons and treatises of the period. Julian therefore slides imperceptibly from the "alle that is spedfulle to vs to wytt and for to knowe, fulle curtesly oure good lorde wylle shew vs what it is with alle the prechyng and techyng of holy chyrch" to an account of what God has shown her and, from there, to her explanation of that revelation.

Her move from a faith defined in external and objective terms to one rooted in experience and filtered through understanding might have been perceived as more troubling had she not so carefully prepared her line of argument. Rather than scorn members of the clergy for their devotional tepidity (something Rolle did not hesitate to do) or suggest the fallibility of Holy Church (as did Wyclif) or castigate her fellow Christians for their worldliness, Julian describes her faith in terms of obedience, fidelity, and kinship. Despite the truth she perceives in and through her visions, she maintains her unity with the beliefs of the Church:

> The furst dome, whych is of goddes ryghtfulnes, and that is of his owne hygh endlesse loue, and that is that feyer swete dome that was shewed in alle the feyer revelation in whych I saw hym assign(e) to vs no maner of blame. And though theyse were swete and delectable, ȝytt only in the beholdyng of this I culde nott be fulle esyd, and that was for the dome of holy chyrch, whych I had before vnderstondyn and was contynually in my syght. And therefore by this dome me thought that me behovyth nedys to know my selfe a synner. And by the same dome I vnderstode that synners be sometyme wurthy blame and wrath, and theyse two culde I nott see in god. And therfore my desyer was more than I can or may telle, for the hygher dome god shewed hym selfe in the same tyme, and therfore (m)e

behovyd nedys to take it. And the lower dome was lernyd me before
tyme in holy chyrche, and therfore I myght nott by no weye leue
the lower dome. (LT 487–88)

Julian places in the foreground the tension she feels between the two
judgments, her own and that of the church, and insists upon her alliance
with the church's judgment about sin. However, the very transparency of
her statement serves a more opaque purpose. First, she uses the word *dom*
to describe two attitudes toward sinners. The word, which meant judgment,
was commonly used to indicate the Last Judgment.[74] It described an act of
administrative justice that was the product of rational inquiry and hence
had the force of law. By using the same term to describe her private revelation and the public ruling of the church, she suggests both the status of her
own revelation and her entirely rational appraisal of it. She also categorizes
the two judgments with the adjectives higher and lower, granting the more
privileged status to what God shows her privately.[75] Second, despite her
avowal of obedience to the faith of Holy Church, she is equally insistent
that she cannot ignore this subjectively worked out faith: "me behovyd
nedys to take it." A few pages later, Julian disingenuously describes herself
as a "simple soul" whose fundamental ignorance of the divine nature can
only be ameliorated by merging herself into the church, "And now I ȝelde
me to my modyr holy chyrch, as a sympyll chylde owyth" (LT 494). Julian
may well affirm her obedience and simplicity, but we need to see such
protestations in relation to the public she conceived of for her writing. By
presenting herself as a child of the church, Julian defuses any response to
the Long Text that might link it to the views of John Wyclif. Since copies of
the works of Rolle containing Lollard interpolations were being circulated,
Julian's avowals of orthodoxy suggest her awareness of current trends and
of the danger of heterodoxy.[76] But, more important, such statements can
also be seen strategically, as screens allowing Julian the opportunity to

---

74. Kurath and Kuhn (1956–).

75. Colledge and Walsh (1978) feel that these two adjectives should not be construed
hierarchically, and yet the passage itself seems to beg for such an interpretation. In addition,
in the next chapter (see 492), Julian suggests that her early grounding in the faith was but
the first stage of a more sophisticated manner of teaching that came to her in her visions.

76. For example, a metrical preface to an early fifteenth-century northern copy of Rolle's
psalter (Bodleian MS Laud. Miscell. 286) notes, first, that there is no heresy in this particular
copy, going on, "Copyd has this Sauter ben: of yuel men of lollardy: And afterward hit has
bene sene: ympyd in with eresy." The writer then says that such copies were used in Lollard
"schools." See Bramley (1884), 1–2.

advance some of her most ambitious arguments, the first expressed in the parable of the Lord and the Servant and the second in her picture of divine maternity. For if Revelation 14, the longest addition Julian made in the Long Text (expanding one chapter to twenty-three), contains a number of testimonies to her simplicity and fidelity, it is also where Julian locates the key arguments of a theology privileging divine mercy and forgiveness and incorporating sin into a singularly loving providential scheme.

Not the least striking aspect of Julian's theology is her method, whose implications are far-reaching. As bolstered as her writing is by rhetorical authorities and as anchored as her thought is in theological and monastic traditions, the Long Text of the *Showings* nevertheless affirms the primacy of spiritual experience by exemplifying the ways in which a life might serve as a text worthy of explication. The tension she expresses between the need to reconcile external truths with internal realities reflects contemporary concerns with the dangers of unauthorized—or unguided—searching. But where Hilton phrases the question in oppositional terms—either the faith of the church or the stirrings of the self—the thrust of Julian's argument is for unity rather than separation. Hilton suggests that intellectual attention paid to the stirrings of subjectivity might too easily lead the devotee astray. The *Showings* offers powerful evidence that we can use the intellect to interpret feelings, that the faith that is taught may exist somehow alongside the faith one learns experientially, and that we need not resolve all questions so stringently. If Chaucer has the Wife of Bath counter male authority with female experience—and thereby replicate a system of binary oppositions— Julian enters the lists of the *débat* and provides another set of answers altogether. She links experience to subjectivity and stresses the relationship between the senses (both spiritual and physical) and the reason, creating a system that is not delimited by binary terminology and can therefore not be explained in oppositional terms. Her work suggests that authority can be applied to experience and intellective knowledge can make highly innovative but not necessarily unorthodox use of those feared "stirrings." By her careful translation of an elite Latin system of reading into English and by her refusal to define categories so strictly, Julian presents a stunningly intellectual defense of the "femininity" excoriated, chastened, and corseted by generations of exegetical censors who sought to control texts, carnal stirrings, and vernacular yearnings.[77]

---

77. By "femininity," I mean those impulses that were grouped under that rubric. I do not mean to suggest Julian's defense of women or of feminism; her excision of literal femininity from the Long Text suggests her disinterest in the obvious. Like Chaucer's Clerk (see Chapter

There is also an important political or social valence to the language with which Julian considers the idea of authority. Unlike Chaucer, Julian was not a firsthand observer of contemporary political or parliamentary developments. However, we should not make the too-easy assumption that she was completely detached from the currents of public opinion or that she did not use and examine the language of her contemporaries and the social codes it embodied. Thus, while we cannot employ the same historical methodology with Julian's work as with Chaucer's, we need to recognize that the terms she chose as a devotional writer were those that had currency when she wrote. There are at least three aspects of Julian's thought and language that make the most sense in the context of late fourteenth-century concerns and codes: her unusual refusal to think in binary terms, which, in turn, governs her handling of the categories of class and gender. Both categories were frequently invoked in discussions of authority, or of threats to it, and invoked in ways that emphasized the fundamental opposition between male and female or between ruler and ruled. Though Julian uses both the language of gender and that of class, particularly in her efforts to explain the nature of God's relation to humankind, by eschewing the oppositional language of her contempories, she offers a radical alternative to the punitory figure of authority who tended to dominate late medieval consciousness. Like Chaucer, Julian applies contemporary terminology in a strikingly original way, using it to think her way through certain issues into conclusions and usages that are very much her own.

The years when Julian was revising the *Showings* were dominated by the subject of authority as it pertained to institutional order. Though the particulars of the political situation could not be so relevant to Julian as they were to Chaucer, the ways in which that situation was described or expressed say much about current usage and terminology, especially the social unease that was expressed through the language of gender.[78] In April 1376, the Good Parliament had publically condemned six of Edward III's worst councillors and banished the king's mistress, Alice Perrers, from the court. John of Gaunt had taken these actions as directly threatening the principle of regal authority and retaliated by controlling the Westminster Parliament of 1377, which then rolled back the reforms of the previous

---

5), Julian uses the topical as a means of engaging with those very principles that underpin the foundations of the ordinary.

78. For a reading of the social strategies that underlie the use of gender in the mystery cycles, see Coletti (1990) (1992).

year's parliament and imprisoned its popular speaker, Peter de la Mare.[79] It was in this same parliament that the bishop of Saint David's, who was a friend of Gaunt's, eulogized the royal family by none too subtly likening Richard, who as heir to the crown awaited the tributes of his subjects, to the Christ child sought from afar by the Wise Men.[80] He thereby drew upon the language of sanctity and held up the child, Richard, as the incarnation of a new order.

Gaunt was clearly right in assuming that the issue under consideration was that of authority, as the account of these events by the author of the so-called Scandalous Chronicle also suggests. Strongly opposed to John of Gaunt, whom he does not hesitate to depict as power-hungry and manipulative, the writer focuses on Edward's infatuation with his mistress as a symptom of a more troubling moral laxity. By accusing Alice Perrers of being well-versed in the arts of flattery and magic, he describes her as enervating the masculine force of the king, as well as insidiously undermining the character of the entire court. The same author's account of Peter de la Mare's release from prison provides an implicit contrast to the flaccidity of regal authority in the person of the speaker, whom the people welcome in the sacramental language of the Mass, "Benedictus, qui venit in nominus Domini!"[81] To the weakness and femininity of the court, the author opposes the salvific force of de la Mare, symbol of a parliament silenced by one scornful of the Commons and driven by his own need for power.

This argument about the nature of authority can be detected in contemporary chronicle accounts of and reactions to other important events of the period, the papal schism, the Rising of 1381, and the Merciless Parliament. In their assumption that the sequence of events known as history is a text capable of explication, the authors of these accounts should be seen as fully engaged exegetes, whose critical language was designed to have its own social impact.[82] Consequently, where the author of the Scandalous

---

79. For contemporary accounts of the Good Parliament, see *Rot. Parl.* (1783), 2:321–60; Galbraith (1927), 82–94; Thompson (1874), 68–108; Walsingham (1863), 1:320–21. For discussions, see Armitage-Smith (1905), 121–31; Holmes (1975); Ormrod (1990b), 35–39; Richardson and Sayles (1981), 377–99; Roskell (1968), 1:31–52, 2:1–14; Waugh (1991), 223–29. For a discussion of John of Gaunt's role in these events, see Goodman (1992), 55–72.

80. See *Rot. Parl.* (1783) 2:361; Armitage-Smith (1905), 146–47.

81. Thompson (1874), 74, 95, 150–51. I discuss these events more fully in Chapter 5. For work on the political uses of the language of gender, see Strohm (1992), chaps. 5, 7.

82. For further thoughts on this issue, particularly as it relates to the Rising, see Pearsall (1989) and, more recently, Justice (1994b). The most sustained argument for the reading of cultural "texts" is presented in the work of Strohm; see Works Cited.

Chronicle accused Edward III's court of effeminacy, Walsingham did not hesitate to echo that earlier description in his account of Richard II's courtiers during the 1380s. Richard's refusal to rely on the advice of older councillors and his tendency to surround himself with the young and the fashionable vexed many contemporary observers, causing them to question Richard's understanding of regal authority.[83] There are other, more oblique, aspersions cast on participants in actual or fictive events. The monk of Saint Albans who wrote the Scandalous Chronicle compares the Londoners who feared the threatened French invasion in 1386 to timid hares—an animal long associated with Venus. He castigates them for their softness and accuses them of being brave only in peacetime.[84] The poet who wrote *Sir Gawain and the Green Knight* depicts Arthur's court as fearfully young and inept when confronted with the Green Knight's adult vigor and scorn for its mannered and and effete ways. In the section on knighthood in the *Vox Clamantis,* John Gower identifies love of women as the cause of that estate's degeneration. In addition, the many references in a wide variety of texts of the Old Testament heroine Judith play out this drama of self-scrutiny by figuring true strength in the very body that captiously drains masculine energy from its supposed conqueror.

The dangers perceived in femininity can also be translated into the even more volatile social arena, for gender categories were used as synecdoche for the concept of hierarchical power that underpinned medieval life.[85] Hence, those who maintained authority over texts, bodies, or peoples enjoyed masculine status in relation to what was read, possessed, or ruled. If contemporary observers feared a sliding femininity at work in the council chambers of kings, they feared even more the unruly stirrings of the body of the state. Nowhere is this loathing for the terrors of fluidity more apparent than in Gower's treatment of the Rising of 1381 in *Vox Clamantis.* In Book 1, which he devotes to an account of the Rising, he describes the

---

83. For remarks about Edward III, see Thompson (1874), appendix, 401. For similar statements about the court of Richard II, see Walsingham (1863), 156. See also discussion of Richard's court in Chapter 5.

84. See Thompson (1874), 370–71.

85. Scott (1988) addresses the ways in which gender can be used as an "analytic category . . . as a way of talking about systems of social or sexual relations . . . as a way of signifying relationships of power"; see particularly, 41–49. Later, Scott (1992) questions the way in which categories like gender that must be historicized have achieved "foundational status." As Aers has pointed out in regard to what are the essentializing gestures of twentieth-century discussions of the feminine as it was used by medieval authors, we need to beware of assuming that authors did not adapt and enrich the language they themselves used.

revolt as a chaotic blurring of those boundaries marking distinctions between classes and kinds. For the poem's narrator, the horror lies in the
formlessless of his vision: field and city, man and beast, lord and peasants
appear not as they were meant to be; even the Tower of London turns out
to have paper walls rather than stone. For Gower, the peasant is not simply
bestial but irredeemable, always waiting to harm the "very man who provided for him."[86] Gower shares with contemporary chroniclers his characterization of the rebels as inarticulate and brutish, an account of them that
is, as Paul Strohm notes, "designed to discredit the social standing, judgment, and objectives of the rebels."[87] By reading the text of the Rising as
a manifestation of baseness or carnality in the social body, contemporaries
indicated a methodology rooted in the oppositional language with which
gender was also construed.[88]

They also indicated their fundamental belief that authority was finally a
synonym for control. To some extent, the best or most compassionate of
the commentators on English society was Thomas Brinton, bishop of Rochester. Brinton was not only sensitive to the tensions within the church and
society, but sensitive to the needs of England's poor. For example, in a
sermon preached probably in 1378 upon the ways in which we can express
love for our neighbors, Brinton points out that the city as a construct
depends upon a recognition of mutual support between Dives and Pauper.
Though Brinton makes no effort to deny the necessarily hierarchical basis
for social order, his remarks about the poor are nonetheless a far cry from
Gower's description of a subhuman mob.[89] In a sermon on the subject of
the Rising of 1381, Brinton began by urging the need for a great penitential
clamor, alluding to the ceremonial noise of petitionary grief that arose
collectively in religious foundations as a means of diverting the effects of
justice. In another sermon on the Rising, Brinton described it as an insurrec-

---

86. Stockton (1962), 94–95. Gower added book 1 to an already completed poem, thereby
indicating just how urgently he felt about those social tendencies expressed through the Peasants' Revolt. On Gower's sense of his social role, see Justice (1994b), chap. 5; Peck (1978);
Yeager (1990).

87. Strohm (1992), 34. For other recent studies of the Rising in relation to its contemporary interpretations, see Crane (1992); Dobson ([1970], 1986); R. Green (1992); Justice
(1994b); Pearsall (1989).

88. Here, see also Strohm (1992), chapter 7; Crane (1992), 215. Crane takes issue with
Lee Patterson's remarks about gender. Although I think she misconstrues Patterson's comments about politics and gender, her argument nonetheless needs to be considered in relation
to Patterson's (1991) remarks, 280–83.

89. See Devlin (1954), 437–38.

tion of servants against masters and therefore as a sign of fundamental or metaphysical chaos: he averred that since servitude was introduced into the world by sin, social hierarchy is a necessary manifestation of divine justice. Seen in these terms, the Rising was doubly heinous; servants not only killed masters, but those who were unfit for rule went on to attempt to become masters.[90] Brinton saw the disorder of the revolt as symptomatic of national sin but also of weakness in the ruling classes, including members of the clergy, whom he does not hesitate to chastize for their worldliness.[91]

I do not mean to set Gower's portrait of the bestial peasant against Brinton's image of the sinful and mistaken servant and do Gower the diservice of leaving him the lone spokesman for law and order. Throughout the period after the Rising, there are many indications of what must have been a desperate need to reassert control—judicially or rhetorically—over the wayward social body. In charging the commissioners who captured and punished the offenders after they had been lulled by the young king's mild and courteous manner, Richard described their decidedly incourteous fates in graphic detail, "secundum legem regni nostri Anglie, vel aliis viis et modis, per decollaciones et membrorum mutilaciones, prout melius et celerius juxta discreciones vestras vobis videbitur faciendum."[92] He specified that those who had split the body politic were to suffer fragmentation and mutilation, translating the terms of political metaphor into a literal judgment on those whose baseness and carnality deserved—nor could apprehend—no better. Richard's words constitute a critical reading of the events surrounding the Rising and underline the intimate relationship between interpretation and action that characterized so much political language during the early modern period. The Parliament Rolls for the years afterward display a nervous preoccupation with subversive behavior in general. From reports of people preaching "on their own authority" (and supposedly spreading "heresies, errors, slander, discord, and dissension between diverse estates"), to the continued punishments for the rebels, to complaints in 1387 and 1388 about the Crown itself and its "defaut de bon governance," there is a general sense that what used to check the impulse to

---

90. See Devlin (1954), Sermons 99 and 101.

91. For similar analyses of the contemporary situation as reflecting a dangerous abrogation of authority by those who ought to lead, see Gower's comments in book 3 of the *Vox Clamantis* as well as the important sermon preached at Paul's Cross in 1388 by Thomas Wimbledon (Owen 1966). See also the numerous examples of prelatical and clerical vice cited by Owst (1966) and Scase (1989), 7.

92. Quoted in Strohm (1992), 56.

disorder did no longer. Thus in 1386, a complaint was brought against the sergeants of arms for oppression and extortion; they were urged to behave as they did in "ancient times" and discharge their offices honorably.[93] Whenever those "ancient times" in fact were, their effect seemed only to linger in the memory.

The implicit relationship between authority and control was further heightened by the social value placed upon such masculine attributes as valor, strength, and bravery. These are all key components of the Plantagenet "myth." In relation to Edward III's reputation for chivalric might, Charles V of France, who possessed a keen political intelligence, was cast into the shadows. Given to patient waiting and negotiation, he was derided by his contemporaries for his unmanliness and lack of chivalry. Like their father, the sons of Edward III were warrior princes who scorned weakness, terror, or illness.[94] As valiant and as shrewd as John of Gaunt was, the full radiance of that myth fell upon his older brother, Edward, the Black Prince, the father of Richard II. The chivalric reputation of the Black Prince was high enough in his lifetime, but his untimely death in June 1376, the year of the Good Parliament, made him the stuff of legend. Whether as a carefully barbed reminder to Richard of his father's manliness or as a response to a more general sense of disorder, the *Life of the Black Prince,* probably written in 1385 and perhaps commissioned by John of Gaunt, held up Edward's prowess and chivalry as standards, juxtaposing them to the venality of courtiers and the weakness of lesser soldiers.[95] An equally potent aura surrounded the bishop of Norwich, Lord Henry Despenser. During the Rising, Despenser personally crushed the revolt against the abbot of

93. I am referring to the records of Parliament for the years 1382, 1383, 1384, 1386, 1387, 1388. See *Rotuli Parliamentorum* (1783). On the subject of "ancient rights" and the ways in which peasants also harkened back to the purities of an earlier age in which these rights were guaranteed by charters, see Faith (1984). In the early chapters of his study of the French Revolution Schama (1989) describes the similarly conservative yearnings of the French not-so-privileged, whose political dissatisfaction was focused on the threats to their well-being posed by mercantilism, by individualism, and by profit. Consequently, the disaffected called for the king to protect and to restore the "ancient" communal rights of the people as a means of combating the nascent capitalism of the age. Schama also notes an almost obsessive need to validate acts of violence with writs or charters.

94. See Armitage-Smith (1905), 66–67 for remarks about Charles V; 83 for the Black Prince's merciless handling of the siege of Limoges. For a study of the ways in which gender categories were used to express the relationships between justice and mercy, see Strohm (1992), chap. 5, "Queens as Intercessors."

95. See Herald (1974). Walker (1990), 57, suggests that Gaunt may have commissioned the *Life* in order to glorify the chivalric triumphs of himself and his men.

Peterborough in Cambridge, and in Norfolk he himself killed some of the rebels who had taken shelter near a church altar. Walsingham's account of the bishop's efforts to crush the rebels in Norfolk presents him as wrathful, fully armed, young, and bloodthirsty. When a year later there was another rising in Norfolk, it was accompanied by a conspiracy to kill the bishop who had sought such reprisals against the local rebels.[96] Despenser's love of the martial arts was not exhausted by internal forays; in 1383 he led the disasterous "crusade" against the French forces in Flanders, arousing the scorn of *politiques* for his military failure and of John Wyclif for his exploitive adaptation of crusader rhetoric, as well as the use of papal indulgences, to further a secular war between England and France. Despenser's display of militarism may have influenced Chaucer's handling of the legend of Saint Cecilia (see chapter 5).

To some extent, the emphasis upon warlike behavior was simply an inextricable feature of a society whose aristocrats subscribed to the values and myths of chivalry.[97] On the other hand, the language that was used to express those values drew quite explicitly upon gender categories as a means of indicating relative status. The underlying humor of *Sir Gawain and the Green Knight* reflects such a system of codes; in the contrast between the Green Knight's vivacity and Bercilak's energy and Camelot's elaborate manners and Sir Gawain's courteous evasions, the poet opposes masculine to feminine as a way of heightening the vulnerability of Arthur's young and glittering court. Julian need not have known either the poem or the *Life of the Black Prince* to have understood something about the ways in which gender categories were used to signify relationships involving power. However, situated as she was in Norwich, she probably knew a good deal about its bishop and about the impact of the Rising of 1381 throughout East Anglia.[98]

Norwich was no backwater city. After London, it was the second in population and in wealth. Furthermore, Norwich's own highly developed

---

96. For these accounts, see Dobson (1970, 1986), 235–37, 259–60, 334. For a discussion of Despenser's martial fierceness, see Edwards (1958); Tuck (1984b). In Capgrave, ed., Hingeston (1858), 170, Capgrave recalls Despenser as an example of bravery.

97. For a discussion of the conflict between the militaristic practice of chivalry and its public ideology see Patterson (1991), chap. 3, "The *Knight's Tale* and the Crisis of Chivalric Identity."

98. See Dobson (1986), 233–34. For a discussion of Norwich as an important component of contemporary networks of intellectual and theological discourse, see Clark (1992). Jantzen (1987), 7–11, describes Julian's Norwich and juxtaposes Julian's message of love to the warlike tendencies of Bishop Despenser.

sense of class distinctions also suggests ways in which its merchant elite looked upward for its system of values. The merchants of that city sought to maintain a clear social distinction between themselves and the craftsmen. The ordinances of Norwich therefore specified that entry to the common council was to be denied to a member of the more humble craft guilds and, furthermore, that if a craftsman became rich enough to qualify for being mayor, he had to renounce his craft.[99] If the social and political world of late medieval Norwich was highly stratified, the intellectual and religious life of the community was characterized by a certain fluidity. In general Norwich shared—or excelled—in the late medieval trend away from established ecclesiastical structures. According to Norman Tanner there were more hermits and anchorites known to have lived there between 1370 and the Reformation than in any other town in England. Furthermore, it was the only town in late medieval England known to have contained a community of laywomen similar to those found on the Continent. Tanner cautiously speculates that the relatively high degree of education among wealthy Norwich families, along with the evidence for widespread lay piety and for economic prosperity may well have helped to create an environment where new ideas were welcomed. He goes on to suggest that the vitality of the Norwich church owed a good deal to the variety and richness of local religious life.[100]

Moreover, the local church was dominated by its vigorous and warlike bishop, whose sense of self was manifested in acts that bespoke his keen understanding of the dynamics worked out through categories of both gender and class. Henry Despenser was born in either 1341 or 1342 of an aristocratic family. He spent his younger years in Italy, where he fought in the army of the pope. In 1370, when he was canon of Salisbury, he was nominated to the bishopric of Norwich. In describing him, John Foxe, for whom Bishop Despenser represented everything wrong with the church of Rome, translates an incident from the spring of 1377 that he found in the *Chronicon Angliae*. As Foxe puts it, when the bishop visited the town of Lynn, he was not contented with the honor ordinarily done to his office, but demanded a "new" and "unusual kind of magnificence." He asked that the mace that normally preceded the town's mayor be borne before him. Both the mayor of Lynn and the citizens warned of the unwisdom of this

---

99. Hilton (1992), 51, 102. For a rich account of the city's mercantile vigor, see also A. Green (1971), chap. 14, "The Common Council of Norwich."

100. Tanner (1984), 55, 58, 66, 110–12, 166. See also Colledge and Walsh (1978), 39–43.

demand. Despenser ignored their warnings, referred scornfully to the common people as "ribaldos," and insisted on carrying out his wish. Deserted by all other residents of Lynn and preceded by one of his own men carrying the mace, Despenser was assaulted at the town gates by those very commons, pelted with stones, and finally forced to accept the intervention of the king in order to appease the wrath of the citizens, who perceived him as exceeding his power and wishing to usurp what was not his.[101] The chronicler's version of the incident proceeds not simply from a dislike of the bishop of Norwich, but from a fundamental awareness that when power separated itself from authority—in this case, spiritual authority—its security could not be guaranteed. In seeking power that was not his to seek, the bishop signified his pride and thereby placed himself, and his office, in jeopardy. Since neither the original author nor Foxe had any love for Despenser, the truth of the account rests more in what it reveals about contemporary tensions as they are expressed in and through contemporary language. Thus, what are spiritual qualities, like pride or wisdom, are expressed through the bishop's attitude toward the "ribalds"; and the spiritual and civil "good" of an order promulgated upon hierarchy underpins the disruptive picture of those same scoundrels and knaves pelting a bishop with stones.[102] That the chronicler accepts the fundamental opposition between ruler and ruled—or the tension built into all social relations—is clear from the language; he implies that what is oppositional is maintained through control, of both the self and the social body.

What might all of this mean for Julian, whose work testifies to her erudition and to her sensitivity to contemporary terms and codes? In their edition of the *Showings* Colledge and Walsh present evidence for her Latinity, for her intimacy with the Vulgate as well as for her knowledge of Augustine, Gregory, and William of Saint Thierry. They also strongly suggest her familiarity with more current texts like *The Treatise of Perfection of the Sons of God, The Cloud of Unknowing, The Scale of Perfection,* and perhaps Chaucer's *Boece* and Langland's *Piers Plowman,* going on to argue that she must have been a nun until about 1393, when, after finishing the Long Text, she entered the anchorhold.[103] This is, of course, speculation. While

101. For details on Despenser's life, see the *Dictionary of National Biography.* For the original, see Thompson (1874), 139–40; Foxe (1965), 2:105.

102. The English noun "ribald" was taken from the medieval Latin word "ribaldos" and was used to designate those of both lower social and moral status, hence retainer or knave or vagabond. The Latin uses "vulgus," "villae," "plebs," and "communes"—all terms of class.

103. See Colledge and Walsh (1978), introduction, 43–59.

it seems unlikely that Julian's life fell into a pattern any neater than most lives, what is especially important about these suggestions is the insistence that Julian must have had access to a library. Since convents were places where women could acquire an education in Latin culture, it makes sense to guess that she, like many other cloistered religious of the period, moved from the conventual to the solitary life. Furthermore, convents were not separate from the worlds around them, but depended on systems of outside support, communication, and labor for their very existence. If Julian were cloistered, it would in no way preclude her awareness of the tensions and issues of the late fourteenth century as they were expressed through current systems of language.[104] I would go even further and maintain that Julian, like most self-conscious and observant writers, did not simply *use* the social and political codes of her day; she exploited and reshaped them in order to arrive at new ways of seeing. In order to appreciate fully the nature of her achievement in the *Showings,* we must broaden our understanding of its context to include events like the Rising of 1381 and the ongoing debate about authority that characterized the social and political—as well as the ecclesiastical—realms. For thirty years of her life, from 1370 to 1406, Henry Despenser ruled the diocese of Norwich. He was a colorful figure, an apt administrator, and a loyal supporter of his king, Richard II. In the end, he was willing to suffer imprisonment by Henry IV for his loyalty to Richard. Spoken of as "youthful" for long after he was young, the bishop personified the aggression, the temper, the noblesse oblige, the power (even when threatened) of the male aristocrat. He publically enacted a quality of "lordship" at the time when lordship appeared under attack. At that same time Julian was writing both versions of the *Showings.*

The two most dramatic and potentially explosive of the inventions that characterize the later version can be found in Revelation 14, which not only contains both her vision of the Lord and the Servant and her account of God's maternity, but joins them successively in a single vision of the divine nature. Julian's bishop was in no literal sense a "source" for these inventions any more than the Rising of 1381 or the Merciless Parliament or Richard's entry into London in 1392 (or Maidstone's version of it) can be called "sources" for the *Showings* (see Chapter 5). However, the visions that she casts as her experience and that serve to authorize her acts of

---

104. On this issue, see Strohm (1992), 116, where he argues that we need not draw a line between Chaucer's Alceste and Queen Anne, but, instead, need to recognize "the environment of interpretive structures within which Alceste was invented and within which Anne seems at least partially to have invented herself."

writing cannot be treated ahistorically, nor can our treatments of them dehistoricize their content and their form. For example, it is highly unlikely that a twentieth-century American would have or recount a vision like that of the Lord and the Servant. Visions take place in the language of the time in which they occur; they speak to those who use that language and can therefore understand the social codes embedded in it. Both texts of the *Showings* give evidence of Julian's sensitivity to those codes. Thus, in the sixteenth revelation where she is oppressed by the devil, she not only smells his stink but hears noise and jangling, which she describes in terms her readers might appreciate: "also I harde a bodely talkyng, as it had been of two bodyes, and both to my thyngkyng talkyd at one tyme, as they had holde a perlement with greate besynes, and all was softe whystryn" (LT 648). She retained almost verbatim from the Short Text this analogy between hearing someone talk at cross-purposes and the sound of a parliament (see ST 270), with the exception that she substituted whispering for "muttering." Similarly, her remarks about the servant's clothing and tasks in the example of the Lord and the Servant, which I shall discuss below, reveal her care to historicize vision, or her intention of using the language of vision as a means of commenting upon a world fixed in its own stultifying tension. After all, it is devil noise that is likened to parliament. Julian lived in and wrote for a world conceived of as hierarchical and frequently described as composed of oppositional pairs. Since it was a fallen world, opposition was assumed to be an inevitable feature of any order issuing from hierarchy because what was beneath demanded some variety of control. Even Brinton, whose discussions of social ills are milder than many of his contemporaries, makes no attempt to deny opposition, merely to ameliorate it by urging on the ruling class a greater sense of responsibility. It is in this sense that figures like Bishop Despenser or events like the Rising of 1381 should be used contextually in seeking to understand Julian's life and art. The descriptions of significant events of the period from 1373 to 1393 and the lives of some of its notables provide evidence for the relevance of oppositional pairs like lord and servant, man and woman, form and formlessness employed as indices of social stability.

For the remainder of the chapter I would like to focus on Revelation 14 and the ways in which Julian's presentation of her material employs and expands contemporary terms and codes as a means of expressing a broader and less constrictive vision of God. In both the table of contents in chapter

1 of the Long Text and the introduction to the fourteenth revelation, Julian describes this revelation as concerning prayer:

> The xiiii is that our lord god is grownd of our beseking. Heer in was seen two fayer properties. That one is rightfull preaier; that other is verie trust, which he will both be one lyke large. And thus our praier liketh him, and he of his goodnes fulfillyth it. (LT 284)

Neither the example of the Lord and the Servant nor the discussion of divine maternity are mentioned in this initial description of the revelation, nor in the early chapters of the revelation itself. Various reasons have been adduced for what may be either silence or omission: Julian may have written the table of contents before she drastically expanded the material in this revelation; the table of contents may apply to the Short Text rather than to the Long; or the entry in fact describes what she is doing in the revelation.[105] Since the entire revelation proceeds from the proposition that God is the ground of our beseeching, Julian needs to work out a way to explain the relationship between humankind and God in prayer. Her first problem is our sinful nature, which she has been taught separates us from God; the second is the degree of trust we can have for a figure who is traditionally described as punishing our defects. The example of the Lord and the Servant can be seen as exploring the first of these problems, the doctrine of God's maternity as ameliorating the anxieties of the second.

By deciding not to privilege these two portions of the revelation in her introductory material, Julian maintains the seamless and determinedly unprovocative quality of the Long Text. References to either class or gender might be construed by authorities as indicating a suspicious heterodoxy, particularly since the earliest legislation for heresy came in the aftermath of the Rising of 1381.[106] There would be no reason to refer to either an example of a Lord and a Servant or an exposition of God's maternity in the table of contents and thereby tempt a reader to excerpt these portions and read them out of context. Instead, and as others have pointed out, each is integral to the *entire* argument of the Long Text; as early as in the first revelation we can find language that foreshadows both explanations.[107] That neither should be severed from its grounding in the social and commu-

---

105. See Colledge and Walsh (1978), introduction, 25, 112–62; Watson (1993), 675–77.

106. See Richardson (1936), 10. See also Dahmus (1952), 79–81.

107. On the seamless nature of the Long Text, see Glasscoe (1983); Heimmel (1982), 82–90; Nuth (1991), 31; Watson (1992b); Windeatt (1977).

nal codes of the late fourteenth century underlines Julian's determination to use the language of her day to write theology, as well as her profound awareness of the delicacy she must bring to her endeavor. As she says early in the revelation, "I saw no wrath but on mannes perty . . . for wrath is nott elles but a frowerdnes and a contraryousnes to pees and to loue. And eyther it comyth of feylyng of myght or [o]f feylyng of wysdom or of feylyng of goodnesse, whych feylyng is nott in god, but it is in oure party" (LT 500). The impulse to singularity that can be detected in feelings of superior might, wisdom, or virtue is that which separates us from ourselves and hence from God. In contrast to social relations predicated upon hierarchical opposition, Julian works out the terms of a theology grounded in loving union.

The care with which she presents her mysterious and compelling vision of the Lord and the Servant indicates how important Julian sees it to her overall intent in the *Showings*. She introduces the account by returning to the tension she experiences between the teachings of Holy Church and her own revelations. In particular, she is concerned about the issue of authority as it relates to sin:

> But yet here I wondryde and merveylyd with alle þe dylygence of my soule, menyng thus: Goode lorde, I see the that thou arte very truth, and I know truly þat we syn grevously all day and be moch blame wurthy; and I may neyther leue the knowyng of this sooth, nor I se nott the shewyng to vs no manner of blame. How may this be? For I knew be the comyn techyng of holy church and by my owne felyng that the blame of oure synnes contynually hangyth vppon vs, fro þe furst man in to the tyme that we come vppe in to hevyn. Then was this my merveyle, that I saw oure lorde god shewyng to vs no more blame then if we were as clene and as holy as angelis be in hevyn. (LT 510–11)

Julian here expresses the conflict she feels between objective and subjective knowledge, using the verbs *to know* and *to see* to underline the distinction she wishes to outline. The brief rhetorical question, "How may this be," points up a bewilderment, which a few lines later she defines as a conflict between her reason and her blindness. She ends the chapter with an anguished question, "A lorde Jhesu, kyng of blysse, how shall I be esyde, who shall tell me and tech me that me nedyth to wytt, if I may nott at this tyme se it in the?" That conflict between what is known and what is seen is resolved by "a wonderfull example of a lorde that hath a servannt," which Julian describes as giving "syght to my vnderstandyng of both." In other words, the example, by showing her, resolves through personal spiritual experience what could not be resolved by the articles of the faith.

By referring to the story of the Lord and the Servant as an "example," Julian skillfully guides a reader's response to it. Since "example" was frequently used synomously with "parable" and with "exemplum" and was freighted with associations of authority, she at once situates the tale generically in a way that directs attention to her critical apparatus and underlines its status within her work.[108] In other words, the term directs us to the tale's allegory even before we read it and hence to the possibility of understanding its higher meaning. Her remarks also make it clear that she will explicate the example, performing the interpretive function she defers to the reader throughout the Short Text. There, she presents her visions as pictures issuing through her but not necessarily interpreted by her. Julian's reading of the example of the Lord and the Servant emphasizes how firmly she asserts her authority as seer and exegete and manifests her determination to sanction her subjective apprehension of truth with her objective methodology. Moreover, Julian's decision to blur the boundaries between lordship and servantship in her explication of the example cannot be detached from the highly charged and oppositional social language of the 1380s. Her careful presentation of the entire piece—text and interpretation—suggests that she intended the example to speak to the complicated nexus of social and religious issues surrounding the subject of dominion.

The example is deceptively simple. Julian describes herself as seeing two persons, a lord sitting solemnly and a servant standing expectantly before his lord. The Lord sends the Servant on an errand. The Servant runs hastily and lovingly to do the Lord's will, but falls into a valley. There, despite all his efforts and his grief, he is trapped and may not even turn his face to look on his lord. Julian notes that she can find no justification for the Servant's extraordinary suffering, especially since his goodwill and desire to please his Lord caused his fall. Neither does she see the Lord as behaving wrathfully toward his fallen Servant. Instead, he pities his distress and searches for a way to give him an even greater gift in return for his suffering. At this point, the "shewyng of the example" vanishes, and Julian is left to replay it in her memory and to seek to understand its meaning.

---

108. For example, see Kurath and Kuhn (1956–). On *exemplum,* see Colledge and Walsh (1978), 513 n. 3; Johnson (1990), 54–56; Scanlon (1994).

Julian asserts control over this particular text by insisting on her own gradual apprehension of its hidden meaning. She begins her gloss by stating that the story has a double meaning, or that the "syght" was shown "double" in the Lord and "double" in the Servant, meaning that she "saw" each component of the example, first, in bodily likeness and then spiritually. She thereby indicates not simply that the story has two interrelated sets of meanings, but that those meanings are inextricably bound up with her own capacity for sight. She alludes to the fundamental subjectivity of her interpretation by stressing that God himself taught her how to understand what she saw, not that she turned to an outside interpreter or to any other external figure of authority. In fact, she heightens our sense of her growing critical acumen by describing her initial confusion about the nature of the vision. Like any painstaking exegete, Julian presents herself as spending years trying to decipher the meaning of the text before her.

Her account of the example is therefore fissured strategically so that we are never far removed from the act of exegesis. After her first account of what she saw, she perceives that the Servant's fall has made it possible for the Lord to reward him more grandly than he otherwise could have. She then notes that the showing itself vanished, but her astonishment at it did not depart. She continues, saying that though she saw some relation between Adam and the Servant, she saw many "dyuerse properteys" that did not apply especially to him. Acknowledging the difficulty of the showing, she says, "In whych mysty example the pryvytes of the reuelacyon be yet moch hyd; and nott with stand(y)ng this I sawe and vnderstode that euery shewyng is full of pryvytes" (LT 519). Julian here applies the language of interpretive inquiry to a private vision that she feels contains the solution to God's attitude toward the sinner. She continues to use hermeneutical apparatus in the cause of subjectivism, specifying three types of contemplative knowledge that help her to understand her visions. That she has been engaged in a long and arduous project is stressed by her remark that it has taken her twenty years ("saue thre monthys") to understand the example, which she then recalls point by point, analyzing each detail in what now is recounted as a vision in technicolor. Where the first version of the example contained only an account of the actions of the Lord and the Servant, the second version—which she retrieves from her memory of the vision itself— is highly specific, containing descriptions of the drape of the clothing, of its precise hues, of skin tones, gestures, and facial expressions. Julian treats each of these points seriously and allegorically, leading her reader through a sort of memorial picture gallery that becomes more significant with each visit. She finally arrives at an understanding of the example, allowing her to see that in the Servant is "comprehended" Adam, or all men, and Christ.

Julian, however, states that what has already been a full treatment of the showing has not begun to exhaust the meanings encoded in the example. She therefore provides the second portion of her exegesis, which presumably corresponds to the spiritual interpretation she mentioned when she introduced the example. There, she asserted that the second "showing" was spiritual, or without bodily likeness. In making the transition between the two types of meaning, she indicates that the first type prepares for the second level of comprehension, "Also in thys merveylous example I haue techyng with in me, as it were the begynnyng of an A B C, wher by I may haue some vnderstondyng of oure lordys menyng, for the pryvytes of the reuelacion be hyd ther in, not withstondyng that alle þe shewyng be full of prevytes" (LT 539). Julian then begins to expand upon the nature of the Trinity, allowing her language to suggest the ways in which what is triune can be one. She recounts Christ's earthly pilgrimage as a process of fragmentation and then describes the sequel to the example of the Lord and the Servant in Christ's reunion with the Father after that process is completed. From the final sentence in chapter 51 affirming trinitarian unity, she moves swiftly to the opening sentence of chapter 52, which reads, "And thus I saw that god enjoyeth that he is our fader, and god enjoyeth that he is our moder, and god enjoyeth that he is our very spouse, and our soule his lovyd wife." By some special intuitive leap, Julian begins to extrapolate the motherhood of God from her spiritual comprehension of the example of the Lord and the Servant.

There are broad social implications underlying Julian's example of the Lord and the Servant, not the least of which is that inherent in her methodology. At each stage of the process of interpretation, Julian insists upon her identity as repository of the full text, upon her own rights of explication, upon the effort she has expended on the task, and upon the truth of her observations. Since she removed any references to her gender from the Long Text, as well as adding the example of the Lord and the Servant along with her account of the motherhood of God, she was obviously not interested in any challenge to authority along the lines of that offered by the Wife of Bath. However, her carefully detailed and logically argued reading of private experience constitutes a more insidious and complicated exploration of the very issue of authority, since she maintains her right as a privately sanctioned individual to read—and to broadcast as truth—the result of subjective inquiry into her own experience. She presents both this experi-

ence and her explication of it as resolving the tension between her interior
knowledge of God and the church's teachings about him. Were she to omit
her many references to Holy Church, to her humble obedience to that
church, or to the anguish she feels over the conflict between faith and sight,
the Long Text of the *Showings* might not appear so pristinely orthodox.
Even her familiarity with and use of key texts of monastic spirituality serves
to blunt the force of Julian's genuine and sometimes startling creativity.
Julian, like Chaucer, understood the necessity of speaking through the
mouthpiece of conventional authority.

Her exploitation of conventional models is integral to the entire conception of the example of the Lord and the Servant. Her language, as well as
the very conception of servantship, is saturated by scriptural allusions and
references.[109] Julian therefore writes with a full and rich assurance that
behind her detailed account of the Lord and the Servant is the figure of the
Suffering Servant foretold by Isaiah. In her account of the ways in which
the Servant figures both Adam and Christ, she draws upon the Pauline
epistles, and for her depiction of Christ as a gardener, upon the tradition
surrounding John's account of the Resurrection where Mary mistakes her
risen Lord for the gardener.[110] Her careful account of the Servant's clothing,
which she later links to the clothing of human flesh that Christ wore during
his earthly ministry, has its roots in the same Gospel tradition that Langland
drew upon for his treatment of Hawkyn, the wedding guest who wears
dirty clothing to the feast, in Passus 13 of the B text of *Piers Plowman*.[111]
For her account of the nature of the Trinity, she is similarly bolstered by
scriptural allusions as well as by the authoritative texts of the Christian
tradition.

And yet, despite her reliance upon scriptural and exegetical authority,
we cannot ignore that Julian chose to add this long section about a Lord
and a Servant, and to blur the lines of distinction between lordship and
servantship, at a time when almost every major figure in England was
discussing lords and servants in radically different terms. In the civil sphere
there was a pervasive effort to sharpen the boundaries between the two as

---

109. For these, see Colledge and Walsh (1978), Revelation 14, notes.

110. For the figure of the Suffering Servant, see Colledge and Walsh (1978), 513–14; for
Paul, see 521; for the representation of Christ as a gardener and the relevance of agricultural
metaphors to the subject of spiritual cultivation, see Johnson (1984), 180–91.

111. See also Cleanness, 11.134–60, in Andrew and Waldron (1978). On clothing as a
sign of physicality, see Colledge and Walsh (1978) 536 n. 249. See also the discussion of
Griselda's clothing, in Chapter 5.

a way of buttressing the notion of dominion and thereby of preserving the ideal of a hierarchically ordered society. For example, the Cambridge Parliament of 1388, which strongly reaffirmed the earlier Statute of Laborers, employed language that suggests how nervously its members contemplated the unrest in the social body. Not only were "Artificers, Laborers, Servants, and Victualers" perceived as greedy and implicitly dangerous, but their potential for traveling from place to place in the realm seemed particularly worrisome. So, along with fixing wages, Parliament reiterated legislation that applied to a different era and sought to fix the laborers of the 1380s within specific geographic places. Lacking a letter of testimonial, any servant found out of his region, was suspect.[112] That geographic waywardness was frowned upon during the late Middle Ages is clear from texts like *The Book of Margery Kempe* where Margery's very presence in cities like Bristol brings official censure. However, during the 1380s, the mobility of servants who cried out against the institution of serfdom and who acted violently against their masters gave special point to official legislation.

Furthermore, as Wyclif's experience proved, any attempt to address issues of *spiritual* dominion and to privilege the humility of service might too easily be translated into accusations that this was an attempt to abolish social degree.[113] Wyclif's Latin treatises on civil dominion and on pastoral office emphasized the need for worthiness in figures of authority and consequently the need for reciprocity of service. For Wyclif, a lord only deserved his office if he saw himself as a servant. Wyclif distinguished between civil and ecclesiastical dominion and did not disallow the principle of hierarchical ordering. Nonetheless, by affirming the idea of reciprocal dominion, he implicitly blurred the boundaries between lordship and servantship.[114] As Johann Loserth has pointed out, the origin of *De Civili Dominio* is most clearly connected with events surrounding the Good Parliament; after 1376 Wyclif began to defend those ideas by which the Good Parliament governed and to criticize the church's involvement with temporal rule. The real issue, of course, was that of church property. Accepting as patron and protector John of Gaunt, who favored increased clerical taxation, Wyclif, who was

---

112. The attempt to stabilize a laboring population that, since the plague, had become increasingly mobile in its search for higher wages was fraught with denials and contradictions. See A. H. Thomas (1929), lxiv, for remarks about the perceived dangers of laborers. On the legislation of the Cambridge parliament, see the analysis by Aers (1988a), 26–35. See also Aston (1984), 312; Clopper (1992); *Statutes of the Realm* (1963), 2:56; Strohm (1992), 62.

113. See Aston (1984), 283. See also my discussion in Chapter 5 of Wyclif and the relationship between dominion and grace he articulated.

114. See Wyclif (1966), introduction, xxiii; 1, chap. 11; Wyclif (1863), 40.

a popular London preacher, continued to promulgate his ideas about dominion even after Gaunt had revoked the resolutions of the Good Parliament.[115]

Whether or not Wyclif's views were misunderstood as promoting social rebelliousness, Julian's "example" of a Lord and a Servant seems a studied act in the context of the social and ecclesiastical rhetoric of the 1380s. Its grounding in the language of Scripture and the ideas of the Fathers notwithstanding, the example speaks with more than a single voice. Julian achieves this texture by at once emphasizing the difference between the appearances of the Lord and his Servant and the entirely loving relationship between them. She describes the Lord as sitting and the Servant as standing before him. Where the Lord wears richly draped blue robes, the Servant "was clad symply, as a laborer whych was dysposyd to traveyle ... hys clothyng was a whyt kyrtyll, syngell, olde and alle defautyd, dyed with swete of his body, streyte syttyng to hym and shorte, as it were an handfull beneth the knee, bare, semyng as it shuld sone be worne vppe, redy to be raggyd and rent" (LT 527–28). Although Julian later allegorizes this clothing as the flesh Christ put on with the Incarnation, her description of it also defines the distance between social degrees in a world where lords dressed and behaved very differently from servants. Julian next recounts her initial reaction to this scene as violating decorem: "This is now an vnsemely clothyng for þe seruant that is so heyly lovyd to stond in before so wurschypfull a lord." With her next sentence, Julian reveals just how inadequate such a response is, since it reflects the manners of a society where clothing defines the man, "And inward in hym was shewed a ground of loue, whych loue he had to the lorde, that was evyn lyke to þe loue that þe lord had to hym."

Her account of the Servant and his clothing is arresting, in part, because she uses it to recall those very distinctions among persons that characterize communal ordering. For late medieval society, clothing was one pronounced sign of social degree. Chaucer, of course, spends much of the General Prologue to the *Canterbury Tales* describing the pilgrims' clothing. In the Clerk's Tale he uses Griselda's clothing as a sign of both social and spiritual status and in a way that points up the conflicts between the tale's levels of meaning. Moreover, in the Prologue to the Canon's Yeoman's Tale, he dramatizes a process of identification that depends upon the narrator's ability to "read" another's clothing:

> Al light for somer rood this worthy man,
> And in myn herte wondren I bigan
> What that he was til that I understood
> How that his cloke was sowed to his hood,
> For which, whan I hadde longe avysed me,
> I demed hym som chanoun for to be.

What Chaucer stages here in slow-motion is an intellective process by which the narrator is able to deduce something from the evidence his senses have collected. His abilities, however, depend on more than raw intelligence; they depend upon the degree of his own socialization. He can read because he is also a member of a highly stratified society.

Similarly, Julian uses the Servant's outward appearance to recount her own species of spiritual deduction:

> for it semyd by his outwarde clothyng as he had ben a contynuant laborer and an hard traveler of long tyme. And by the inward syght that I had both in the lorde and in the servant, it semyd that he was a newyd, that is to sey new begynnyng for to traveyle, whych servannt was nevyr sent out before. (LT 529)

Julian here offers two ways of reading the Servant's clothing, both of which gesture toward contemporary social anxiety. First, she amplifies the phrase "contynuant laborer" with "hard traveler." The pun on travel/travail does, as Colledge and Walsh point out in their note to this passage, function as a complicated scriptural allusion. However, the reference to a longtime laborer *and* traveler is an interesting choice in light of the late fourteenth-century concern with the dangerous and forbidden mobility of laborers. She then goes on to describe this servant as seeming to begin something for the first time. Her phrasing of the questions prompted by the Servant's appearance would have triggered further speculations by a late medieval reader. Is he then a longtime laborer who moves from place to place, taking on new jobs in each locale? What could not be countenanced by actual medieval agricultural workers—who were suspected of being the most radical group—can of course be accepted theologically, for the "work" of God's redemption of humankind is at once continual in human history and newly worked out in the Incarnation. However, Julian's use of details of clothing, her pun on travel, and her references both to longtime and newly appointed workers send more than simple scriptural messages, especially at a time when the contemporary terminology for social ranks was becoming increasingly more precise and complex.[116]

Julian's handling of this scene illustrates her thoroughly orthodox theological sensibility *and* her arresting creativity. As she continues to explore the meanings of the details in this picture, she provides a profoundly moving account of the divine nature in the regard the Lord has for his Servant (Adam or Christ or all people), a love fully returned by the Servant. However, the tenderness with which she depicts the laborer is far removed from the bestial face of Labor we find in so many contemporary descriptions. She at once heightens the sense of the Servant's toil and ennobles it: "And then I vnderstode that he shuld do the grettest labour and the hardest traveyle that is. He shuld be a gardener, deluyng and dykyng and swetyng and turnyng the erth vp and down, and seke the depnesse and water the plantes in tyme" (LT 530–31). Her language here is poised between the exegetical treatments of Christ as gardener found in treatments of the *Noli me tangere* scene of John 20 and the realities of manual labor as they must have been present to her contemporaries. Although her purpose is genuinely theological, it also has social implications. She composed the example during the years when Froissart placed in John Ball's mouth a sermon rejecting the concept of a social balance between lords and serfs: "For what reason do they hold us in bondage? Are we not all descended from the same parents Adam and Eve? And what can they show or what reason can they give why they should be more masters than ourselves?"[117] More insiduously than any actual or imagined rebel, Julian erases the oppositional boundaries between master and servants, using the social language of the 1380s to express a view of divinity that seeks no horrific dismemberment for its wayward servants.

Julian by no means attempts to level social degrees. She, however, employs language that was particularly meaningful during a time of anxiety about social stability. Since the language of class was used to describe social tension throughout the last twenty years of the century in works like the *Canterbury Tales,* the *Vox Clamantis,* and *Piers Plowman,* Julian's use of

---

116. See Poos (1991), 21. On the social and religious relevance of the image of the laborer, see Clopper (1992) and Kirk (1988).

117. Cited in Hilton (1985a), 138. For further discussion of the writing ascribed to John Ball, see R. F. Green (1992).

it should not be seen as a radical departure or as a revolutionary social statement. On the other hand, the example should be seen as more than her own version of a New Testament parable—or perhaps it *is* her version of a parable, in the sense that Julian, like Langland, saw the ways in which the Gospel writers presented Jesus against the background of a society whose values were misplaced. As David Aers has said earlier, "Time and again the Gospels show his life and words as an unacceptable challenge to dominant institutions and traditions." Moreover, Julian's example would have been disturbing for her contemporaries in ways it cannot be for late twentieth-century readers for whom any overt references to social degree are embarassing and class therefore rarely acknowledged as a strictly defined category. In the Servant, Julian describes a person drawn from the margins of her own society—an itinerant worker? an agricultural laborer, whose clothes are ragged and sweat-stained?—and performs an act of exegesis upon that body that leads us to understand the nature of Christ by means of that picture. Where her contemporaries assigned brutish and barely sensate qualities to those who occupied its margins, Julian finds Adam's face, our face, the face of God's love. Nor does she seek to excise the impulse to sin that was associated with our bodily margins; there, too, she finds what unites us with God.

For Julian sin is the reality dividing Servant from Lord; therefore she must begin to understand something of the nature and purpose of sin in the divine scheme of things. Although there is nothing unorthodox about her approach to sin, her willingness to see it as lamentable rather than contemptible distinguishes her from most of her contemporaries. Depictions of sin tended to emphasize its deformity and to liken sin to a hidden and putrid disease that will respond only to penitential purgation.[118] In addition to emphasizing the deleterious effects of sin on the individual, medieval treatments of sin stressed its effect on the community, providing portraits of the seven vices like those in *Piers Plowman* that are designed to reflect the ways in which vice destroys the fundamental unity of the social body. Medieval discussions of sin also focused on the realities of divine wrath and punishment as reminders of the justice that awaited the obdurate and impenitent sinner. The emphasis upon sin is common to both orthodox and heterodox writers and preachers. For example, the

---

118. See, for example, Brandeis (1900), 72; Holmstedt (1933), 72; Patterson (1991), 377; Wenzel (1989), 45–46. For a discussion of Julian's theology of sin, see D. N. Baker (1994), chap. 3.

Athanasian Creed, a portion of which looms large in *Piers Plowman*, focuses upon judgment in ways that the Nicene Creed does not. Thus, Piers's
Pardon reads, "Qui bona egerunt ibunt in vitam eternam; / Qui vero mala
in ignem eternum."[119] One fourteenth-century manuscript containing a
translation of the psalter as well as Wyclif's commentary on the Athanasian
Creed presents the creed as functioning as a similar sort of guarantee of
salvation. The scribe has echoed the opening of the creed and written that
if every man kept it "hool," he would have eternal life. Wyclif's own
commentary provides little comfort for the individual anxious about the
state of his or her soul; he only serves to emphasize the patriarchal character of the creed itself.[120] Caught between a recognition of human frailty as
it was meticulously analyzed and codified and the demands of heavenly
justice, the medieval Christian must have found a good deal of solace both
in the sacrament of penance and in the possibility of doing enough good
works to merit prayers after death from the community of the living. In
the weekly commemoration of benefactors, in the annual "general mind"
in which the name and memory of "good doers" was called out, in funeral
practices, and in other activities, the parish created a text that perpetuated
the concept of the Christian community held together by its consciousness
of sin.[121]

Julian's emphasis is different. She freely acknowledges the ugliness of sin,
but discovers it in the face of the devil, who for a while thrusts his face
into hers (see Revelation 16). In fact, she contrasts the stench and deformity
of this face to the inherent beauty of her own soul:

> And then oure good lorde opynnyd my gostely eye and shewde me
> my soule in þe myddys of my harte. I saw þe soule so large as it
> were an endlesse warde, and also as it were a blessyd kyngdom;
> and by the condiciions þat I saw there in I vnderstode þat it is a
> wurschypfulle cytte, in myddes of that cytte (sitts) oure lorde Jhesu,
> very god and very man, a feyer person, and of large stature, hyghest
> bysschoppe, most solempne kynge, wurschypfullest lorde. (LT
> 639–40)

---

119. Langland (1979), IX, 288–89. My thanks to H. Angsar Kelly for answering my questions about the Athanasian Creed, which was recited everyday at Prime in the Sarum Rite.

120. British Museum MS Add. 10,046, f.125r. Compare the emphasis in Chaucer's *Parson's
Tale* and in Erbe (1905).

121. See Burgess (1988); Rosenthal (1972), 10. I am also drawing upon my notes of a
paper given by Clive Burgess on the parishes in late medieval Bristol that he gave in October
of 1992 at the Institute for Historical Research at the University of London.

This beatific description of her soul is an extension of the example of the Lord and the Servant. There, she emphasizes, not the penalties attending the Servant's fall, nor his deformity, but his essential nobility and abiding love for his master. If we think of the Servant as related in one way to Adam as she instructs, her emphasis is upon the Servant's pain in falling, his inability to help himself, and his sorrow in not being able to look upon his Lord.[122] Nor does she discuss the Lord as a figure of wrath or justice. Instead, she depicts the face of that Lord as filled with mercy, pity, sorrow, and love for his poor servant. Julian's human faces may be sad or lost, but they are neither diseased nor ugly. This is especially striking in the context of her times. Civil authorities prescribed policies of containment for the body politic. Parliament consistently reaffirmed earlier statutes and, what is more, did so using phrases like "made in the time of King Edward" or "statutes made before this time." The phrases suggest ways in which the past was used to validate measures confining, punishing, and limiting what had become dangerously mobile. If the civil authorities constricted the unruly body, ecclesiastical authorities purged it or pruned it, encouraging a self-scrutiny that can seem at times like self-hatred.[123] For ugliness, Julian substitutes beauty, for willfulness, helplessness, for disobedience, error, and for bestiality, nobility. Finally, for the wrath of the father, she offers the loving embrace of the mother.

If Revelation 14 concerns prayer and has two conditions, as Julian remarks in chapter 41, the example of the Lord and the Servant must be intended to explore the first of those conditions, "ryghtfulle prayer." Julian expands on this by having God say to her "I am grounde of thy besekyng" (LT 461). She ends the example of the Lord and the Servant by underlining the unity she now perceives between the persons of the Trinity and between the divine and human natures:

> Now is the spouse, goddys son, in pees with his lovyd wyfe, whych is the feyer maydyn of endlesse joy. Now syttyth the son, very god and very man, in his cytte in rest and in pees, whych his fader hath dyʒte to hym of endlesse purpose, and the fader in the son, and the holy gost in the fader and in þe son. (LT 545)

She begins the next chapter of this revelation with the sentence, "And thus I saw that god enjoyeth that he is our fader, and god enjoyeth that he is

---

122. See Colledge and Walsh (1978), 515ff.
123. See Patterson (1991), 378–79.

our moder, and god enjoyeth that he is our very spouse, and our soule his lovyd wyfe" (LT 546). As David Aers has also pointed out, her use of "thus" links the two sections by indicating that her exposition of the maternity of God is an extension of that of the Lord and the Servant. God our Lord, Christ our Servant have become our mother, our spouse. Julian thereby begins her magnificent description of God's maternity, which must correspond to the second of the two conditions of prayer, "seker trust" (LT 461).

As Caroline Walker Bynum has demonstrated, Julian's use of maternal language as a key aspect of her trinitarian theology is based upon the conventions of monastic devotion. In this sense, there is nothing heterodox about Julian's description of God as our mother, since there were other writers who drew upon such language as a means of exploring the concepts of divine mercy and spiritual nurture. Nor is there any indication that women authors were more likely to employ the terms of maternity. On the contrary, women authors tended to focus more on the figure of Jesus the Bridegroom or to empathize with the life of the Virgin Mary. Male writers, notably Saint Bernard of Clairvaux, were primarily responsible for elucidating images of a nurturing, maternal God.[124] In her discussion of divine maternity, Bynum links this phenomenon to the increasing feminization of language occuring from the twelfth century, a process that she insists needs to be contextualized and seen in relation to the immediate concerns of each writer. Bynum's contribution to our understanding of the relationship between gender and medieval spirituality emphasizes both the persistent use of gender categories to justify intellectual positions or dilemmas and the continual reconstruction of those categories over time. Julian's careful employment of the language of divine maternity in the Long Text of the *Showings* should be seen as one more example of the ways in which spiritual writers exploit conventional stances and modes in terms that are meaningful to their particular periods of time. Thus, while it is crucial to recognize the orthodoxy of her approach, it is equally important, as David Aers has emphasized in his study of gender, to understand the ways in which Julian's picture of God our Mother is integral to a design in the Long Text by which she sought to reformulate the current language of authority.

The changes Julian made in the Short Text of the *Showings* indicate her sensitivity to the implications of invoking gender. As I have already noted,

---

124. See Bynum (1982), chap. 4. See also Bradley (1991), 136, for remarks about Julian's tendency to avoid what were the conventional images of the female mystic.

she removed all references to her own gender. She thereby substantially altered her self-presentation in the Long Text. Rather than the female visionary who serves as a medium for revelation and who is then transcribed or given form by another, she represents herself as both text and exegete. As the author of her own story she assumes an active role. Furthermore, in Chapter 10 of the Short Text, describing her fearful apprehension of Christ's human sufferings during the Passion, Julian makes a passing reference to her own mother: "My modere that stode emangys othere and behelde me lyftyd vppe hir hande before m(y) face to lokke mynn eyenn, for sche wenyd I had bene dede or els I hadde dyede; and this encresyd mekille my sorowe, for nouȝt withstandynge alle my paynes, I wolde nouȝt hafe beenn lettyd for loove that I hadde in hym" (ST 234). The description focuses attention upon the seer herself and upon her imitative response to the Passion. Julian's mother stands with others regarding Julian's "dying" as the Virgin stood similarly surrounded while her Son gave himself for the world's sins. However, since Julian identifies herself as a woman visionary early in the Short Text, the reference also feminizes the scene by heightening the incipient emotionalism of the Short Text.

In the much-expanded Long Text version of this passage, Julian excises the explicit references to gender and, instead of focusing upon her own role as sufferer and daughter, analyzes Christ's pain and her reactions to it. By discussing the human aspects of Christ's suffering, she touches on a subject intimately bound up with that of gender. Since Christ took his human nature from his mother, his capacity to experience pain is but one of the gifts Mary passed on with her flesh. As so many documents of late medieval spirituality proclaim, we can begin to merge with Christ by seeking those experiences that unite us to him. Eve's reviled and feeble flesh is thereby transformed to Mary's triumphant weakness; the very femininity scorned becomes glorified in the Incarnation. Correspondingly, the emotionalism and carnality identified as female can be seen as avenues to a devotional intensity that supersedes the powers of reason. As some writers point out, Christ first revealed his risen self to the women who loved him, especially to Mary Magdalene.[125] Julian's exploration of Christ's pain serves as synec-

---

125. Jesus' women followers were especially important to some Wycliffite preachers and commentators. For example, Oxford Bodleian MS Bodley 243, which contains two of the Wycliffite *Glossed Gospels*, Luke and John, discusses the Resurrection scene recorded in John 20 as exemplifying the stronger love of these women. The authors of the Wycliffite sermon cycle edited by Hudson and Gradon (1988–90) were extremely sensitive to the use of gender as an indicator of spiritual devotion; see 1:430; 2:174, 280–81; 3:199. On Mary Magdalene, see Johnson (1984), 148–61.

doche for our own frail and carnal apprehension of sacrifice. However, as David Aers has argued, Julian uses her apprehension of pain as the gateway to a heightened understanding of joy. She ends by emphasizing not weakness and suffering but strength and triumphant love. Her revision of this scene depends upon the language and categories of gender without being constricted by references that would fix its range of meanings in any sort of hegemonic strategies.

More important, Julian's decision to remove references to literal femininity from the Long Text allows her to develop a trinitarian theology that incorporates the feminine into what is more often described as a masculine zone of power. She therefore defines the concept of motherhood as transcending any actual relationship: "Thys feyer louely worde: Moder, it is so swete and so kynde in it selfe that it may not verely be seyde of none ne to none but of hym and to hym that is very mother of lyfe and of alle" (LT 598). Throughout her discussion of divine maternity, she describes motherhood not simply in the conventional terms of nurture, but in the language of power. Maternity is the source of wisdom, knowledge, and mercy; it is the ground of our being; it is our origin and our end; it is our teacher; it is an active agent in the working out of providential design.[126] Where so many medieval accounts of the feminine emphasize weakness, Julian describes, not simply feminity, but maternity, and describes it in terms of strength. In fact, Julian seems not interested in femininity, only in maternity; hence, less in gender than in the office attached to gender. Her account of maternity, which is as arresting as her use of the contemporary language of labor to describe Christ, should be seen as strategic. Since authority implies relation, any refiguration of divine authority necessarily involves a reformulation of the entire system of power relations. By assigning such properties to divine authority, which she has previously depicted as a Lord who has a Servant, she inevitably provides a perspective upon sin that gives it the bewildered face of the human Servant/Child.

Julian thereby offers a solution to the problem of intentionality that preoccupied many of her contemporaries. If I can take the liberty to counterpose Julian's grieving Child to Chaucer's Pardoner or to Langland's Hawkyn, we can begin to understand why her presentation of God's motherly face seems so radical within the context of late fourteenth-century treatments of authority.[127] Through the Pardoner, Chaucer presents the

---

126. See Colledge and Walsh (1978), 593, 598.

127. On the sin of despair and the terrible self-consciousness and unexpiated guilt Chaucer dramatizes through the Pardoner, see Patterson (1991), 380–421, whose discussion of these issues informs my own.

human consciousness as the awful site where knowledge of sin and expectation of judgment intersect, as the comfortless landscape of despair. Langland's efforts to explore the human apprehension of guilt likewise hint at the tolls of self-awareness. In place of the despair we can detect beneathe the surface of the Pardoner's "leve moder let me in," or Hawkyn's seemingly insurmountable problems with cleansing, Julian counters, "Synne is behouely, but alle shalle be wele, and alle shalle be wele, and alle maner of thynge shalle be wele" (LT 405). This sentence from Revelation 13 anticipates the example of the Lord and the Servant and the explication of divine maternity, which are found in Revelation 14. In both her description of sin as necessary and her assurance that all shall be well, she anticipates her picture of a sorrowing but helpless servant, whose fall is mourned lovingly by his lord. In the gentle and soothing language that Julian uses throughout both texts of the *Showings* she adumbrates a picture of the divine that is finally revealed when she begins to describe the properties of God our Mother in the fourteenth revelation of the Long Text. I do not mean to suggest that Julian does not encourage the reader to search the conscience or to take sin seriously, but by likening the sinner to the child, she locates sin within a larger cycle of spiritual growth.

Julian's sleight of hand is masterly; in place of the feeble frail female visionary whose mother watches her spiritual agony she substitutes the anonymous voice of the human child soothed by God its Mother. (The tenderness of this relationship is somewhat heightened in the Paris manuscript, which consistently uses the pronoun "she" for the soul, suggesting an inherent likeness between the soul and God.[128]) The shift encapsulates her overarching concern with unity. Recently medieval scholars have begun to modify the thesis of Philippe Ariès that the lines between adulthood and childhood were blurred throughout the Middle Ages and to argue that childhood was indeed seen as a separate stage of life.[129] As the lyric copied into John of Grimestone's preaching book suggests, children were regarded with a good deal of affection then as now:

Children ben litel, brith and schene,
and eþe for to fillen,

---

128. For Aers' discussion of *anima*, see Chapter 3.

129. See Ariès (1962), chap. 2, "The Discovery of Childhood." For more recent work that counters the thesis that the Middle Ages had not yet "discovered" childhood, see Hanawalt (1986a), chap. 11, "Childhood"; Patterson (1991), 363–64; Patterson (1989), 133, 160–75. For late medieval texts suggesting the types of distinctions drawn between childhood and

Suetliche pley3ende, fre of 3ifte,
and eþe for to stillen.[130]

In praising innocence the speaker suggests his own footing in the land of experience and implictly accepts the responsibility of helping to tutor the child in the arts of adult living. In need of satisfaction and comfort, the child also needs nurture and guidance in order to grow. Precisely this emphasis upon growth marks Julian's handling of the metaphor of childhood throughout the *Showings*. Not only are adults accepting of the mistakes of childhood, but they regard childish errors as necessary stages in the acquisition of knowledge.

Fundamental to the focus upon spiritual growth in the *Showings* is Julian's depiction of two types of mother-child relationships. The first reflects the habit of referring to the Church as Mother, hence as the nurturer of the fledgling soul. In this sense, the mother is also a figure of punishment.[131] References to Holy Church as mother, teacher, and guide seem to predominate in the Short Text, which contains no explication of divine maternity. In this version, Julian presents herself as submitting to the guidance of Holy Church, which she tends to identify with God. Nonetheless, her corresponding identification of the consciousness of sin with the teachings of Holy Church and of merciful recognition with Jesus anticipates the hints in the Long Text that God's maternal regard far supersedes that of his church.[132] Only when she begins to expound a trinitarian theology that incorporates male and female attributes into a single figure of loving authority does Julian offer a picture of a second type of mother-child relationship. Within the terms of this second type of bond, consciousness of sin is less pressing a concern than consciousness of love. Love is so important to Julian's thought because she describes it as that force whereby the soul is kept whole and united ("onyd") with God. Since the soul is the manifestation of the divine nature in us, by coming to know ourselves, we come to know God:

---

adulthood, see Furnivall (1868), particularly *The Babees Book* (c. 1475); *The Young Children's Book.*

130. Wilson (1973), 50. The lyric, which is also in Latin, occurs on f. 38v.

131. See, for example, Wenzel (1989), 81. The author of the *Chastising of God's Children*, in Colledge and Bazire (1957), 98–114, characterizes the mother as a figure of love and punishment. The emphasis in both works on correction is dramatically different from Julian's.

132. For characterization of the church in the Short Text, see, for example, Colledge and Walsh (1978), 243, 244, 252, 258, 267, 275.

A hye vnderstandyng it is inwardly to se and to know that god, whych is oure maker, dwellyth in oure soule, and a hygher vnderstandyng it is and more, inwardly to se and to know oure soule that is made dwellyth in god in substance, of whych substance by god we be that we be. (LT 562)

Julian does more here than describe the soul's union with the divine. By affirming the soul's substantial identity with God as a species of higher knowledge, she suggests that spiritual growth is growth toward a recognition of oneness or likeness. Our relationship with God our Mother is therefore related to but different from our relationship with earthly parent figures. The human child grows toward a recognition of oneness in sin; the innocence of childhood is a condition of its temporality, a condition we leave behind us as we are initiated into knowingness and self-consciousness.[133] On the other hand, the *spiritual* child, the *anima*, grows toward a recognition of the love that unites it to its mother. The distinction is crucial within the context of Julian's thought: by refusing to use the language of opposition, she locates her exposition of trinitarian theology in a realm where similarity is the basis for her rhetoric.[134]

Almost any passage in the *Showings* yields rich evidence of Julian's refusal to oppose systems to one another. If she at times distinguishes between modes of knowing, she does not admit any fundamental division. Hence, in Revelation 16, she presents an astonishing *credo* of transcendant unity:

Oure feyth is a lyght, kyndly comyng of oure endlesse day that is oure fader, god, in whych lyght oure moder, Cryst, and oure good lorde the holy gost ledyth vs in this passyng lyfe. This lyght is mesuryd dyscretly, nedfully stondy(ng) to vs in the nyght. The lyghte is cause of oure lyfe, the nyght is cause of oure payne and alle oure woo, in whych woe we deserve endlesse mede and thanke of god, for we with mercy and grace wylfully know and beleue oure lyghte goyng therin wysly and myghtely. And at þe end of woe, sodeynly

---

133. Patterson (1989) has written evocatively on Chaucer's use of childhood as a reminder of a lost innocence that may be available in moments of poetic or spiritual recognition.

134. Heimmel (1982), 94, has also made the point that Julian refuses simple terms of opposition. There are a number of fine studies of Julian as a theologian. See D. N. Baker (1994); Jantzen (1987); Leech (1988); Nuth (1991); Palliser (1992); Pelphrey (1982); Pezzini (1990).

oure eye shalle be opynyd, and in clernes of syght oure lyght shalle
be fulle, whych lyght is god, oure maker, fadyr, and holy gost in
Crist Jhesu oure savyour.

Thus I sawe and vnderstode that oure feyth is oure lyght in oure
nyght, whych lyght is god, oure endlesse day. (LT 723–25)[135]

All critics of the *Showings* find themselves transformed into abject readers
by the brilliance of the prose, so it is probably self-indulgent of me to quote
this passage at length. And yet, where is it possible to break it? Like so
much of Julian's best writing, the sentences form one seamless web held
together by her masterly use of *is*, which she uses to establish the inherent
unity between God and the soul, between darkness and light, and between
privation and plenty. The final sentence records her own response to this
series of Johannine statements, "I saw and vnderstode." Yet she does not
oppose seeing to understanding, but joins what are two distinct modes of
knowing in one proclammation.

Julian's refusal to use the language of excision or of opposition is central
to her purpose as both a writer and a thinker; she ends her text by ringing
changes on the sentence, "loue was his menyng." Neither the terms employed by contemporary devotional writers, by preachers, nor by social
critics seem adequate to the task of explaining the relationship between
humankind and God. In the Long Text, Julian goes well beyond contemporary usage, employing terms that were conventionally treated as opposed
pairs, but, at the same time, refusing to emphasize the distance between
head and heart, authority and experience, gloss and text, masters and servants, male and female, father and mother. Her prose, like her thought,
insists on a reformulation of our terms of conversation. Rather than establish terms that seek to contain—and inevitably delimit—the objects they
signify, Julian creates a system wherein identities flow almost imperceptibly
into one another. In so doing she provides an arresting and creative response
to her contemporaries, who too often defined chaos and sin as a fluidity
that threatened to overtake those controls established by all forms of authority. If we seek to isolate and contain what we fear in ourselves, Julian
collapses both fear and authority into love.

---

135. Watson (1992b), 87, has also remarked on Julian's "almost deliberately flexible" use
of terminology.

CHAPTER FIVE

Chaucer and the Postures of Sanctity

LYNN STALEY

The relevance of the *Canterbury Tales* to the social and political world of the late fourteenth century has never been questioned. However, the terms by which both Chaucer and his world have been described and the questions those terms have been used to formulate have inevitably reflected current critical and social concerns. In recent years there has been a renewed interest in the degree of Chaucer's political and social involvement with an age whose tensions are increasingly the focus of inquiry. Our sense of Chaucer, the author, has begun to accommodate a similar acceptance of fissure.

Rather than the Chaucer whose works are implicitly assimilated to the novel, with its harmonies of structure, theme, and character, we tend more often to recognize in Chaucer's poetry, and particularly in the *Canterbury Tales,* evidence of incompletion, fragmentation, and of process.[1] The issue of deliberate irresolution is crucial: through the tales Chaucer continues to debate and explore his own relationship as a poet to the social body and to its most visible embodiments of authority and order. The struggle Langland's work reveals between a Pentecostal utopian vision and the sight of actual institutions compromised by a mercantilist ethic and a punitive conception of justice may well have set the terms for Chaucer's lifelong exploration of the components of community.[2] However Chaucer's aesthetic, as well as his social and political position, and hence his implied audience, were different from Langland's. Chaucer lived and worked in the world of the exigent; his poetry reflects his keen sense of political realities and consequently of the needs for compromise, for ambiguity, and for deflection. These may be strategies of self-protection, but they are also the tools of art. Where Langland presented stark pictures of what Aers has called "the collective rejection of justice," Chaucer offered tales that obliquely dramatize his increasingly dark analysis of the mechanisms by which society might be reformed. If we can find very few explicit references to contemporary events in Chaucer, we can nonetheless find the issues that fueled contemporary conflicts refigured in the fiction of the tales. Chaucer frequently domesticates and privatizes social and political conflict; though such ironic metamorphoses appear to contain the dangers posed by social or theological insurrection, they force a listener or a reader to recognize

---

1. Charles Owen has argued that Chaucer's poem might more happily be called the Book of the Tales of Canterbury and what we have a working draft that was carefully assembled and pieced together by early fifteenth-century scribes and scribal workshops, who imposed their own sense of form upon the fragments. See Owen (1982); Pearsall (1992). For the classic statement supporting the order articulated through the Ellesmere manuscript, see L. D. Benson (1981).

Along with a renewed interest in historicism (and a renewed sense of how historical inquiry might work), I should also notice a school of Chaucerian studies that increasingly (and wrongly, to my mind) categorizes historical scholarship as imperialistic, and thus as hostile to feminist or psychoanalytic criticism. It would be naive to think that the "politics of the holy" did not also govern the trends in literary criticism. For a response to such antihistoricist tendencies, see Aers (1995).

2. See Cooper (1987); Mann (1973), 208–12. In a paper given at the New Chaucer Society in 1992, Anne Middleton also suggested ways in which Chaucer positioned himself in relation to Langland.

the unmentionable and thus add another level of sound to the murmur of the pilgrims.[3]

Chaucer, however, was far more than a passive transmitter of cultural and social ideas and symbols. Though oblique, he was a shrewd social and political analyst, one capable of asking genuinely provocative questions about the figuring of authority and its problematic relationship to political power. From the late 1370s through 1390s, or between the last years of the reign of Edward III and those of Richard II, English institutions were under seige rhetorically (and sometimes actually) and consequently their "guardians" felt the need to legitimate the very bases of their assumption of authority. This process of definition can also be described as a conversation in which the terms of sanctity were the object of negotiation. In their efforts to jockey for political leverage, the king, the church, and Parliament each sought to appropriate the language of devotion. Chaucer was of course privy to this conversation and refracted it in the writing that engaged him throughout this same period. He, however, did so, not by a poetics of replication, but by using the codes of his own world as a means of exploring those destructive impulses that underlie social and civil institutions. In three of the *Canterbury Tales*—the Second Nun's Tale, Chaucer's own Tale of Melibee and the Clerk's Tale—he approached this subject in remarkably similar ways but with dramatically different emphases and results. Each of these tales describes a section of Chaucer's long meditation upon the conversation about authority that went on during the last quarter of the fourteenth century. Taken together, the tales trace a progression in Chaucer's political thought and suggest that, like Langland, Chaucer found his imagination stymied by an endemic mercantilism that threatened finally to meld all degrees of social distinction into a disorderly, self-interested, and finally unworkable unit.

All three tales are translations of "authoritative" texts that employ exemplary women—Cecilia, Prudence, and Griselda—to embody a moral meaning. It is through such traditionally innocuous forms and modes that Chaucer tends to speak with the greatest freedom. Convention—whether

---

3. For discussions of Chaucer's literary strategies of deflection, see Ganim (1990); Patterson (1991), esp. 280–83; Pearsall (1992), 109, 122–23; Strohm (1989), 159ff. In contrast to my own emphasis in this chapter upon Chaucer's growing preoccupation with fissures in the social body, Strohm (1979), argues for a view of the *Canterbury Tales* as presenting a "mixed commonwealth of styles" and of voices and impulses, ultimately as describing a coherence that includes difference.

literary or cultural—offers a disguise, particularly if a writer wishes to examine the nature of authority from within the confines of a hierarchical society. Taking on the role of a translator of a saint's legend, of a Boethian fiction, or of an allegory of spiritual testing appears an inoffensive enough occupation; similarly, with the fictions of gender. Throughout his career, Chaucer used gender relations as a way of analyzing the dynamics of a highly structured and power-oriented society in which women were deprived of any actual political power.[4] Chaucer could as safely and as deviously identify with a woman as he could with the role of translator; in neither guise did he appear to apportion power to himself. Nor did he overtly challenge existing institutions and forms if he lodged moral authority in a Cecilia, a Prudence, or a Griselda, whose class puts her at even a farther remove from power. But through his recasting of traditional materials, Chaucer explored a political situation of increasing complexity and decreasing possibility. Although both the Second Nun's Tale and the Melibee point up the political implications that underlie all individual acts and thus establish their fictions in the ambiguities of the actual, neither tale obviates remedies for the problems it explores. Both tales are rooted in speech as a mode of persuasion. Both Cecilia and Prudence seek to convert through a discourse that refigures the concept of power by insisting that it be linked with authority. Cecilia does not convince Almachius, but, as Chaucer knew, it was the church's ability to win kings to its side that set the course for subsequent history. And, for many during the last decades of the fourteenth century, if reform were to come, it could come only through kings whose assumption of ethical leadership would relieve the church of its involvement with the world and revitalize the institutions of the state.[5] On the other hand, Griselda, with the exception of one startlingly knowledgeable speech, does not challenge Walter; her effectiveness, such as it is, lies in her evenhanded and finally undervalued rulership (which is delegated to her by Walter) and in her silence. Whatever possibilities may be latent in his earlier attempts to imagine community are strikingly absent in a tale I would describe as one of Chaucer's most radical statements of political despair. For all its devotional emphasis, the Clerk's Tale is rooted in the grim realm of realpolitik, where factions are held tenuously together by the need for power and prosperity and where the sanctified is finally only a commodity like any other.

---

4. For studies of literary uses of gender as explorations of medieval social codes, see Aers (1980), chaps. 5, 6; Crane (1994); Strohm (1992), "Treason in the Household."

5. See Wilks (1972) and McGrade (1991).

The medieval language of political power was a system of codes rich in metaphor, heavily nuanced, frequently indirect that was designed to construct the image of a world held together in harmonious hierarchy.[6] However, power, like any commodity, can never be stable, and the period from the late 1370s to the early 1390s marks shifts in the understanding of the balances of political power that inform the ways in which Chaucer phrases his exploration of power and authority. Though the subject of Richard II's authority was certainly the focus for a good deal of political action during the 1380s, culminating in the attempt of the Wonderful Parliament of 1386 to curb the king's power and the punitive acts of the Merciless Parliament in 1388, regality too narrowly defines what was a broadly conceived topic. The preoccupation with the nature of social or political authority can also be seen during the 1370s and particularly in the events surrounding the Good Parliament in 1376. Furthermore, the period was a crucial one for Chaucer himself. During the 1370s he traveled twice to Italy and several times to France on diplomatic business, campaigned in France with the troops of John of Gaunt, was appointed to a customs post in the port of London, and received annuities both from John of Gaunt and from the king. He was thus in a position and of an age to begin to think about the various components of authority as they affect power relations.

It is also the decade in which the Commons began to find its voice and to describe itself as having a collective mission. The step from consciousness to a consideration of the relationship between representation and consent and between agency and authority can be a short one. The history of parliamentary development is long, and parlimentary consciousness hardly appeared full-grown in a single decade. But as parliamentary historians point out, it was during the reign of Edward III that a house of commons definitely emerged. Moreover, Commons began—rhetorically, at least—to identify itself with the "community of the realm," and hence to describe itself as a body acting for the good of the commonwealth. (Though the members of Commons acted for the "commonwealth" only by their very narrowly conceived definition of it, which is to say they acted for the good of themselves and their class whom they represented, it is the rhetoric of representation and its reverberations throughout Chaucer's work that interests me.)[7] During the reigns of Edward I and Edward II, Parliament

---

6. The work that has been done on the relationship between language and political myth is large. My work here is indebted to the following studies: P. Brown (1992); Bloch (1975), introduction; Geertz (1973).

7. For remarks pertaining to Chaucer's experience of parliament, see Prestwich (1983); Richardson and Sayles (1981), chap. 24, "The Commons and Medieval Politics."

had functioned as a representative body in the granting of taxes, in bringing petitions before the Crown, and in assenting to legislation. In the deposition of Edward II, Parliament had added its voice to those of the prelates, the magnates, and the lesser nobility. As Michael Prestwich notes, the official announcement of Edward's abdication employed an intentionally comprehensive formula and joined the entire social hierarchy in a single phrase, "common council and assent of prelates, earls, barons, and other nobles, and all the community of the realm."[8] It thereby brought into prominence those who represented that community.

The representative situation that Chaucer would have known, who was himself a member from Kent during the Wonderful Parliament of 1386, reflected Edward III's needs as a warrior-king. Since Edward continually needed money to fund his war with France, Commons served as an important mediating body, negotiating between the king's fiscal needs and the grievances of persons in the shires.[9] However, the terms of this relationship shifted slightly during the years of Edward's reign. As G. L. Harriss notes, after the Black Death, which drastically winnowed the labor supply and thus altered the balance of power between landlord and tenant, the allegiance of members of Commons inclined even more toward their social and political betters, the parliamentary block representing the interests of the nobility. Rather than seeking to protect the poor in their shires from predatory taxation, they began to support forms of taxation that would "tap the new found prosperity of the lower classes."[10] The relationship between shires' representatives and shires was further complicated by the dynamics of the process of selection.[11] Knights of the shire were chosen by shire communities, which assembled in county courts. These assemblies were dominated by local magnates and their bailiffs, but village reeves and villagers also were present and fundamental to the business of election. Fiscal needs played their part in the beginning of the representative process;

---

8. Prestwich (1983) 13.

9. G. L. Harriss (1976), 42; Prestwich (1983), 15.

10. Harriss (1976), 55. For a study of labor and attempts to regulate the labor supply (as well as prices) to counteract the effects of inflation, see Putnam (1908). Putnam argues that the orignal rationale for the Statute of Laborers was neither unintelligent nor malign but was an attempt to check an ill-understood economic crisis. The Black Death not only hastened the breakdown of the old system but accelerated economic and social changes throughout the community (217–23). For an application of the ways in which the laboring classes profited from the more vigorous economy of the late fourteenth century, see Hilton (1985a); Patterson (1991), 246–58.

11. For an analysis of the following, see Prestwich (1983).

local communities were frequently less concerned with the issue of representation than with the economics of sending a knight to parliament. At the same time, the magnates ceased to see the manipulation of Commons as a valuable parliamentary technique, further anchoring the interests of members from Commons to their shires and thus to the economic business of representation. By the later years of Edward III, Commons in some areas, like the local administration of justice or the vexing issue of purveyance, described itself as acting on behalf of the "community"; on questions involving labor, it more explicitly aligned itself with elite interests, thus with the magnates, the gentry, and the smaller landlords. Furthermore the shires' increasing assertion of self-governance helped to develop the process by which its representatives brought petitions from the Commons to the king, inevitably suggesting ways in which the strictly local was tied to the greater interests of the realm.[12]

The complicated dynamics of representation and consent naturally informed the shifting language of political ritual.[13] For example, the deposition of Edward II dramatically affected the relationship among political interest groups, changes that, in turn were written into revisions of the *ordo* for the coronation of a monarch.[14] The *ordo* for the coronation of Richard II was based upon the 1308 text, which proclaimed the king's divine and hereditary rights, but the alterations in that text suggest a newly defined sense of the balance of powers. Though the sources for the 1377 revision make no explicit mention of election, in certain manuscripts of the ordo of 1308 a clause had been inserted directing that after the sermon, a question should be put to the people. The 1377 revision went even further and directed the archbishop to inquire from the four corners of the "theatre" whether the people would give their *voluntas* and *consensus*. During these questions, the king was supposed to stand and look in all four directions until the people acclaimed him. At Richard's coronation, this process came after his pledge, thereby underlining the relationship between inheritance, regal responsibility, and popular obedience. Implicit in the staging of this moment was the notion of a bilateral covenant that rested on the agency of both parties, king and people; however, it remained a notion, or a hint, the very ambiguity of which could be interpreted in accordance

---

12. See Maddicott (1981), 72.

13. For a study of political ritual as a language, see Koziol (1993), especially the introduction and chap. 9.

14. Schramm (1937). See also the important essay by H. G. Richardson (1960). For the ceremony, see Legg (1901), chap. 13, "Liber Regalis."

with partisan politics. Similarly, the questions that were put to the king were intended to suggest his relationship to the law, but the succeeding phrase, "which the people shall choose" underlined Parliament's power. The king's party in 1377 was unhappy about his taking an oath that bound him to administer future legislation by the people ("Concedis vistas leges et consuetudines esse tenendas et promittis per te eas esse protegendas et ad honorem Dei corroborandas quos vulgus elegeret, secundum vires tuas?").[15]

Their unease with this final and newly written question to which the king must accede not only identifies political ritual as a form of public theater, but defines ritual in terms of ambiguity and conflict, as a text whose exegesis was directly related to power relations. In the texts of royal pageantry from the reign of Richard II to that of Elizabeth I, we can read an ongoing debate about such relations, a debate frequently authored by the very "people" whose tribute to their sovereign the pageant supposedly represented.[16] Thus significant moments during Richard's reign were marked by pageantry that commented upon that event as affecting or manifesting the king's power: his coronation in 1377, the coming of Anne of Bohemia to England in 1382, and the restoration of London's liberties in 1392.[17] As the coronation *ordo* illustrates, dramas staged in the "theater" of the realm are designed not as static ceremonies, but work out or dramatize tensions inherent in all hierarchical relationships. They thus attempt to define community as process, as the product of what is a ceaseless tug-of-war about the distribution of power.

Commons was an important component of this process. During the late 1370s and the 1380s, Commons grew even more self-conscious about its role, as the manuscript history of the early fourteenth-century treatise, "Modus Tenendi Parliamentum" suggests. The "Modus," which is the earliest systematic discussion of Parliament, was studied and edited by M. V. Clarke and assigned to the reign of Edward II, probably in or about 1321.[18] In it the importance of the Commons is underscored because, unlike the

---

15. For a fuller account of these events, see Schramm (1937), 170–72, 207, 212. The quotation is on 172. R. H. Jones (1968) suggests that Richard's later years can be read as an attempt to recast the terms of his coronation ritual.

16. See, for example, Bergeron (1971); Johnson (1990), 14–18, 144–56; Kipling (1985), 83–103; Wickham (1959), 1:62–71; Withington (1918), 1, chap. 3. I also thank Gordon Kipling for his generous reply to my questions.

17. For descriptions of these, see Wickham (1959). The most interesting of these, the 1392 pageant, was based upon the two preceding, but with changes that capture something of the political tension of 1392. For discussion of this 1392 pageant, see below, this chapter.

18. Clarke (1936); Taylor (1968).

magnates, members of Commons are "representative": in them is vested the power of the community of the realm. Written to glorify Parliament, the "Modus" defines that body in terms of its two functions: representation and consent.[19] That a treatise circumscribing regal power with parliamentary responsibility should have been written during the unhappy reign of Edward II makes sense. But, as both Clarke and John Taylor point out, interest in the treatise really began with the accession of Richard II to the throne. In manuscripts it is associated with documents containing the coronation of Richard II, and from the late fourteenth century on, it became the standard description of Parliament. By the fifteenth century, the "Modus" was used as a parliamentary handbook and was frequently transcribed with the Statutes of the Realm.[20] It is also during this period, particularly after the Good Parliament of 1376 and its banal aftermath in the Parliament of 1377, that Commons became acutely aware of the responsibilities (and perhaps dangers) it incurred by taking itself seriously as a representative body and not simply as a consenting one. In Chaucerian terms, a species of mythmaking was under way: Commons was in the process of creating a voice that could articulate its own version of political truth by co-opting the notion of communal sancity.

As T. F. Tout noted, the dates 1376 and 1388 encapsulate the two most striking parliamentary victories before the Lancastrians.[21] Both victories were short-lived. John of Gaunt regained control of Parliament in the name of the Crown in 1377, and Richard bided his time before asserting his own regal power after the damage inflicted on him by the appellants in the Merciless Parliament. But in the events surrounding such historic moments there are more important lessons, particularly for a writer of Chaucer's habits and social position, than simple victory. What was under discussion was the complicated subject of authority, not simply regal authority and power, but representative authority. Though in the Good Parliament, the Commons represented itself as moving against privilege in order to winnow the inner circle around the senile Edward III, Commons did not seek to bring down the government or to attack the principle of hierarchical ordering that underpinned it. Instead, it self-consciously described itself as seeking to restore good government to the realm. And, in fact the brief success of the Good Parliament rested on parliamentary tradition going back to

---

19. See Clarke (1936), 244, 246–47.
20. Clarke (1936), 348, 365; Taylor (1968).
21. Tout (1970), 299.

the beginning of Edward's reign as well as on the disatisfactions that were a feature of that reign during its final decade when Edward removed himself from the business of governing.[22]

Throughout the 1370s those dissatisfactions were focused by the broad issue of authority as it manifested itself in taxation. The anticlericalism of the period took on a added edge after 1375 when the Crown sanctioned Gaunt's need for papal support for his own Iberian aspirations and reversed what had been national policy, allowing the pope to tax the English church without getting much in return. Since during the early 1370s, Commons had called for the removal of clerical ministers and had even suggested that church property be nationalized, Edward's change of mind, which coincided with both an economic downturn and significant losses to the French, was very unpopular.[23] Moreover, Edward was no longer the shrewd ruler whose consciousness of his own image and whose political skills had forged alliances that worked to his benefit.[24] Instead, he had retreated from public life and had dispersed his own power among members of his inner circle, whose self-interestedness was the true focus of parliamentary concern. If the "king" needed money to fund an unprofitable war, then those who were to consent to raising already oppressive taxes wanted to know who would spend the money. Though the indictments of royal ministers that issued from the Good Parliament were reversed by the Parliament of 1377, which was to some extent controlled by John of Gaunt, the lessons of that Parliament could not be so easily erased. Commons had asserted itself and begun to forge an identity as the conscience of the realm. It had rhetorically aligned itself with the principle of good government. It had established an important precedent for the indicting and trying of royal ministers and had slowly, through debate, worked out the procedures for doing so. It had, both metaphorically and actually, found its voice.[25]

It spoke with the voice of the upright man. For the first time in its history, Commons employed a speaker to mediate between itself and the king.[26] That speaker was the steward of the earl of March, Sir Peter de la Mare, whose reputation for wisdom and eloquence earned him the respect of his

---

22. For a study of Edward III, see Waugh (1991). For the Good Parliament, see Holmes (1975).

23. Heath (1988), 142–43; Waugh (1991), 221–22.

24. On Edward's consciousness of his own image, see Ormrod (1990b), 45.

25. See G. L. Harriss (1981), 60; Waugh (1991), 226.

26. Roskell (1968), 2:1–14. For accounts of de la Mare as speaker, see Galbraith (1927), 82–90; Holmes (1975), 101–5; Ormrod (1990b), 35–37; Waugh (1991), 201, 224.

contemporaries, "miles sapiens et facundus nomine Petrus de Lamare, in cujus ore sententia omnium dependebat."[27] Not only was Peter de la Mare praised in the Latin of the chronicles, but popular songs were composed in his honor. When, after having been imprisoned for his prominent part in the Good Parliament, he was released in 1377, early in the reign of Richard II, Thomas Walsingham reports that the people hailed him with the sentence used to welcome Christ into the Mass, "Benedictus, qui venit in nomine Domini!"[28] Although the *Chronicon Angliae* (or the so-called Scandelous Chronicle) is heavily biased against John of Gaunt, at whose instance Peter de la Mare was arrested by October 1376 and imprisoned in Nottingham Castle, the incident should not be discounted. Whatever its factual basis, the description of de la Mare's welcome by the citizens of London—which deliberately echoed regal acclamations—hints at the ways in which the language of religious and political ritual could be used to comment upon and redefine a situation. Since in the last parliament of Edward III's reign and in the first of his own reign the bishop of Saint David's, a friend of Gaunt's, had compared the young Richard II to the Christ child, going on to urge the king's subjects to bring liberal subsidies for the defense of the realm, the popular acclamation for the mature and politically astute Peter de la Mare may have been intended to send a complicated message about what constitutes moral authority.[29]

Peter de la Mare was not the only figure to emerge from Commons as a sort of representative man. Again from Walsingham comes the account of Sir Thomas Hoo's dream, the only medieval shire knight for whom there is a documented attitude about a political issue.[30] What Walsingham describes is a classic "literary" dream vision, whose very artfulness underlines the flimsiness of the borders among politics, art, and history. The dream supposedly took place in the early days of the Good Parliament, when the Commons was debating the king's need for better counsel. Hoo fell asleep pondering means by which the abuses that seemed rife in the kingdom

---

27. This description is John Malvern's, the continuator of Higden's *Polychronicon;* see Higden (1994), 8:426. See also Walsingham (1863), 1:321.

28. Thompson (1874), 150–51. For Walsingham's account of the Good Parliament, see 68–108. See Tout (1970), 305, for a discussion of de la Mare's popular support.

29. As David Aers has pointed out to me, Adam of Usk reports that the same sacral acclamation was used to criticize Henry IV in 1401, suggesting how well the chroniclers understand the language of devotion that was available for political exploitation. See Thompson (1876), 65, 189.

30. My phrasing here is drawn from Goodman (1968), 139. For Walsingham's account of Hoo's dream, see Thompson (1874), 70–72. See also Holmes (1975), 136.

might be eradicated. In his dream he found himself in the chapter house of Westminster Abbey, where Commons usually met. On the ground he saw seven gold florins. When he could not find their owner, one of the monks explained that the seven gold coins represented the seven gifts that the Holy Spirit had given to the knights "for the utility and reformation of the state of the kingdom."[31] Upon awakening, Hoo told the other members of Commons about his vision. Hoo was a well-respected and well-connected knight, a minor landowner, a former soldier, whose piety is marked by his closeness to the Westminster monks. However, these also constitute political affiliations, as Walsingham's rough treatment of John of Gaunt illustrates. Moreover, Hoo's dream—or the written account of it—contains those crucial elements of the dream vision that denote an allegorical form in which the message encoded in the dream is intimately related to the moral identity of the dreamer. Hoo has a dream in which he finds windfall gold and acts out his own selflessness by not profiting from those seven gold florins left lying on the pavement. After his unsuccessful search for the owner of actual gold, the most prominent of the monks in the choir of Westminster, who performs the function of the guide or teacher, tells him he has found metaphoric gold. Hoo is thereby distinguished from the inner circle around the king, who do appropriate what they find; and the monks are distinguished for their ongoing observance of the *opus Dei*, the work they do even as Hoo and his colleagues labor in the chapter house for the good of the king and the realm. The dream—which is a kind of political fiction and perhaps a collaborative one at that—thus binds Westminster and Commons together as bodies of special wisdom and counsel. Implicitly, Commons is presented as the medium through which sapience—interpreted by the church—is proffered to the king.

What is being imaged here, as in the several contemporary descriptions of Peter de la Mare, is the moral authority of the knight of the shire, who is presented as the spokesman for the community. For example, in 1377, Peter de la Mare had spoken out against those who deceived and penalized the poor.[32] In so doing, he rhetorically aligned himself with the shire, whose interests he represented. Figures like de la Mare or Hoo—whatever the intricacies of their actual factional allegiances—were used by the chroniclers as embodiments of the values of the community of the realm. The

---

31. Translated in Holmes (1975), 136.
32. See *Rot. Parl.* (1783), 3:100. For a wonderful analysis of the complex series of class tensions that contributed to the Rising of 1381, see Searle and Burghart (1972); on 387 they refer to this incident.

fact that they detach themselves from the Latin chronicles in which they are embedded and seem to step forward with personalities that even now can engage us demonstrates ways in which the monks who wrote the histories trafficked in sacred images. Such cameo portraits almost demand a John of Gaunt against whom the holy might be defined. With his breeding, his unparalleled wealth and power, his reputation for arrogance and temper, John of Gaunt could be used to symbolize what ought not to control government, nor overinfluence the prince.[33] For too many, Gaunt represented a privilege of class, wealth, and power that took no care of the "people"; the savagery of the riots that broke out against him both in 1377 and in 1381 amply demonstrate his alienation from the popular mood.

Notwithstanding Gaunt's ability to roll back the parliamentary indictments of 1376 within three months of their passage and restore to power the victims of the Good Parliament, including Alice Perrers, the profiteering mistress of Edward III, Commons had arrived at a significant moment of self-definition. In the very act of self-definition, Commons moved increasingly into the field of historic consciousness. For one thing, as G. L. Harriss notes, it is in the thirty years following the Good Parliament, that the activities of Commons are better recorded and more widely chronicled than at any time before the age of Elizabeth I, another significant moment in the history of the House of Commons. The corrective role that it had chosen for itself guaranteed its continued importance as a mediator between the king and the people and as the "natural counsellor" to the king.[34] In the first Parliament of Richard II's reign, Commons continued to focus upon the concept of privilege by reminding the young king of the importance of merchants and of "persones de diverses estatz" to the state of the realm, urging him to broaden the scope of those to whom he turned for counsel.[35] Commons continued the attack on privilege by returning to Alice Perrers, earlier reinstated by John of Gaunt, but after Edward's death without supporters at court. This time she was tried and indicted in earnest. Commons also picked up its earlier complaints over the perennially vexing issue of maintenance and the threat to public justice posed by the private armies of the rich, over papal jurisdiction, and over the equity of tax levies. If the record of Richard's first parliament can initially seem status- and profit-

---

33. See Armitage-Smith (1905); Given-Wilson (1986), 146–54, 159–60; Goodman (1986); Goodman (1992), esp. chap. 15; Walker (1990).

34. Harriss (1981), 60; Waugh (1991), 228. For a differently focused assessment, see Ormrod (1990b), 169–70.

35. *Rot. Parl.* (1783), 3:5. See also Searle and Burghart (1972), 379.

driven, submerged in a text about money and merchandizing is a text about a country for which the old tripartite hierarchical model of community makes hardly any sense. The record reads like an apologia for Commons as the proper body of counsel, since only Commons recognizes and understands the composition of Richard's nation.[36]

Perhaps in the merry chaos of another political dream vision, the *Parliament of Fowles,* Chaucer ironically echoed social faction by translating it into the language of the many, the mother tongue: "Have don, and lat us wende!" or "Kek kek! kokkow! quek quek!" or "Al this nys not worth a flye!"[37] For Walsingham's elegant narrative of Sir Thomas Hoo's dream of representative responsibility or Langland's fable of the rats convened in the name of "common profit," Chaucer substitutes the "representative" multivocal clamor of the Commons against the privileges of nobility.[38] Between his judicious exploitation of the conventions of French court poetry, his already well-developed sense of irony, and the self-interested shouts of the birds, who can tell at which target he aims? Chaucer's *Parliament of Fowles* (PF) is usually dated between 1377–78 and 1380–81. Both dates are connected to marriage negotiations for Richard: the first to the unsuccessful attempt to betroth Richard to the daughter of Charles V of France and the second to the beginning of negotiations leading to the marriage of Richard and Anne of Bohemia.

As Larry D. Benson has pointed out, Chaucer gives a good deal of weight to the political aspects of Cicero's *Dream of Scipio,* which he uses as a proem to his bird parliament. With its overt emphasis upon the notion of the common profit, the *Dream of Scipio* explicitly defines the individual in relation to public duty:

> "Know thyself first immortal,
> And loke ay besyly thow werche and wysse
> To commune profit, and thow shalt not mysse
> To comen swiftly to that place deere
> That ful of blysse is and of soules cleere."
>
> (PF 73–77)

---

36. For the entire text, see *Rot. Parl.* (1783), 3:5–31.

37. For both an account of previous attempts to date the poem and the best contextualization of the *Parliament of Fowles,* see Larry D. Benson (1982). McCall and Rudisall (1959), 279, have also suggested a link between the two parliaments.

38. On the language of Langland's rats and contemporary political writing, see J. A. W. Bennett (1957), 33.

Scipio here tells the narrator that self-consciousness prompts labor and, in turn, that labor for the "commune profit" is the means of entry to the place where the self can experience true bliss and clarity. But Scipio's certainty—in a movement mirrored in the first fragment of the Canterbury book, which likewise moves abruptly from an expression of classical and non-Christian political ideals to the confusion of contemporary political activity and tension—obtains only momentarily and is refracted into the two succeeding sections of the *Parliament of Fowles*.[39] In his account of the garden of Nature, which includes the Temple of Venus, and in the wonderful picture of the bird parliament that concludes the poem, Chaucer refuses to circumscribe experience in precisely the way Scipio suggests. Instead, he uses the occasion of the poem—the prospect of a royal wedding—to explore or simply to present the broader and ultimately unresolvable tensions inherent in social groupings. By placing in a single canvas the feckless, book-bound narrator, the imperious Scipio the Elder, the abundant garden of primordial nature, Venus disheveled lying with her porter, Richesse, and the tenuous order of Nature's gathering of birds, Chaucer disallows any simple or reductive definition of social order or of the individual's relation to it. What Scipio says may well be true, but the goddess Venus and her servant who is also her bedmate remain in the same frame as the noble Scipio. Not only does Venus blur the lines of social distinction, she complicates those of moral distinction. Scipio directs the narrator to a *locus amoenas* where desire is fulfilled by responsibility; Venus embodies the site of desire itself:

> Hyre gilte heres with a golden thred
> Ibounden were, untressed as she lay,
> And naked from the brest unto the hed
> Men myghte hire sen; and, sothly for to say,
> The remenaunt was wel kevered to my pay,
> Ryght with a subtyl coverchef of Valence—
> Ther was no thikkere cloth of no defense.
> (PF 267–73)

Chaucer here describes Venus as a text every bit as potent and as mysterious as that of Cicero's *Dream of Scipio*, a work Macrobius had enclosed securely within his gloss. From the waist up, she is uncovered so that "men

---

39. I am indebted here to Pearsall's fine discussion of the poem (1992), 122–27. For a discussion of the poem's presentation of unresolved tensions, see Aers (1981).

myghte hire sen." But the "remenaunt" is subtly veiled.[40] The primary
meaning of "remenaunt" was that remaining portion, frequently in reference to a story, a text, or a document. In both her aspects, Venus demands
a beholder, a voyeur, or an exegete; and if the narrator of the *Parliament
of Fowles* is inept at the task, the brilliantly visual experience he recounts
is a text as elusively available to its viewers as the Venus who occludes our
sight. If Venus and Scipio may at first seem to inhabit separate spheres, the
third section of the poem works against binary or reductive interpretations.
Nature reminds the birds (and presumably the reader) that they are assembled there because she pricks them with "pleasaunce," that instinct Chaucer
has just a few lines earlier personified in the group around the disruptive
Cupid:

> Tho was I war of Plesaunce anon-ryght,
> And of Aray, and Lust, and Curteysie,
> And of the Craft that can and hath the myght
> To don by force a wyght to don folye—
> Disttigurat was she, I nyl nat lye;
> And by hymself, under an ok, I gesse,
> Saw I Delyt, that stod with Gentilesse.
>
> (PF 218–24)

Similarly the ritualized action of the bird parliament does not so much
"contain" the chaos of instinctual desire as figure the explosive and ambiguous needs that at once threaten attempts at community and underlie them.
Scipio locates authority in the self's recognition of its ties to community;
the *Parliament of Fowles* throws open to question the very process by which
the self distinguishes between private and public needs.

The preoccupation with the nature and components of civil authority
was likewise central to discussions of the church, which was deeply impli-
cated in the brokering of secular power. Whether or not clerical corruption
actually increased during the decade, anticlerical sentiment gained a measure of legitimation. England was not alone in questioning the basis for the
church's authority, but in John Wyclif, who was not yet classified as heretical in the 1370s, it had a thinker and, above all, a writer who brought

---

40. Spearing (1993), 216–17, provides a trenchant reading of this passage. See Dinshaw
(1989), esp. chap. 5, "Griselda Translated," for an exploration of the relationship between
gender and reading.

together a previously disparate group of reformist views.[41] Throughout most of the 1370s Wyclif focused his polemics upon the church's secular authority and temporal wealth. He probably wrote his *De Civili Dominio* during the mid-1370s. The work challenged the whole notion of authority by following Richard Fitzralph in linking dominion to *spiritual* authority, specifying that no one in a state of mortal sin can hold dominion.[42] Fitzralph had defined lordship in relation to the *imitatio Christi*, thereby drawing a distinction between lordship and possessionship. Since for Fitzralph only God had authority, any earthly lordship is contingent and temporary, founded only in grace. Fitzralph's treatise was, of course, prompted by the controversy over the mendicant orders, but his ideas of lordship and authority had unsettling implications for a church where secular power and property had become inseparable from spiritual power. Wyclif's reformulation of some of Fitzralph's ideas in *De Civili Dominio,* which occupies the third, fourth, and fifth places in the series of twelve books that make up his *Summa in Theologia,* had its own political edge. In defining sanctity against contemporary practice and by explicitly questioning those very categories that were used to define social order, Wyclif furthered the conversation about the nature of authority that preoccupied Commons during those same years.[43] Though a few years later, in *De Officio Regis,* Wyclif confined his attack on property and secular power to the church, the implications of *De Civili Dominio* are more broadly social. He aimed at the church in describing secular authority as one of the necessary but evil effects of the Fall, but the consequences of the argument cannot be so narrowly constricted.

Wyclif's views on church property made him potentially useful to the Crown, and John of Gaunt pressed him into service in 1377, by asking him to write a reply to the query of Richard II's Great Council about papal revenues.[44] That his disapproval of the wealth of the "court of Rome" and

---

41. See Coleman (1981b), 213ff.; Hudson (1978), introduction; McFarlane (1953), 89ff.; McKisack (1959), 290; Peck (1986); B. Robertson (1968), 133–35.

42. For Fitzralph, see Poole (1890); Scase (1989), chap. 3.

43. In his introduction to the fourth volume of the *De Civili Dominio,* Johann Loserth suggests that the treatise is closely connected "with the agitation of men's minds brought about by the proceedings of the Good Parliament" (v). For another discussion of Wyclif's ideas about authority in relation to the Good Parliament, see Holmes (1975), 170–74. Michael Wilks has recently suggested that we ought to turn to Wyclif's biblical commentaries, written during this same period, for the most radical expressions of his reformist views. See Wilks (1994), esp. 50–52.

44. For the text of Wyclif's reply, see Myers (1969), 656–57.

the practice of simony made him unpopular with the papacy is hardly surprising. But it was only after the Great Schism in 1378, which set aside the principle of church unity, that Wyclif began to attack the very idea of papal primacy.[45] The schism dramatized many of the tensions inherent in the church's almost inextricable involvement with the world of secular authority. Though the worldliness and mercantilism of the Avignon Curia were well known,[46] before the schism, the popes had attempted to work in the interests of peace between England and France. However, in Rome, in April 1378, Bartolomeo Prignano, archbishop of Acerenza and Bari, became Pope Urban VI. In August of that same year, a faction of the cardinals had declared that election void and elected Clement VII, thereby creating two popes, one at Rome and the other at Avignon.[47] The schism not only made a mockery of the principle of church unity, it pointed up the degree to which the church had bound itself to the fortunes of secular powers. Since England supported Urban VI while France and her allies supported Clement VII, each pope now had a vested interest in a particular country. The Anglo-French struggle seemed to perpetuate the schism, and the schism seemed to ensure a continuation of a war that was increasingly draining for both sides.[48]

These fundamental absurdities became even more obvious when one pope designated as a "crusade" a military venture against forces loyal to the other pope. In England, in the late spring and summer of 1383, the ignominious crusade of Henry Despenser, bishop of Norwich, against French forces in Flanders underlined the ways in which spiritual and secular powers might work against success in either arena.[49] The Commons was

---

45. For Wyclif's reaction to the Schism, see both the introduction and the texts gathered in *John Wyclif's Polemical Works* (Buddensieg 1883). Throughout these works, Wyclif places emphasis upon the ideal of the unity of the church. See also McFarlane (1953), 89; Matthew (1880), xv–xviii. Of the sermons, see particularly, "Of the Leaven of Pharisees" and "De Papa."

46. See, for example, the address to the king from Commons in 1376 in Myers (1969), 655–56) asking for the expulsion of papal tax-collectors and for the revival of the statutes of provisors and *praemunire*.

47. For contemporary English accounts of the events, see Knighton (1965), 128; Leslie Macfarlane (1953); Stow (1977), 49; Walsingham (1965), 1:380–87.

48. I am not suggesting the single effect of the schism on the outcome of the peace negotiations, but rather that the church's moral position was severely compromised by "diplomatic" exigencies. See Keen (1973), 212–13, 257; McKisack (1959), 146, 405; Palmer (1972), 14. For the English decision to support Urban VI, see *The Statutes of the Realm* (1963), 2:11.

49. For an account of Despenser's Crusade, see Gaylord (1960); McKisack (1959), 429–33; Perroy (1933), 166–209. See also Keen (1973), 275; D. W. Robertson (1968), 154; Palmer (1972), 10, 47; Tuck (1985), 181–83. In 1379, Urban VI had already launched a "crusade" against Clement VII.

not in a mood to subsidize a major expedition against the French in Flanders.[50] Bishop Despenser was therefore allocated just enough money to recruit a force on which the pope conferred the status of a crusade: anyone fighting for a year, or anyone who would devote sums or pay to the bishop sufficient wages to keep a warrior fighting for a year was granted an indulgence usually allowed to those who set off for the war in the Holy Land. Such a crusade could be financed by the alms of those who purchased plenary remission; the money and jewelry that poured in suggests the shrewd marketing strategy of the bishop and his supporters.[51] Not only was the crusade a military failure, but it was a moral failure. Wyclif's reaction to the financing of the expedition was pronounced: in his view, the church had thereby put itself in the position of authorizing the killing of fellow Christians and had done so by trading a spiritual commodity for a financial gain.[52]

Manuscripts of Wyclif's works are notoriously rare, owing to the scrupulous care with which English censors sought to edit the historical record. Furthermore, Wyclif's Latin works can seem laboriously written; he wrote not for the monk but for the professor and the theologian. However, Wyclif's influence cannot be directly correlated either with the number of manuscripts we have of his works or the relative aridity of his Latin prose. He broadcast his ideas through the streets of London, spreading them through the city's churches. Oral influence cannot be quantified, but the evidence for Wyclif's popularity as a preacher—along with the contemporary association between Wyclif and the "populist" doctrines promulgated by the itinerant preachers of the English Rising—suggests that the Parliament Rolls recount only the most acceptable version of the story.[53] What was a conversation about the nature of both spiritual and secular authority and about the uses of representation and consent among knights of the

---

50. On the financial burdens the war imposed on Englishmen and their corresponding unwillingness to endure greater taxation to support further ventures, see Palmer (1972), 8–11.

51. For contemporary accounts, see Knighton (1965), 198–201; Walsingham (1965), 2:71, 76; Hector and Harvey (1982), 34–35. Knighton (198) describes the hidden treasure of the realm as in the hands of its women. See also Gower's critique in the Prologue to the *Confessio Amantis;* Peck (1978), 15–18.

52. For Wyclif's reaction, see "Of the Leaven of Pharisees," "Of Prelates," and "The Office of Curates," in Matthew (1880). On page 491, Matthew quotes from Wyclif's *Exposition of Matthew 24* in reference to the pope's liberal indulgences on behalf of the Flanders campaign. See also "De Fundatione Sectorum," "De Dissensione Paparum," and "Cruciata" in Buddensieg (1883). See also D. W. Robertson (1968), 154.

53. Aston (1984), 1–47. See also Armitage-Smith (1905), chap. 8; Hudson (1988), chap. 2, 9; Wilks (1972), 124; Wyclif (1966), ix, x.

shire and burgesses took a noisier form when it was transferred to the city
and translated into the city's language.

In the legend of Saint Cecilia—which belongs roughly to the same early
period though it was later recast into the Second Nun's Tale—Chaucer
focuses upon spiritual authority and its problematic relation to secular
power. The causal relationship between faith or self-knowledge and works
that Chaucer articulates through Scipio is also central to his prologue to
the legend of Saint Cecilia. But though Chaucer ostensibly uses the narrator
of the saint's legend—as he had used Scipio—to express an initial simplicity
and clarity, a far more diffuse dialectic governs the prologue to the legend
of Saint Cecilia, as well as its relation to the legend itself.[54] The three
parts of the prologue adumbrate a progression from idleness to prayer to
purposeful activity, a motion consonant with the trinitarian operations of
the divine upon the human soul. Thus the narrator implies that his act of
translation serves both as a remedy for the heaviness that afflicts him and
as proof of spiritual change, a species of successful alchemy in sharp contrast to the illusory alchemical processes the Canon's Yeoman discloses in
the succeeding tale.[55] But, as Chaucer implies through the prologue, far
more is involved in the process of translation than worthy and salvific
labor.[56]

Chaucer's version of the legend is usually dated between 1373 and
1386.[57] It is generally accepted that Chaucer decided to include the legend
in the Canterbury book relatively late in the Canterbury period, probably
in the 1390s, when he was composing the Canon's Yeoman's Prologue and
Tale. It is also accepted that he wished to link the two tales, since in all of

54. For studies of the relationship between prologue and tale that stress the unity between
them, see Clogan (1972); Collette (1976); Kolve (1981); Peck (1967).

55. Russell Peck has argued that the Prologue to the Tale changes the context for the life
of Saint Cecilia by linking the contemporary Christian through the saint with the sanctity of
the Blessed Virgin. See previous citation. For studies linking the two tales, see Grennen (1966);
G. Olson (1982a); Rosenberg (1968).

56. See Copeland (1992), for a discussion of the historical and theoretical framework of
vernacular translation. Copeland argues that in the fourteenth century the act of translation
was grounded in that of invention, or in interpretation and refiguration.

57. In the Prologue to the Legend of Good Women (1386–87), Chaucer, seeking to justify
his literary services to women, lists a legend of Saint Cecile among his works. Most Chaucerians hold that this legend could not have been written before about 1373. Arguing its "immatu-
rity of style and the closeness of its translation," Robinson dated it shortly after 1373, and
Fisher dates it around 1374. However, Ridley argues for a later date, sometime in the middle
period. See Robinson (1957), 755; Fisher (1989), endpaper; Ridley (1987), 942. On the other
hand, Howard (1978) regards the style as "up to a par" (292) with Chaucer's later work.

the manuscripts that contain both tales, the Canon's Yeoman's Prologue begins with the line "Whan ended was the lyf of Seinte Cecile."[58] Chaucer's legend of Saint Cecilia reveals an underlying concern for the status, or moral authority, of the church that cannot be detached from the conflicts of the decade preceding its composition. Both of the most outstanding literary works of this period, the B-text of *Piers Plowman* and Gower's *Vox Clamantis* display some of the strategies with which these writers sought to express their concern for what they saw as the increasing secularization of the church.[59] Chaucer's strategies are neither those of Gower nor Langland, but his legend of Saint Cecilia is equally informed by contemporary perceptions of the moral or spiritual authority of the church.[60] If we place the composition of the legend of Saint Cecilia toward the later period of its probable dating, linking it to works like the *Troilus* and probably the story of Palamon and Arcite that would also become a Canterbury tale, we cannot afford to ignore the likely political relevance of the legend, nor its position in the development of Chaucer's political thinking.[61]

Chaucer's account of Saint Cecilia, at once oblique and pointed, exemplifies his preoccupation with contemporary issues and raises subjects that appear even more problematic when that legend is placed in the Canterbury book. He exploits the key elements of the legend—Cecilia's opposition to paternalism, her reinterpretation of the marriage contract, her spiritual and intellectual leadership, and her confrontation with secular authority—in

---

58. Though it is generally accepted that Chaucer intended to assign the tale of Saint Cecilia to the Second Nun, Blake (1985), 33, 87, notes that the attribution is probably scribal. The Canon's Yeoman's Prologue refers only to the previous tale, not to the teller.

59. For references to the Schism in the B-Text, see Prologue, 136; xv, 171; xvii, 234; for references to the papacy and war, see xix, 407–55; xxi, 428–29. See Myers (1969), 602–6, for remarks about the elaborate apparatus of church courts and officials that had developed by the late fourteenth century. See also Leff (1961). For an extensive study of the theme of reform in the literature succeeding the Peasants' Revolt, see Peck (1986).

60. On this subject, see Giffin (1956), 29–48, and Hirsh (1977), 129–46. Giffin sees the tale as written around 1383 to celebrate Adam Easton's nomination as Cardinal Priest of Santa Cecilia in Trastevere, which was being built on the traditional site of the saint's house. Easton was the East Anglian Proctor of the Black Monks at the Curia and a staunch supporter of Urban VI. Hirsh links the tale to the schism itself, suggesting that the tale's concern with the unity of the church may reflect Chaucer's concern for contemporary disunity.

61. Throughout the 1370s and the early 1380s, Chaucer traveled frequently on government business, much of it connected with negotiations between England and France. He was several times in Italy and was, in fact, in Milan at the time of the announcement of the election of Clement VI. Robertson speculates that he and Sir Edward Berkely may have brought the news of the schism home with them. See Crow and Olson (1966); D. W. Robertson (1968), 142.

ways that emphasize his grasp of Wycliffite debates about the status of the church. Thus, though through the tale, he presents or mediates a set of problems ultimately relevant to the worldly status and hence to the spiritual authority of the church, he does so by "thinking with" Saint Cecilia, whose ancient sanctity provides a screen for his exploration of otherwise charged subjects.[62] Through her he can explore both the simple purity and the nascent compromise of the early church, using her legend to mask a technique whereby statements often work in opposite directions simultaneously.

Just as the legend is designed to challenge a church whose authority was increasingly translated into the terms of secular power, Chaucer's prologue to the life of Cecilia locates the work within a particular range of considerations. The prologue is generally taken as Chaucer's own prologue to a life of Cecilia, which he wrote perhaps before he conceived of a Canterbury book. He thus characterizes the speaker as male ("I, unworthy sone of Eve"; line 62) and focuses upon the labors of the translator as writer, rather than as "pilgrim" or "teller."[63] Some of the phrasing in the prologue suggests that he might have been working on it during the same period in which he was writing *Troilus and Criseyde*. For example, he describes the devil as leading the idle man "right by the lappe," wording that echoes a gesture used frequently in *Troilus* to indicate mastery or control. In addition, in the narrator's invocation to the Virgin in which he asks for her aid, he twice calls out "Now help." Chaucer uses the same wording in his account of Troilus's panicked prayer to Venus before his first night in Criseyde's bed (*Troilus*, III, 715–35). Troilus's comic pleas for help finally cause Pandarus to exclaim, "'Thow wrecched mouses herte,'" after which he brings Troilus into Criseyde's bedchamber "by the lappe."

In addition to phrasing that links it to a period of intense political thought and writing, the prologue more overtly suggests that, even before he made the decision to move it into the Canterbury book, Chaucer saw the entire work as inherently provocative. In particular, his handling of the subject of translation indicates his awareness of current political conversa-

---

62. The term is that of Claude Lévi-Strauss but filtered through P. Brown (1988), 153. See also Brown's discussion of Gregory of Nyssa's portrait of his sister, Macrina, 297ff. Though some scholars still see the tale as classically and simply opposed to the modern murkiness staged in the Canon's Yeoman's Prologue and Tale, increasing attention is being paid to the tale's complexities. See, for example, Hirsh (1990) and Collette (1976).

63. For comments about this phrase, see *The Riverside Chaucer* (1987), explanatory notes, 943 n. 62.

tions. Though in the 1380s the subject of translation was not the dangerous topic it became after Arundel's Constitutions were published in 1409, it was nonetheless associated with the controversial views of Wyclif and his followers and consequently demanded a certain amount of rhetorical care.[64] Chaucer's description of the process of translation is at once utterly conventional and potentially radical. He first asks the Virgin to use him as a medium of transcription for the life of Saint Cecilia ("do me endite"; VIII, 32), employing the verb "do" in a causative sense. At the end of the invocation, he again downplays his own agency in the making of the legend. There, he begs our pardon for not taking the effort to compose the story more subtly ("This ilke storie subtilly to endite"; VIII, 80), since he has translated the work of another, "For bothe have I the wordes and sentence / Of hym that at the seintes reverence / The storie wroot" (VIII, 81–83). Within the fiction of the prologue, the translation represents an answer to the narrator's prayer for the Virgin's pardon for his sluggishness and sinful condition. The activity it exemplifies is a sign of his redemption through grace and thus a labor for which he can take no credit (nor presumably any blame). Though Chaucer's stanzas provide a Christian translation of classical invocations to the gods or Muses, in linking good translation to spiritual illumination ("for that feith is deed withouten werkis, / So for to werken yif me wit and space, / That I be quit fro thennes that most derk is!" VIII, 64–66), they sound a Wycliffite note. In his exposition of Matthew 23 and 24 (whose apocalyptic message Wyclif claimed as his own), Wyclif linked the ability to understand and to communicate the meaning of Scripture to grace. He thereby sought to undermine the priestly monopoly upon scriptural interpretation by making comprehension a gift of grace, a sign of *spiritual* authority unbounded by the hegemonic power of the church.[65] This claim would be extended even farther by the author of the General Prologue to the Wycliffite Bible, which was written in the mid-1390s. In the fifteenth chapter of the General Prologue, the author ends his panegyric for translation of the Scriptures by insisting that the translator must not only study his subject matter, but endeavor to "lyue a clene lif, and be ful deuout in preiers . . . that the Holi Spiryt, autour of wisdom, and kunnyng, and truthe, dresse him in his werk, and suffre him not for to erre."[66] As in Chaucer's prologue to the legend of Saint Cecilia, translation is at once a

64. For a discussion of the politics of translation, see Hanna (1990); Hudson (1982); Hudson (1988), 136–37, 166–68; Hudson (1986); Staley (1994), 129–46.

65. See Wilks (1994), 50–51.

66. *Holy Bible* (1850), general prologue, 1:60.

labor and a sign of the transformative actions of grace upon a sinful man, re-dressed in knowledge and truth.

Chaucer seems to blunt any possible force his semi-Wycliffite account of translation might have by using it to introduce a translation of a saint's life and by aligning himself as translator with marginal and powerless feminin-ity. The energies of the Wycliffite translators were directed at translation of Scripture, and particularly of the Gospels, not at the transmission of secondary "sources."[67] By translating the life of Saint Cecilia into the ver-nacular, Chaucer carefully located himself within the community of ortho-doxy. Like the earlier authors of the Katherine group or like such later figures as Osbern Bokenham and John Capgrave, Chaucer assigned himself a humble and a socially acceptable task that might serve as an insignia of his own status in that community. By going on to identify himself with the Canaanite woman who compared herself to the dogs gathering up crumbs from the master's table (see VIII, 59–61), Chaucer further indicates his lowly and insignificant position. Adopting the guise (or more properly the gender) of the powerless, he prays for illumination by the Virgin in order that he might transcribe the work of another. Though Chaucer appears to contain the effect of his description of translation by disclaiming either his singularity or his power, the issue he has raised and its associations with Lollardly prepare the way for a deeply ambivalent account of Cecilia's life.

The legend itself—despite or because of Chaucer's disclaimers—is a far from simple performance. With its emphasis upon the saint's virginity and devotion, confrontation with authority, her courage, and, finally, her mar-tyrdom and death, the life of Saint Cecilia is a conventional-enough tale of the early church.[68] In English literature, *St. Marherete, St. Juliene, St. Kath-erine,* as well as the works of Bokenham and Capgrave all evince a similar interest in the ideal of female chastity and sanctity. It is their devotion to Christ the Bridegroom that gives these women power to defy figures of familial and secular authority and to become emblems of the sort of radical reversal that transforms weakness into strength. These stories are frequently fantastic, in the sense that the heroines undergo extraordinary tortures at the hands of increasingly frustrated males, whose dominion is undercut by the rhetorical acuity and physical endurance of their female opponents.[69] The tales of Saint Cecilia that Chaucer inherited and used are traditional

---

67. See the preface to *Holy Bible* (1850), xiv–xv.

68. For remarks about the components of female sacred biography, see Heffernan (1988), esp. 188. See also Braswell (1986).

69. On these conventions, see Heffernan (1988), 188, 197, 261, 265.

in this sense, but the story contains more than voyeurism or sadism or simple praise for a virgin martyr.[70]

That the Saint Cecilia legend contains hints of a radical social and spiritual restructuring can be seen in a work like *The Life of Christina of Markyate,* a twelfth-century biography of a contemporary saint, whose determination to lead a cloistered life led her into open conflict with her parents, as well as with local ecclesiastical and secular authorities.[71] Despite her early vow of virginity, Christina's wealthy and influential parents betrothed her to Burhred, a young man of local standing. Her parents grew frustrated with her refusal to consider marriage and one night let Burhred into her bedroom, hoping that he would take her by surprise. Her biographer depicts Christina as a variety of wise virgin, dressed and awake and more than ready for the bridegroom:

> . . . she welcomed the young man as if he had been her brother. And sitting on her bed with him, she strongly encouraged him to live a chaste life, putting forward the saints as examples. She recounted to him in detail the story of St. Cecilia and her husband Valerian, telling him how at their death they were accounted worthy to receive crowns of unsullied chastity from the hands of an angel. Not only this: but both they and many others after them had followed the path of martyrdom and thus, being crowned twice by the Lord, were honoured both in heaven and on earth. "Let us, therefore," she exhorted him, "follow their example, so that we may become their companions in eternal glory. Because if we suffer with them, we shall also reign with them."[72]

Christina goes on to suggest to Burhred a marriage contract like that between Cecilia and Valerian: she will not publicly embarrass him but will go home with him if he will take a vow to live chastely, in anticipation of becoming a religious in a few years' time. She offers him, in the eyes of the world, a sham marriage; she will abet him in deceiving the world. Moreover, she positions herself as the dominant figure in this marriage, since it is her wish for chastity and devotion to Christ that would shape the sort

---

70. For Chaucer's sources for the *Second Nun's Tale,* see Gerould (1941), 664–84; Reames (1978–79; 1980; 1990).

71. See Talbot (1959). Talbot's introduction is particularly helpful. I have discussed this work elsewhere, see Staley (1994), 41–44.

72. Talbot (1959), 51.

of relationship she offers to Burhred. Although Christina never realizes that "new" marriage with Burhred, she and the hermit Roger share a cell for four years, basing their chaste relationship on their mutual love for Christ. The monk of Saint Albans who wrote the life of Christina certainly understood the radical undertones provided by the example of Cecilia. Cecilia offers a complete reversal of accepted social norms: she deceives her parents and others about her marriage; she dominates her husband; she engenders none but spiritual offspring; she belongs to an underground sect outlawed by Roman law.[73] She not only presents a challenge to authority (something she shares with many saints), she offers a new ordering of hierarchies far more threatening than any of the Wife of Bath's solutions to contemporary relationships. The threat Cecilia poses to a hierarchy that is typically gendered as male was likewise recognized by the author of *A Book to a Mother* (c. 1380), who refers to Saint Cecilia, along with Katherine, Lucy, and other maidens who shall arise at the last day and "condempne such bodiliche stronge men þat despisen chastite and Cristes techinge."[74]

Chaucer did not have to know the *Life of Christina of Markyate* to perceive those elements in the legend of Saint Cecilia that made it so potentially powerful a statement. As Sherry Reames has demonstrated, Chaucer drew upon two sources for his own version of the legend.[75] Up to line 344, where Cecilia ends her instruction of Tiburce, Chaucer followed closely the account in the *Golden Legend*. For the remainder of the tale, he drew upon what Reames has provisionally called the Franciscan abridgment, a much briefer Latin version of the legend to be found in a widely used lectionary of Franciscan provenance. As Reames has noted, there were many Latin versions of the legend of Saint Cecilia available to Chaucer, and his decision to translate as a single legend versions found in two separate sources was significant. His choice of the latter source, the Franciscan abridgment, is especially important, since, unlike most versions of the life of Saint Cecilia,

---

73. For remarks about the importance of Cecilia in the Middle Ages, see Kolve (1981). Kolve notes (140–41, 151–52) that Cecilia was linked to the ideals of virginity and martyrdom, going on to discuss her "spiritual fecundity" and the centrality of her marriage to her iconography. For some illuminating remarks about the subversive nature of the Second Nun's Tale, see J. Scattergood (1987).

74. Cited in Colledge and Walsh (1978), 1:205 n. 48. Julian, who says that she heard the story of Cecilia in church, took Cecilia as one of her models, wishing for three wounds in imitation of Cecilia's three neck wounds. See the Short Text, 1:204–6, and discussion in the chapter following.

75. See Reames (1990).

it gives increased emphasis to Cecilia and to her combativeness.[76] Reames's accounts of Chaucer's handling of these two sources suggest much about Chaucer's understanding of the uses of this particular saint's legend; by his acts of translation, Chaucer subtly reshaped the legend in order to highlight Cecilia herself. She dominates Chaucer's account in ways she does not other medieval English lives of Cecilia.[77] Through her Chaucer presents a picture of a church at once starkly simple and Christlike and potentially compromised. It is a picture whose shadows are those of the church as Chaucer experienced it.

The Second Nun's Tale offers a picture of the primitive church as a group joined by love for Christ and belief in the Gospel, shepherded by Urban, to whose sacramental powers Cecilia sends her "children," her husband and her brother-in-law. Chaucer depicts a church that, in fact, serves as a new society, the codes and relationships of which reverse those of pagan society. Chaucer's handling of Cecilia and her marriage signals the radically new nature of this relationship. First, he strengthens what is an already strong portrait of Cecilia in the source he followed for the first half of the tale by omitting the early reference to Cecilia's fears about her wedding night. Where the *Golden Legend* describes her as fasting and praying before her marriage and as commending her fears to God, Chaucer says only, "Every seconde and thridde day she faste, / Ay biddynge in hire orisons ful faste" (VIII, 139–40).[78] As Reames has noted, in the latter part of the tale, Chaucer follows the Franciscan abridgment, which drastically cuts the speeches of both Valerian and Tiburce.[79] While the editing does not deny them their martyrdom, it places Cecilia center-stage as the spokesperson for the Christian faith, since she emerges as the tale's true preacher.

Chaucer's handling of the marriage between Cecilia and Valerian underscores the unconventional nature of their accord. He first sketches in the conventions of courtship and marriage by subtly embellishing the text of the *Golden Legend*. Where his source merely notes that a young man named Valerian was betrothed to her, Chaucer's wording does more than describe an event: "And whan this mayden sholde unto a man / Ywedded be, that was ful yong of age, / Which that ycleped was Valerian" (VIII, 127–29). His use of *sholde,* as well as the passive construction, intimates

---

76. Reames (1990), 347–48. For another discussion of this combativeness, see Beichner (1974).

77. See Bokenham (1988), 203–25; Lovewell (1898).

78. See Gerould (1941), 672.

79. Reames (1990), 339.

the weight of social custom in noble Roman households. A few lines later, in describing her wedding night, Chaucer writes, "The nyght cam, and to bedde moste she gon / With hire housbonde, *as ofte is the manere*" (VIII, 141–42; emphasis added), substituting a reference to custom for one to the "sweet silences of the bedchamber," found in his Latin source.[80]

Such instances point up Chaucer's strategy as a translator, for he exploits those themes that are embedded in the text itself. His translation serves as a particularly intelligent and well-focused interpretation of a text, a reading that offers a picture of the church as composed of individual relationships (based on personal conversions) that replace the conventions of secular society. Thus, the "fruit" of Cecilia's wedding night is the rebirth of her husband as a Christian.[81] In thanking God for Cecilia's busyness in converting her husband, Urban suggests the idea of spiritual fecundity, "Domine Ihesu Christe, seminator casti consilii, suscipe seminum fructus quos in Cecilia seminasti."[82] Chaucer translates the sentence as, "Almyghty Lord, O Jhesu Crist . . . / Sower of chaast conseil, hierde of us alle, / The fruyt of thilke seed of chastitee / That thou hast sowe in Cecile, taak to thee!" (VIII, 191–94). By describing the seed as a seed of chastity, Chaucer underlines the wordplay of the Latin *seminator, seminum, seminasti.* When Valerian returns to Cecilia newly "cristned" (VIII, 217) by Urban, the angel's gift of two crowns of lilies and roses to Cecilia and Valerian seems to consecrate a new marriage in a private ceremony that celebrates a differently directed union, one that will find its fulfillment in martyrdom. Chaucer suggests this by saying that the angel gave one crown to Cecilia and the other to Valerian, "hir make" (VIII, 224). His choice of a word more normally used to describe physical union is designed to underline the hierarchical relationship between physical and spiritual union the tale adumbrates. Similarly, his translation of the Latin *cognatum,* which Cecilia uses to greet Tiburce, her actual brother-in-law, as her brother in Christ, as *allye* (VIII, 292), captures the fairly comprehensive connotations of kinship and alliance contained in the original. Finally, the final picture of Cecilia as nurturer suggests ways in which she has created a family that owes its loyalties to no earthly kinship line. Thus Chaucer describes her as teaching the faith to those she had "fostred" and as preaching to them during the final three days of her life.

---

80. "Venit autem nox in qua suscepit una cum sponso suo cubiculi secreta silencia"; Gerould (1941), 672.

81. For other remarks about spiritual fruitfulness, see Grennan (1966); Kolve (1981), 151–52; Reames (1980), 40–41.

82. Gerould (1941), 672.

Like a spiritual *mater familias,* she gives her goods to her "children" and asks Urban to make a church of her house (VIII, 540–46).

The sense that Cecilia offers those around her an alternate system of language and sight is borne out by her trial scene. As Reames has noted, Chaucer followed the Franciscan abridgment in drastically editing the final part of the life of Saint Cecilia, abridging the brothers' trial scene, their conversations with Maximus, their executions, and Cecilia's long speech to the ministers. In so doing, he threw Cecilia's trial, which was left virtually uncut, into prominence.[83] He also highlighted Cecilia's aggressiveness. Since Chaucer chose for his source a text that removed anything that might detract from Cecilia, he inevitably focused attention upon a heroine who seems to follow no pattern of accepted female behavior. She quibbles with Almachius's literal-minded questions; she instructs him in rhetoric; she insults his power; finally, she takes the initiative and begins questioning her accuser, going on to correct his semantics. Chaucer captures the staccato pace of the original, with its terse dialogue punctuated by "Almachius dixit . . . Caecilia respondit." In effect, she tells Almachius that he must redefine his system of reality; she asserts a sharp division between the systems and codes of earth and heaven. What Almachius values—his power (VIII, 435), his judicial codes (VIII, 445), and his gods (VIII, 488–90)—are valueless. His power she redefines as a "bladdre ful of wynd" (VIII, 439), his ordinances as making wickedness of innocence (VIII, 464–65), and his gods as merely "images" made of stone (VIII, 509, 500). Her argument, which affirms the reality of the incorporeal and the blindness and folly of those who find a reality in what is mutable and unreal, suggests an unresolvable tension between the church and the world.[84]

It is this tension, along with Cecilia's substitution of Christian values for worldly codes, that makes her life so potentially useful to a poet like Chaucer. If we compare Chaucer's version of her life with any of the Middle English versions, or with his Latin sources, it is clear that Chaucer succeeds so brilliantly, not by adding to the tale, but by editing what is superfluous to the point he wishes to make. Both his choice of source-texts and his editing are acts of interpretation and refiguration designed to provide an image of the holy that points up the emptiness of imperial systems that locate value in power. His portrait of Cecilia throws into sharp relief those

---

83. See Reames (1990), 340–41, 359–60.

84. For remarks about the impossible ideal figured in the Second Nun's Tale, see Howard (1978), 290–92. See also Dean (1984).

characteristics that link her with the radical simplicity of the early church, and ultimately with Christ. Cecilia thus stands in sharp contrast to the institutions, values, and codes of imperial, secular Rome; a key part of her story is the conflict between Christian and Roman society. By Chaucer's time, of course, no such conflict existed. In fact, the Curia frequently resembled Almachius's court more than Urban's and Cecilia's collection of kindred souls.[85] If Chaucer indeed first wrote his life of Saint Cecilia in the period between 1373 and 1385, his attempt to provide an image of those values the community holds sacred was even more strategic. Hagiography, as Peter Brown has reiterated, cannot be divorced from its social context; hagiography ultimately concerns power, or the nature of authority.[86] Thus, while Chaucer did not invent the legend of Saint Cecilia, his decision to translate it—and to choose the sources that he did—was significant, since he chose to recount and to create a tale containing an implicitly radical series of messages.

However, what appears a simple and clear-cut confrontation between opposing systems is complicated by the final two stanzas of the tale. After giving away her goods to those she has nurtured, Cecilia speaks to Pope Urban:

> "I axed this of hevene kyng,
> To han respit thre dayes and namo
> To recomende to yow, er that I go,
> Thise soules, lo, and that I myghte do werche
> Heere of myn hous perpetuelly a cherche."
>
> Seint Urban with his deknes prively
> The body fette and buryed it by nyghte
> Among his othere seintes honestly.
> Hir hous the chirche of Seint Cecilie highte;

---

85. If Giffin is correct and Chaucer did translate the legend of Saint Cecilia as a gesture toward Adam Easton (see note 23), a grim irony may underlie Chaucer's inclusion of the legend in the *Canterbury Tales*. In discussing Easton's loyalty to Urban VI, Macfarlane notes that, as a cardinal, Easton was later imprisoned and tortured by Urban VI (11 January 1385) for his alleged part in a plot against the pope. Imprisoned unjustly, Easton nonetheless maintained his conviction of the legitimacy of Urban's right to the papacy. See Macfarlane (1953), 78 n. 4. For another discussion of Chaucer's handling of the contrast between imperial Rome and "God's invisible kingdom," see Curtis (1986), who sees the Second Nun's Tale as disembodied, as "archival."

86. See P. Brown (1981; 1982).

Seint Urban halwed it, as he wel myghte;
In which, into this day, in nobel wyse,
Men doon to Crist and to his seint servyse.

(VIII, 542–53)

The last two lines, which bring the life of Saint Cecilia into the present, where in "nobel wyse" men do service to Christ and his saint, raise a number of important questions.[87] What construction does Chaucer here intend? Does he intend a graceful reference to the building of Santa Cecilia in Trastevere? Does he intend a subtle compliment to Adam Easton, named cardinal priest of that church between December 1381 and December 1384, who might then take an interest in the ecclesiastical problems of his fellow East Anglians?[88] Does he intend to remind his audience that the church was no longer either simple or one? Does he intend the "noble wyse" of present-day worship to recall the poem's opening lines, describing Cecilia who "Was comen of Romayns and of noble kynde" (VIII, 121), thus linking his world with that of Rome? Is it significant that his narrator finds light for his darkness and work for his sloth in a private labor that connects him, not to the contemporary fellowship of the church, but to the spirit of the early church? If Cecilia can accuse Almachius of making gods of stone, of worshiping only images, of what might she accuse the church during the period from 1373 to 1385? But it is by her simple act of benefaction that Cecilia initiates a process of increasing complexity, a process Wyclif and others would decry in the gift of Constantine remembered on the feast day of Saint Sylvester. Urban, in fact, was credited with being the first pope to take rents and temporal possessions for the church, which before that time had existed in apostolic poverty.[89] It is, of course, that subject of rents and temporal possessions that so concerned Chaucer's contemporaries when they contemplated the relationship between the church and society. Where most versions of the life of Saint Cecilia end by stating the date of her martyrdom and asking the saint to intercede for the audience, Chaucer

---

87. The Franciscan abridgment reads, "Domum autem eius in eternum nomini sancte ecclesie consecravit, in qua beneficia domini exuberant ad memoriam sancte Cecilie usque in hodiernum diem"; Reames (1990), 361.

88. See Giffin (1956), 34–38.

89. See Bonet (1949), 53, 83–84. According to Coopland, Bonet drew this information from Bartholomew of Lucca. See also P. Olson (1986), 150–51n. Olson also refers to Bonet. For an account of the formulation of the ideal of the primitive church, see Glenn Olsen (1969). See also the end of Book 2 of the *Confessio Amantis,* where Gower recounts the tale of Constantine and Sylvester. For a discussion of this passage, see Peck (1978), 77.

ends a tale of clarity with a decidedly muddy detail. His decision to translate this particular saint's life—and to manipulate the variety of sources he did—at a time when the church was all too involved in the secular game of power seems a deliberate attempt to provide an image of the church when popes and governors did not play for the same stakes.[90] However, Chaucer cannot be accused of taking an overtly polemical stance. He shapes his translation of Cecilia's life but does not change it into what it is not. He does not use it to recommend a sweeping program separating the powers of the church from those of the state. And yet Almachius's eagerness to silence Cecilia most nearly resembles the attitude of the English church toward its Wycliffite critics, who even at this point spoke of themselves as martyrs of a primordial church.[91] He does not advocate women preachers. But neither does he criticize Cecilia's ecclesiastical voice. He does not urge that the church divest itself of its temporalities. And yet the legend contains the outlines of a Christianity as radically simple as any image created by John Wyclif in this period.[92]

That Chaucer recognized the political and social ambiguities inherent in his translation is further suggested by his decision to include it in the Canterbury book. If the legend seems a subtle exploration of some of the inconsistencies inherent in the institution of the church, by pairing it with the Canon's Yeoman's Prologue and Tale, Chaucer points up both the differences and the affinities between the primitive church and its contemporary incarnation. The clarity, the coolness, the clear-cut choices depicted in the Second Nun's Tale contrast sharply to the murky colors, the heat and sweat, and the ill-defined conclusions described in the Canon's Yeoman's Prologue and Tale. It is not Cecilia, clearly arguing the truth of Christ, who effects spiritual change, but a more earthy figure, Harry Bailey, whose shrewd questioning of the Yeoman elicits finally a tale of the "truth" behind alchemical conversion. We have in Harry neither preacher nor priest, but a figure who can ask our world's questions:

> "Why is thy lord so sluttissh, I the preye,
> And is of power bettre clooth to beye,

---

90. For two articles exploring Ricardian poets in relation to the subject of social mediation see Middleton (1978); Strohm (1979). For a searching look at some of Langland's strategies, see Middleton (1990).

91. See Wilks (1994).

92. For discussions of the Wycliffite program, see Hudson (1988), 389. For remarks about the ways in which Chaucer invokes ideals linked to Lollardy, see 390ff. See also Peck (1986),

If that his dede accorde with thy speche?"
                                            (VIII, 636–38)

"Where dwelle ye . . ."
                                            (VIII, 656)

"Why artwo so discoloured of thy face?"
                                            (VIII, 664)

If Cecilia displays a gift of spiritual sight linked to the medieval conception of wisdom, Harry Bailey is gifted with powers of observation that ally him with worldly wisdom.[93] But while we note the discrepancies the two tales suggest between the primitive and the modern church, we are nonetheless aware that Harry's wisdom is not to be scorned. At Boghtoun under Blee (VIII [G] 556), where the Canon and his Yeoman join the pilgrimage, we have come a long way from the world of pagan Rome; and the complexities of the Canon's Yeoman's tale intensify the stark outlines of the tale of the Second Nun while also bringing out the submerged tensions of the tale of Saint Cecilia. Cecilia's "lineage" is the modern church; her gift to Pope Urban is ultimately no different from countless bequests throughout the centuries separating her world from Chaucer's. The church composed of gulled priests and deceptive canons traces itself back to Cecilia in the tale of the Second Nun. The suburbs once inhabited by Urban and "the povre folkes that ther dwelle" (VIII [G] 174) are now peopled by robbers and thieves, including the canon and his yeoman (VIII [G] 657–60).[94] The crown of martyrdom, symbol of victory over the world, that Cecilia offers her converts is no longer available in a world where the church has become the world.

Chaucer's decision to add the legend of Saint Cecilia to the Canterbury book and to pair it with the Yeoman's account of alchemical failure and duplicity allowed him to confront theological or ecclesiastical issues as they pertained to questions of social order and justice. The picture he presents of Cecilia before Almachius is a scene that would be played out in Lollard accounts of confrontations with figures of ecclesiastical authority, the most famous of which is Thorpe's trial before Archbishop Arundel, which David

---

118, 126. Reames points out (1990, 344) that Wyclif used this incident as proof that the laity could perform minor sacraments.

93. On Cecilia and spiritual sight, see Collette (1976).

94. For a discussion of Chaucer's use of the suburbs as loci of subversion in these two tales, see J. Scattergood (1987).

Aers has already discussed.[95] Cecilia, like Christ before Annas and Caiphas, retains her dignity even as she questions the very basis of Almachius's assumption of authority. If the church, as many late medieval texts proclaim, had become the crucifier, the prince must assert his own moral authority and restore the "true" church by relieving it of its temporalities. The succeeding prologue and tale of the Canon's Yeoman continue to question the nature of the church's authority by exploring the realities of change. First, as I have implied above, the only alchemy that takes place in the tale is that enacted between Harry Bailey and the Yeoman. In his ability to deduce the Yeoman's true state and to elicit a confession of sorts from him, Harry reveals himself as far more adept at the arts of transformative dialogue than most of the clergy on the pilgrimage. This sort of change, or spiritual reversal, was the type that Wyclif and his followers were only too glad to admit, since it took place in the heart of the individual.

The confession that follows removes the veil between celebrant and devotee and reveals as illusory the operations performed in crucibles for the adoring eyes of the greedy. The Yeoman uses the language of alchemy to proclaim what Wyclif had stated in the language of theology—that substance cannot be changed without accident, that change took place only in the heart of the worshiper.[96] The Yeoman does more than reveal mystery as finally empty; he reveals the power behind the mystery as impotence. Lee Patterson has outlined the ways in which alchemy was seen as both a verbal and a social practice, and discussed Chaucer's handling of its pursuit as exemplifying his own ambivalence about the iconoclastic urge to emancipate the self from the past, which can also lead to disillusionment and despair. Patterson draws a sharp distinction between the primitive clarity of the tale of the Second Nun and the modern ambiguity of the Yeoman's performance.[97] Patterson has contributed much to our understanding of

95. See also Kendall (1986), esp. 57–67; Staley (1994), 138–50.

96. See Catto (1985a; 1992); Rubin (1991), 14–35. My wording is deliberate here: I want to suggest the allusiveness of the tale's language but do not want to lock it into a Lollard allegory. In a paper delivered at the meeting of the New Chaucer Society in 1994, Wendy Scase also discussed the association made by contemporary Wycliffites between transubstantiation and alchemy. For a discussion of Wyclif's views on the eucharist, especially as they involved letting the laity in on what were clerical matters—in other words, his interest in the vernacular—see Aston (1987). As Wyclif and others well knew, though the doctrine of transubstantiation pertained to belief, it could not be separated from the broader topic of power, since it was an act performed by an elite caste for the "nurture" of those who had no power to "feed" themselves. On this issue, see Beckwith (1993).

97. Patterson (1993a). Chaucer's use of sexual language to describe the "ecstasy" (or lack thereof) that accompanies alchemical success underlines the complex web of associations that serve to figure power in the social world of late medieval London.

the contexts for alchemical literature, but, rather than lock the tales into a binary opposition, I suggest we see Chaucer as using the pair to explore the problematic relationship between authority and power, between the past and the present, between the individual and the institutions that circumscribe individual action. Both tales provoke questions about the use of power, particularly ecclesiastical power, and challenge its authority through dramatizations of individual agency. Such questions and challenges are of course warp and woof of the fabric of dissent from Wyclif to Bunyan and on to our own days. But Chaucer is not so neatly categorized as a dissenter, nor is the tale of Cecilia his last word on authority. Harry Baily may find out the most and usher us into a realm where we long for but cannot achieve the object of our desires, but Harry is also a merchant. His vision is limited by his desire, and we already know from his words in the prologue to the Monk's tale that the "governour" is powerless in his own home.

By exploiting the conventions of gender, whereby woman was linked to disorderly desires and the so-called woman on top to reversed hierarchies, Chaucer embodies a radical refiguration of social and spiritual systems in Cecilia herself, who offers a redefinition of human relationships.[98] In the most fundamental sense, the tale is "up-si-doun." In fact, if Chaucer were to have translated what is implicit in the tale into a program of church reform, he might have found himself, like John Wyclif in 1377, needing to justify himself before Bishop Courtenay of London.[99] Cecilia's apostolic poverty, the critique of the present-day church she implicitly offers, her aggressiveness, and her preaching make her as threatening a figure as Wyclif. If the Parson's dislike of swearing can cause Harry Bailey to smell a "Lollere" in the wind (II [B1] 1173), why does not the tale of Saint Cecilia create even more comment? Cecilia's gender, her virginity, and her sanctity defuse certain types of responses, just as Chaucer's claim that he translated the work of another, or was inscribed upon by the Virgin herself, prevents us, even now, from reading the tale as a program for reform. Chaucer's indirect strategy, along with his deliberate fashioning of an outsider's identity, allowed him to occupy a position that gave him scope to explore a set of problems that grew even more complex during the first half of the reign of Richard II, when the issue of secular authority could at times seem more pressing than that of ecclesiastical.

---

98. See particularly, Davis (1975), 124–51.

99. For a discussion of the constraints on the writing of satire and theological statement in the period 1378–1406, see Simpson (1990a); Spearing (1985), 89–92.

The events of the 1380s—particularly the popular violence of the Rising of 1381 and the judicial violence of the Merciless Parliament—should not be dissociated from the previous decade's concern with the nature of authority. For if, as both Fitzralph and Wyclif stated, Sir Thomas Hoo's dream implied, and the work of the Good Parliament demonstrated, authority should rest on grace or worthiness, society's order was in jeopardy. Recent studies of the Rising of 1381 are providing strong evidence for the intelligence, sense of strategy, and capability of those who spearheaded the revolt. Contemporary descriptions of the rebels characterized them as brutish, their motivations as venal and greedy, and their acts as triumphs of sheer force and numbers.[100] However, these accounts, taken together with careful considerations of the rebels' movements and intended targets, suggest, as Nicholas Brooks has argued, that we have "read" the Rising as the chronicle writers wished us to. We have thereby denied its leaders the intelligence necessary to plan and carry out swiftly an attack of such magnitude.[101] By painting them as subhuman peasants, those who wrote the histories composed scenarios that owed their logic to a hierarchically ordered society wherein chaos ensued if hierarchy was disturbed. The chronicle writers thus provided a picture of a fixed and exclusive society that accommodated change only within assigned categories. Kings may become bad kings; courtiers may become knights of the bedchamber rather than of the battlefield; peasants may rebel against their lords. By transgressing social boundaries, the rebels could be seen to threaten the conceptual framework of community itself.

---

100. See Crane (1992); Green (1992); Pearsall (1989); Strohm (1992), chap. 2. For a contrasting view of the rhetorical strategies of contemporary accounts of the Rising, see Justice (1994b).

In addition to the above-cited recent studies of the Rising as a sort of vast cultural text, there are a number of excellent historical studies of the Rising. My brief remarks should be seen as signposts pointing to far more ambitious treatments of the event within the frame of political history. For recent work from which I have drawn my characterization of the Rising as symptomatic of tensions produced by the Hundred Years' War, especially as they were focused by the charge of abuse of power or authority, see Aston (1994); Cornford (1984); Dobson (1986); Hilton (1973); Kaeuper (1988); Madicott (1986; 1987); Ormrod (1990a); Searle and Burghart (1972); Wilks (1972). See also Rot. Parl. (1783), 3:98–121, for an account of the November–December Parliament of 1381, in which the speaker, Sir Richard Waldgrave accounted for the Rising by pointing to administrative corruption and oppressive taxation. The record of this parliament is a fascinating one. Though its language is generally pacific, its recommendations are at once shrewd and tough, targeting the mismanagement of the privileged rather than the venality of the masses. See Ormrod's excellent analysis (1990a), 23–26.

101. Brooks (1985), 256. See also Cornford (1984). See also note 100.

As told by contemporaries, Wat Tyler's famous conversation with the young King Richard is a tale of the chaos of a boundaryless world. Though none is as detailed as that in the *Anonimalle Chronicle,* the various chronicle accounts of that incident all include some way in which Tyler offended the fundamental decorem upon which society rested. Fittingly for a leader who requested the abolition of serfdom and the disestablishment of degree, Tyler is described as playing with a dagger "like a boy" in the king's presence, as approaching the king on horseback, as keeping his head covered, or as rinsing out his mouth in front of the king. The encounter between Tyler and the king is thus used to particularize the nature of the more general chaos enacted in the streets of London, where the heads of significant figures of civil and ecclesiastical authority already decorated London Bridge.[102] The chroniclers present the rebels as desecrating what was by its very nature set apart. The violence that took the lives of select figures of secular power, that destroyed collections of legal records, that released prisoners, and that murdered resident aliens throughout the city is somehow epitomized by the picture of Wat Tyler treating the young king of England as though he were a comrade. Age thereby assaults youth; tilers behave as if they were kings; experience trangresses innocent majesty. The street had become a sort of theater for acts of violation and sacrilege.[103]

The picture presented by the chroniclers has its own deeply significant philosophic and cultural point, but it also disallows agency and thus the sort of hard-headed political and social appraisals that can prompt institutional change. By "institutional," I mean here to indicate the king. All of Commons' petitions, as well as the demands of the rebel leaders and much of the thrust of formal political writing in general, was directed toward the figure whose assumption of authority could effect truly creative change. Wyclif had perceived the centrality of the monarch in the late 1370s and

---

102. See the accounts assembled by Dobson (1986), 3.

103. A similar dynamic drove many of the equally symbolic acts of the French Revolution, such as the king's treatment after the capture at Varennes or the revolutionaries' takeover of the queen's private chambers. Princess Joan had been affronted in her own apartments; see Dobson (1986), 171–72. What was being staged, of course, was a violation of "sacred" space. In the movie, *La Nuit de Varennes,* the distance between the two ways of looking at the world is brilliantly captured when it is finally revealed what is in the mysterious parcels the royal servants have so carefully guarded—the crowns of the king and queen, the symbols of their sacral offices. When the crowns are uncovered, one of the ladies-in-waiting bows to the crowns (notwithstanding the fact that the royal couple is there in the flesh) and says "sa majesse." For a rich and perceptive treatment of the cultural implications of the French Revolution that has much to teach us about the Rising of 1381, see Schama (1989).

had even hinted at the possibility of a new order of political beings brought together as equal subjects under the Crown. In such a reformed world, the English church, stripped of its secular power and holdings, would be reduced to its essentials and acquire the spiritual authority that it lacked at present.[104] About the same time that Chaucer was working on the legend of Saint Cecilia, in which he provided a picture of such a church, John of Gaunt was using Wyclif to attack ecclesiastical privilege. Wyclif promulgated his ideas through his sermons, which, as Wilks has pointed out, were not intended to make revolution a popular act but to ensure popular support for his ideas.[105] Chaucer's picture of the early church and of Cecilia's simplicity is indeed dangerously close to the notion of Wycliffite authority. Cecilia's authority issues from her faith for which she is martyred. Chaucer's depiction of Cecilia's bold defiance of secular power (or his decision to translate that particular legend) curiously refigures Wyclif's contemptuous reaction to the attempts of some clerics to image themselves as imitating Becket's martyrdom by defending church properties against the king. As Wyclif rudely pointed out, defense of property could not make a martyr.[106] The society Cecilia inhabits, like Wyclif's vision of a new social order, is without fixed boundaries and can include anyone who believes.

I am not here aligning Chaucer with Lollardy, but, instead, arguing that he used his poetry to ask questions about urgent social issues that were inevitably related to the politics of devotion or sanctity. His legend of Saint Cecilia is at once an early probe into the subject of spiritual authority as it was articulated in the early 1380s and a work he thought interesting enough to insert into the Canterbury book at a later date. There, its questions become far more pressing, particularly in relation to the Canon's Yeoman's Prologue and Tale. The subject of authority, as Chaucer formulated it, cannot be neatly conceptualized as an inquiry into ecclesiastical authority in relation to secular power. Thus, Almachius is less like a prince than a "prince" of the church. However, as the tale *also* suggests, the need for reform is produced by Cecilia's own generative presence and gift. If the tale of Cecilia demonstrates no moment of unalloyed purity, that of the Canon's Yeoman looks forward to no quintessential transfiguration but figures the evanescent motion of grace upon the individual. The two tales thus describe the terms of reform while questioning its likelihood. Or, put

---

104. See the probing article by Wilks (1972), esp. 119–21.
105. Wilks (1972), 124–25.
106. On Wyclif's language, see Holmes (1975), 171.

another—and Wycliffite—way, can individual and institutional reform ever be separate topics? The mercantilist ethic of the common alchemist corrupts the language of selfhood that can be found in alchemical texts as surely as the gifts of the faithful undermine the mission of the church.[107] If the church must seek to be unimplicated in the world's pursuit of goods, the leaders of that world must accept their roles as agents of reform. To this end, Chaucer recognized what his fellows in Commons also knew: that the merchant had come of age, that the world was not tripartite (if it ever had been), that responsibility and thus authority obtained not simply to kings but to those who advised them.

In the Melibee, the Canterbury tale he assigned to himself, he explored some of the problems involved in an understanding of civil authority that must rest on more than might. To this end, he uses Dame Prudence as a means of defining a view of royal agency that depends upon the intertwined concepts of representation and consent. W. M. Ormrod has argued convincingly that the political debates of 1386–87, which culminated in the Merciless Parliament of 1388, were continuations of the concern with leadership voiced by Commons directly after the Peasants' Revolt.[108] Not only can that political conversation be extended back into the 1370s, but in Chaucer the age had an observer and analyst of rare historical sensitivity.[109] The barely leashed sexual energy that underlies the *Parliament of Fowles* and the judicially sanctioned violence of a Roman courtroom in the legend of Saint Cecilia offer glimpses of the ways in which social forms and codes can restrain but not subdue the will. But in the Rising of 1381 and the Merciless Parliament, Chaucer would have had examples of a true breakdown of social or moral control. For "rustics" (as the chroniclers labeled them), it was one thing to murder an archbishop or a sergeant at arms. But for Parliament to enact similarly violent penalties upon bad or inept counsellors changed the terms by which society is categorized and thus understood. In relation to the violence of the 1380s, Chaucer took a characteristically idiosyncratic stance. Rather than focus upon the violence itself, he focused upon the process by which violence was allowed to predominate—or upon the dangers of abrogating regal authority.

---

107. For an account and analysis of this language, see Patterson (1993b).

108. Ormrod (1990a), 30.

109. For studies that rigorously historicize Chaucer's poetry, see Knight (1986); Patterson (1991); Strohm (1989); Wallace (1990; 1991; 1992). In "The Textual Environment of Chaucer's 'Lak of Stedfastnesse,'" Strohm (1992) also focuses on the political atmosphere of the late 1380s and the ways in which Chaucer's poem functions as advice to Richard within the context of this period.

Since Richard II's coronation in 1377, criticism had been directed at his advisers; as he grew older, criticism was directed toward his patronage of a new courtier nobility that had to some extent supplanted the established aristocracy in royal access, and thus in influence. As Anthony Tuck notes, for the first four years of Richard's reign, such criticism had come mainly from Commons. But, from the autumn parliament of 1383 onward, aristocratic hostility towards both the king and his courtiers became more open, culminating finally in the Parliament of October 1386.[110] This dissatisfaction with the king's advisory inner circle was manifested in the continuous parliamentary uneasiness about the expenses incurred by the royal household: from 1381 on, there were demands in Parliament for investigation into the expenditures of the household.[111] Richard's hostile response to the actions taken by Parliament in 1386, whereby revenues were taken out of the king's control and placed in the hands of a council appointed for a year, created a situation where violent, rather than constitutional, methods seemed the next logical step.[112] In absenting himself from Westminster and in directly challenging parliamentary authority, Richard helped to solidify support for his opponents, thereby precipitating the sequence of events that began at Radcot Bridge on 20 December 1387 and ended, temporarily at least, in the Merciless Parliament of 1388, which saw the exile or the execution of the king's favorites.

The three important chroniclers of Richard's reign—Henry Knighton, Thomas Walsingham, and the Westminster chronicler—along with poets like John Gower all suggest a profound concern with the nature of secular authority figures.[113] Chaucer himself was in as privileged a position to observe, and presumably to analyze, the political scene as anyone during this period. Whether Chaucer was residing in London or in nearby Kent during the early years of the decade, as a member of a peace commission for Kent from 1385 until 1389 and as one of Kent's two representatives to Parliament in 1386, he would have been directly involved with some of the more important figures and issues of a decade that some have described as a turning point in Richard's reign. Furthermore, as a member of the "king's party," Chaucer could have had no liking for the censure and violence

---

110. A. Tuck (1973), 86–87.
111. Keen (1973), 276.
112. See Keen (1973), 276–81; A. Tuck (1973), 87.
113. See Stockton (1962) for a cogent introduction, as well as translations of the *Vox Clamantis* and the *Cronica Tripertita*. See also Pichaske and Sweetland (1977); Schlauch (1945).

directed toward some of his friends and close associates.[114] Given what must have been a frightening and a tumultuous experience, his literary activity during this same period suggests his tendency to analyze rather than to excoriate. *Troilus* is usually assigned a date in the mid-1380s and *The Legend of Good Women* seems to have been written not long after. *Boece* is likewise linked to this period of Chaucer's literary career. Of *The Canterbury Tales,* the Knight's Tale, the Physician's Tale, the Melibee, and perhaps the Monk's Tale are commonly dated early in the *Canterbury* period and thus in the mid to late 1380s.[115]

W. W. Lawrence, Gardiner Stillwell, and, more recently, V. J. Scattergood and R. F. Yeager have pointed up the ways in which the tale must have seemed to glance at contemporary affairs, particularly crucial issues concerning England's relationship with France.[116] That Chaucer was privy to the tug between the king's interest in fostering peaceful relations with France and the more bellicose sentiments of those surrounding the duke of Gloucester and the earl of Arundel seems more than likely, since in July 1387 a letter of protection was made out for Chaucer to accompany William Beauchamp, captain of Calais, to Calais on the king's business. Though the reason for the trip is not known, it may have been concerned with the twin issues of peace and trade; Beauchamp had recently been involved with negotiating a resumption of trading agreements that had been interrupted by the French War, and Chaucer had had some experience with such negotiating parties before.[117]

While the theme of peace is certainly important to the Melibee, the tale seems designed to offer a more sweeping analysis of England's domestic

---

114. For accounts of Chaucer's life during this period, see "Chaucer's Life" by Martin M. Crow and Virginia E. Leland in *The Riverside Chaucer* (1987), xxii–xxiii; Crow and Olson (1966), 44–53, 61–62, 348–401; Pearsall (1992), 203ff. For two discussions of Chaucer's activities in relation to the foreign affairs of the same period, see also D. W. Robertson (1985); V. J. Scattergood (1981).

115. For discussions of the dating of Chaucer's works, see the comments in both the introduction and the explanatory notes in *The Riverside Chaucer* (1987).

116. Lawrence (1969); V. J. Scattergood (1981); Stillwell (1944); Yeager (1987). P. Olson (1986), 113–23, likewise feels the Melibee is a "peace work." For some interesting suggestions about the relevance of Wyclif's political theories to the Melibee, see Jeffrey (1984), 138. For cogent discussions of Franco-English relations during this period, see Palmer (1972), chaps. 5 and 6; D. W. Robertson (1985).

For other studies of the Melibee that suggest the tale's importance to the overall scheme of *The Canterbury Tales,* see Howard (1976), 309–16; Lawler (1980), 102–8; Owen (1977), 124–29; Patterson (1989); Pearsall (1985), 285–88; Ruggiers (1979). Finally, for a cogent discussion of the Melibee in relation to Chaucer's prose, see Lawler (1984).

117. See V. J. Scattergood (1981), 294. For another view, see Pearsall (1992), 206–7.

situation. Chaucer found in Renaud de Louens' adaptation of Albertano of Brescia's *Liber consolationis et consilii* a treatise whose straightforward moral message of consolation and prudent counsel seems designed for a more intricate political purpose.[118] The affinities between the tale and Boethius's *Consolation of Philosophy* are obvious; both works are thinly veiled allegories offering moral counsel to a figure who has lost the ability to understand or to control his immediate situation. But where Lady Philosophy offers Boethius advice of a metaphysical nature, Prudence offers Melibeus counsel that is intended to help him alter a secular and political situation that is poised on the brink of chaos. Thus, rather than help him come to terms with a condition he cannot change, she teaches him how to become an agent of positive change. When her advice is distilled into a series of precepts, it becomes clear just how clearheaded a political couselor she is.

Prudence's advice is ultimately concerned with the idea of leadership. She begins by undercutting two tenets of a predominantly male and hierarchical society: the belief in force and the disbelief in a woman's ability to give wise advice. Thus where the majority of Melibeus's "greet congregacion of folk" (VII, 1004) have urged him to turn his grief into anger and seek vengeance upon his enemies, Prudence argues against hasty action. Melibeus responds by refusing to be governed, or to appear to be governed, by a woman, thereby giving Prudence the opening she needs to shift the grounds of their discussion from the relative merits of peace or war to the more practical problems associated with the creation and maintenance of viable social units. Though she is certainly an advocate of deliberate action, her real concern is with the nature of power and thus with the ways in which political power can be manifested and sustained for the good of all.

Her initial thrust—the choice of good advisers—is one with a good deal of relevance for English affairs during the decade of the 1380s.[119] However, she focuses less on the actual counselors than on the process by which they are chosen, and thus on Melibeus's moral judgment and capacity for true authority: "I wol enforme yow how ye shul governe yourself in chesynge of

---

118. For the text of both works, see Severs (1941b). I use "political" here to refer to the broader issues associated with the workings of social institutions and to designate "the priority of local intentions and topical circumstances." The latter phrase I have borrowed from Patterson (1987), 58 n. 29.

119. Stillwell (1944), 441. In a paper delivered at the 1994 meeting of the New Chaucer Society, David Wallace argued that the *Melibee* was intended as advice for advisers, for wives and friars. However, the tale seems to underline the need for kings (or leaders) to choose good advisers.

youre counseillours" (VII, 1114). Before attempting to choose an advisory council, a leader should ask God for wisdom, then make sure he himself is without anger, greed, or hastiness. After warning him to keep his own council, she tells him what not to look for in an advisory body, a body that she insists must be kept small in order to be effective. In telling Melibeus to avoid fools, flatterers, and old enemies, Prudence suggests a keen sense that all human relationships are, for better or worse, based on power. Considering the realities of human nature, it is best to assume that fools, flatterers, and former enemies are less than trustworthy. For example, of the latter she says, "For sikerly, though thyn enemy be reconsiled, and maketh thee chiere of humylitee, and lowteth to thee with his heed, ne trust hym nevere. / For certes he maketh thilke feyned humilitee moore for his profit than for any love of thy persone, by cause that he deemeth to have victorie over thy persone by swich feyned contenance, the which victorie he myghte nat have by strif or werre" (VII, 1185–86).

Not only does Prudence not offer Melibeus starry-eyed advice, but she points out the ways he himself erred as the head of the council he formerly called upon for advice. He has brought his own "ire, coveitise, and hastifnesse" (VII, 1246) into the council chamber and has thereby neglected an objective attitude before his councillors that is likely to elicit wise advice. Instead, he has let them see his inclination to make war on those who have wronged him. However, she then begins to offer him more positive advice that is designed to overturn his rather elementary approach to political problems.

Prudence is a pragmatist, and her words are directed at the creation of a strong social unit. She thus urges him to keep his person (VII, 1298) by employing intelligent defensive measures: he should be wary of deceivers and maintain friends rather than fortifications. Both pieces of advice turn Melibeus back on himself, on his vigilance and discretion, and on his ability to inspire loyalty and friendship. Thus, while her advice sounds innocuous enough, proverbs like "Ovyde seith that 'the litel wesele wol slee the grete bole and the wilde hert.' And the book seith, 'A litel thorn may prikke a kyng ful soore" (VII, 1325)—which significantly enough is one of the few additions Chaucer made to the tale—are designed to alert harts and not weasels to the threats small things can pose to the great.[120] The kingly hart

---

120. On this line, see the explanatory notes in *The Riverside Chaucer*, 926. For Ovid's "viper," Chaucer substitutes a weasel. He also adds the final portion of the proverb. The French text reads, "Et Ovide ou *Livre de Remède d'Amours* dit, 'La petite vivre occist le grant thorel; et le chien, qui ne pas moult grant, retient bien le sanglier.'" See Severs (1941b), 588,

must remain alert to dangers to his safety. Prudence goes on to urge a new way of thinking upon her more reactionary husband, arguing against personal vengeance and for the use of law, that is, for brains rather than brawn. She blames him for thinking highly of his position and his wealth, instead counselling work and the proper use of riches. She ends by advising peace with his adversaries because peace is a means to the higher end of social unity (see VII, 1676ff.).

Prudence, however, goes about restoring order by admitting the facts of the situation before her. Melibeus has been truly wronged. She does not ignore his claims to injury but insists that the guilty must acknowledge their guilt and repent. Second, Melibeus and his friends must accept both the acknowledgment and the repentance in good faith. Chaucer's handling of this section of the tale is particularly interesting, for he adds a sentence in which the guilty parties, after submitting to Melibeus as lord, emphasize the quality of his mercy: "For wel we knowe that youre liberal grace and mercy strecchen hem ferther into goodnesse than doon oure outrageouse giltes and trespas into wikkednesse, al be it that cursedly and dampnabley we han agilt agayn youre heigh lordshipe" (VII, 1825). That Melibeus doesn't understand what they mean by grace and mercy is clear when he tells Prudence that, in accepting their repentance, he will disinherit them of all their goods and exile them forever. Once more, Prudence must reeducate him, urging upon him loss rather than gain, meekness and debonairness rather than might and vengeance. Just as the end of Prudence's counsel is designed to emphasize the need for mercy, diplomacy, and liberality in responsible and informed rulers, so the end of the tale is intended to point up the more general reversal that has taken place in Melibeus himself.

The additions Chaucer made to the ending of Le Livre de Mellibee et Prudence are revealing, since they suggest his strategic interest in implanting the theme of reversal within a conventional medieval moral tale. Whereas his French source ends by saying, "Quant Mellibee ot oÿ toutes les paroles Dame Prudence et ses sages enseignemens, si fut en grant paix de cuer et loa Dieu, qui lui avoit donné si sage compagnie," Chaucer goes well beyond expressing Melibeus's thanks for having been granted such a wise wife.[121] The Chaucerian version of this sentence reads:

---

line 540. For another discussion of Chaucer's use of the proverb and possible reasons for substituting a weasel, see Rowland (1971), 46.

121. For the French text, see Severs (1941b), 614, lines 1169–79. This change is not noted in the notes for The Riverside Chaucer (1987).

Whanne Melibee hadde herd the grete skiles and resouns of dame Prudence, and hire wise informaciouns and techynges, / *his herte gan enclyne to the wil of his wif, considerynge hir trewe entente, / and conformed hym anon and assented fully to werken after hir conseil,* / and thonked God, of whom procedeth al vertu and alle goodnesse, that hym sente a wyf of so greet discrecioun. (VII, 1869–1872; emphasis added)

The three clauses that Chaucer adds here are designed to emphasize the subtle hierarchical shift that has taken place in Melibeus and to do so by suggesting a rational progression. Thus, Melibeus's heart inclines; he considers her intent; he finally conforms and assents to her counsel. The process itself is in marked contrast to his manner of reaching decisions earlier in the tale. There, decisions emerge from subjective responses; now, he moves from inclination to assent through consideration. While the process certainly suggests his moral or rational education, phrases like "the wil of his wif" and "to worken after hir conseil" imply a more radical reversal. For these are exactly the guidelines pilgrims like the Wife of Bath work so hard to establish as the basis for marital harmony, a harmony that only masks a deeper and more fundamental disorder. But in the context of the Tale of Melibee, such a reversed hierarchy signals a shift from strict justice and the harsh laws of war to merciful adjudication and diplomacy. Similarly, the final sentence, which is also Chaucer's addition, plays upon the theme of mercy, stressing the reality of heavenly mercy in the face of human imperfection: "For doutelees, if we be sory and repentant of the synnes and giltes which we han trespassed in the sighte of oure Lord God, / he is so free and so merciable / that he wole foryeven us oure giltes / and bryngen us to the blisse that nevere hath ende." His emphasis here, as in the tale of Prudence and Melibeus, links repentence with mercy; the awareness of guilt and the true intent of the penitent activates the bounty of God's mercy. Chaucer thus closes the tale by implying that our impulses to penance, on the one hand, and mercy, on the other, help to bring our earthly relationships and societies into closer alignment with their heavenly referent.

There seem to be at least two sets of issues at stake in Chaucer's choice and handling of *Le Livre de Mellibee et Prudence*: political and literary. Politically, Chaucer's decision to translate this treatise seems especially apt when we consider the domestic events of the final years of the 1380s and the controversy that focused on the subjects of the king's authority and on his relationship to his inner circle of advisers. Much of this controversy converged on the figure of Robert de Vere, the earl of Oxford, whom Richard created duke of Ireland in 1386. According to Walsingham, scandalous rumors circulated about the king's taking the extraordinary step of elevating De Vere to duke.[122] In Parliament that fall, there were accusations against the chancellor, Michael de la Pole, and, once more, there were odd rumors—in this case, rumors of occult influence—circulating about the degree of influence such advisers had over the king.[123] As both Henry Knighton and Thomas Walsingham make clear, these accusations from both the nobles and the Commons were not simply directed at individual persons but at the broader and more important issues of undue influence and of royal responsibility. Thus the altercation between the king and Parliament over the dismissal of Michael de la Pole indicated just how far Richard had allowed himself to become alienated from Parliament.

Those grievances Parliament brought before Richard in a parliamentary address of 1386 would reappear in a more serious form in the Merciless Parliament of 1388.[124] The fact that Richard did little or nothing to remedy the political situation in 1386 points up his own inability to recognize the weaknesses in a political situation of his own making. The address itself can be read as a demand that Richard recognize the bond between himself and his Parliament. Its members remind him of the very sanctity of their own body by pointing out that there should be a yearly Parliament, assembled for the purposes of maintaining peace, of righting wrongs, of seeing to the health of the realm, and of providing the king with council. They insist that, according to ancient statutes, the king may not of his own will alienate himself from Parliament. To this, Richard replied by raising the specter of the king of France, suggesting that he might ask his aid against the insurgents. Richard's words touched off another speech from his Parlia-

---

122. Walsingham (1863) says, "tantum afficiebatur eidem, tantum coluit et amavit eundem, non sine nota, prout fertur, familiaritatis obscoenae; submurmurantibus caeteris nobilibus et baronibus, ac indigne ferentibus tantae promotionis appetitum in viro tam mediocri, quem non plus caeteris commendabant vel generis sui sublimitas vel reliquarum virtutum dotes" (148). The point of irritation seems to be less the subject of vice than that of De Vere's "middling" generic and moral stature. See also A. Tuck (1985), 115, who says that De Vere "seemed to epitomize in person all that was objectionable about Richard's court."

123. See Knighton (1965), 216. See also Ainsworth (1990), 197.

124. For a text of the parliamentary address of 1386, see Knighton (1965), 216–220; Rot. Parl. (1783), 3:215–24. For a less detailed account of these events, see Walsingham (1863), 149–53. For a discussion of the Parliament of 1386 in relation to earlier parliaments, see Palmer (1971).

ment, this one slightly more militant. After pointing out the folly of looking to France, they raise the twin evils of heavy taxation and bad advisers. They end by once more recalling the authority of ancient statutes, pointing out that if the king does not fulfill his part of the bond between them, they can depose the king, urging him to abandon his present counselors and turn to Parliament for advice.

This interchange may well reflect some of the unresolved tensions that lingered from Richard's coronation in 1377. The coronation oath that Richard took subtly downplayed the role of divine election in order to emphasize the nature of the bond between king and Parliament.[125] The ceremony thus proclaimed that the bond between king and people was a contractual one.[126] It is precisely this contractual agreement between ruler and ruled that seems to have formed the core of the controversy between Richard and his Parliament in the 1380s. Richard was perceived as ignoring his responsibilities as king by not choosing his advisers from among the old nobility and by not recognizing the function of Parliament.

From the Parliament of 1386 until that of 1388, the political atmosphere in England remained uneasy. Though Richard acceded to Parliament's demands, dismissing Michael de la Pole and agreeing to the formation of a council of nobles who would oversee the kingdom for a year, he abandoned Westminster, created a rival council of his own, and spent most of his time in the Midlands and in Wales.[127] He also posed a legal challenge to parliamentary rights by posing a series of questions concerning recent events to a handpicked group of justices, including Robert Tresilian, chief justice of the King's Bench. The justices satisfied the king by reinforcing the concept of regality and the role of royal prerogative. More significant yet for the *Melibee,* they recommended that those who contravened or compelled the king should be punished capitally as traitors.[128] It is during

125. For a detailed account of these revisions, see Schramm (1937), 170–72. See also McKisack (1959), 399.

126. There is a particular irony inherent in the relationship between Richard and his parliament and between Edward II and his. As A. Tuck points out (1973, 71), Richard seems to have been drawn to the figure of Edward II and to have spent a good deal of time reflecting upon some of his methods of administration. He also made sure that his anniversaries were properly observed by the monks at the abbey where Edward was buried and, in the 1390s, attempted to have his ancestor canonized.

127. See Knighton (1965), 221–32, for an account of the articles of arraignment against Michael de la Pole and of the terms established between Richard and Parliament. See also Walsingham (1863), 148–53. For a detailed account of the events of the following year, see Keen (1973), 280ff.; McKisack (1959), 442–47.

128. For the text of these questions and answers, see Knighton (1965), 237–40; *Rot. Parl.* (1783), 3:233–34. For a discussion of these questions, see Keen (1973), 281.

1387 that we find, particularly in Walsingham's chronicle, an increased attention to the continuing closeness between Richard and Robert de Vere, by then the duke of Ireland. Froissart reported that de Vere was compared to a rapacious otter in a fishpond or to a wife squandering her husband's wealth. His favorite was thought to keep the king from more serious pursuits and, in fact, to undermine the chivalry of the court. As Walsingham noted gloomily, knights are more devoted to Venus than to Bellona, more at home in the bedchamber than in the field, and more likely to use language than lances in defense.[129] While Walsingham is certainly not the final authority on the domestic situation of 1387, his picture of a king somehow bound by magic spells to an unworthy favorite, whose undue influence saps the king of his royal authority and thus robs the country of its king, nonetheless suggests that the situation was certainly no better than in 1386. Moreover, his strategic use of the language of gender serves to heighten the theme of disorder in his account of Richard's government.

These resentments, together with the news of the king's legal challenge to Parliament's prerogatives, solidified support behind the king's opponents. In November 1387, Parliament and the magnates who controlled it wanted Robert De Vere, Michael de la Pole, Robert Tressilian, Nicholas Brembre, and Archbishop Neville tried for treason. After much bickering between Richard and his opponents, the duke of Ireland raised a force in Chester, which was defeated at the battle of Radcot Bridge in Oxfordshire by the forces of the king's opponents, the duke of Gloucester and the earls of Arundel, Warwick, Derby, and Nottingham.[130] In the subsequent parliament, the Merciless Parliament, many of those most closely bound to the king were condemned to death or exile.

From the thirty-nine articles of accusation brought against the five most tightly linked to Richard, it is clear that both the nobles and the Commons perceived the crisis as one of authority. Though Robert De Vere, Michael de la Pole, Robert Tressilian, Nicholas Brembre, and Archbishop Neville were accused of some crimes relating to greed, for example, of receiving from the king goods and gifts of property, for the most part, the charges

---

129. "Et hii nimirum milites plures erant Veneris quam Bellonae, plus valentes in thalamo quam in campo, plus lingua quam lancea praemuniti, ad dicendum vigiles, ad faciendum acta martia somnolenti"; Walsingham (1863), 156. For Froissart, see the discussion in Ainsworth (1990), 198.

130. Mine is a truncated account. For the details of the deteriorating situation between the king and the several interest groups now aligned behind his opponents, see both Knighton (1965), 240–56, and Walsingham (1863), 161–69. See also Keen (1973), 282; McKisack (1959), 447–53; Tuck (1973), 114.

against them concerned their undue influence over the king. The articles of accusation are careful to characterize Richard as young and inexperienced rather than as venal or vain, thereby focusing less upon his own responsibilities as sovereign than upon the deleterious effects of bad advisers. Thus the five are charged with alienating Richard from his lords and other counselors, of binding him to them by oaths he need not and should not take, of turning the people from Richard through their bad advice, and of meddling with English justice by hindering the people legally and by falsely counselling the king so that he ceased to uphold the laws of his own land.[131] The gravity of the charges really turns on the degree of control they were perceived to have had over Richard, who is cast as a creature of others, rather than as a figure of regal authority, as the recurring phrase "caused him to" ("ont fait le roy," "firent le roy") suggests. Ironically, of course, Richard was forced by these same accusers to accede to their demands and to ratify Parliament's death sentences against his former men, whom Parliament was accusing of tempting the king into altering the power structure of the nation.[132]

Seen in relation to the domestic situation of the late 1380s, Chaucer's Tale of Melibee can be described as a shrewd piece of political analysis and advice. On the surface, the tale appears consciously detached from the politics of its time; for example, Chaucer deletes, "And Solomon says, 'Woe to the land that has a child as a lord and whose lord dines in the morning'" (Eccl. 10:16) from a series of proverbs that Prudence directs at her husband.[133] Though he omits lines that might be construed as explicitly referring to the king, he adds others, such as the reference in line 1325, where he quotes Ovid as saying that "the litel wesele wol slee the grete bole and the wilde hert." The proverb seems especially meaningful, since Chaucer substituted the weasel (related, of course, to the otter to which de Vere was compared) for the viper he found in his source. As Beryl Rowland notes in reference to Chaucer's comparison of Alison in The Miller's Tale to a weasel, the weasel was considered a playful little animal, but also a creature of ill-omen, associated with lust, trickery, and witchcraft.[134] Since those were

---

131. For the text of these articles, see Hector and Harvey (1982), 236–69; Knighton (1965), 271–92.

132. Walsingham (1863), 174–75, notes, "Deinde exactum est juramentum a Rege, ad standum regulationi procerum; et non solum a Rege, sed a cunctis regni incolis, idem juramentum est expetitum."

133. See the explanatory notes in The Riverside Chaucer (1987), line 1199, for a discussion of this omission.

134. Rowland (1971), 29.

qualities attributed to Robert de Vere by the contemporary chroniclers,
Chaucer's substitution of the weasel is possibly significant; the hart, of
course, was the beast Richard chose and unveiled at the Smithfield tournament of 1390 to adorn the royal heraldic devices and badges of livery.
Whether such omissions and additions were intended to function as screens
for or as covert signs of Chaucer's political intentions, the thrust of the
entire tale seems aimed, not simply at a political situation, but specifically
at Richard himself.[135] Most obviously, Prudence is primarily concerned
with the process by which counselors are chosen and counsel solicited. At
no point does she suggest that Melibeus consider taking action without the
advice of others, thus implicitly underlining the contractual nature of the
relationship between a ruler and the ruled. But her handling of an issue as
charged as that of counsel is far more astute than that found in either the
chronicles or in the poetry of John Gower. Where he and the chroniclers
tend to excuse Richard and focus upon the active and willful role played
by his advisers, Chaucer's Tale of Melibee explores the responsibility a ruler
has for the bad advice he receives and takes; in other words, it focuses
upon a relationship that is less manipulative than it is complicit.[136] Thus
Prudence spends almost no time blaming Melibeus's advisers for urging
him toward vengeance, focusing instead upon the method by which he
chose his advisers and upon his mishandling of the scene of counsel. In so
doing, she suggests his own disclaimer of responsibility as a ruler; he be-
haves less as a figure for authority than as a private citizen, whose personal
wrongs demand an immediate and subjective response.

In fact, if we choose to look at the Tale of Melibee as directed at the
domestic crisis of the late 1380s, it emerges as a strong, if carefully crafted,
statement about the nature of regal responsibility. Most important, the
remedies Prudence advises are less institutional than they are personal. Even
Chaucer's decision to give the name Sophie, or wisdom, to the daughter
who is nameless in his original suggests the personal nature of Melibeus's
wound. Though the tale demands that we maintain the fiction of treating

---

135. R. F. Green (1980), 142–43, 145–46, 166ff., discusses both the *Consolation of Philosophy* and the Melibee as forms of advice to kings.

136. In addition to the Chronicles, see book 6 of the *Vox Clamantis*, which focuses upon
the king. As Stockton (1962), 11, notes, the book originally excused the king from responsibility, laying England's troubles upon the king's advisers. In revising his poem, possibly around
1393, Gower shifted some of the blame to Richard. For later and harsher views of Richard,
see also *Richard the Redeless* or *Mum and the Sothsegger*. As Gower's revisions likewise
suggest, political poetry of the 1390s gave Richard a good deal less credit than it had ten
years previously.

this crime as a crime against his property and therefore as related to the issue of social authority or power, Melibeus's damaged wisdom is an individual matter (with vast institutional or social implications). What Prudence teaches him to do through her own wise counsel is to exercise control, not over others through force, but over himself by cultivating his sense of measure, of justice, and of mercy. The wisdom she helps him to heal is a quality that, while certainly modeled upon the abstract or celestial virtue, nonetheless is firmly rooted in rational and objective thought.

The name Chaucer assigns to the wounded daughter allows him to use her on the tale's two levels, as an instance of the wrong Melibeus has suffered at the hands of others and as a figure for the wrong he has done himself. It is at this juncture that the tale reveals its particular toughness as political advice. If we adhere, for a moment, to the literal fiction of the Tale of Melibee, it is clear that Chaucer makes no attempt to gloss over the fact that Melibeus has suffered an injury. His house has been breached, his wife beaten, and his daughter wounded. Though Prudence reproves him or his excessive grief, her remarks nonetheless indicate the necessity of reading the tale on the literal, as well as on the figurative, level. She thus uses terms like "the wrong that thou hast receyved" (VII, 1393) and "this vileynye" (VII, 1404) when discussing Melibeus's injury. But the tale's literal fiction is most important in relation to her discussion of justice. She first warns her husband against unseemly vengeance, saying, "ye shul venge yow after the ordre of right; that is to seyn, by the lawe and noght by excesse ne by outrage" (VII, 1528), and advising against defense of violence by violence (VII, 1533), in sharp distinction to the advice Richard had received from the justices in 1387. In her diplomatic mission to Melibeus's enemies, she underscores the reality of the crimes they have committed against him, urging them to repent of their wrongs, "that hem oughten have greet repentaunce / of the injurie and wrong that they hadden doon to Melibee hir lord, and unto hire, and to hire doghter" (VII, 1732).

But the full burden of the tale's literal message falls on Melibeus himself, since it is he who must see the wisdom of replacing strict justice with merciful adjudication. Prudence therefore argues against his plan of disinheriting and exiling his now repentant neighbors:

> "Certes . . . this were a crueel sentence and muchel agayn resoun. /
> For ye been riche ynough and han no nede of oother mennes good /
> and ye myghte lightly in this wise gete yow a coveitous name, /
> which is a vicious thyng. . . . / And therfore it were bettre for yow

to lese so muchel good of youre owene than for to taken of hir good
in this manere, / for bettre it is to lesen good with worshipe than it
is to wynne good with vileynye and shame." (VII, 1835–40)

Such advice depends upon the tale's literal fiction, or upon the recognition
of an actual injury. Prudence can only urge Melibeus toward an awareness
of the benefits of mercy if she agrees that he has been wronged. Moreover,
Chaucer can only argue in such terms if we agree to the same fiction;
otherwise, the mercy that Prudence describes has only the value of a theoretical virtue. While Chaucer and his audience certainly believed in the
theory of mercy, the tale itself loses a good deal of its strength if we detach
it from the realm of the actual. It is one thing to speak abstractly of imitating God's mercy, quite another to seek to make that mercy relevant to
actual and injurious circumstances, as Prudence does near the very end of
her discourse. Her emphasis upon mercy as a political necessity in relation
to actual crimes committed against Melibeus is all the more pointed if we
see the tale as related to the political circumstances of the 1380s, or as a
carefully veiled analysis of the situation that existed between Richard II
and his subjects. Prudence implicitly suggests that Richard has indeed suffered an injury, that those who have sought to check his prerogatives are
not blameless and might well deserve the sort of strict justice that Melibeus
wishes to exact, the justices had advocated, and Richard surely contemplated. But she argues against such acts of justice on the grounds of political
expediency, offering him advice that allows him to take firm control of a
situation that threatens to control him.

On the other hand, Chaucer's decision to give Melibeus's daughter the
name of Sophie, or wisdom, concentrates the focus of the tale's figurative
level of meaning upon Melibeus himself and thus upon his responsibility
for the injuries he has suffered. It is Chaucer's interest in maintaining both
a literal and a figurative level of meaning that lies behind the seemingly
inconsistent handling of the figure of Sophie. These are inconsistencies that
he found in his source, but that he implicitly points up by his naming of
Sophie in the first sentence of the tale. For example, Prudence says to her
husband, "And therfore, sire, if ye wol triste to my conseil, I shal restoore
yow youre doghter hool and sound. / And eek I wol do to yow so muche
that ye shul have honour in this cause" (VII, 1109–10).[137] Her words make
sense only in relation to a figurative injured daughter, or in relation to

---

137. Chaucer here renders a faithful translation of the original.

Melibeus's damaged wisdom. Such inconsistencies become even more apparent when Prudence first considers the possible causes of Melibeus's injury, among them his enemies' hatred and malice (VII, 1395–1407). She follows up what is a discussion of a literal wrong by dwelling upon his lack of moral vigilance, which has made him vulnerable to attacks from man's three enemies, the flesh, the world, and the devil: "thou hast suffred hem entre in to thyn herte wilfully by the wyndowes of thy body, / and hast nat defended thyself suffisantly agayns hire assautes and hire temptaciouns, so that they han wounded thy soule in fyve places; / this is to seyn, the deedy synnes that been entred into thyn herte by thy fyve wittes" (VII, 1422–24). This sentence lays the blame for the attack on Melibeus himself. Prudence suggests her husband's fundamental responsibility for his predicament by using both verbs and adverbs that underline his inability to defend himself from assaults and temptations. Though her allegorical reading of the attack may seem heavy-handed to the modern reader, it gives ballast to the tale's powerful message of individual moral responsibility.

However, Chaucer's interest in heightening the tale's figurative meaning is even more provocative in relation to the political atmosphere of the 1380s. By naming Sophie, he at once emphasizes the interior nature of Melibeus's wound and downplays the need to dwell upon a legalistic emphasis on what constitutes just reparation. If Melibeus has indeed been wounded in his "fyve wittes," only Melibeus can restore what Melibeus has himself lost. Moreover, Chaucer's decision to delete such proverbs as "Woe to the land that has a child as a lord" seem intentionally disarming when we consider the possible political applications of Chaucer's handling of such figures as Sophie. The tale is focused upon the ruler's responsibility for maintaining a peaceful and fruitful relationship between himself and his subjects. The wrongs that Melibeus has suffered reflect his own incapacities and inattention to the moods and needs of his "neighbors." What the Tale of Melibee finally suggests is the astute and balanced nature of Chaucer's political analysis: he is not loath to blame Melibeus's neighbors for actual crimes, but he is most interested in illustrating how Melibeus might remedy a situation for which he is ultimately responsible. The fundamental message of the Tale of Melibee is directed at England's very heart, its king. The peace that comes of Dame Prudence's advice can come only as the result of Melibeus's recognition that order is his responsibility to restore. Furthermore, it is an order squarely based upon the assumption that political or social institutions are contractual by nature, that he must establish and maintain a relationship at once hierarchical and harmonious between himself and his subjects. He can only accomplish such a task if he is willing to see himself as bound by and to others—hence the importance of counsel—and as needing to maintain himself as a rational, objective leader of the whole body politic.

Albertano of Brescia's tract afforded Chaucer the literary screen that he needed for such a message. First, it gave him once more the literary role of the translator, or of the compiler.[138] Such a role, as Minnis points out, allowed him to deny any personal responsibility or authority for what were the ideas of other men, and to take responsibility only for their arrangement. Not only does the Tale of Melibee afford Chaucer such a defense, particularly since his translation diverges only rarely, albeit significantly, from his original, but the fact that its primary spokesperson is Dame Prudence (clearly a descendant of Lady Philosophy) gave him a second line of defense. If the other Canterbury pilgrims project themselves into their tales, frequently identifying with a figure whom they see as the hero of their stories, it is only logical to assume that Chaucer might have followed a similar strategy with the tale he assigns to the pilgrim Geoffrey. If so, the tale's only true "hero" is its heroine, Prudence. Chaucer thereby availed himself of a double blind, choosing a female spokesperson for a tale of political advice and analysis. Speaking from behind or within the tale's moral center, Chaucer rebukes both his contemporaries and his king, but in a way that maintains his cover as a reporter or compiler, a cover that is key to his self-characterization throughout *The Canterbury Tales*. Taken together with its mate, *Sir Thopas,* with its picture of bellicose chivalric buffoonery, the Tale of Melibee points up the tensions of the political and social atmosphere of the 1380s. In the Tale of Melibee, Chaucer offers a remedy as levelheaded as any Richard may have received.[139] He is urged to take the advice of a woman, or a translator, of someone without any genu-

---

138. Minnis (1984), 191–210.

139. *Sir Thopas* is, of course, undated although Manly, on fairly shakey grounds, placed it in the early 1380s; see the explanatory notes to *Sir Thopas* in *The Riverside Chaucer* (1987). On the pairing of *Sir Thopas* and The Tale of Melibee, see especially, V. J. Scattergood (1981); Yeager (1987). Though most studies of *Sir Thopas* are concerned with the tale's stylistic satire, both Scattergood and Yeager feel that in his "drasty rymyng" Chaucer takes aim at some of the absurdities of the contemporary knightly class, particularly at the element of that class intent on maintaining peace through war. The work of Scattergood and Yeager, along with my own, suggests that Chaucer's decision to link these two tales under his name, whenever that decision was made, was designed to link the issues of chivalric and regal responsibility. Patterson (1989) has more recently treated the Melibee as exemplifying one perspective upon Chaucer's understanding of the social practice of writing. Patterson sees the tale, which he too links to the figure of the poet in the role of adviser to kings, as a mode that Chaucer

ine political power, and cultivate his wisdom, becoming master of himself and thus the master of men. In so doing, Chaucer offers truly inverse counsel, cutting at the roots of both the literary and the political expectations of his age. He thereby positions himself, along with Prudence, on the periphery of events, far-sighted, astute, and artfully disguised by the inherent limitations of the role he has chosen for himself.

There is, moreover, a more fundamental—and ultimately darker—irony to the pilgrim Geoffrey's performance. The very form through which he chose to speak was rooted in the trials of the powerless. Boethius is a victim of imperial injustice; his need of wisdom does not cancel out the inequities of his situation. Chaucer's use of the Boethian fiction to advise his king inverts the traditional figuring of the *consolatio*. Rather than place in the foreground a powerless figure at the mercy of figures more powerful than he—a Black Knight checked by death or an unlucky lover—Chaucer accomplishes a sleight of hand and places the king in the chair of the commoner. Moreover, as the Boethian genre consistently teaches, the only means by which we leave that chair is by the power we find in our wills to change ourselves from victims, from fools of Fortune, to sovereigns. Chaucer thereby translates not simply a treatise but a form, altering its configurations, and passing it on more dangerous than he found it. He uses it, not to console a king's prisoner, but to address the king himself, and uses it to teach a king how to avoid becoming a prisoner of his own need for power.

There is consequently more at stake here than the events surrounding the Merciless Parliament. Chaucer's complicated handling of the subject of authority in relation to agency and council indicates that he saw the Merciless Parliament as but one instance of a longer process by which the understanding of authority was refigured to include the subject of representation from the last years of Edward to the early 1390s, when the Clerk's Tale was probably composed. It is in the Clerk's Tale that he most (in)directly confronts the complicated relationship between power and authority as they apply to the social body. In so doing, he again appropriates both the screen of a translated text and an inherited code of gender relations to throw into sharp relief the assumptions upon which order was supposedly

---

ultimately rejected. He takes *Sir Thopas* (which he links to the poet's function as a minstrel who exists to ratify social identity) as a serious exploration of the poet's social relationships. In the end, Patterson rejects the picture of Chaucer as continuing to speak with a political voice, choosing to see him as increasingly private, writing for history, rather than about it. Obviously I disagree, but Patterson's essay contains many important points and insights.

founded. Rather than define the social body in terms of its fundamental
unity, the Clerk divides that fictionalized wholeness into its separate parts.
The Clerk is the only pilgrim who offers a model for the social structure
through which can be posed genuinely hard questions about the realities
of power. As such, it is a far more sophisticated performance than either
the legend of Saint Cecilia or the Tale of Melibee. Through the Clerk's
complicated handling of the story of Griselda, Chaucer allows darker questions into his book. By separating (and not rejoining) authority from power,
the tale depicts a starkly polarized world where representation is neither
effective nor, for the most part, disinterested. The decision to recount the
story of Griselda and the precise way in which her story is shaped reflect
Chaucer's astute reading of political relationships.

The Clerk ends his story by telling us what the tale is not intended to do,

> This storie is seyd, nat for that wyves sholde
> Folwen Grisilde as in hymylitee,
> For it were inportable, though they wolde,
> But for that every wight, in his degree,
> Sholde be constant in adversitee
> As was Grisilde. . . .
>
> (vi, 1142–47)

In suggesting that his tale is bearable only if read allegorically, the Clerk
inevitably points to what he left out of his tale, to what is otherwise unap-
parent. And indeed for most modern readers the tale's metaphysics seem a
poor return on the ventures of either life or art. As Derek Pearsall has
remarked, the picture of marriage as tyranny, as "the exercise of absolute
power over a powerless subject is not a convenient analogy for the comfortable relationship of a loving God and a grateful subject."[140] It is in the
juncture between the literal apprehension of the story of Griselda's patient
suffering of her husband Walter's inexplicable cruelty and its figurative
application that the Clerk's Tale has acquired its critical literature. Elizabeth
Salter's early work on the Clerk's Tale established the terms of this critical
conversation by pointing up the ways in which the tale's allegory does not
fit its fictional vehicle.[141] More recently, Anne Middleton has pointed out
that the tale "has become in modern times perhaps *The Canterbury Tales'*

---

140. Pearsall (1992), 255. See also Wetherbee (1989a), 13, 90–95.
141. Salter (1962a).

supreme test of its readers' interpretive powers."[142] Charlotte Morse has reiterated the ways in which the tale spoke to the yearning of earlier readers for *exempla* of wisdom, fidelity, and patience, but it elicits a more violent and hostile reaction among twentieth-century readers who fault the Clerk for telling a story whose impact and meaning depend upon an acceptance of gender as hierarchically and repressively ordered.[143]

Two different but related schools of critical thought have begun to change the ways in which we are coming to understand our own reaction to the Clerk's Tale. Readings of Chaucer that focus on his handling of gender as a means of exploring contemporary social codes and feminist analyses of gender relations within his works have significantly broadened our view of the relevance of women, of sexual and social relationships, and of the misogyny we were all trained to accept as part of the medieval landscape.[144] We are consequently less willing to dismiss our anger at Walter and more willing to scrutinize the Clerk's uneasy and frequently ambiguous relationship to the subject of gender relations. Second, studies of the political valences of the tale of Griselda as it was passed from Boccaccio to Petrarch have suggested Chaucer's participation in an elaborate literary conversation about tyrannical power.[145] Both types of approaches take as their starting points the disunity the tale's two levels of meaning produce and go on to explore the possible meanings of disunity or instability. They consequently focus attention upon Chaucer's reasons for choosing to translate into English a tale already in use as a register of social tension.[146]

As these studies suggest, we should trust the violent reaction the tale elicits from modern readers as indicating something else in it besides a message of spiritual endurance and acceptance. The question is finally not the appropriateness of two radically different responses to the tale of Griselda. The question turns on Chaucer's motives for encouraging two opposed levels of meaning, since their disjunction directs us to the hotly

---

142. Middleton (1980), 121.

143. Morse (1985).

144. For example, see Aers (1978–79); Aers (1988a); Dinshaw (1989); Hansen (1992); Mann (1991); Martin (1990); Strohm (1992), chap. 7, "Treason in the Household."

145. Grudin (1989); Wallace (1990).

146. For the texts, see Severs (1941a, 1942). See also Golenistcheff-Koutouzoff (1933). For Philippe de Mézières's translation of the tale (c. 1384–88), see Golenistcheff-Koutouzoff (1937). De Mézières also refers to the tale in an even more overt political context in his *Letter to King Richard II*, written in 1395; see Coopland (1976). For important remarks about the textual history of the tale, see Middleton (1980); Morse (1985). See Lerer (1993), chap. 3, for comments about the fifteenth-century manuscripts in which the Clerk's tale appears.

debated subjects of authority and power. The Clerk of Oxford at once uses Griselda to define authority and presents that authority as unavailable to a contemporary society that does not value what is not immediately quantifiable. Griselda therefore threatens not simply Walter, or hegemonic principles in general; she calls into question the entire status quo that emanates from a source of political power. That level of meaning, the allegorical or the spiritual, to which the Clerk directs his audience at the end of his tale also provides Chaucer with the means of indicting secular institutions for their utter lack of authority. In fact, the very machinery that undergirds the spiritual meaning of the tale is essential to what is a more disturbing political meditation.

To return to the Clerk's strictures on interpretation: By insisting on an allegorical or spiritual meaning for his tale, the Clerk directs attention to those very points at which the allegory falters. The changes he makes in the sources he used suggest his awareness of the tale's inherent inconsistencies.[147] First, the Clerk inserts himself into his own narrative by underlining the troubling nature of the tale he has borrowed, encouraging us to read Walter as both mysterious or irrational and cruel in a way that his sources do not do. Second, he drastically enlarged the role of the people, thus altering the relationship among the tale's various parts in ways that inevitably affect narrative balance, perspective, and, consequently, a reader's response. Here, as in the legend of Saint Cecilia, he reveals his own dexterity as a reader or critic. He expands upon what is implicit—though unrealized and thus undeveloped—in both of his sources. The French and Latin accounts describe a confrontation between two forces, Griselda and Walter. The role of the people is incidental. But Chaucer gathers the diffuse references in his sources into a single monolithic force to which he applies one of two nouns, *people* or *folk*.[148] Though the French version of the tale does employ the noun *people,* neither of Chaucer's sources reveals the consistent focus upon the people that Chaucer establishes by the repetition of these two nouns. Where both the Latin and the French versions are as likely to refer to "those standing near" or to "those observing," or, more abstractly yet to Walter's growing reputation for cruelty (Walter's bad *fama* in this case serving as a metonymy), Chaucer describes a single force, point of view, and voice that he designates as "the people." This has the effect of

---

147. On the tale's relationship to its sources, see also Middleton (1980); Morse (1985); Grudin (1989); Wallace (1990).

148. See my early essay (Johnson 1975) that discusses one level of meaning inherent in Chaucer's use of the people.

writing out the minor nobles and the courtiers of the Petrarchan tale.[149] Rather than the clutter of an Italian court with its various classes and interlocking relationships, the Clerk sketches in a world composed of the aristocratic Walter, his wife, and his people, both, of humble origin.

The Clerk characterizes the people as unstable. Soon after having sworn their inner and outer obedience to him, the people begin to doubt his promise to marry. Once they experience Griselda's concern for them, they love her. When the people assume Walter is a murderer, their love turns to hatred and they begin to murmur against him, "For which, where as his peple therbifore / Hadde loved hym wel, the sclaundre of his diffame / Made hem that they hym hatede therfore" (IV, 729–31). Later, when they see the beauty of Walter's "new wife," they admire him, saying "That Walter was no fool, thogh that hym leste / To chaunge his wyf, for it was for the beste" (IV, 986–87).[150] The tale's happy ending returns them to a state of docile obedience, in which they remain for Walter's life and for that of his son, who succeeds him in "reste and pees" (IV, 1136).

Both the Clerk's strategic intervention into his own tale and his careful blocking of the people as unstable and self-interested combine to focus our attention upon Griselda as a foil—both to the people's fickleness and to Walter's apparent changeability. Though at the end of the tale, he interprets Griselda as the Christian soul, throughout the narrative, he surrounds her with symbols linking her to Christ.[151] When Walter comes for her, Griselda is carrying a water pot, which she sets down "in an oxes stalle." After she is dressed for her wedding, the Clerk remarks that it does not seem as though she were born and reared in an "oxe-stalle." The references to the ox's stall, which are not in his sources, implicitly assimilate Griselda to the

---

149. De Mézières includes barons, once more suggesting that the tale always speaks to the issue of power relations. See Golenistcheff-Koutouzoff (1933), 158.

150. Wallace (1990), 200–202, sees this incident and the following pronouncement upon popular changeability ("O stormy peple. . .") as an instance of rupture in Commons, a rupture that has been created by Walter's tyranny. Justice (1994b), 227 n. 118, however, sees the two points of view as merely indicative of the fundamental valuelessness that characterizes the popular voice. I think the situation Chaucer describes is yet more grave, for the "peple" (who welcome the novelty of a new lady "of hir toun") are opposed to "sadde folk" (the voice behind the "O stormy peple" stanza), and neither has any ability to check Walter's behavior, nor any wish to do so.

151. Condren (1984) argues that the tale presents Griselda as a figure for Christ who is tempted and tested by blind humanity, embodied in Walter. However, Condren's reading simply substitutes one spiritual allegory for another. Rather than search for a means of harmonizing the tale's conflicting elements, I suggest we accept the conflict between the two levels of meaning as part of Chaucer's intent and thus of the tale's force.

Christ child, born among the beasts and reared in poverty. At the same time, the Clerk emphasizes Griselda's "translation." By dressing her richly and by combing her hair, the women who enrobe Griselda for her wedding enact a ritual of social and spiritual change. Like a queen en route to her coronation or like a soul newly dressed, Griselda's progress from hut to palace is accomplished by means of symbols deeply woven into medieval culture. Griselda does what Hawkyn cannot: she wears new clothes to her wedding feast.[152] The Clerk translates those ideals of the *imitatio Christi* that are also embodied in Cecilia—chastity, fruitfulness, charity, integrity, care for the common good, and faith—into the secular Griselda.[153]

But here, the Clerk's allegory breaks down. In a sense, the Clerk cannot have it so many ways: How can Griselda carry the burden of being the virtuous soul translated from a low form of existence to a higher one and the image of Christ without violating the Clerk's suggestion that Walter is "like" God? Or, put another way, how can her clothes mean? If Griselda's new clothes signify her translation from commoner to queen, her marriage to the husband of all souls, why are we not distraught when she puts them off? She equates her old clothes with her primordial purity, her nakedness with her virginity:

> My lord, ye woot that in my fadres place
> Ye dide me streepe out of my povre weede,
> And richely me cladden, of youre grace.

---

152. As both the contemporary poems *Purity* and *Piers Plowman* illustrate, clothing was used as an indicator of the spiritual state. The New Testament guest who wears dirty clothing to the wedding feast (see Matthew 22) is a type of the unrepentant soul. Clothing was also an important symbol in political ritual. For example, in 1390, Richard II made a gift of a pair of red-velvet shoes to the monks of Westminster to replace those lost at his coronation. The abbey stored the coronation regalia and clearly both the king and the monks thought the shoes important enough to warrent replacing. See Hector and Harvey (1982), 414–17. For another study emphasizing translation as an elaborate literary metaphor, see Wallace (1990).

153. On this aspect of Griselda, see Mann (1991), 158. Although I agree with many of Mann's remarks about Griselda's allegorical dimension, I do not think either the portrait or the tale so harmonious as she does; nor do I see Griselda and Constance as similar, thus allowing us to equate suffering femininity with Christlikeness. That Chaucer himself perceived the complications inherent in the language of gender and of devotion is apparent if we compare Griselda to Constance. The Clerk's picture of Griselda is less one of the suffering woman (and certainly not analogous to the passive femininity so central to the Man of Law's performance) than of the outsider, separated by class and gender from power, who nonetheless retains control over each situation. Though I assimilate her to Christ, I do so through the figure who underlies the more radical, social gospel that Aers has articulated above. For a perceptive reading of the Man of Law, see Wetherbee (1989b).

To yow broghte I noght elles, out of drede,
But feith, and nakednesse, and maydenhede . . .
                              (IV, 862–66)

Wherfore, in gerdon of my maydenhede,
Which that I broghte, and noght agayn I bere,
As voucheth sauf to yeve me, to my meede,
But swich a smok as I was wont to were,
That I therwith may wrye the wombe of here
That was youre wyf . . .
                              (IV, 883–88)

Where his sources focus upon the rich clothes and jewels Griselda leaves behind her as simply as any good dealt her by Fortune, Chaucer places his greatest emphasis upon her poverty, her formerly poor clothes, as signs of her unalloyed identity. The rich clothes define her as a wife and consort, but "swich a smok as I was wont to were" defines her inner reality, a maidenhead gone forever (as Harry Bailey reminds his group at the beginning of the Man of Law's tale), but nonetheless remanent in the smock she wears to cover the womb that bore Walter his apparently dead children. Chaucer may well be recalling—or having Griselda echo—Saint Jerome's view of marriage as a skin or covering, hence as a protection from the solitary condition of human life, and of nakedness as a symbol of virginity.[154] If so, the allusion encapsulates the fissure between the tale's two levels of meaning. If we are to see the relationship between Walter and Griselda as *like* that between God and the soul, as the Clerk insists, Griselda's long speech makes no sense. Nor does it make any sense in relation to the earlier scene of clothing. How can Griselda enhance her status by slipping back into Hawkyn's old clothes, especially since her new clothes were invested with such meaning previously? The clothes that typically figure soiled humanity in this context Chaucer uses to indicate Griselda's all-encompassing humanity, her redemptive Christlikeness, her willing resumption of lower status in a society whose sumptuary laws were used to define social boundaries. However, in relation to Walter the *ruler,* who speaks "boistously" "in open audience" to Griselda, and whom the Clerk consistently questions and judges, Griselda's willing assumption of vulnerability, her integrity, and her control make an enormous amount of sense. Her "femininity" defines Walter's "masculinity": like that of Al-

---

154. From Epistle 128 cited in Miles (1989), 66.

machius, it is bombast, the noise of power. If she is, in part, a figure for Christ, she can only be a figure for the Christ who opposed himself to hostile systems of power, who spoke for the common profit, who answered his judges only in the most measured and rational sentences, and who concealed his nature in the vesture of flesh.

Chaucer's version of the tale of Griselda depends upon a narrator who at once points up its inconsistencies and underlines the tale's spiritual lessons. The Clerk's literal or emotional comments, which encourage us to view Walter simply as cruel, if taken at face value, tempt us—like the people—to react to Walter and his actions rather than to emulate Griselda, who acts freely and creatively. The key to her freedom is knowledge, a knowledge Griselda herself gives evidence of possessing with her startling words to Walter on the eve of his marriage to his new wife:

> "O thyng biseke I yow, and warne also,
> That ye ne prikke with no tormentynge
> This tendre mayden, as ye han doon mo;
> For she is fostred in hire norissynge
> Moore tendrely, and to my supposynge,
> She koude nat adversitee endure
> As koude a povre fostred creature."
>
> (IV, 1037–43)

Griselda here gives notice that she is no gull, no unwitting victim of Walter's temptations or of the Clerk's irony, but a figure who, in living by the spirit of the bargain she contracted with Walter before her marriage, lives by love and therefore by knowledge. On the other hand, the people have broken both their literal and metaphoric agreement with Walter. Though they have not engaged in active rebellion, they have complained against Walter's right to make decisions and, upon seeing his intended new wife, have turned against the wife they swore to accept and honor. The very words Walter uses to restrict their activities "neither grucche ne stryve" foreshadow their role as the antitype of Griselda. Their impatience only serves to highlight her patience, since as the tale finally implies, both Griselda and the people are subjected to the same test, whose object is patience.

On the level of metaphysics, what the Clerk—or Petrarch—implies about the inscrutability and terror of human existence is a more realistic solution to existence (ultimately more comforting) than attempts to explain away the unexplainable. In comparison to the Clerk, pilgrims like the Man of

Law hold out cheap answers and illusory comfort to the problems of real adversity.[155] Experience can prove the worth of the Clerk's Tale, as it also proves the appropriateness of his refusal to provide us with the answer we seek. He, instead, in the contrast between Griselda and the people, depicts two modes of response to a power we cannot expect to understand. The obvious correlative here is the book of Job. In the end, Job is granted no real explanation for his suffering, simply the dazzling reminder of God's superior power in the awesome list of questions with which God answers Job's query. Job is thus answered only in terms of his own limited perspective: he was not there when God made the whale or when the stars sang together. Used in this way, the story of Job is not a political tale; it privatizes suffering and operates on the level of the individual process of enlightenment and acceptance. However, the very harshness and mysteriousness of the Clerk's spiritual allegory become deeply disturbing when we translate it into the realm of political or social relations. It is when we cease to see Griselda's patience as Job-like and begin to see it as Christlike, that the tale acquires a broader social or political valence. Those same three components of the Clerk's Tale—people, Griselda, and Walter—that combine to provide a tough spiritual lesson can also be used to define a grim political situation.

The Clerk's Tale may end with injunctions to read the tale spiritually, but it begins in a veiled conversation about the social function of poetry.[156] In asking the Clerk to tell his tale, Harry Bailey first tells him not to tell a spiritual tale ("To make us for oure olde synnes wepe" [IV, 13]) and to reserve high style for addressing kings (IV, 18). The Host thus specifies both subject matter ("som myrie tale") fitting to the "play" of the contest and style ("Speketh so pleyn at this tyme . . . That we may undrstonde" [19–20]). The Clerk replies in language worthy of a king's adviser,

> I am under youre yerde,
> Ye han of us as now the governance
> And therfore wol I do yow
>   obeisance,
> As fer a resoun axeth, hardily.
>   (22–25)

---

155. On this issue, see Wetherbee (1989b).

156. On this opening and the ways in which Chaucer uses it to compose a community, see Lerer (1993), 29–31; Middleton (1980); G. Olson (1982b), 160–61; Wallace (1990).

He signals his obedience to the ordering principle of the pilgrimage: for the duration of the "play," the Host, and not, for example the Knight or the Monk or the Parson, rules the roost.[157] But he qualifies the degree of his consent with the phrase, "as fer as resoun axeth" and goes on to tell a tale that employs "spiritual" matter as a mode of political address.

The Clerk is similarly "obedient" to his ostensible Petrarchan source. First, he uses more than a single source, drawing as well upon the French *Le Livre Griseldis,* and perhaps upon Boccaccio's original. Second, as we have seen, in the act of translating he reshapes the tale. In addition to heightening the role of the people, the Clerk himself points out Walter's inscrutability, thus opening him up to the widest sort of interpretation. For example, both Petrarch and the author of *Le Livre Griseldis* follow Boccaccio in quickly characterizing Walter as given to the pleasures of the chase and therefore as unmindful of the future ("incuriosissimus futurorum").[158] The Clerk expands this opening description of Walter from what is only about six lines in both of his sources to three stanzas and, in the process, manages to imply a good deal about the prerequisites for good rule. The Clerk not only expresses his disapproval for Walter's carelessness but glosses it in moral terms:

> I blame hym thus: that he considered noght
> In tyme comynge what myghte hym bityde,
> But on his lust present was al his thoght,
> As for to hauke and hunte on every syde.
> Wel ny alle othere cures leet he slyde,
> And eek he nolde—and that was worst of alle—
> Wedde no wyf, for noght that may bifalle.
>
> (IV [E] 78–84)

The Clerk is subtly disobedient to his master Petrarch here. His phrasing, which combines elements from both of his sources, points up not simply Walter's inattention but his more dangerous tendency to negligence and self-regard. By pairing the phrases "hunte on every syde" and "cures leet he slyde," rhyming *syde* with *slyde,* he juxtaposes Walter's "lust present"

---

157. See also Lerer (1993) and Olson (1982b).

158. Severs (1942), 256. The French is a bit more expansive and is probably where Chaucer got his emphasis upon passing time: "et en somme noble en toutes manieres, fors tant qu'il ne vouloit que soy jouer et esbatre et passer temps ne ne consideroit point au tempts ne es choses a venir" (257).

to his "cures," a noun used to describe pastoral as well as social responsibility. The emphatic phrasing seems also to catch the echo of contemporary voices, since in 1386 a group of burgesses had complained about the lack of justice in the realm, listing Richard's love of hunting as a sign of his irresponsibility and political naïveté.[159]

Chaucer's handling of the next scene, in which Walter's subjects ask him to take care for their future by marrying, continues to play with the notion of social responsibility, but does so by glancing at the subject of representation. Both of his sources say that Walter's people choose one of their number who has greater authority and who knows how to talk to him.[160] The scene in the Clerk's Tale suggests a different type of social tension:

> Oonly that point his peple bar so soore
> That flokmeele on a day they to hym wente,
> And oon of hem, that wisest was of loore—
> Or elles that the lord best wolde assente
> That he sholde tell hym what his people mente,
> Or elles koude he shewe wel swich mateere—
> He to the markys seyde as ye shul heere . . .
>   (IV [E] 85–91)

This stanza contains two words that I would describe as part of Chaucer's private political lexicon: *flokmeele* and *assente*. The word *flokmeele*, meaning "in groups," seems a peculiarly Chaucerian choice, since the term inevitably evokes other significant "flocks": the flock the Host gathers together for the trip to Canterbury and the more literal flock whose welfare Chaunticleer almost fatally impedes. The word implies the need for a figure of authority. Chickens or sheep or birds, the nouns for which flock is a signifier, are creatures whose very lack of reason demands a point of reference. As Chaucer's other references to representative bodies suggest, he gave little credence to the sort of "wisdom" that might issue from groups.[161] Chaucer, however, does not play the part of flattering Placebo and disparage the flock in order merely to endorse rulership. Chaunticleer must learn to use his wits before he can ensure his flock's security.[162] "Flokmelle" may also be intended to recall that flock of birds who gathered early in another

---

159. See Ainsworth (1990), 188.
160. See Severs (1942), 256–57.
161. See, for example, McCall and Rudisall (1959).
162. See Ganim (1990); Johnson (1985).

decade and whose "order" captured something of the tension in the social body between the concept of the public good and the reality of individual desire. In other words, Chaucer's use of the word seems both to deny and admit the seriousness with which we should take such bodies. Moreover, in the following lines he adumbrates what is a process of parliamentary prerogative whose underlying rationale is left ambiguous. The people in the Clerk's Tale do not simply select a figure at once sage and eloquent; they select someone who is wise *or* able to encourage Walter to listen to "what his peple mente" *or* who can elaborate on the people's concerns. Chaucer's audience would have recognized that Walter's people elect a *speaker* who presents the people's care for its future in a way that allows Walter to change his behavior.

Chaucer's use of the word *assente* is equally freighted with political and social associations. *Assente* could be used to designate a private or a formal agreement; it could also describe mutual consent or, more simply, an opinion. Chaucer uses the word in the first sense when, before he takes away her daughter, Walter asks Griselda "that ye to me assente as in this thyng" (IV, 494). In the General Prologue Chaucer employs the communal connotations of the word when by "oon assent," the pilgrims accept the Host as governor, judge, and recordkeeper (I [A] 813–14). In the Knight's Tale, Chaucer allows for its full range of meanings, since the Knight uses it to imply the need to align the individual with the concept of the popular good. He therefore describes the Athenians as ceasing to mourn for Arcite "by oon general assent" at which point they summon a parliament to decide matters of alliance. Afterward, Theseus summons Emelye and Palamon and delivers to them the famous First Mover speech in which he opposes individual "wilfulnesse" to the orderly mutability of the universe. He then says to Emelye, "Suster . . . this is my fulle assent, / With al th'avys heere of my parlement," urging her to take Palamon for husband and for lord, to show her "wommanly pitee." In effect, he asks her to bend her will to his own opinion and to the mutual accord of Parliament by giving her formal agreement to a marriage that has now become a symbol of the tentative settlement between mortality and order. Theseus thus asks Emelye to marry and thereby become the agent who brings Thebes into alliance with Athens, the Venerian body politic into harmony with Athenian wisdom. In so doing she will also subject Diana to communal laws. In reversing the direction of the request, the Clerk subordinates the question itself. In this tale the flock asks the assent of its leader: the people, who are consistently described as short-sighted, offer Walter, as Theseus offers Emelye, marriage as a remedy against time. The Clerk returns to the substance of the Knight's Tale, thus pointing up those very limitations inherent in the Knight's version of social order.

The Knight's Tale can serve as a touchstone for our postmodernist sensitivity to irresolution and conflict. Where the Knight's Tale was too often seen as an early answer to the social conflicts staged throughout the Canterbury pilgrimage, recent studies of the tale figure it as the first of a series of complicated questions about social order and the individual's relation to that order. Thus, though they focus on different aspects of the Knight's Tale, Marshall Leicester, Barbara Nolan, and Lee Patterson all point to the ways in which the Boethian surface of the Knight's Tale of hierarchical ordering only tenuously contains the unruliness the Knight and his chivalric code are theoretically supposed to neutralize. The Knight's half-ironic appraisal of the structuralist architectonics of his performance, his understanding or misunderstanding of the history he recounts, and the tale's fundamental relationship to such literary models as the *roman antique* all provide means of entry into a realm of ambiguity and instability.[163] As Chaucer seems to have suspected, for the Knight and those who share a faith in an order based upon beautiful fictions, the game is already more than half-lost.[164] Whether we agree with Leicester that the Knight himself acknowledges the limits of these fictions or with Patterson that he fails to understand the nature of the historical and social reality he composes, it is almost impossible to accept the tale as the standard against which the disorder of the tale-telling is measured.[165] But it is in this tale that Chaucer begins to ask the series of complicated and unresolved questions about social and individual order that impell the book.

By simply opposing wilfulness to necessity or by proposing in Theseus the Jovian principle of order to which the various components of the social body must relate or risk a reputation for wilfulness, the Knight considers social order only in relation to disorder. His carefully polarized picture of the commonweal allows only the simplest questions about social order into his tale. The Miller responds to this picture with a parody of the story of

---

163. Leicester (1990), 221–382; Nolan (1992), chap. 7; Patterson (1991), chap. 3. These are among the lengthiest recent studies of the Knight's tale. For other important studies, see Aers (1980), chap. 7; Neuse (1962); Neuse (1991), 105–28; Pearsall (1992), 151–59; Salter (1962a).

164. I owe the phrase to Nolan (1992), 280.

165. Wetherbee (1989a) also feels that the Knight himself is aware of the complexities of his tale, 43.

Palamon and Arcite: he substitutes Nicholas and Absalom for the courtly lovers, puts a "beard" on Emelye, and locates the action in the profit-oriented and inquisitive peasant community rather than in the distant city of Athens.[166] Robin interprets communal harmony not as a state achieved through a process of rational evaluation and assent but as a much more tenuous balance effected between individual appetite and the communal drive for stasis. He may challenge the Knight's fiction by plunging us into the economic and social conflicts of Chaucer's England, but he leaves intact the assumptions upon which the Knight's understanding of society is founded.

The Clerk challenges the Knight's vision of order by reconsidering those elements that make up the social body. Rather than Theseus, the Clerk presents Walter. He omits the warring aristocrats entirely. For the Athenian parliament that inclines unanimously to Boethian harmonies, he offers "the people."[167] For Emelye, the chivalric prize, the object of male desire and fear, he depicts Griselda, whose silence and strength are far more daunting to male majesty than the chastity of any romantic heroine. From the very beginning of his tale, it is clear that the Clerk has more to do than block in a top-heavy and anachronistic picture of the state. If the way in which the question is phrased predicts the answer or the range of possible answers to it, the differences between the Knight's and the Clerk's Tales could not be more striking. The Knight begins with a carefully composed and static portrait of Theseus in whom he embodies the ideals of medieval chivalric rule. But the Clerk begins in a way much more ambiguous and provocative.[168] Where in the versions of Boccaccio, Petrarch, and that found in *Le Livre de Griseldis*, attention is immediately focused only on Walter and upon his political power, the Clerk divides his focus to include both Walter and the people. In so doing, he underlines the ways in which representative responsibility and consent are intimately related to regal assent and responsibility. If I were to translate the dynamics of his tale into the crudest possible terms, I would say that it depicts a world where Commons is too easily swayed by appearance and self-interest and where the monarch is unchecked either by private codes or by his relations and subjects.

As reductive as such a translation is, it nonetheless provides a point of entry into the personal and political issues that lie behind Chaucer's deci-

---

166. Knight (1986), 90; Schweitzer (1986), 27.

167. Wallace (1990), 202, has also noted the relationship here with Commons.

168. I am here extending P. Brown's (1992) remarks about political rhetoric in chap. 1 of *Power and Persuasion in Late Antiquity*.

sion to translate his version of the story of Griselda into the language of late fourteenth-century England. In sharp contrast, Chaucer's contemporary Philippe de Mézières first used the story of Griselda to endorse the private virtues of mastery of the self and, a few years later, to extole wifely docility. (He translated the story sometime between 1384 and 1389, and in his *Letter to King Richard,* written in 1395, wished Richard a wife like Griselda.) His version of the story encourages a nonprovocative reading, one intended to maintain orderly hierarchies based on strictly defined boundaries between classes and genders.[169] The Clerk's Tale, along with other tales from the "marriage-group," is commonly ascribed to the period from about 1390 to 1394. For Chaucer himself, this was a period of change, of what Derek Pearsall has labeled "new beginnings."[170] In July 1389, he was appointed to a busy administrative post as clerk of the king's works. The post, which paid well, demanded a good deal of time and energy. He served in this office until June 1391, when he either resigned or was asked to resign. Thereafter, during a period of enormous creativity and productivity when he was occupied with writing the bulk of the *Canterbury Tales,* his annual income came from various annuities and presents. The records also suggest that for most of the 1390s he was living in Kent, probably in Greenwich, about six miles from London. Thus, while he was working on the *Canterbury Tales,* he was free to consider his subject matter from a sort of double vantage point; his physical distance from London was matched by the spiritual distance of his semi-retirement. As a man who had been involved with public issues all of his life and whose interests had allied him with the Crown to greater or lesser degrees, Richard's majority must have presented Chaucer with a curious spectacle of power.

In May 1389, Richard resumed his regality and began to lay the foundations for a state centered around a strong, even autocratic, monarchy.[171] Though earlier studies of Richard described him as an irrational and neurotic figure, more recently historians of the period have begun to consider him as a royal theorist and strategist. Consequently, increasingly attention is being paid to Richard's reasons for attempting to locate power so thoroughly in the king and thus to his handling of the political situation in the

169. See Philippe de Mézières, *Letter to King Richard II,* in Coopland (1976), 37, 42. See also Morse (1985), 77–80; Williamson (1985), 393–408.

170. Pearsall (1992), 214–26.

171. Barron (1971); Eberle (1981); Galbraith (1982); R. H. Jones (1968); A. Tuck (1985), 197–222. For another view, see Taylor (1971). For a study of tyranny and tyrants, both Italian and English, in relation to Chaucer, see Wallace (1991).

years succeeding the Merciless Parliament. Richard's actions seem now more canny and calculating. For example, after the Merciless Parliament he needed to establish a basis for his assumption of regal dignity and power. Through the Tale of Melibee Chaucer counsels that a ruler maintains power through authority. Though Prudence is realistic about the exigencies of rule, she consistently locates responsibility for good rule in the ruler, or in his willingness to accept that responsibility. Richard seems to have decided on another course. It was certainly to his benefit to encourage faction in order to position himself centrally in relation to those factions. Therefore, in an effort to break the alliance between the nobility and the Commons that had had such harsh results in the Merciless Parliament of 1388, he sided with the Commons on two important issues: the war with France and the need to curb livery and maintenance.[172] Even as he sought to dislodge the magnates from the private armies that were the source for their power, he attempted to create strong bonds between the monarch and the nobility. Thus, in the Smithfield Tournament of 1390 he unveiled his badge of the White Hart, through which he would bind members of the nobility to him in a royal livery.[173] Furthermore, Richard clearly sought to stamp a particular impression upon his age. In the lavish appointments, manner of living, fashions, and entertainments of his court and in the art and architecture of the Ricardian period can be detected a particular style, the impress of the royal identity.[174] What can seem merely thoughtlessness and prodigality—charges that were leveled at Richard by the chroniclers— may, in fact, be a strategy for centering cultural as well as political power in the monarchy.

Simple power was, of course, not the object of negotiation; there are and there were varieties of power. In the late Middle Ages the economic power that was an important component of the commonweal resided in the city and in the merchants who controlled the medieval city. In 1392 what Caroline Barron describes as a long-standing grudge between Richard and the city of London broke out into open hostilities when the citizens of London refused the king a loan.[175] In May of that year he issued a writ informing the London sheriffs that the court of common pleas had been removed to York; then he removed the chancery, the exchequer, and the inmates of Fleet Prison. A few weeks later, Richard sent a writ summoning the mayor,

172. A. Tuck (1973), 134.
173. Storey (1971), 131–52.
174. See Eberle (1981).
175. Barron (1971). See also Thrupp (1989), chap. 1.

the sheriffs, and all aldermen to appear before him at the end of June. Richard had them imprisoned, replaced the city government, and levied a huge fine on the city. Barron's analysis of this episode is particularly astute and apposite to the issues raised through the Clerk's Tale. She suggests that Richard's pardon of the city later that summer was designed to point up his mercy, that his harsh tactics were the foil to his gesture of forgiveness. However, as Barron also points out, the king pardoned the fines (though he demanded 10,000 pounds as the cost of the pardon) and restored the city's liberties only conditionally with the proviso "until the king shall otherwise ordain."[176]

Money was not the sole price of pardon. As the monk of Westminster puts it, Richard demanded that "on the day appointed for his progress, which was 21 August, they should come out to meet him and receive him at Wandsworth with appropriate pomp, each city craft in its own livery and mounted on horseback, to escort him with all honour through the city to Westminster."[177] The Westminster chronicler describes the citizens as carrying out these conditions to the letter. They not only thronged (22,000 on horse and an "unaccountable" number on foot) to meet him, but elaborately staged his re-entry into the city. At Wandsworth, the "first encounter" ("In primo namque occursu") they presented him with a sword and the keys of the city. At London Bridge, they presented him with two coursers and the queen with a palfrey. Both horses were magnificently saddled. The city was decorated and hung with various cloths in Richard's honor. At Fish Street, two beautiful young men censed him with golden thuribles. At Eastcheap, two boys dressed as angels presented Richard and Queen Anne with two crowns. From there the king and queen processed to Temple Bar, where they were presented with a gold table "worth 100 marks." At Westminster, the royal pair laid aside their crowns to kiss the Gospels held out to them by the prior and monks of the Abbey. The king entered the church, made his devotions before the shrine of Saint Edward, and returned to his palace. The next day he attended a banquet held by the Londoners in his honor where he received another table, this one worth five hundred marks. Afterwards Richard seated himself on his throne and returned to the city what he had taken away, with, of course, some provisions.[178]

---

176. Barron (1971), 190–91.

177. Hector and Harvey (1982), 504–5.

178. I have drawn my account from the Westminster Chronicle. For other accounts, see Higden (1964), 8:268–70; Smith (1972); Suggett (1947). It is interesting—particularly in light of similar accounts of Richard in the 1380s—that contemporaries do not lay the blame on

The pageant suggests the intricate way in which regal power was under-
written by mercantile wealth. The city manifested its rights and its might
in the magnificence with which it decked itself and in the worth of the
presents it gave to Richard. Its acts are quantifiable, and the Westminster
monk does not hesitate to note how much the gifts are worth. Neither did
the city present itself to Richard with ritual gestures of supplication and
humiliation, such as going barefoot to meet him; but, instead, the crafts
rode out in organized prosperity to welcome back a runaway king.[179] Richard, however, wanted a final gesture, one, perhaps, in the direction of
history. He requested that the Carmelite friar, Richard Maidstone, record
the pageant in a Latin poem.[180] The *Concordia* is consequently not an
account of the pageant—and indeed it differs radically from other contemporary accounts of the event—but a reading of it, an interpretation of its
script in terms of contemporary political language. It describes the reconciliation as taking place between the city of New Troy and its spouse, its
king and its master. Torn apart by evil counsel, the two now enact a moment of marital reunion. Richard is presented as beautiful, merciful, kindly,
and pious and the city as gaily decked like a bride to receive her husband
and lord. Maidstone's account, which is far more detailed than that found
in the Westminster Chronicle, elaborately plays with this drama of courtship and reconciliation between two magnificent figures, the well-appointed
wife and the kingly husband. He records for Richard (and for posterity) a
picture of Richard as frozen in perpetual youth, as, at once, Paris, Troilus,
Absalom, *and* Solomon and of New Troy as the site of bounty. In putting
together such a disastrous set of figures, Maidstone most likely intended to
instruct as well as to praise his prince, implicitly urging him to maintain
control by maintaining his "masculine" wisdom. He thereby offers Richard
an obverse portrait of himself as triumphant over both the powers of time
and of rebellion.

What happened between Richard and the citizens of London, as between
Richard and his courtiers is a prolonged conversation about goods and
power. The language of marriage that Maidstone employs functions as a

---

the king *or* on the city for the original conflict, but, instead, blame Richard's counsellors for
misleading him. See, for example, Hector and Harvey (1982), 496–97.

179. For an analysis of the rituals of supplication as they relate to political order, see Koziol
(1993), esp. chap. 9. For other pertinent discussions of royal pageantry, see Cannadine and
Price (1987). For studies of English royal pageants, see Bergeron (1971), 9–122; Kipling
(1985); Staley (1994), 165–68.

180. For discussions of this poem see Kipling (1985); Smith (1972), introduction; Strohm
(1992), 107–11; Wickham (1959), 64ff.

trope for royal power: the bridegroom longs to enter the bridal chamber, where he will restore "your" liberties. What is tacitly acknowledged and barely masked by the Solomonic language is the recognition that all marriages have a price. Patricia Eberle has suggested that the subject of goods was equally important to contemporary representations of Richard's relations with the nobles. Eberle argues that the negative emphasis upon the fashion and the lavishness of Richard's court that can be found in works like "Richard the Redeless" did not simply criticize the worldliness of the court but was intended to comment upon the court as failing to offer any resistance to royal power. Eberle sees the author of this poem as criticizing the court for allowing the king to dominate even matters of fashion: the court implicitly encouraged him to subordinate all law to his own will and pleasure and thus to engage in inherently tyrannical acts.[181] What seem to be at stake in the 1392 pageant and in Richard's relations with his courtiers are the terms of power, which Richard wished to locate in the king. But in each case, power is figured solely as a manifestation of wealth. It is not also linked to moral authority. Though there is obviously something very wrong about power when it is linked only to wealth rather than also to authority, I am less interested in reading Richard than in reading Richard as Chaucer read him. And, in relation to the late fourteenth-century "ideals" of representation and consent that Chaucer would have recognized, something is dangerously askew in a state when money appears to be the only check on royal prerogative.

The picture of the commonweal that is submerged in the Clerk's Tale is similarly unbalanced. Walter's immediate relations, who presumably are able to command resources similar to his own, are presented as helping Walter to perpetrate his cruel fictions. The people may *grucche* at him, but they are satisfied by finite goods—a happy ending, material satisfaction, peace, the stability they initially demanded of Walter—the bread and circuses of the medieval commonweal. The church, like Walter's relations, participates in the hoax:

> Whan that his doghter twelve yeer was of age,
> He to the court of Rome, in subtil wyse
> Enformed of his wyl, sente his message,
> Comaundynge hem swiche bulles to devyse

---

181. Eberle (1981), 171–72. Richard described the law as residing in the heart of the king; *Rot. Parl.* (1783), 3:416.

As to his crueel purpos may suffyse—
How that the pope, as for his peples reste,
Bad him to wedde another, if hym leste.

(IV, 736–42)

Where Boccaccio, Petrarch, and the author of *Le Livre de Griseldis* make
it clear that the letter is a forgery and the pope not involved, Chaucer
describes a more ambiguous situation. Though the next stanza specifies
that these bulls are to be counterfeit, Chaucer implies that the Curia is
complicit in the project, that it counterfeits its own bulls. Even his phrasing,
"court of Rome," underlines the dangerous similarities between worldly
and spiritual courts as places that merely endorse the royal will. The only
force that checks Walter by calling his bluff is the object of his cruelty.
With the words, "This is ynogh, Grisilde myn," the game stops.[182]

The Clerk presents Griselda in relation to two different but related systems of value. Both were construed through the language of gender, and
both have decided implications for Chaucer's scrutiny of contemporary
social codes. First, as a woman, Griselda embodies what is of value to
society, insofar as society (in this case one dominated by the masculine)
defines itself in terms of what it values. Chaucer's use of the feminine to
scrutinize the nature of social relationships can be seen throughout his
works. From the formel eagle in *The Parliament of Fowls* to Criseyde to
the heroines of *The Legend of Good Women* Chaucer uses gender and
gender relations to analyze a society dominated by impulses gendered as
male that inevitably depend upon the feminine for self-definition. To put it
in bird talk, without the formel eagle, what is the point of the chivalric
enterprise? Early in the Canterbury book he signals the importance of
gender to his dramatization of social tension by locating in Emelye what is
at once prized and feared by chivalric society. Second, the Clerk construes
Griselda as more than the focus for complicated male drives and desires.
Her poverty and her virtue designate her as a signifier for another level of
holiness: the symbols with which he surrounds her inevitably recall the
Christ who challenges the world's power and wealth.[183] He uses Cecilia in
such a way: in her he embodies a church whose allegiances are spiritual
and whose identity cannot be translated into the Roman language of power.

---

182. The "game" also began this way: after Griselda gives her promise to Walter before
their marriage, he says, "This is ynogh, Grisilde myn" (IV, line 365). Mann (1991) also notes
this repetition (153).

183. In her study of Chaucer, Mann (1991) links Griselda to Christ (chap. 4, esp. 152–53).

But Griselda is a far more commanding figure—socially and spiritually—than either Emelye or Cecilia; her power derives from the Clerk's use of her to refigure the concept of social and spiritual authority.

In terms of the medieval language of gender, what is male was construed as rational and potent and what is female as irrational and in need of restraint. Throughout his works, Chaucer plays variations upon these constructions, as he does in those works I have discussed. Neither the male eagles, Almachius, or Melibee emerge as particularly rational or potent and are seriously upstaged by the ladies who refuse to engage in male demonstrations of might and noise. As court lady, as image of the church, or as philosophical adviser none of these figures actually threatens male dominion. Only Griselda poses a serious challenge to power and has authority in both spheres. She is wife and mother and Christ figure. She presents an image of the holy translated to the social and political sphere. Griselda fulfills the function implicitly demanded of Emelye and has the children who will guarantee the stability of Walter's line. Furthermore, the Clerk's handling of Griselda's social function epitomizes her care for the common good in a way that evokes the concern for representation and consent that so preoccupied political conversation during the last quarter of the fourteenth century. Like his sources, Chaucer notes the people's praise for Griselda for her obedience, discretion, and virtue. But he extends the political implications of her virtue he would have found in his sources by describing her as a figure of judicial equity:

> Nat oonly this Grisildis thurgh hir wit
> Koude al the feet of wyfly hoomlinesse,
> But eek, whan that the cas required it,
> The commune profit koude she redresse.
> Ther nas discord, rancour, ne hevynesse
> In al that land that she ne koude apese,
> And wisely brynge hem alle in reste and ese.
>   (IV, 428–34)

Griselda's allegiances thus go in two mutually concordant directions. Through marriage she is bound to Walter; through birth, she is bound to the people. Chaucer consequently describes her as fulfilling both sets of obligations. She is virtuous, obedient, discreet, and dignified; she is also wise, equitable, and pacific. In contrast to the people, who select a speaker and petition to Walter, who, in fact, go through the motions of parliamentary representation, Griselda actually represents the common good, works for it, and consents to it as it is mediated to her through Walter. At no point does she work for her own good. It is tempting to see her as a throwback to earlier figures who embodied representative authority, like Peter de la Mare and Thomas Hoo. Neither prosperous merchants nor courtly fashion-plates, these men were presented in language that anchored social concerns in spiritual. Similarly, Chaucer uses Griselda to define the holy in social terms. The very disjuncture between the tale's "two levels of meaning" is an inextricable part of its meaning. If Peter de la Mare could be welcomed back to the city in the language of sacral entry, why should Chaucer not add details to his portrait of Griselda that juxtapose her to the Christ? He thereby evokes, however, no figure of suffering, emaciated "femininity," but the Christ who lived among the poor, who spoke out against power, who allowed himself to be broken by it, but who triumphed over it.

Chaucer assimilates the feminine to the divine but, in so doing, points up moral courage and strength and their relation to poverty. Griselda is intimidating in many of the ways in which the Jesus of the mystery plays intimidates his captors. His silence, his dignity under torture, his willing assumption of suffering, and his understanding of the dynamics of power are attributes of his absolute authority. Like Christ, Griselda appears less victim than master of the man who apparently masters her. Walter, like Annas and Caiphas or Herod, seems more "feminine," less rational, than does Griselda. In fact, in relation to contemporary gender codes, Griselda appears the most "masculine" of the figures in the tale and more truly threatening to tyrannical power. The people may be many, but they are fickle, and the nobles are quiescent with Walter's designs. Only Griselda refuses the role of weeping, wounded femininity that her circumstances would seem to demand and that the people seek to encourage with their laments for her plight. Where they wish her to throb with injustice or to melt with grief, she remains upright. She thereby at once excites our admiration and repels us, for Chaucer has written our response into the Clerk's translation of Petrarch's tale. Only when Griselda learns that her children are returned to her does she give way to emotion by fainting and by holding onto her children so tightly that it is hard for them to slip away from their overcome mother (see IV, 1079–1103). Chaucer much expands this section from the meager and relatively pat versions in his sources. His additions, including Griselda's fainting, underline Walter's tyrannical cruelty and the strain under which Griselda has been living for so many years. They also

dramatize her silent and never-ending love for her children and her extraordinary dignity. The combined effect—her silence and her swooning love—
allows him to eschew the sentimentality the people encourage but to validate her capacity for love and suffering. Her triumph does not simply lie
in her suffering, but in the way she chooses to suffer. Her agency does not
reside in meaningless action any more than does that of the Christ of the
Passion plays. Finally, by juxtaposing her powerlessness and silent love to
Walter's power, Chaucer insists on an image of the divine that emerges
from the radical (or modern?) "social" gospel that was used to challenge
existing social hierarchies.

The tale suggests that the language of religion and of politics cannot be
separated any more than the two realms can be seen as unconnected. Nor
can power be wrenched from its roots in authority without serious consequences. As such, the Clerk offers his listeners a terrifying performance, one
that—fittingly enough—the Merchant rushes to countermand. The Clerk's
handling of the tale is terrifying on two counts. To Chaucer's first audience,
the subjects of Richard II, the tale must have held up a realistic mirror:
there is no guarantee that the "game" (of testing or of power?) won't
happen again. Walter, though he doesn't say so, does not promise not to
do it again; more important, there remains no one in the tale capable of
checking him. The only check on him is the authority vested in Griselda
by her ability to endure adversity without swaying. While it is true that we
cannot, even after great suffering, wrest a writ from the universe guarantee-
ing our freedom from future grief and pain, we do not expect our kings to
operate with such inscrutability. As the late medieval coronation ceremony
figured it, regal power was a manifestation of divine and hereditary authority that was underpinned by popular acclaim. The Clerk thus asks the
question the Knight will not allow: What happens if Theseus is neither
wise nor stable? In a typically Chaucerian manner, he does not give a
final answer but offers only a scenario by translating Petrarch's story of
"spiritual patience."

There is another way in which the tale is terrifying. Chaucer's most
significant addition to the tale of Griselda comes at the end, where the
Clerk turns from the tale itself to address his audience.[184] It is at this point
that Chaucer directly links the tale of Griselda to the community of which
he himself formed a part:

---

184. Middleton (1980, 148–50) has wonderfully discussed these stanzas as elaborate play.
I agree, but I think the play is more dangerous than we think.

But o word, lordynges, herkneth er I go:
It were ful hard to fynde now-a-dayes
In al a toun Grisildis thre or two;
For if that they were put to swiche assayes,
The gold of hem hath now so badde alayes
With bras, that thogh the coyne be fair at ye,
It wolde rather breste a-two than plye.

(IV, 1163–69)

The Clerk complains that there are no more "wives" like Griselda. The modern wife is concerned only with power, not with authority. He compares the scarcity of true "wives" to a sort of currency crisis, a crisis that England itself experienced through the late fourteenth century because of the scarcity of gold and silver.[185] He thus reminds his audience that in this age, marriage and money are inseparable. But he also suggests that even the "coynes" that bind communities together are tokens of devaluation. He follows this stanza of complaint with the famous phrase, "For which heere, for the Wyves love of Bathe— / Whos lyf and al hire secte God mayntene," introducing the *Lenvoy de Chaucer* that concludes the tale of Griselda with a song of bitter sarcasm.[186]

What is the Wife of Bath's "secte"? In Middle English *secte* could refer to a class of people, to those of a certain way of thinking, to gender, to a system of religious belief, or to a faction. The word thus described a clearly defined interest group. In the *Lenvoy* Chaucer presents that interest group as female, urging wives to be active and emulate the Wife of Bath in pride, dominance, garrulity, and ferocity. If Griselda's sanctity, her power as a Christian example, gave Chaucer the space to look at tyranny, the sarcastic praise of a "femininity" embodied most vividly in the Wife of Bath, whose mercantilism is evident throughout her prologue, allows him to turn his attention to the king's bedmate, his subjects, his "wife." In contrast to the people who doubt and murmur but are bought off by the prospect of more gain, Griselda, the true wife, remains faithful to the terms of her marriage agreement.[187] Late fourteenth-century politics certainly had faction enough, *sectes* enough, but did it have figures of authority? Were there any

---

185. Ormrod (1990a), 27.

186. For discussion of the manuscript evidence for the status of this stanza, see Johnson (1989), 132–33.

187. In relation to this issue, two essays are particularly helpful in their insistence that "wives" function as signifiers of communal values. See Hahn (1992); Wilks (1982).

of whom could be said, "Benedictus qui venit nomine domini"? Or was Commons now filled only with false Griseldas?

By the time he decided to translate the legend of Griselda as the tale of the Clerk, Chaucer had come a long way from the quacking of ducks and the posturing of eagles. Though the view the *Parliament of Fowls* provides of the state and of the relationship between the individual and social order is not simple, it is nonetheless simple in relation to what can be found in the Clerk's Tale. The story of Palamon and Arcite is a more complicated performance, but it becomes even more complex as the first tale in the *Canterbury Tales*. In that position, Chaucer could use it as a sort of preliminary statement, a version of society whose phrasing, configurations, concepts, and codes reappear throughout the tales. Moreover, by assigning the tale to the Knight, he could delimit its scope. Here, teller matters not so much in terms of voice or "personality" but because the teller can be used to define the limits of a particular fiction. The Clerk's Tale constitutes the most intelligent and knotty of the responses to the Knight's Tale. By a careful reworking or re-reading of his sources, Chaucer returns to the Knight's Tale and to the substance of issues at which the Miller and his kind could only grudge.[188] Petrarch may be dead and "nayled in his cheste" (IV [E] 29) and Griselda and her patience dead and buried in Italy, but the story the Clerk took from his Italian progenitors is intimately related to Chaucer's analysis of an age subtly and decisively different from that in which Chaucer probably first translated the *Teseida* into the work that we know as the Knight's Tale. The society the Knight carefully constructs, the Clerk deconstructs into its separate and potentially volatile parts. In so doing he not only separates the concept of authority from that of power but locates his performance in the dangerous and unstable realm of political relations where there are more questions than there are answers.

More important, Chaucer uses the Clerk to ask questions through the tale that the Knight will not allow. The Knight is at great pains to explain such things as Arcite's death or social or personal conflict, to rationalize the apparently irrational, as Boccaccio does not do in the *Teseida*. Since the Knight is working with a model of the state as, like the universe, emanating from a point of order or a First Mover, he must locate disorder in

---

188. On the political implications of the peasant tales, see Patterson (1991), 264–70, 273–79. I am suggesting that we see the Clerk as taking up in a far more radical way those issues Patterson suggests are silenced through an elaborate strategy of domestication.

the whims or passions of the individual will. Moreover, he identifies willfulness with the feminine, subsuming all that is not Theseus's "order" under
a simple rubric. In this sense, Emelye's desire "noght to ben a wyf and be
with childe" poses the most willful of threats to dynastic enterprises. By
wishing for freedom, she wishes not to experience mastery. When this image
of beauty that produces desire and weakness in the male warrior, speaks
against hierarchical ordering, the Knight responds by destablizing that image through a series of puns on *queynte*.[189] He thereby reduces the goddess
seen out the prison window to a sexual function and Emelye's allegiance
to Diana to an urge every bit as disruptive to society's future and order as
any posed by Venus herself. The graceful picture of reciprocal and interde-
pendent harmony with which the Knight concludes the tale begs much more
difficult questions about society's means of achieving order.

The Clerk begins his tale where the Knight ended his. For the Clerk,
marriage is not the denouement. He does not locate his tale within the
conventions of romance, where marriage or music functions as a trope for
an order restored or renewed. In his tale, marriage is the very issue, the
problem to be explored. He thereby extends the Wife of Bath's suggestion
that the fundamental issue embedded in the subject of marriage is authority
and its relation to power. But the implications of the Clerk's Tale are far
graver than of the Wife's. He at once suggests the intimate relationship
between regal power and authority and representation and consent *and*
offers no prospect of achieving anything like an ideal situation. Finally
neither the people nor Walter can be trusted, nor are there any Griseldas
left among us who can mediate in the name of concord and equity. If Harry
Bailey wishes Goodelief would emulate Prudence's rare moderation or if
Cecilia's clarity of values seems sadly lacking in a world of warring popes
and self-interested prelates, Griselda is even more elusive and daunting an
ideal. However, by refusing to ignore the moral or social ambiguities inherent in each of these tales, Chaucer maintains them and their heroines in
the realm of uncertainty and thus in the complexities of the political and
social world he saw around him.

As he suggests through his handling and positioning of the three translated tales of Melibee, Saint Cecilia, and Griselda, we do not live in a world
of nicely opposed concepts but in London, whose suburbs, court, and halls

---

189. This, of course, is a vexed issue. For a sampling of opinion, see Benson (1985); Crane
(1990), 55. For an extended argument that Chaucer's puns serve such a destabilizing purpose,
see Delany (1994).

of government hold a variety of unworthy impulses in uncertain suspension. I would go so far as to say that Chaucer may well have thought—or have come to think—that de la Mare or Hoo never existed as they were portrayed, that Griselda is indeed long dead. I would go even farther and say the Clerk's tale "answers" another Oxford scholar who argued for a strongly king-centered state as the prerequisite for reformation. To Wyclif and all others who looked for new worlds, Chaucer offers this one, which is described in the idealized language of Solomon's marriage song but, in fact, is held together by the coin of the realm, undervalued, bendable, and mostly brass.

Epilogue

DAVID AERS AND LYNN STALEY

Where the body is, there will the eagles be gathered together.
—Matthew 24:28

We have chosen to look at some of the texts from the last twenty-five years of the fourteenth century. Concentrating on such a brief period has enabled us to explore in some detail just what is meant by "heterogeneity" or "multi-vocality" or "complexity" in late medieval culture, terms that have begun to displace the myths of homogeneity, unity, and freedom from conflict that shaped so much of the work done by literary medievalists from 1950 into the early 1980s. As our work demonstrates, late-fourteenth-century authors certainly felt varying degrees of communal pressure, but they nonetheless were able to express divergent views and explore issues relating to both power and authority without facing the legal strictures that came into being with the reign of Henry of Lancaster and the second episcopacy of Thomas Arundel.[1] The most erudite level of discussion—and thus the greatest recorded body of evidence for the diversity of late-fourteenth-century English culture—went on at the universities, where the first impact of John Wyclif's challenge to existing ecclesiastical and theological structures was felt.[2] However, the university was not an isolated community, and much of the recorded discussion in the Latin of the schools spilled over into contiguous devotional and political communities.[3] Our work provides evidence for understanding some of the ways in which fourteenth-century writers saw themselves as participating in that same widespread and complicated conversation about the nature of sanctity.

1. See Watson (1995).
2. See Catto (1992).
3. See Hudson (1986); Hudson (1988).

Since attempts to define and, inevitably, appropriate the holy underlay medieval attempts to image authority, the late-fourteenth-century conversation about the concept of sanctity is a means of entry into a debate the
consequences and implications of which would reach well into the fifteenth
century and beyond.

David Aers argues that medieval images of the "humanity of Christ"
need to be seen as historically contingent versions of the holy. That writers
and theologians might conceive of other ways of presenting that sacred
humanity is manifested, as Aers points out, in the work of Wyclif and other
Lollard writers, in Langland, and in Julian of Norwich. Fundamental to
his argument is the recognition that the late fourteenth century participated
in a multileveled conversation about the relationship between power and
authority that was frequently worked out through the language of images.
Moreover, to say that the concept of the *imitatio Christi* functioned as an
ideal for Christian medieval culture is not to endorse a single way of presenting that ideal. Not only were choices available, but it is beginning to
appear that those choices were recognizably meaningful in the broader field
of late medieval political consciousness. If to offer an alternate model of
the holy is to dissent—or to suggest a language for dissent—we need to
explore not simply the images a writer used but his or her reasons for
choosing one image rather than another. As Aers's analysis of the language
of suffering emphasizes, we cannot ignore the historical specificity of
Julian's imagery any more than we can speak of Langland's vision of Christ
without knowing the common tongue of the late fourteenth century. Moreover, we need to recognize ways in which an image might appear to be
serenely conventional when, in fact, convention can be used strategically
and pointedly as a means of opening up a subject of potential threat to
prevailing systems of order.

Lynn Staley focuses on two writers who, though not normally paired,
offer contemporaneous examples of some of the complexities of this late-
fourteenth-century conversation about the configuration of authority and
its relationship to power. Both Julian of Norwich and Geoffrey Chaucer in
some sense owed their livelihoods to dominant ecclesiastical and political
institutions. Both were vulnerable to communal pressure and esteem, and
dependent in a number of ways on those more powerful than they. To some
extent, both Chaucer and Julian were *relatively* marginal to the blocs that
"employed" them; Julian's marginality was compounded by her gender
and, possibly, by her lay status.[4] Though neither ought to be described as

---

4. David Aers's work on late-fourteenth-century literature, as well as his chapters in this
volume, focuses on the ways in which writers relate to or seek to evade the codes (and

heterodox, the writings of both—and during roughly the same period of time—suggest two profoundly intelligent minds at once grappling with the need to think independently of dominant codes and the inherent regulations imposed by conventional models *and* avoiding any decisive rupture with the codes themselves. Moreover, we can find strong evidence in both writers for the ways in which political or social considerations were expressed through the language of devotion.

Finally, and this bears directly on Aers's inquiry into the humanity of Christ, neither Julian nor Chaucer seems interested in inviting a purely affective response to the suffering they frequently foreground in their works. In current scholarship such suffering is often associated with the feminization of Christ and with the glorification of weakness. Although both employ the language of gender with remarkable dexterity, they do so in ways that undercut any simple means of understanding either gender or suffering or the possible connection between the two. Put another way, Julian's emphasis is as remote from that of Richard Rolle or Nicholas Love as is Chaucer's. Instead, both Julian and Chaucer place their greatest emphasis upon knowingness. Suffering, of the sort eulogized by the Prioresse or by the Man of Law, is not enough; nor is femininity to be canonized for its utterly nonresistant endurance, an endurance that thus refuses to offer any direct and prophetic challenge to the revered structures of worldly power. By their careful handling of the feminine as most effectively linked to knowledge, they signal their awareness—inevitably political— that the call to Christ is a call to consciousness. It is a call that poses serious risks to all civil or ecclesiastical structures that are based on the assumption that powerlessness can be mythologized or weakness sanctified in ways that are congruent with entrenching and protecting a might separate from authority.

As these examples suggest, dissent brings with it consciousness. Those who differ with prevailing models are implicitly diverging from the views expressed through those models. The knowledge—or self-consciousness— of the dissenter brings what was submerged into the open. Once the conversation about models becomes a struggle to define the right model, the terms, or the risks, significantly change, as they did in England in the fifteenth and sixteenth centuries. There is enough evidence to suggest that Thomas Arundel—like his *bête noire* John Wyclif—understood that to present

---

attendant pressures) of dominant social structures. See Works Cited. For Chaucer and the issue of marginality, see also Pearsall (1992) and Strohm (1989).

Christ as socially engaged was to present him as socially transgressive.[5] We might well speak of the Lancastrian regime (including the Lancastrian church) as strategically "producing" devotional language and imagery. Like Griselda, who indicates her own grasp of Walter's threat to ordinary humanity—and thus the role she herself has been playing—by advising him not to test his new wife as he had done his old, Julian of Norwich, Chaucer, and Langland signal their conscious participation in an elaborately coded conversation. Their search for alternate models for sanctity indicates their engagement with contemporary tensions, as well as their awareness of the social or political implications with which devotional images are freighted. Their very use of those images constitutes an expansion and an enrichment of a language that could still be used to explore the ambiguities inherent in the concepts of authority, power, and holiness.

The ultimate value of our joint enterprise rests in the variety of questions generated by our inquiry into some of the authors of late fourteenth-century English culture. We will therefore end by passing on some of our own questions to the academic community that is itself in the midst of a massive and multidisciplinary unraveling of claims about that culture's homogeneity.[6]

Perhaps one of the most provocative and associational topoi in the language of today's academy is that of the body. Aers argues that the presentation of Christ as victim that seems to dominate our present understanding of late medieval spirituality was, in fact, only one of the choices available to the fourteenth-century author, artist, or devotée. The transformations in late medieval figurations of Christ were inextricably bound up with the movements of power, with a cultural politics in which, of course, gender played an important role. Indeed, how to represent the humanity of Christ was an issue in an ongoing dialogue within and without the orthodox Church from the high Middle Ages through the Reformation, a dialogue in which Milton's confessed inability to complete his poem on "The Passion" is a particularly eloquent moment (published, 1645; written in the early 1630s). This being the case, we need to know far more than we yet do about the social contexts in which different representations of Christ were created and to which they were meaningful. Here we will certainly

---

5. Hughes (1988) presents strong evidence for Arundel's acute understanding of the many challenges with which the Church was presented. Watson (1995) greatly augments this picture.

6. The publication of Eamon Dufy's *The Stripping of the Altars* has sharpened the nature of this discussion. See, for example, Aers, "Altars of Power," (1994c).

need micro-histories.[7] By choosing to focus not on the body of Christ but on the works and sayings of Christ, an author inevitably altered the metaphoric field on which he or she might draw. What is in some ways startling about fourteenth-century treatments of Christ is their variety. We cannot as easily move from a discussion of Christ to a focus upon the suffering, punctured body as we can later in the medieval period. Why? Is the emphasis on Christ's fragmented physicality, suffering, and rejoining bound up in ways we do not quite understand with the Lancastrian rhetoric and consciousness of nationhood? Or is the fifteenth-century focus on the body a symptom of an anxiety about the loss of community, however imaginary, that that rhetoric continually affirms and celebrates?[8]

Moreover, if in the late fourteenth century such choices regarding the depiction of Christ were indeed available, those choices were being made knowingly with a particular reading or viewing public in mind and as part of an identifiable cultural, spiritual politics. Do we understand such readers or viewers in terms of class or gender or both? For example, Felicity Riddy and Carol M. Meale have argued for both aristocratic and religious female reading communities, identifying a number of texts—including Julian's *Showings,* the Vernon manuscript, and Chaucer's tale of the Prioress—as best understood within the contexts of those communities.[9] Were texts that focused on the physical, suffering, or affectivity consciously directed at a female public? How then do we read Chaucer's portrait of the Prioress in the General Prologue in relation to the bloody tale that she tells or approach Julian's careful reworking of the Short Text of the *Showings?* While we maintain that late-fourteenth-century people were being forced into an awareness of choices in crucial areas of devotion and iconography, there remains a question of degree, of focus: How sharply, or how pervasively were the political and social implications of affective devotional writing and image-making considered? If affective devotional texts were linked to women, were they seen by the clergy, and *perhaps* by women too, as lesser, something Chaucer may suggest by his characterization of the Prioress as of a lower social rank and of dubious spiritual stature?[10]

---

7. Beckwith (1993) has pointed the way here in her study of the fifteenth-century context for representations of Christ's body.

8. See Aers (1992), chap. 6; Staley (1994), chap. 5.

9. Meale (1993); Riddy (1993).

10. See, for example, Cooper (1989), 37–39; Mann (1973), 128–37. At the 1992 meeting of the New Chaucer Society, a special session, organized by Thomas Hahn, was devoted to the Prioress. Papers by Miri Rubin, Denise L. Despres, Gavin I. Langmuir, Heather Findlay, Jeremy Cohen, and Thomas Hahn focused on the ways in which Chaucer seems to use the

Our work on Julian of Norwich also raises a number of questions. Aers argues that Julian created a text whose complex rhetorical and theological strategies supersede (and undermine) the traditional affective forms on which they draw. Julian's employment of affective images and motifs needs then to be understood as indicating something about her own awareness of the social implications of affective prose as well as suggesting her growing desire to write for as broad a public as possible. Moreover, as Staley argues, we need to establish a more historical context for Julian and her sense of the function of devotional prose. If she is polemical, can we afford to separate her theological argument from its social implications? Ought we to look more closely at devotional prose in order to understand the complicated nexus of social, religious, and political impulses that drove its authors and inspired its readers?[11] In addition, our work suggests Julian's consciousness of the strictures under which a woman wrote. The constraints Julian felt were different than those acknowledged by earlier writers such as Hrosvitha or Hildegard of Bingen. The growing pressure on women religious throughout the thirteenth and early fourteenth centuries and the increasingly narrow channels for their energies and talents certainly had an impact on women's voices.[12] However, the greatest challenge for an English woman writer was offered by John Wyclif himself, whose doctrines were frequently presented by his opponents as threatening the harmonies of a hierarchically gendered world.[13]

Aers argues that, like all representations of Christ's humanity, those in *Piers Plowman* have to be understood as part of particular, historically contingent webs of conflicts and questions. Only when this is done can we grasp the spiritual and political implications of the choices Langland made in his figurations of Christ's humanity and, quite as importantly, choices he made to *set aside* certain dominant images and conventions. We must seek to identify the ways in which *Piers Plowman* fuses themes and images pertinent to the conflicts that underlay devotional iconography, spirituality, and politics in postplague England. The poem's remarkable reception history—for it was claimed as an authorizing text by the rebels of 1381, by Lollards, by Protestants, as well as by orthodox Catholics—witnesses as

---

tale to signal moral, social, and religious inconsistencies. See also Fradenburg (1989); Ferster (1990).

11. The work of Peter Brown (see Works Cited) is central to this issue.

12. See the work of Leff (1967) and Lerner (1972) as they touch on the history of women's religious movements.

13. See Blamires (1989; 1993).

much to its exceptional critical openness as it does to the colonizing interpretative practices of its readers. However, although *Piers Plowman* has
certainly had its share of exegetes, there are wide-ranging questions still to
be explored, concerning both the poem itself and its place in the culture of
discourse to which it belongs. Prominent among these is the need to understand more about the roles of gender in the poem.[14] What are the implications of the virtual (and extraordinary) absence of the Blessed Virgin Mary
from *Piers Plowman*? How can Langland even compose the series of *vitae
Christi* within *Piers* without devoting some prolonged attention to Christ's
mother?[15] How do we read the way his *vitae Christi* exclude the role of
the loyal women disciples—Mary Magdalene, Mary the mother of James
and Joseph, and the mother of the sons of Zebedee—who had followed
Jesus from Galilee? Unlike the men who followed Jesus, these women neither denied him nor fled, but faithfully took care of him (see Matthew
27:55–56; Luke 8:1–3). It was to these women that Jesus appeared in the
Resurrection before he disclosed himself to men (see Matthew 28:1–11).[16]
How do we understand a poem that finally dispenses with all female mediators and teachers or evaluates the passionate love that Will comes to feel
for Piers, his chosen guide?

Staley argues that, like Langland, Chaucer employed the language of
sanctity as a way of thinking his way through an increasingly knotty political situation. She suggests that he deliberately employed terms that were
being exploited in the social and political arenas of his own day in order
to dramatize the implications of a situation that, for him, could only be
altered through Richard's assumption of his own agency in relation to that
of other bodies, the Commons or the Church. She locates the *Clerk's Tale*
within a progressively bleak sequence of works that use a common language
to explore the oppositional relationship between authority and power.
Rather than focus the tale solely on Richard and the subject of tyranny,
Staley includes in its sweep parliamentary Commons and a materialism
that served to cement the members of the social body together into an
apparent unity.[17] That Commons presented itself in socially sanctified terms

---

14. See Aers (1994a); Lees (1994); Murphy (1994).

15. For a consideration of the role Mary played in the late-fourteenth-century literary
imagination, see Collette (1994).

16. For Lollard commentary on these incidents, see the remarks in Staley (1994), 102, 126.

17. David Wallace's recent essays on Chaucer, which will form part of his forthcoming
book, *Chaucer and Polity,* suggest that Chaucer used many of the *Canterbury Tales* to investigate the contrasts between tyranny and republicanism that were manifest in contemporary
Italian politics, particularly in the ideological and political tensions that characterized the

throughout the period may once have provided Chaucer with a certain amount of ironic pleasure, but by the time he wrote the *Clerk's Tale* his irony had become fairly dark. Her discussion emphasizes the need to sensitize ourselves to the nuances of late-fourteenth-century English political rhetoric. What types of conversations, or negotiations, were conducted using the language of the holy? What types of questions can we ask of Griselda? Why does Chaucer not present a tale along the lines of the Slaughter of the Innocents, in which a woman fights to preserve her children? Is he advocating Griselda's nascent stoicism rather than the affective piety of the Prioress or the furious activity that the Wife of Bath endorses in her complex rhetorical performance? Or is he dramatizing the political limitations of such stances? What are the implications of his choice in recounting the tale of Griselda rather than a more militant (and obviously provocative) story? What does it suggest that he gave the bloody tale of the little clergeon to a female narrator and that of the stoic Griselda to a male teller? How are we to approach Chaucer's attitude toward images and issues relating to gender, politics, and devotion in the *Second Nun's Tale,* the *Melibee,* and the *Clerk's Tale* when we consider their probable dates of composition and their positions in the manuscripts of the *Canterbury* book?

Can we speculate more generally about the ways in which treatments of gender may have had hidden political associations? For example, in the "uses" to which Cecilia was put by Chaucer, Julian of Norwich, the early Wycliffites, Nicholas Love, and the author of the Longleat sermons, do we have evidence of part of a submerged conversation regarding the boundaries between lay and clerical activities that is carried on through her figure?[18] What such questions underline is the necessity of understanding categories like gender as historically or socially contingent. We cannot simply talk about a writer's attitude toward the feminine without reference to what types of associations the feminine had *and* in which contexts. We cannot assume that all late-medieval religion had an affective emphasis. Julian's picture of God Our Mother exists in the same space as Rolle's

---

relationship between Milan and Florence. (On Italian political thought, see Skinner [1978], esp. 77–79.) I cannot do justice here to Wallace's careful argument, but we see Chaucer as less drawn by the Florentine republicanism of the Italian political theorists such as Salutati than as preoccupied by the venal impulses he saw underlying English political institutions. Finally, we do not think that after a certain point Chaucer saw a solution to the problems he analyzed.

18. See above, Chapter 4 n. 18; Watson, "Censorship and Cultural Change" (1995). Other figures like Susanna or Judith also need investigation. For example, see Staley (1994), 47, 139, 141.

description of the Christ shot full of holes like a dovecote, but the choice of one picture rather than the other had implications that are ultimately related to those very issues of power and authority.

Our study raises further questions about the literary culture of the late fourteenth century. For example, what questions arise when we think about collections like the Vernon manuscript, the works of the *Gawain*-poet, and the Lollard sermon cycle as taking shape during roughly the same ten years?[19] The Vernon manuscript is a careful gathering of a number of devotional and penitential texts, including the *South English Lengendary*, an augmented midland version of the expanded *Northern Homily Cycle*, the *Speculum Vitae*, the *Prick of Conscience*, the *Prikke of Love*, several works by Rolle, the A Text of *Piers Plowman*, and a number of penitential works. Its very size testifies to the years and resources that went into its composition, as well as to the degree of planning and organization involved in placing so many texts together in a single, great volume. Such a codex also can be read as a social statement, whose deliberate orthodoxy and conventionality must be located within the context of the types of conversations we have described in this book.[20] The Vernon manuscript—with its frequently lugubrious penitential treatises—seems especially significant when we juxtapose it to the Wycliffite sermon cycle, which Hudson dates probably in the 1390s. Where the Vernon manuscript, probably copied during the mid 1380s (and perhaps compiled for nuns), is the product of monastic culture and resources and can suggest much about elite reading communities during the period, the sermon cycle is directed toward a lay public, one whose social diversity bespeaks a different sort of devotional impulse.

The two collections seem to tempt us toward generalizations based on class and on gender in relation to class; gatherings like the *Pearl* manuscript suggest that we might proceed more cautiously. If, as Derek Pearsall has suggested, the poems of the *Pearl* manuscript are not only the product of monastic culture but evince the link between the world of monastic learning and that of magnate culture, can we also locate the poems within the context of the debates of the late fourteenth century?[21] With their persistent focus on royalty and hence on the basis for regal authority, the poems explore a subject of intense concern throughout the period. Are such in-

---

19. See *The Vernon Manuscript* (1987); Pearsall (1990); Hudson and Gradon (1988–90).
20. See Heffernan (1990); Brown (1994).
21. Pearsall (1981). One of the most ambitious of recent attempts to historicize these poems is that of Michael Bennet (1983).

stances intended to resonate with (or to comment on) Wyclif's own views
of reform as a movement instigated by the voice of the true preacher but
finally emanating from a strong figure of secular rule, the king? Although
its invectives against clerical impurity and warnings against uncleanness
are as conventional and, at times, as gloomy as any to be found in the
Vernon manuscript, the poet's choice of biblical texts needs further contextualization.[22] Until we know more about what Anne Hudson has described
as a Lollard sect vocabulary, we cannot know how to evaluate the poet's
choice of scriptural *loci*. *Sir Gawain* seems more understandable within the
context of works such as *Troilus and Criseyde* and Chaucer's own analysis
of the dynamics of statecraft and rule, but what of Gawain's entirely private
act of penitential recreation in relation to the Wycliffite critique of confessors and confession?[23] *Pearl*, perhaps the most richly gorgeous and iconic
of the four poems, also persistently questions its own visual apparatus.[24]
The *Gawain* poet's handling of sanctity as manifested through gender or
gendered characteristics likewise demands further historicization and contextualization.[25] Despite the religious emphasis of three of the poems, the
poet does not offer a picture of a suffering, "feminized" Christ or even of
victimized femininity. Instead, he presents pictures of a majestic Godhead,
a feast-giver, a bridegroom, an all-powerful figure who holds the whale in
his hands, and of female figures who are at times far more astute than
figures such as Gawain or the *Pearl* dreamer. How should we read his
presentation of divinity or his handling of gender?[26] Can we use either as
a means of evaluating the intended audience for these poems?

   We do not mean to suggest that the *Gawain* poet was a Wycliffite.
Instead, we mean to underline our ignorance of the subtleties of late-
fourteenth-century conversation and, to return to Pearsall's original obser-

---

   22. For relevant recent work on such vocabularies, see Barr (1994) and Delany (1994),
117–23.
   23. See Aers (1988a), chap. 4, for comments on the split the poet articulates between
private and communal codes.
   24. Most recently, see, for example, Aers (1993); Rhodes (1994); Stanbury (1991).
   25. For recent work, see Dinshaw (1994); Frantzen (1991); Heng (1991; 1992).
   26. By "gender" we mean to include all sexual relationships within a social context. For a
reading of sexuality and its uses by the author of these poems, see Dinshaw (1994). Dinshaw
reads evidence for sexuality in a far more literal manner than we. She, in fact, argues that the
possibility of homosexual relations implicitly raised by the "exchange of kisses" between the
Host and Sir Gawain fits into a powerful argument for the order of a heterosexual society.
Instead, our own approach suggests that such questions should be addressed by seeking to
understand, as precisely as possible, just what the images and acts could signify *within a
certain historical and cultural field*.

vation, to point out the urgency of recovering a cultural context that is far more complicated and nuanced than we have previously thought. The poems in the *Pearl* manuscript are only one—albeit a major—example of works that need to be read in relation to our deepening understanding of the late fourteenth century and the inquiry into rhetorical consciousness.[27] As Aers suggests in his treatment of Langland, the issue was not a simple question of orthodoxy or heresy. There were still many conflicting, even contradictory, ways of being orthodox and would be until the publication of Arundel's *Constitutions* in 1409 and after.[28] Hence there is a real difference between what was likely—or possible—during the late fourteenth and the fifteenth centuries. Julian's *Showings*, Love's *Mirror,* and Kempe's *Book of Margery Kempe* trace a history of devotional prose that is also a history of cultural change and repression. However, between Julian of Norwich and Nicholas Love lie years during which the Wycliffite translation of the Bible was completed and produced in expensive volumes intended for lecterns or, perhaps, bishop's libraries; deluxe manuscripts of the Wycliffite "glossed Gospels" were commissioned and executed; and ornamented versions of Richard Rolle's translation of the psalter with Wycliffite interpolations were copied not for the artisan reader but obviously for someone of both learning and affluence.

The silence and alienation that Louise Fradenburg finds so powerfully expressed in the *Manciple's Tale* may represent Chaucer's closing statement about naked power and the poet's vulnerability in the face of that power, but the *Tale* does not close out the conversation in which Chaucer participated.[29] As responses to the rebels of 1381 demonstrate, the late fourteenth century was certainly not a period where freedom of speech was anybody's right.[30] However, it is clear that it offered an arena for certain types of conversations that could not have been held in the fifteenth century. Or, to use the language we ourselves have borrowed, who was the Christ and for whom did he speak and live? Our work points not to a uniform vision that can supply an answer to this question, but to a recognition of differences. For William Langland, Geoffrey Chaucer, and Julian of Norwich, Christ certainly suffered death, was buried, and rose again. But he also wore the clothes of the laborer, sought to redress the world's ills, redeemed

---

27. We also include texts like *The Seige of Jerusalem* here, especially considering Ralph Hanna's work on contextualizing that poem. See Hanna (1992).
28. See Watson (1995).
29. Fradenburg (1985).
30. See Aers (forthcoming); Justice (1994).

through an all-powerful love, challenged the power of the world, and consequently chose his Passion, but did so graciously, joyously, courageously,
and dangerously. "Was it enough. . ." Julian's Christ says to her, "Did I
suffer enough, are you satisfied?" Through Christ Julian proclaims not the
anguish of the broken pierced body but triumphant power and the pure
pleasure of willed sacrifice. Unlike Julian, Langland pays sustained attention to human agency and political/ethical responsibility in the judgments
against Christ, the torturings, and the killing. For Langland—as in Lollardy—this Christ is also a dangerous memory: the "freedom" he brings is
agonistic and thus constitutes a real threat to any existing institution that
purports to be his mystical body. Unlike both Julian and Langland, Chaucer
is not a christocentric writer. He seems often to use devotional images and
motifs as ways of pointing up their ambiguous and too-often worldly uses.
What appears clear cut, such as the picture of Cecilia's piety and strength,
becomes less so when her history is assimilated to that of the Church in
the world. Griselda may be an example of fidelity and patience when we
consider her as a type of soul, but, when we alter our perspective and
consider her Christ-likeness in relation to an earthly Walter's bombast and
power, we are left with a difficult set of political meditations that are rooted
in spiritual considerations. What hope is there for the virtues embodied in
Prudence or Cecilia or Griselda in a world that traffics so blithely in false
images and debased coinage? Julian, Langland, and Chaucer can offer vig-
nettes of the holy that are sometimes more radical than many we—or
our authoritative establishments—contemplate today. However, Chaucer
himself implies that these are not *pieces* that can be fitted into any coherent
pattern. Piers, Griselda, servants and masters, Walsingham's version of
Peter de la Mare, the true king, the true priest should all be seen as efforts to
constitute sanctity using the vernacular of late-fourteenth-century England.
Then as now, the struggle for the holy is a struggle over christening rights.

Works Cited

Primary Sources

Acta Sanctorum . . . editio novissima. 1863. Ed. J. Carnandet et al. Paris: Palme, 1863.

Allen, Hope Emily, ed. 1927. *Writings Ascribed to Richard Rolle.* London: Oxford University Press.

———, ed. 1931 and 1963. *English Writings of Richard Rolle.* Oxford: Clarendon Press.

Andrew, Malcolm, and Ronald Waldron, eds. 1978. *The Poems of the Pearl Manuscript.* York Medieval Texts, 2d series. Berkeley and Los Angeles: University of California Press.

Angela of Foligno. 1985. *Il Libro Della Beata Angela de Foligno.* Edizione critica. Edited by L. Thier and A. Calufetti. Rome: Editiones Collegii S. Bonaventurae ad Claras Aquas.

———. 1993. *Angela of Foligno: Complete Works.* Translated by P. Lachance. New York: Paulist Press.

Augustine. 1954. *In Ioannis Evangelium tractatus CXXIV.* Edited by D. R. Willems. Turnhout: Brepols.

———. 1958. *On Christian Doctrine.* Translated by D. W. Robertson. Indianapolis, Ind.: Bobbs-Merrill.

———. *De doctrina christiana.* 1962. Edited by I. Martin and K.-D. Daur. Turnhout: Brepols.

———. 1986. *Homilies on the Gospel of John; Homilies on the First Epistle of John; Soliloquies.* Edited by P. Schaff. Grand Rapids, Mich.: Eerdmans.

Beadle, R., ed. 1982. *York Plays.* London: Arnold.

Beadle, R., and P. M. King, eds. 1988. *York Mystery Plays: A Selection.* Oxford: Clarendon Press.

Bible. 1964. *The Holy Bible translated from the Latin Vulgate . . . (Douai, A.D. 1609; Rheims, A.D. 1582).* London: Burns and Oates.

Bible. 1966. *The Jerusalem Bible.* London: Darton, Longman and Todd.

Biblia Sacra Iuxta Vulgatem Versionem. 1983. Stuttgart: Deutsche Bibelgesellschaft.

Bokenham, Osbern. 1988. *Legendys of Hooly Wummen.* Edited by Mary S. Serjeantson. Early English Text Society 206. London: Oxford University Press, 1938; repr. Kraus.

Bonet, Honoré. 1949. *The Tree of Battles*. Translated by G. W. Coopland. Cambridge: Harvard University Press.

Bramley, H. R., ed. 1884. *The Psalter or Psalms of David and Certain Canticles with a Translation and Exposition in English by Richard Rolle of Hampole*. Oxford: Clarendon Press.

Brandeis, Arthur, ed. 1900. *Jacob's Well*. EETS 115 London: Kegan Paul, Trench, Trübner.

Buddensieg, Rudolf, ed. 1883. *John Wyclif's Polemical Works*. London: Trübner.

Capes, William W., ed. 1916. *Registrum Johannis Trefnant*. London: Canterbury and York Society.

Capgrave, John. 1858. *Liber de Illustribus Henricis*. Edited by F. C. Hingeston. London: Rolls Series.

Chandos, Herald. 1974. *Life of the Black Prince*. Edited by Mildred K. Pope and Eleanor C. Lodge. Oxford, 1910; repr. New York: AMS Press.

Colledge, Edmund, and James Walsh, eds. 1978. *A Book of Showings to the Anchoress Julian of Norwich*. 2 vols. Toronto: Pontifical Institute of Mediaeval Studies.

Colledge, Eric, and Joyce Bazire, eds. 1957. *Chastising of God's Children*. Oxford: Basil Blackwell.

Coopland, G. W., ed. 1976. *Philippe de Mézières' Letter to King Richard II*. New York: Barnes and Noble.

Cornford, Barbara, ed. 1984. *The Rising of 1381 in Norfolk*. Gorleston, Norfolk: Huggins.

Crampton, Georgia Ronan, ed. 1993. *The Shewings of Julian of Norwich*. Kalamazoo, Mich.: Medieval Institute Publications.

Cristin the mervelous [*Christina mirabilis*]. 1885. "The life." In "Prosalegenden: Die Legenden des MS Douce 114," edited by C. Horstmann, *Anglia* 8:119–34.

Crow, Martin M., and Clair C. Olson, eds. 1966. *Chaucer Life Records*. Oxford: Oxford University Press.

Devlin, Sister Mary Aquinas, ed. 1954. *The Sermons of Thomas Brinton, Bishop of Rochester (1373–1389)*. Camden Third Series. 2 vols. London: Royal Historical Society.

Dobson, R. B., ed. 1986. *The Peasants' Revolt of 1381*. London: Macmillan 1970. Reprint.

Erbe, Theodor, ed. 1905. *Mirk's Festial: A Collection of Homilies*. EETS, extra series 96. London: Kegan Paul, Trench, Trübner.

Fisher, John H., ed. 1989. *The Complete Poetry and Prose of Geoffrey Chaucer*. New York: Holt, Rinehart and Winston.

Foxe, John. 1965. *The Acts and Monuments*. 8 vols. New York: AMS Press.

Furnivall, Frederick J., ed. 1868. *Early English Meals and Manners*. EETS 32. London: Kegan Paul, Trench, Trübner.

Galbraith, V. H., ed. 1927. *The Anonimalle Chronicle 1333 to 1381*. Manchester: Manchester University Press.

Gower, John. 1962. *The Major Latin Works of John Gower*, trans. E. W. Stockton. Seattle: University of Washington Press.

Guillaume de St. Thierry. 1973. *The Golden Epistle of Abbot William of St. Thiery.* Translated by Walter Shewring. Introduction by Justin McCann. London: Sheed and Ward.

Harvey, Ralph, ed. 1896. *The Fire of Love and The Mending of Life or The Rule of Living.* EETS 106. London: Kegan Paul, Trench, Trübner.

Hector, L. C. and Barbara Harvey, eds. and trans. 1982. *The Westminster Chronicle.* Oxford: Clarendon Press.

Heyworth, P. L., ed. 1968. *Jack Upland, Friar Daw's Reply and Upland's Rejoinder.* Oxford: Oxford University Press.

Higden, Ranulph. 1964. *Polychronicon.* 9 vols. Edited by Joseph Rawson Lumby. London: Kraus Reprint.

Hilton, Walter. 1991. *The Scale of Perfection.* Translated by John P. H. Clark and Rosemary Dorward. New York: Paulist Press.

Hoccleve, Thomas. 1970. *Hoccleve's Works: The Minor Poems.* Edited by F. J. Furnivall and I. Gollancz. Revised by J. Mitchell and A. I. Doyle. EETS 61, 73. Oxford: Oxford University Press.

Hodgson, Phyllis, ed. 1944. *The Cloud of Unknowing and the Book of Privy Counselling.* EETS 218. London: Oxford University Press.

Holmstedt, Gustof, ed. 1933. *Speculum Christiani: A Middle English Religious Treatise of the Fourteenth Century.* EETS 182. London: Oxford University Press.

The Holy Bible . . . made from the Latin Vulgate by John Wycliffe and His Followers. 1850. 4 vols. Edited by Josiah Forshall and Sir Frederic Madden. Oxford; New York: AMS Press.

Horstmann, C., ed. 1885. "Prosalegenden: Die Legenden des MS Douce 114." *Anglia* 8:102–96.

———, ed. 1895–96. *Yorkshire Writers.* 2 vols. London: Swan Sonnenschein.

Hudson, Anne. 1993. *Two Wycliffite Texts: The Sermon of William Taylor 1406 and The Testimony of William Thorpe 1407.* EETS 301. Oxford: Oxford University Press.

Hudson, Anne, and Pamela Gradon, eds. 1988–90. *English Wycliffite Sermons.* 3 vols. Oxford: Clarendon Press.

Jacques de Vitry. 1994. *The Life of Marie d'Oignies.* Translated by M. H. King. Toronto: Peregrina.

Kempe, Margery. See Meech and Allen.

Knighton, Henry. 1965. *Chronicon.* Edited by J. R. Lumby. London, 1895; repr. Kraus Reprint.

Kurath, Hans, and Sherman M. Kuhn. 1956– . *Middle English Dictionary.* Ann Arbor: University of Michigan Press.

Langland, William. 1979. *Piers Plowman, an Edition of the C-Text.* Edited by Derek Pearsall. Berkeley and Los Angeles: University of California Press.

———. 1988. *Piers Plowman: The B Version.* Edited by G. Kane and E. T. Donaldson. London: Athlone.

Legg, Leopold G. Wickham. 1901. *English Coronation Records.* Westminster: Archibald Constable.

Love, Nicholas. 1992. *Mirror of the Blessed Life of Jesus Christ: A Critical Edition.* Edited by M. G. Sargent. New York: Garland.

Lovewell, Bertha E. 1988. *The Life of St. Cecilia from MS. Ashmole 43 and MS. Cotton Tiberius E. VII with Introduction, Variants, and Glossary.* Yale Studies in English. Boston: Lamson, Wolffe.

Lydgate, John. 1911. *The Minor Poems of John Lydgate.* Edited by H. N. Mac-Cracken. EETS 107. London: K Paul Trench, Trübner.

Mary of Oignies. 1885. "The Life." In "Prosalegenden: Die Legenden des MS Douce 114," edited by C. Horstmann, *Anglia* 8:134–84; *see also* Jacques de Vitry.

Matthew, F.D., ed. 1902. *The English Works of Wyclif,* EETS 74. London: Trübner.

Mechtild of Hackeborn. 1979. *The Booke of Gostlye Grace of Mechtild of Hackeborn.* Edited by T. A. Halligan. Toronto: Pontifical Institute.

Meditationes Vitae Christi. See Peltier (1868) and Ragusa and Green (1961).

Meditations on the Supper of our Lord, and the Hours of the Passion. 1875. Edited by J. M. Cowper. EETS 96. London: N. Trübner.

Meech, Sanford Brown, and Allen, H. E. ed. 1940 and 1961. *The Book of Margery Kempe.* With prefatory notes by Hope Emily Allen. EETS 212. London: Oxford University Press.

Millett, Bella, and Jocelyn Wogan-Browne, eds. 1990. *Medieval English Prose for Women.* Oxford: Clarendon Press.

Monk of Farne. 1957. "The Meditations of the Monk of Farne." Edited by H. Farmer. *Analecta Monastica* 4:141–245.

———. 1961. *The Monk of Farne; The Meditations.* Translated by a Benedictine of Stanbrook. London: Darton, Longman and Todd.

Myers, A. R., ed. 1969. *English Historical Documents, 1327–1485.* New York: Oxford University Press.

Ogilvie-Thomson, S. J., ed. 1988. *Richard Rolle: Prose and Verse.* EETS 293. Oxford: Oxford University Press.

Owen, Nancy H. 1966. "Thomas Wimbledon's Sermon: 'Redde racionem villicaciones tue.'" *Medieval Studies* 28:176–97.

Peltier, A. C., ed. 1868. *Meditationes Vitae Christi.* In *Bonaventurae Opera Omnia,* 12:509–630. Paris: Vives.

Poole, Reginald Lane, ed. 1890. *Johannis Wycliffe: De Dominio Divino Libri Tres to which are added the first four books of the Treatise "De Pauperie Salvatoris" by Richard Fitzralph Archbishop of Armagh.* London: Trübner.

Ragusa, Isa, and R. Green, eds. and trans. 1961. *Meditations on the Life of Christ.* Princeton: Princeton University Press.

The Riverside Chaucer. 1987. Edited by Larry D. Benson, general editor. Boston: Houghton Mifflin.

Robinson, F. N., ed. 1957. *The Works of Geoffrey Chaucer.* 2d ed. Boston: Houghton Mifflin.

Rolle, Richard. 1963. *English Writings of Richard Rolle.* Edited by H. E. Allen. Oxford: Clarendon Press.

Ross, W. O. 1940. *Middle English Sermons.* Edited by Ross. EETS 209. London: Oxford University Press.

Rotuli Parliamentorum. 1783. 6 vols. London.

Severs, J. Burke, ed. 1941a. "The Clerk's Tale." In *Sources and Analogues of Chaucer's Canterbury Tales,* edited by W. F. Bryan and Germaine Dempster, 288–332. Chicago: University of Chicago Press.

———. 1941b. "The Tale of Melibeus." In *Sources and Analogues of Chaucer's Canterbury Tales,* edited by W. F. Bryan and Germaine Dempster, 560–614. Chicago: University of Chicago Press.

———. 1942. *The Literary Relationships of Chaucer's "Clerkes Tale."* Yale Studies in English 96. New Haven: Yale University Press.

Simmons, T. F., ed. 1879. *The Lay Folk's Mass Book.* EETS 71. London: N. Trübner.

Skeat, W. W., ed. 1968. *The Vision of William concerning Piers the Plowman together with Richard the Redeless.* 2 vols. Oxford: Oxford University Press.

Smith, Charles Roger, ed. and trans. 1972. *Concordia Facta Inter Regem Riccardum II et Civitatem Londonie per Fratrum Riccardum Maydiston.* Ph.D. dissertation, Princeton University.

Statutes of the Realm. 1963. 2 vols. London, 1816. Reprint.

Stockton, Eric W., trans. 1962. *The Major Latin Works of John Gower.* Seattle: University of Washington Press.

Stow, George B., ed. 1977. *Historia Vitae et Regni Ricardi Secundi.* Philadelphia: University of Pennsylvania Press.

Talbot, C. H., ed. 1959. *The Life of Christina of Markyate.* Oxford: Clarendon Press.

Tanner, N. P., ed. 1977. *Heresy Trials in the Diocese of Norwich, 1428–31.* Camden Fourth Series, vol. 20. London: Royal Historical Society.

Taylor, William. 1993. *The Sermon of William Taylor, 1406.* In *Two Wycliffite Texts,* edited by A. Hudson. EETS 301. Oxford: Oxford University Press.

Thomas of Chobham. 1968. *Summa Confessorum.* Edited by F. Broomfield. Louvain: Nauwelaerts.

Thomas, A. H., ed. 1929. *Calendar of Plea and Memoranda Rolls preserved among the Archives of the Corporation of the City of London at the Guildhall, A.D. 1364–1381.* Cambridge: Cambridge University Press.

Thompson, E. M., ed. 1874. *Chronicon Angliae, Auctore Monacho Quodam Sancti Albani (1328–1388).* Rolls Series. London: Longman.

———, ed. and trans. 1876. *Chronicon Adae de Usk, A.D. 1377–1401.* London: John Murray.

Thorpe, William. 1993. *The Testimony of William Thorpe.* In *Two Wycliffite Texts,* edited by A. Hudson. EETS 301. Oxford: Oxford University Press.

The Vernon Manuscript. A Facsimile of Bodleian Library, Oxford, MS. Eng Poet a.1. 1987. With an Introduction by A. I. Doyle. Cambridge: D. S. Brewer.

Walsingham, Thomas. 1863. *Historia Anglicana.* Edited by Henry Thomas Riley. London: Longman, Green, Longman, Roberts, and Green. Reprinted London: Kraus, 1965.

Wenzel, Siegfried, ed. 1989. *Fasciculus Morum: A Fourteenth-Century Preacher's Handbook.* University Park: Pennsylvania State University Press.

Wilkins, David, ed. 1737. *Concilia Magnae Britanniae et Hiberniae.* 4 vols. London; Brussels, 1964. Vol. 3.

Wyclif, John. 1863. *Tractatus de Officio Pastorali*. Edited by G. V. Lechler. Leipzig.
———. 1876. *Dialogus Sive Speculum Ecclesie Militantis*. Edited by A. W. Pollard. London: Wyclif Society.
———. 1886. *De Ecclesia*. Edited by J. Loserth. London: Wyclif Society.
———. 1887. *De Officio Regis*. Edited by A. W. Pollard and C. Sayle. London: Wyclif Society.
———. 1888. *Sermones*. Edited by J. Loserth. 4 vols. London: Wyclif Trübner. Vol. 2.
———. 1893. *Tractatus de Blasphemia*. London: Wyclif Society.
———. 1913. *Opera Minora*. Edited by J. Loserth. London: Wyclif Society.
———. 1966. *Tractatus de Civili Dominio*. 4 vols. Edited by Reginald Lane Poole. London: Wyclif Society, 1885; repr. Johnson, 1966.

Secondary Sources

Aers, D. 1975. *Piers Plowman and Christian Allegory*. London: Arnold.
———. 1978–79. "Criseyde: Woman in Medieval Society." *Chaucer Review* 13:177–200.
———. 1980. *Chaucer, Langland, and the Creative Imagination*. London: Routledge and Kegan Paul.
———. 1981. "*The Parliament of Fowls*: Authority, the Knower and the Known." *Chaucer Review* 16:1–17.
———, ed. 1986. *Medieval Literature: Criticism, Ideology and History*. Brighton, Sussex: Harvester.
———. 1988a. *Community, Gender, and Individual Identity: English Writing, 1360–1430*. London: Routledge.
———. 1988b. "Rewriting the Middle Ages: Some Suggestions." *Journal of Medieval and Renaissance Studies* 18:221–40.
———. 1990. "Reading *Piers Plowman*: Literature, History and Criticism," *Literature and History*, second series, 2: 20–34.
———, ed. 1992. *Culture and History, 1350–1600*. Hemel Hempstead: Harvester Wheatsheaf.
———. 1993. "The Self Mourning: Reflections on Pearl." *Speculum* 68:54–73.
———. 1994a. "Class, Gender, Medieval Criticism, and *Piers Plowman*." In *Class and Gender in Early English Literature*, edited by B. J. Harwood and G. R. Overing, 59–75. Bloomington: Indiana University Press.
———. 1994b. "Justice and Wage-Labor after the Black Death: Some Perplexities for William Langland." In *Work and Culture in the Middle Ages*, edited by A. Frantzen and D. Moffat, 169–90. Cambridge: Brewer.
———. 1994c. "Altars of Power: Reflections on Eamon Duffy's *The Stripping of the Altars*." *Literature and History* 3:90–105.
———. 1995. "Gayle Margherita, *The Romance of Origins: Language and Sexual Difference in Middle English Literature* (Philadelphia: University of Pennsylvania Press). Review, *Speculum*, 70:992–95.
———. Forthcoming. "*Vox populi* and the Literature of 1381." In *The Cambridge*

History of Medieval Literature, edited by D. Wallace. Cambridge: Cambridge University Press.

Ainsworth, P. F. 1990. *Jean Froissart and the Fabric of History: Truth, Myth, and Fiction in the "Chroniques."* Oxford: Clarendon Press.

Alford, J., ed. 1988. *A Companion to Piers Plowman.* Berkeley and Los Angeles: University of California Press.

Allen, D. G. 1988. "The Premature Hermeneutics in *Piers Plowman.*" In *Allegoresis,* edited by J. S. Russell, 49–66. New York: Garland.

Ariès, P. 1962. *Centuries of Childhood: A Social History of Family Life.* Translated by R. Baldick. New York: Vintage.

Armitage-Smith, S. 1905. *John of Gaunt.* New York: Scribner.

Ashley, K. M. 1978. "Divine Power in the Chester Cycle and Late Medieval Thought." *Journal of the History of Ideas* 39:387–404.

Ashton, J. 1991. *Understanding the Fourth Gospel.* Oxford: Clarendon Press.

Astell, A. W. 1990. *The Song of Songs in the Middle Ages.* Ithaca: Cornell University Press.

Aston, M. 1960. "Lollardy and Sedition, 1381–1431." *Past and Present* 17:1–44.

———. 1984. *Lollards and Reformers: Images and Literacy in Late Medieval Religion.* London: Hambledon.

———. 1987. "Wyclif and the Vernacular." In *From Ockham to Wyclif,* edited by A. Hudson and M. Wilks, *Studies in Church History, Subsidia,* 281–330. Oxford: Basil Blackwell.

———. 1993. *Faith and Fire: Popular and Unpopular Religion, 1350–1600.* London: Hambledon.

———. 1994. "Corpus Christi and Corpus Regni: Heresy and the Peasants' Revolt." *Past and Present* 143:3–47.

Baker, D. N. 1994. *Julian of Norwich's "Showings": From Vision to Book.* Princeton: Princeton University Press.

Baker, D., ed. 1978. *Medieval Women.* Oxford: Blackwell.

Bannet, E. T. 1993. *Postcultural Theory: Critical Theory after the Marxist Paradigm.* London: Macmillan.

Barker, P. S. D. 1982. "The Motherhood of God in Julian of Norwich's Theology." *Downside Review* 100:290–304.

Barron, C. M. 1971. "The Quarrel of Richard II with London, 1392–7." In *The Reign of Richard II: Essays in Honour of May McKisack,* edited by F. R. H. DuBoulay and C. M. Barron, 173–217. London: Athlone.

Beckwith, S. 1986. "A Very Material Mysticism: The Medieval Mysticism of Margery Kempe." In *Medieval Literature: Criticism, Ideology and History,* edited by D. Aers, chap. 3. Brighton, Sussex: Harvester.

———. 1992. "Ritual, Church and Theatre: Medieval Dramas of the Sacramental Body." In *Culture and History, 1350–1600,* edited by D. Aers, chap. 3. Hemel Hempstead: Harvester Wheatsheaf.

———. 1993. *Christ's Body: Identity, Culture, and Society in Late Medieval Writings.* New York: Routledge.

Beer, F. 1992. *Women and Mystical Experience in the Middle Ages.* Woodbridge: Boydell.

Beichner, P. E. 1974. "Confrontation, Contempt of Court, and Chaucer's Cecilia." *Chaucer Review* 8:198–204.

Bell, R. M. 1985. *Holy Anorexia.* Chicago: University of Chicago Press.

Belting, H. 1990. *The Image and Its Public in the Middle Ages.* New York: Caratzas.

Benjamin, W. 1969. *Illuminations.* New York: Schocken Books.

Bennett, J. A. W. 1957. *The Parliament of Foules.* Oxford: Clarendon Press.

———. 1982. *Poetry of the Passion.* Oxford: Clarendon Press.

Bennett, J. M. 1987. *Women in the Medieval English Countryside.* Oxford: Oxford University Press.

———. 1992. "Medieval Women, Modern Women: Across the Great Divide." In *Culture and History, 1350–1600,* edited by D. Aers, chap. 5. Hemel Hempstead: Harvester Wheatsheaf.

Bennett, M. J. 1983. *Community, Class and Careerism: Cheshire and Lancashire Society in the Age of "Sir Gawain and the Green Knight."* London: Cambridge University Press.

Benson, L. D. 1981. "The Order of *The Canterbury Tales.*" *Studies in the Age of Chaucer* 3:77–120.

———. 1982. "The Occasion of *The Parliament of Fowls.*" In *The Wisdom of Poetry: Essays in Early English Literature in Honor of Morton W. Bloomfield,* edited by L. D. Benson and S. Wenzel, 123–44. Kalamazoo: Medieval Institute Publications.

———. 1985. "The 'Queynte' Punnings of Chaucer's Critics." In *Studies in the Age of Chaucer, Proceedings, no. 1: Reconstructing Chaucer,* edited by P. Strohm and T. J. Heffernan, 23–47. Knoxville: University of Tennessee Press.

Benson, R. L., and G. Constable, eds. 1982. *Renaissance and Renewal in the Twelfth Century.* Oxford: Clarendon Press.

Bergeron, D. M. 1971. *English Civic Pageantry, 1558–1642.* Columbia: University of South Carolina Press.

Biddick, C. 1993. "Genders, Bodies, Borders: Technologies of the Visible." *Speculum* 68:389–418.

Blake, N. F. 1985. *The Textual Tradition of the Canterbury Tales.* London: Edward Arnold.

Blamires, A. 1989. "The Wife of Bath and Lollardy." *Medium Ævum* 68:224–42.

———. 1994. "Questions of Gender in Chaucer, from *Anelida* to *Troilus.*" *Leeds Studies in English,* n.s., 25:83–110.

Blamires, A., and C. W. Marx. 1993. "Woman Not to Preach: A Disputation in British Library MS Harley 31." *Journal of Medieval Latin* 3:34–63.

Blanch, R. J., ed. 1969. *Style and Symbolism in Piers Plowman.* Knoxville: University of Tennessee Press.

Bloch, M., ed. 1975. *Political Language and Oratory in Traditional Society.* London: Academic Press.

Bloomfield, M. W. 1961. *Piers Plowman as a Fourteenth-Century Apocalypse.* New Brunswick: Rutgers University Press.

Boitani, P., and A. Torti, eds. 1990. *Religion in the Poetry and Drama of the Late Middle Ages in England.* Cambridge: Brewer.

Borg, M. J. 1984. *Conflict, Holiness and Politics in the Teachings of Jesus.* New York: Mellen.

Bourdieu, P. 1977. *Outlines of a Theory of Practice.* Cambridge: Cambridge University Press.

Bourquin, G. 1978. *Piers Plowman.* 2 vols. Lille: University of Lille Press.

Bowers, J. M. 1992. "Piers Plowman and the Police: Notes Toward a History of the Wycliffite Langland." *Yearbook of Langland Studies* 6:1–50.

Bradley, R.. 1976. "The Motherhood Theme in Julian of Norwich." *Fourteenth-Century English Mystics Newsletter* 2:25–30.

———. 1978. "Patristic Background of the Motherhood Similitude in Julian of Norwich." *Christian Scholars Review* 8:101–13.

———. 1990. "The Goodness of God: A Julian Study." In *Langland, the Mystics, and the Medieval English Religious Tradition,* edited by H. Phillips, 85–96. Cambridge: Brewer.

———. 1991. "In the Jaws of the Bear: Journeys of Transformation by Women Mystics." *Vox Benedictina* 8:117–75.

Braswell, L. 1986. "Chaucer and the Art of Hagiography." In *Chaucer in the Eighties,* edited by J. Wasserman and R. J. Blanch, 209–22. Syracuse: Syracuse University Press.

Brennan, T. 1993. *History After Lacan.* London: Routledge.

Brigden, S. 1989. *London and the Reformation.* Oxford: Clarendon Press.

Brooks, N. 1985. "The Organization and Achievements of the Peasants of Kent and Essex in 1381." In *Studies in Medieval History Presented to R.H.C. Davis,* edited by H. Mayr-Harting and R. I. Moore, 247–70. London: Hambledon.

Brown, E., Jr. 1994. *Studies in the Vernon Manuscript.* Reviewed in *Studies in the Age of Chaucer* 16:241–45.

Brown, P. 1981. *The Cult of the Saints: Its Rise and Function in Latin Christianity.* Chicago: University of Chicago Press.

———. 1982. *Society and the Holy in Late Antiquity.* Berkeley and Los Angeles: University of California Press.

———. 1988. *The Body and Society: Men, Women, and Sexual Renunciation in Early Christianity.* New York: Columbia University Press.

———. 1992. *Power and Persuasion in Late Antiquity: Towards a Christian Empire.* Madison: University of Wisconsin Press.

Burgess, C. 1988. "'A fond thing vainly invented': An Essay on Purgatory and Pious Motive in Later Medieval England." In *Parish, Church, and People: Local Studies in Lay Religion, 1350–1750,* edited by S. J. Wright, 56–84. London: Hutchinson.

Burrow, J. 1965. "The Action of Langland's Second Vision." *Essays in Criticism* 15:373–84. Reprinted in *Style and Symbolism in Piers Plowman,* edited by R. J. Blanch, chap. 11. Knoxville: University of Tennessee Press, 1969.

Butler, J. 1990. *Gender Trouble: Feminism and the Subversion of Identity.* London: Routledge.

———. 1993. *Bodies that Matter: On the Discursive Limits of "Sex."* London: Routledge.

Bynum, C. W. 1982. *Jesus as Mother: Studies in the Spirituality of the High Middle Ages.* Berkeley and Los Angeles: University of California Press.

———. 1987. *Holy Feast and Holy Fast.* Berkeley and Los Angeles: University of California Press.

———. 1991. *Fragmentation and Redemption: Essays on Gender and the Human Body in Medieval Religion.* New York: Zone Books.

———. 1995. *The Resurrection of the Body in Western Christianity, 200–1336.* New York: Columbia University Press.

Cadden, J. 1993. *Meanings of Sex Differences in the Middle Ages: Medicine, Science and Culture.* Cambridge: Cambridge University Press.

Callinicos, A. 1987. *Making History: Agency, Structure and Change in Social Theory.* Cambridge: Polity Press.

———. 1989. *Against Postmodernism.* Cambridge: Polity Press.

Cameron, E. 1984. *The Reformation of the Heretics: The Waldenses of the Alps, 1480–1580.* Cambridge: Cambridge University Press.

Camille, M. 1980. *The Gothic Idol: Ideology and Image-Making in Medieval Art.* Cambridge: Cambridge University Press.

———. 1992. *Image on the Edge: The Margins of Medieval Art.* London: Reaktion.

Cannadine, D., and S. Price, eds. 1987. *Rituals of Royalty: Power and Ceremonial in Traditional Societies.* Cambridge: Cambridge University Press.

Carroll, M. P. 1986. *The Cult of the Virgin Mary.* Princeton: Princeton University Press.

Carruthers, M. J. 1990. *The Book of Memory: A Study of Memory in Medieval Culture.* Cambridge: Cambridge University Press.

Catto, J. I. 1985a. "John Wyclif and the Cult of the Eucharist." In *The Bible in the Medieval World,* edited by K. Walsh and D. Wood, 43–55. Oxford: Blackwell.

———. 1985b. "Religious Change Under Henry V." In *Henry V,* edited by G. L. Harriss, chap. 5. Oxford: Oxford University Press.

———. 1992. "Wyclif and Wycliffism at Oxford, 1356–1430." In *The History of the University of Oxford,* 2 vols., edited by J. I. Catto and R. Evans, 2:175–262. Oxford: Clarendon Press.

Cheltham, F. 1984. *English Medieval Alabasters, with a Catalogue of the Collection in the Victoria and Albert Museum.* Oxford: Phaidon.

Chenu, M. D. 1968. *Nature, Man and Society in the Twelfth Century.* Translated by J. Taylor and L. K. Little. Chicago: University of Chicago Press.

Clark, J. 1992. "Late Fourteenth-Century Cambridge Theology and the English Contemplative Tradition." In *The Medieval Mystical Tradition in England,* Exeter Symposium V, edited by M. Glasscoe, 1–16. Cambridge: Brewer.

Clarke, M. V. 1936. *Medieval Representation and Consent.* London: Longmans, Greene.

Clogan, P. M. 1972. "The Figural Style and Meaning of *The Second Nun's Prologue and Tale.*" *Medievalia et Humanistica,* n.s., 3:213–40.

Clopper, L. M. 1992. "Need Men and Women Labor? Langland's Wanderer and the Labor Ordinances." In *Chaucer's England: Literature in Historical Context,* edited by B. A. Hanawalt, 110–32. Minneapolis: University of Minnesota Press.

Coleman, J. 1981a. *English Literature in History, 1350–1400*. London: Hutchinson.

———. 1981b. *Piers Plowman and the Moderni*. Rome: Letture di Pensiero e d'Arte.

———. 1992. *Ancient and Medieval Memories*. Cambridge: Cambridge University Press.

Coletti, T. 1990. "Teaching the Corpus Christi Plays: A Feminist Approach." In *Approaches to Teaching Medieval Drama*, edited by R. K. Emmerson. New York: Modern Language Association.

———. 1993. "Purity and Danger: The Paradox of Mary's Body and the Engendering of the Infancy Narrative in the English Mystery Cycles." In *Feminist Approaches to the Body in Medieval Literature*, edited by L. Lomperis and S. Stanbury, 65–95. Philadelphia: University of Pennsylvania Press.

Colish, M. 1983. *The Mirror of Language: A Study in the Medieval Theory of Knowledge*. Revised ed. Lincoln: University of Nebraska Press.

Colledge, E. 1975. "Fifteenth- and Sixteenth-Century English Versions of 'The Golden Epistle of St. Bernard.'" *Medieval Studies* 37:122–29.

Collette, C. 1976. "A Closer Look at Seinte Cecile's Special Vision." *Chaucer Review* 10:337–49.

———. 1990. "Critical Approaches to the Prioress's Tale." In *Chaucer's Religious Tales*, edited by C. D. Benson and E. Robertson, 95–110. Cambridge: Brewer.

———. 1994. "Chaucer's Discourse of Mariology: Gaining the Right to Speak." In *Art and Context in Late Medieval English Narrative*, edited by R. P. Edwards, 127–47. Cambridge: Brewer.

Collinson, P. 1982. *The Religion of Protestants: The Church in English Society, 1559–1625*. Oxford: Oxford University Press.

Condren, E. J. 1984. "The *Clerk's Tale* of Man Tempting God." *Criticism* 26:99–114.

Cooper, H. 1987. "Langland's and Chaucer's Prologues." *Yearbook of Langland Studies* 1:71–81.

———. 1989. *The Canterbury Tales*. Oxford Guides to Chaucer. Oxford: Oxford University Press.

Copeland, R. 1992. *Rhetoric, Hermeneutics, and Translation in the Middle Ages: Academic Traditions and Vernacular Texts*. Cambridge: Cambridge University Press.

———. 1994. "Why Women Can't Read: Medieval Hermeneutics, Statute Law, and the Lollard Heresy Trials." In *Representing Women: Law, Literature, and Feminism*, edited by S. S. Heinzelman et al., 253–86. Durham: Duke University Press.

Crane, S. 1990. "Medieval Romance and Feminine Difference in *The Knight's Tale*." *Studies in the Age of Chaucer* 12:47–63.

———. 1992. "The Writing Lesson of 1381." In *Chaucer's England: Literature in*

Historical Context, edited by B. A. Hanawalt, 201–21. Minneapolis: University of Minnesota Press.

———. 1994. *Gender and Romance in Chaucer's "Canterbury Tales."* Princeton: Princeton University Press.

Crompton, J. 1968–69. "Leicestershire Lollards." *Leicestershire Archaeological and Historical Society, Transactions* 44:11–44.

Cross, C. 1978. "'Great Reasoners in Scripture': The Activities of Women Lollards." In *Medieval Women,* edited by D. Baker, 359–80. Oxford: Blackwell.

Crossan, J. D. 1991. *The Historical Jesus: The Life of a Mediterranean Jewish Peasant.* Edinburgh: Clark.

Curtis, P. 1986. "Some Discarnational Impulses in the *Canterbury Tales.*" In *Medieval English Religious and Ethical Literature: Essays in Honour of G.H. Russell,* edited by G. Kratzmann and J. Simpson, 128–45. Cambridge: Brewer.

Dahmus, J. H. 1952. *The Prosecution of John Wyclif.* New Haven: Yale University Press.

Davis, N. Z. 1975. *Society and Culture in Early Modern France.* Stanford: Stanford University Press.

Dean, J. 1984. "Dismantling the Canterbury Book." *PMLA* 100:746–62.

Delany, S. 1994. *The Naked Text: Chaucer's "Legend of Good Women."* Berkeley and Los Angeles: University of California Press.

Derrida, J. 1978. *Of Grammatology.* Translated by G. Spivak. Baltimore: Johns Hopkins University Press.

———. 1988. *Limited Inc.* Edited by G. Graff. Evanston: Northwestern University Press.

———. 1994. *Spectres of Marx.* Translated by P. Kamuf. New York: Routledge.

———. 1995. *The Gift of Death.* Translated by D. Wills. Chicago: University of Chicago Press.

Dews, P. 1987. *Logics of Disintegration: Post-Structuralist Thought and the Claims of Critical Theory.* London: Verso.

Dickson, L. 1993. "Reflection in the Mirror: Feminine Discourse in *The Wife of Bath's Prologue* and *Tale.*" *Studies in the Age of Chaucer* 15:61–90.

Dinshaw, C. 1989. *Chaucer's Sexual Poetics.* Madison: University of Wisconsin Press.

———. 1994. "A Kiss is Just a Kiss: Heterosexuality and Its Consolations in *Sir Gawain and the Green Knight.*" *Diacritics* 24:205–26.

Dollimore, J. 1991. *Sexual Dissidence: Augustine to Wilde, Freud to Foucault.* Oxford: Clarendon Press.

Dronke, P. 1984. *Women Writers of the Middle Ages.* Cambridge: Cambridge University Press.

Duffy, E. 1992. *The Stripping of the Altars: Traditional Religion in England, 1400–1580.* New Haven: Yale University Press.

Dugmore, C. W. 1958. *The Mass and the English Reformers.* London: Macmillan.

Dyer, C. 1989. *Standards of Living in the Later Middle Ages.* Cambridge University Press.

Eberle, P. J. 1981. "The Politics of Courtly Style at the Court of Richard II." In

Court and Poet: Selected Proceedings of the Third Congress of the International Courtly Literature Society, edited by G. S. Burgess, 168–78. Liverpool, 1980; Liverpool: Francis Cairns.

Edwards, R. A. 1958. "Henry Despenser: The Fighting Bishop." *Church Quarterly* 159:26–38.

Ellis, R. 1980. "Revelation and the Life of Faith: The Vision of Julian of Norwich." *Christian* 6:61–71.

Emmerson, R. K. 1994. "'Yernen to rede redeles?' *Piers Plowman* and Prophecy." *Yearbook of Langland Studies* 7:28–76.

Faith, R. 1984. "'The Great Rumour' of 1377 and Peasant Ideology." In *The English Rising of 1381,* edited by R. Hilton and T. Aston, 43–73. Cambridge: Cambridge University Press.

Ferster, J. 1990. "'Your Praise Is Performed by Men and Children': Language and Gender in the *Prioress's Prologue* and *Tale.*" *Exemplaria* 2:149–68.

Finke, L. 1992. *Feminist Theory, Women's Writing.* Ithaca: Cornell University Press.

Fletcher, A. J. 1987. "John Mirk and the Lollards." *Medium Ævum* 55:217–24.

Foucault, M. 1979. *Discipline and Punish.* Translated by A. Sheridan. Harmondsworth: Penguin.

———. 1980. *Power/Knowledge.* Edited by C. Gordon. New York: Harvester Wheatsheaf.

———. 1981. *The History of Sexuality: An Introduction.* Translated by R. Hurley. Harmondsworth: Penguin.

———. 1984. *The Foucault Reader.* Edited by P. Rainbow. New York: Pantheon.

———. 1988. "Technologies of the Self." In *Technologies of the Self,* edited by L. H. Martin. Amherst: University of Massachusetts Press.

Fradenburg, L. O. 1985. "The Manciple's Servant Tongue: Politics and Poetry in *The Canterbury Tales.*" *ELH* 52:85–118.

———. 1986. "The Wife of Bath's Passing Fancy." *Studies in the Age of Chaucer* 8:31–58.

———. 1989. "Criticism, Anti-Semitism and the *Prioress's Tale.*" *Exemplaria* 1:69–115.

———. 1990. "'Voice Memorial': Loss and Reparation in Chaucer's Poetry." *Exemplaria* 2:169–202.

Frank, R. W. 1951. "The Pardon Scene in *Piers Plowman.*" *Speculum* 26:317–31.

———. 1957. *Piers Plowman and the Scheme of Salvation.* New Haven: Yale University Press.

———. 1990. "*Meditationes Vitaè Christi:* The Logistics of Access to the Divinity." In *Hermeneutics and Medieval Culture,* edited by P. J. Gallacher and H. Damico, chap. 3. Albany: State University of New York Press.

Frantzen, A. Forthcoming in *PLMA.* "The Disclosure of Sodomy in 'Cleanness.'"

Frantzen, A., ed. 1991. *Speaking Two Languages.* Albany: State University of New York Press.

Frantzen, A., and D. Moffat, eds. 1994. *Work and Culture in the Middle Ages.* Glasgow: Cruithne.

Gaffney, W. 1931. "The Allegory of the Christ-Knight in *Piers Plowman.*" *PMLA* 46:155–68.

Galbraith, V. H. 1982. *Kings and Chroniclers: Essays in English Medieval History.* London: Hambledon.

Gallacher, P. J., and H. Damico, eds. 1990. *Hermeneutics and Medieval Culture.* Albany: State University of New York Press.

Ganim, J. 1990. "Chaucer and the Noise of the People." *Exemplaria* 2:71–88.

Gaylord, A. 1960. "Chaucer's Squire and the Glorious Campaign." *Papers of the Michigan Academy of Sciences, Arts, and Letters* 45:341–61.

Geertz, C. 1973. *The Interpretation of Cultures: Selected Essays.* New York: Basic Books.

Gerould, G. H. 1941. "The Second Nun's Prologue and Tale." In *Sources and Analogues of Chaucer's Canterbury Tales,* edited by W. F. Bryan and G. Dempster, 664–84. Chicago: University of Chicago Press.

Gibson, G. McM. 1989. *The Theater of Devotion: East Anglian Drama and Society in the Late Middle Ages.* Chicago: University of Chicago Press.

Gibson, J. 1992. "Could Christ Have Been Born a Woman? A Medieval Debate." *Journal of Feminist Studies in Religion* 8:65–82.

Giffin, M. 1956. *Studies in Chaucer and His Audience.* Hull, Quebec: Editions "L'Eclair."

Gillespie, V. 1987. "Strange Images of Death: The Passion in Later Medieval English Devotional and Mystical Writing." *Analecta Cartusiana* 117:111–59.

Given-Wilson, C. 1986. *The Royal Household and the King's Affinity.* New Haven: Yale University Press.

Glasscoe, M. 1983. "Means of Showing: An Approach to Reading Julian of Norwich." *Analecta Cartusiana* 106:155–77.

———. 1989. "Visions and Revisions: A Further Look at the Manuscripts of Julian of Norwich." *Studies in Bibliography* 42:103–19.

———. 1992. *The Medieval Mystical Tradition in England.* Cambridge: Brewer.

———. 1993. *English Medieval Mystics: Games of Faith.* London: Longman.

Godden, M. 1984. "Plowmen and Hermits in Langland's *Piers Plowman*." *Review of English Studies* 35:129–63.

———. 1990. *The Making of Piers Plowman.* London: Longman.

Goldberg, P. J. P. 1992. *Women, Work and Life Cycle in a Medieval Economy: Women in York and Yorkshire c. 1300–1520.* Oxford: Oxford University Press.

Golenistcheff-Koutouzoff, E. 1933. *L'Histoire de Griseldis en France au XIVe et au Xve Siècle.* Paris: Librairie E. Droz.

———. 1937. *Etude sur "Le Livre de la Vertu du Sacrement de Mariage et Reconfort des Dames Mariées" de Philippe de Mézières.* Belgrade: Svetlost.

Goodman, A. 1968. "Sir Thomas Hoo and the Parliament of 1376." *Bulletin of the Institute of Historical Research* 41:139–49.

———. 1986. "John of Gaunt." In *England in the Fourteenth Century: Proceedings of the 1985 Harlaxton Symposium,* edited by W. M. Ormrod, 67–87. Woodbridge, Suffolk: Boydell.

———. 1992. *John of Gaunt: The Exercise of Princely Power in Fourteenth-Century Europe.* New York: St. Martin's.

Gradon, P. 1980. "Langland and the Ideology of Dissent." *Publications of the British Academy* 66:179–205.

Graff, G. 1987. *Professing Literature*. Chicago: University of Chicago Press.

Gravdal, K. 1991. *Ravishing Maidens: Writing Rape in Medieval French Literature and Law*. Philadelphia: University of Pennsylvania Press.

Green, A. S. 1971. *Town Life in the Fifteenth Century*. Boston, 1894; reissued New York.

Green, R. F. 1980. *Poets and Princepleasers: Literature and the English Court in the Late Middle Ages*. Toronto: University of Toronto Press.

———. 1992. "John Ball's Letters: Literary History and Historical Literature." In *Chaucer's England: Literature in Historical Context*, edited by B. A. Hanawalt, 176–200. Minneapolis: University of Minnesota Press.

Grennen, J. E. 1966. "St. Cecilia's Chemical Wedding." *JEGP* 65:466–81.

Grudin, M. P. 1989. "Chaucer's *Clerk's Tale* as Political Paradox." *Studies in the Age of Chaucer* 11:63–92.

Hahn, T. 1992. "Teaching the Resistant Woman: The Wife of Bath and the Academy." *Exemplaria* 4:931–40.

Hanawalt, B. 1986a. *The Ties That Bound: Peasant Families in Medieval England*. New York: Oxford University Press.

———. 1986b. *Women and Work in Preindustrial Europe*. Bloomington: Indiana University Press.

———. ed. 1992. *Chaucer's England*. Minneapolis: University of Minnesota Press.

Hanna, R., III. 1990. "The Difficulty of Ricardian Prose Translation: The Case of the Lollards." *Modern Language Quarterly* 50:319–39.

———. 1992. "Contextualizing *The Siege of Jerusalem*." *Yearbook of Langland Studies* 6:109–22.

———. 1994. "'Meddling with Makings' and Will's Work." In *Late-Medieval Religious Texts and Their Transmission*, edited by A. Minnis, 85–94. Cambridge: Brewer.

Hansen, E. T. 1988. "The Wife of Bath and the Mark of Adam." *Women's Studies* 15:399–416.

———. 1992. *Chaucer and the Fictions of Gender*. Berkeley and Los Angeles: University of California Press.

Harbert, B. 1990. "Langland's Easter." In *Langland, the Mystics and the Medieval English Religious Tradition*, edited by H. Phillips, 57–70. Cambridge: Brewer.

Harriss, G. L. 1976. "War and the Emergence of the English Parliament. 1297 to 1360." *Journal of Medieval History* 2:35–56.

———. 1981. "The Formation of Parliament." In *The English Parliament in the Middle Ages*, edited by R. G. Davies and J. H. Denton, 29–60. Philadelphia: University of Pennsylvania Press.

Harwood, B. J. 1992. *Piers Plowman and the Problem of Belief*. Toronto: University of Toronto Press.

Harwood, B. J., and G. Overing. 1994. *Class and Gender in Early English Literature; Intersections*. Bloomington: Indiana University Press.

Heath, P. 1988. *Church and Realm, 1272–1461*. London: Fontana.

Heffernan, T. J. 1988. *Sacred Biography: Saints and Their Biographers in the Middle Ages.* New York: Oxford University Press.

———. 1990. "Orthodoxies' *Redux: The Northern Homily Cycle* in the Vernon Manuscript and Its Textual Affiliations." In *Studies in the Vernon Manuscript,* edited by D. Pearsall, 75–88. Cambridge: Brewer.

Heimmel, J. P. 1982. *"God is Our Mother": Julian of Norwich and the Medieval Image of Christian Feminine Divinity.* Salzburg Studies in English Literature. Salzburg: University of Salzburg.

Heng, G. 1991. "Feminine Knots and the Other Sir Gawain and the Green Knight." *PMLA* 106:500–14.

———. 1992. "A Woman Wants: The Lady, Gawain, and the Forms of Seduction." *Yale Journal of Criticism* 5:101–34.

Hilton, R. H. 1973. *Bond Men Made Free: Medieval Peasant Movements and the English Rising of 1381.* New York: Viking.

———. 1975. *The English Peasantry in the Later Middle Ages.* Oxford: Clarendon Press.

———. 1985a. *Class Conflict and the Crisis of Feudalism: Essays in Medieval Social History.* London: Hambledon.

———. 1985b. "Ideology and Social Order in Late Medieval England." In *Class Conflict and the Crisis of Feudalism: Essays in Medieval Social History,* 246–52. London: Hambledon.

———. 1992. *English and French Towns in Feudal Society: A Comparative Study.* Cambridge: Cambridge University Press.

Hirsh, J. C. 1977. "The Politics of Spirituality: The Second Nun and the Manciple." *Chaucer Review* 12:129–46.

———. 1990. "The Second Nun's Tale." In *Chaucer's Religious Tales,* edited by C. D. Benson and E. Robertson, 161–70. Cambridge: Brewer.

Holmes, G. 1975. *The Good Parliament.* Oxford: Clarendon Press.

Howard, D. R. 1978. *The Idea of the Canterbury Tales.* Berkeley and Los Angeles: University of California Press.

Howell, M. C. 1986. *Women, Production and Patriarchy in Late Medieval Cities.* Chicago: University of Chicago Press.

———. 1988. "Citizenship and Gender: Women's Political Status in Northern Medieval Cities." In *Women and Power in the Middle Ages,* edited by M. Kowaleski, 37–60. Athens: University of Georgia Press.

Hudson, A., ed. 1978. *Selections from English Wycliffite Writings.* Cambridge: Cambridge University Press.

———. 1982. "Lollardy: The English Heresy." *Studies in Church History* 18:261–83.

———. 1985. *Lollards and Their Books.* London: Hambledon.

———. 1986. "Wyclif and the English Language." In *Wyclif in His Times,* edited by A. Kenny, 85–103. Oxford: Clarendon Press.

———. 1988. *The Premature Reformation: Wycliffite Texts and Lollard History.* Oxford: Clarendon Press.

———. 1994. *"Laicus litteratus:* The Paradox of Lollardy." In *Heresy and Literacy,*

1000–1530, edited by P. Biller and A. Hudson, 222–36. Cambridge: Cambridge University Press.

Hughes, J. 1988. *Pastors and Visionaries: Religion and Secular Life in Late Medieval Yorkshire.* Wolfeboro, N.H.: Boydell and Brewer.

Irigaray, L. 1985. *Speculum of the Other Woman.* Translated by G. C. Gill. Ithaca: Cornell University Press.

Jacquart, D., and C. Thomasset. 1988. *Sexuality and Medicine in the Middle Ages.* Translated by M. Adamson. Princeton: Princeton University Press.

James, M. 1983. "Ritual, Drama, and Social Body in the Late Medieval English Town." *Past and Present* 98:3–29.

Jantzen, G. M. 1987. *Julian of Norwich, Mystic and Theologian.* New York: Paulist Press.

Jeffrey, D. L. 1984. "Chaucer and Wyclif: Biblical Hermeneutic and Literary Theory in the XIVth Century." In *Chaucer and Scriptural Tradition,* edited by D. L. Jeffrey, 109–40. Ottawa: University of Ottawa Press.

Johnson, L. S. *See also* Staley, L..

Johnson, L. S. 1975. "The Prince and His People: A Study of the Two Covenants in the *Clerk's Tale.*" *Chaucer Review* 10:17–29.

———. 1984. *The Voice of the Gawain-Poet.* Madison: University of Wisconsin Press.

———. 1985. "'To Make in Som Comedye': Chaunticleer, Son of Troy." *Chaucer Review* 19:225–44.

———. 1989. "*The Clerk's Tale* and the Arts of Narrative Manipulation." *Mediaevalia* 11 (1989 for 1985):121–38.

———. 1990. *The Shepheardes Calender: An Introduction.* University Park: Pennsylvania State University Press.

Jones, R. H. 1968. *The Royal Policy of Richard II: Absolutism in the Later Middle Ages.* New York: Barnes and Noble.

Jones, W. R. 1973. "Lollards and Images: The Defense of Religious Art in Later Medieval England." *Journal of the History of Ideas* 34:27–50.

Justice, S. 1994a. "Inquisition, Speech, and Writing: A Case from Late-Medieval Norwich." *Representations* 48:1–29.

———. 1994b. *Writing and Rebellion: England in 1381.* Berkeley and Los Angeles: University of California Press.

Kaeuper, R. W. 1988. *War, Justice and Public Order: England and France in the Later Middle Ages.* Oxford: Clarendon Press.

Kay, S., and M. Rubin. 1994. *Framing Medieval Bodies.* Manchester: Manchester University Press.

Keen, M. H. 1973. *England in the Later Middle Ages.* London: Methuen.

Kendall, R. D. 1986. *The Drama of Dissent: The Radical Poetics of Nonconformity, 1380–1590.* Chapel Hill: University of North Carolina Press.

Kenny, A. 1990. *John Wyclif.* Oxford: Oxford University Press.

Kerby-Fulton, K. 1990. *Reformist Apocalypticism and "Piers Plowman."* Cambridge: Cambridge University Press.

Kieckhefer, R. 1984. *Unquiet Souls: Fourteenth-Century Saints and Their Religious Milieu.* Chicago: University of Chicago Press.

Kipling, G. 1985. "Richard II's 'Sumptuous pageants' and the Idea of the Civic Triumph." In *Pageantry in the Shakespearean Theater,* edited by D. M. Bergeron, 83–103. Athens: University of Georgia Press.

Kirk, E. D. 1988. "Langland's Plowman and the Recreation of Fourteenth-Century Religious Metaphor." *Yearbook of Langland Studies* 2:1–21.

Knight, S. 1986. *Geoffrey Chaucer.* Oxford: Basil Blackwell.

Kolve, V. A. 1981. "Chaucer's Second Nun's Tale and the Iconography of Saint Cecilia." In *New Perspectives on Chaucer Criticism,* edited by D. M. Rose, 137–76. Norman, Okla.: Pilgrim Books.

Koziol, G. 1993. *Begging Pardon and Favor: Ritual and Political Order in Early Medieval France.* Ithaca: Cornell University Press.

Kristeva, J. 1982. *Powers of Horror: An Essay in Abjection.* Translated by L. S. Roudiez. New York: Columbia University Press.

Kuczynski, M. P. 1995. *Prophetic Song: The Psalms as Moral Discourse in Late Medieval England.* Philadelphia: University of Pennsylvania Press.

Laclau, E., and C. Mouffe. 1985. *Hegemony and Socialist Strategy.* London: Verso.

Ladurie, E. le Roy. 1978. *Montaillou: Cathars and Catholics in a French Village.* Translated by B. Bray. London: Scolar.

Lane, B. G. 1984. *The Altar and the Altarpiece: Sacramental Themes in Early Netherlandish Painting.* New York: Harper and Row.

Laqueur, T. 1990. *Making Sex: Body and Gender from the Greeks to Freud.* Cambridge: Harvard University Press.

Lawler, T. 1980. *The One and the Many in the "Canterbury Tales."* Hamden, Conn.: Archon.

———. 1984. "Chaucer." In *Middle English Prose,* edited by A. S. G. Edwards, 293–96. New Brunswick: Rutgers University Press.

Lawrence, W. W. 1969. "The Tale of Melibeus." In *Essays and Studies in Honor of Carleton Brown* (1940). Freeport, N.Y.: Books for Libraries Press, 100–110.

Leech, K. 1988. "Hazelnut Theology: Its Potential and Perils." In *Julian Reconsidered,* by K. Leech and Sister Benedicta (Ward), 1–10. Oxford: SLG Press.

Lees, C. A. 1994. "Gender and Exchange in *Piers Plowman.*" In *Class and Gender in Early English Literature,* edited by B. J. Harwood and G. R. Overing, 112–30. Bloomington: Indiana University Press.

Leff, G. 1961. "Heresy and the Decline of the Medieval Church." *Past and Present* 20:36–51.

———. 1967. *Heresy in the Later Middle Ages.* 2 vols. New York: Barnes and Noble.

LeGoff, J. 1984. *The Birth of Purgatory.* Translated by A. Goldhammer. Chicago: University of Chicago Press.

Leicester, H. M, Jr. 1990. *The Disenchanted Self: Representing the Subject in the "Canterbury Tales."* Berkeley and Los Angeles: University of California Press.

Lepow, L. 1990. *Enacting the Sacrament: Counter-Lollardy in the Towneley Cycle.* Toronto: Associated University Presses.

Lerer, S. 1993. *Chaucer and His Readers: Imagining the Author in Late-Medieval England.* Princeton: Princeton University Press.

Lerner, R. E. 1972. *The Heresy of the Free Spirit in the Later Middle Ages.* Berkeley and Los Angeles: University of California Press.

Lochrie, K. 1991a. "The Language of Transgression: Body, Flesh and Word in Mystical Discourse." In *Speaking Two Languages,* edited by A. Frantzen, chap. 5. Albany: State University of New York Press.

———. 1991b. *Margery Kempe and Translations of the Flesh.* Philadelphia: University of Pennsylvania Press.

Lomperis, L., and S. Stanbury, eds. 1993. *Feminist Approaches to the Body in Medieval Literature.* Philadelphia; University of Pennsylvania Press.

Lukács, G. 1971. *History and Class Consciousness.* London: Merlin.

Lyotard, J-F. 1984. *The Postmodern Condition.* Translated by G. Bennington and B. Massumi. Minneapolis: University of Minnesota Press.

Macfarlane, L. 1953. "An English Account of the Election of Urban VI, 1378." *Bulletin of the Institute of Historical Research* 26:75–85.

Macy, G. 1984. *The Theologies of the Eucharist in the Early Scholastic Period.* Oxford: Clarendon Press.

Madicott, J. R. 1981. "Parliament and the Constituencies, 1272–1377." In *The English Parliament in the Middle Ages,* edited by R. G. Davies and J. H. Denton, 61–87. Philadelphia: University of Pennsylvania Press.

———. 1986. "Poems of Social Protest in Early Fourteenth-Century England." In *England in the Fourteenth Century: Proceedings of the 1985 Harlaxton Symposium,* edited by W. M. Ormod, 130–44. Woodbridge, Suffolk: Boydell.

———. 1987. "The English Peasantry and the Demands of the Crown." In *Landlords, Peasants and Politics in Medieval England,* edited by T. H. Aston, 285–359. Cambridge: Cambridge University Press.

Mann, J. 1973. *Chaucer and Medieval Estates' Satire: The Text of Social Classes and the "General Prologue" to the "Canterbury Tales."* Cambridge: Cambridge University Press.

———. 1991. *Geoffrey Chaucer.* Feminist Readings Series. Atlantic Highlands, N.J.: Humanities Press International.

Marrow, J. 1979. *Passion Iconography in Northern European Art of the Late Middle Ages and Early Renaissance.* Kortrijk: Ghemmert.

Martin, P. 1990. *Chaucer's Women: Nuns, Wives, and Amazons.* Iowa City: University of Iowa Press.

Marx, K. 1970. *Capital: A Critique of Political Economy.* Vol. 1, *Capitalist Production.* London: Lawrence and Wishart.

McCabe, H. 1991. *God Matters.* Springfield: Templegate.

McCall, J. P., and G. Rudisall Jr. 1959. "The Parliament of 1386 and Chaucer's Trojan Parliament." *JEGP* 58:276–88.

McFarlane, K. B. 1953. *John Wycliffe and the Beginnings of English Nonconformity.* London, 1952; New York: Macmillan.

McGann, J. J. 1988. *Social Values and Poetic Acts.* Cambridge: Harvard University Press.

McGrade, A. S. 1991. "Somersaulting Sovereignty: A Note on Reciprocal Lordship and Servitude in Wyclif." In *The Church and Sovereignty, c. 590–1918:*

Essays in Honour of Michael Wilks, edited by D. Wood, 261–68. Oxford: Basil Blackwell.

McKisack, M. 1959. *The Fourteenth Century, 1307–1399.* Oxford: Clarendon Press.

McLellan, D. 1993. *Unto Caesar: The Political Relevance of Christianity.* Notre Dame: University of Notre Dame Press.

McNiven, P. 1987. *Heresy and Politics in the Reign of Henry IV: The Burning of John Badby.* Woodbridge, Suffolk: Boydell.

Meale, C. M. 1993. "'. . . alle the bokes that I haue of latyn, englisch, and frensch': Laywomen and Their Books in Late Medieval England." In *Women and Literature in Britain, 1150–1500,* edited by C. M. Meale, 128–58. Cambridge: Cambridge University Press.

Middleton, A. 1978. "The Idea of Public Poetry in the Reign of Richard II." *Speculum* 53:94–114.

———. 1980. "The Clerk and His Tale: Some Literary Contexts." *Studies in the Age of Chaucer* 2:121–50.

———. 1982a. "The Audience and Public of *Piers Plowman.*" In *Middle English Alliterative Poetry,* edited by D. Lawton, chap. 7. Cambridge: Brewer.

———. 1982b. "Narration and the Invention of Experience: Episodic Form in *Piers Plowman.*" In *The Wisdom of Poetry,* edited by L. D. Benson and S. Wenzel, 91–122. Kalamazoo, Mich.: Medieval Institute.

———. 1990. "William Langland's 'Kynde Name': Authorial Signature and Social Identity in Late Fourteenth-Century England." In *Literary Practice and Social Change in Britain, 1380–1530,* edited by L. Patterson, 15–82. Berkeley and Los Angeles: University of California Press.

Miles, M. R. 1989. *Carnal Knowing: Female Nakedness and Religious Meaning in the Christian West.* Boston: Beacon.

Minnis, A. G. 1984. *Medieval Theory of Authorship: Scholastic Literary Attitudes in the Later Middle Ages.* London: Scolar.

Moi, T. 1985. *Sexual/Textual Politics.* London: Methuen.

Moore, R. I. 1987. *The Formation of a Persecuting Society.* Oxford: Blackwell.

Morris, C. 1972. *The Discovery of the Individual, 1050–1200.* London: S.P.C.K.

———. 1980. "Individualism in Twelfth-Century Religion: Some Further Reflections." *Journal of Ecclesiastical History* 31:195–208.

Morse, C. C. 1985. "The Exemplary Griselda." *Studies in the Age of Chaucer* 7:51–86.

Murphy, C. 1994. "Lady Holy Church and Meed the Maid: Re-Envisioning Female Personifications in *Piers Plowman.*" In *Feminist Readings in Middle English Literature: The Wife of Bath and All Her Sect.* Edited by R. Evans and L. Johnson. London: Routledge.

Murray, A. 1978. *Reason and Society in the Middle Ages.* Oxford: Clarendon Press.

Nelson, C., and L. Grosberg, eds. 1988. *Marxism and the Interpretation of Culture.* Urbana: University of Illinois Press.

Neuse, R. 1962. "The Knight: The First Mover in Chaucer's Human Comedy." *University of Toronto Quarterly* 31:294–315.

———. 1991. *Chaucer's Dante: Allegory and Epic Theater in "The Canterbury Tales."* Berkeley and Los Angeles: University of California Press.

Newman, B. 1987. *Sister of Wisdom: St. Hildegard's Theology of the Feminine.* Berkeley and Los Angeles: University of California Press.

———. 1990. "Some Medieval Theologians and the Sophia Tradition." *Downside Review* 108:111–30.

———. 1995. *From Virile Woman to Woman Christ.* Philadelphia: University of Pennsylvania Press.

Nolan, B. 1992. *Chaucer and the Tradition of the "Roman Antique."* Cambridge: Cambridge University Press.

Norris, C. 1990. *What's Wrong with Postmodernism?* Hemel Hempstead: Harvester Wheatsheaf.

Nuth, J. M. 1991. *Wisdom's Daughter: The Theology of Julian of Norwich.* New York: Crossroad.

Oberman, H. O. 1963. *The Harvest of Medieval Theology: Gabriel Biel and late Medieval Nominalism.* Cambridge: Harvard University Press.

Olsen, G. 1969. "The Idea of the Ecclesia Primitiva in the Writings of the Twelfth-Century Canonists." *Traditio* 25:61–86.

Olson, G. 1982a. "Chaucer, Dante, and the Structure of Fragment VIII (G) of the *Canterbury Tales.*" *Chaucer Review* 16:222–37.

———. 1982b. *Literature as Recreation in the Later Middle Ages.* Ithaca: Cornell University Press.

Olson, P. 1986. *The "Canterbury Tales" and the Good Society.* Princeton: Princeton University Press.

Ormrod, W. M. 1990a. "The Peasants' Revolt and the Government of England." *Journal of British Studies* 29:1–30.

———. 1990b. *The Reign of Edward III.* New Haven: Yale University Press.

Owen, C. A. 1977. *Pilgrimage and Storytelling in the Canterbury Tales.* Norman: University of Oklahoma Press.

———. 1982. "The Alternative Reading of *The Canterbury Tales:* Chaucer's Text and the Early Manuscripts." *PMLA* 97:237–50.

Owst, G. R. 1966. *Literature and Pulpit in Medieval England.* 2d ed. Oxford: Basil Blackwell.

Oxford Socialist Discussion Group, ed. 1989. *Out of Apathy: Voices of the New Left Thirty Years On.* London: Verso.

Palliser, M. A., O.P. 1992. *Christ, Our Mother of Mercy: Divine Mercy and Compassion in the Theology of the "Shewings" of Julian of Norwich.* New York: de Gruyter.

Palmer, J. J. N. 1971. "The Parliament of 1365 and the Constitutional Crisis of 1386." *Speculum* 46:477–90.

———. 1972. *England, France and Christendom, 1377–99.* Chapel Hill: University of North Carolina Press.

Paster, G. K. 1993. *The Body Embarassed.* Ithaca: Cornell University Press.

Patterson, Lee. 1978. "*The Parson's Tale* and the Quitting of the *Canterbury Tales.*" *Traditio* 34:331–80.

———. 1983. "'For the Wyves Love of Bathe': Feminine Rhetoric and Poetic Resolution in the *Roman de la Rose* and the *Canterbury Tales*." *Speculum* 58:656–95.

———. 1987. *Negotiating the Past: The Historical Understanding of Medieval Literature*. Madison: University of Wisconsin Press.

———. 1989. "'What Man Artow?': Authorial Self-Definition in *The Tale of Sir Thopas* and *The Tale of Melibee*." *Studies in the Age of Chaucer* 11:117–75.

———, ed. 1990. *Literary Practice and Social Change in Britain, 1380–1530*. Berkeley and Los Angeles: University of California Press.

———. 1991. *Chaucer and the Subject of History*. Madison: University of Wisconsin Press.

———. 1992. "Court Politics and the Invention of Literature: The Case of Sir John Clanvowe." In *Culture and History, 1380–1450*, edited by D. Aers, 7–41. London: Harvester.

———. 1993a. "Making Identities in Fifteenth-Century England: Henry V and John Lydgate." In *New Historical Literary Study*, edited by J. N. Cox and L. J. Reynolds, chap. 3. Princeton: Princeton University Press.

———. 1993b. "Perpetual Motion: Alchemy and the Technology of the Self." *Studies in the Age of Chaucer* 15:25–60.

Pearsall, D. 1981. "The Origins of the Alliterative Revival." In *The Alliterative Tradition in the Fourteenth Century*, edited by B. S. Levy and P. E. Szarmach, 1–24. Kent: Kent State University Press.

———. 1985. *The Canterbury Tales*. London: Allen and Unwin.

———. 1988. "Poverty and Poor People in *Piers Plowman*." In *Medieval English Studies presented to George Kane*, edited by E. D. Kennedy, R. Waldron, and J. S. Wittig, 167–86. Wolfeboro, N.H.: Brewer.

———. 1989. "Interpretative Models for the Peasants' Revolt." In *Hermeneutics and Medieval Culture*, edited by P. J. Gallacher and H. Damico, 63–70. Albany: State University of New York Press.

———. 1990. *Studies in the Vernon Manuscript*. Cambridge: Brewer.

———. 1992. *The Life of Geoffrey Chaucer: A Critical Biography*. Oxford: Blackwell.

Peck, R. A. 1967. "The Ideas of 'Entente' and Translation in Chaucer's *Second Nun's Tale*." *Annuale Mediaevale* 8:17–37.

———. 1978. *Kingship and Common Profit in Gower's "Confessio Amantis."* Carbondale: Southern Illinois University Press.

———. 1986. "Social Conscience and the Poets." In *Social Unrest in the Late Middle Ages*, 113–48. Binghamton, N.Y.: Center for Medieval and Early Renaissance Studies.

Pelphrey, B. 1982. *Love Was His Meaning: The Theology and Mysticism of Julian of Norwich*. Salzburg Studies in English Literature. Salzburg: University of Salzburg.

———. 1989. *Christ Our Mother: Julian of Norwich*. London: Darton, Longman and Todd.

Perroy, E. 1933. *L'Angleterre et le Grand Schisme d'Occident*. Paris: Librairie J. Mounier.

Petroff, E. A. 1986. *Medieval Women's Visionary Literature.* Oxford: Oxford University Press.

————. 1991. "Women's Bodies and the Experience of God in the Middle Ages." *Vox Benedictina* 8:91–115.

Pezzini, D. 1990. "The Theme of the Passion in Richard Rolle and Julian of Norwich." In *Religion in the Poetry and Drama of the Late Middle Ages in England,* edited by P. Boitani and A. Torti, 29–66. Cambridge: Brewer.

Phillips, H., ed. 1990. *Langland, the Mystics and the Medieval English Religious Tradition.* Cambridge: Brewer.

Pichaske, D. R., and L. Sweetland. 1977. "Chaucer on the Medieval Monarchy: Harry Bailly in *The Canterbury Tales.*" *Chaucer Review* 11:179–200.

Poos, L. R. 1991. *A Rural Society after the Black Death, Essex 1350–1525.* Cambridge: Cambridge University Press.

Powell, E. 1989. *Kingship, Law, and Society: Criminal Justice in the Reign of Henry V.* Oxford: Clarendon Press.

Prestwich, M. 1983. "Parliament and the Community of the Realm in Fourteenth-Century England." In *Parliament and Community,* Irish Historical Studies 14, edited by A. Cosgrove and J. I. McGuire, 5–24. Belfast: Appletree Press.

Putnam, B. H. 1908. *The Enforcement of the Statute of Laborers During the First Decade After the Black Death.* Studies in History, Economics, and Public Law 32. New York: Columbia University Press.

Rahner, K. 1969 (1974). *Theological Investigations.* Vol. 6. Translated by K.-H. and B. Kruger. London: Darton, Longman and Todd.

————. 1975. *A Rahner Reader.* Edited by G. A. McCool. New York: Seabury.

Reames, S. L. 1978–79. "The Sources of Chaucer's 'Second Nun's Tale.'" *Modern Philology* 76:111–35.

————. 1980. "The Cecelia Legend as Chaucer Inherited It and Retold It: The Disappearance of an Augustinian Ideal." *Speculum* 55:38–57.

————. 1990. "A Recent Discovery Concerning the Sources of Chaucer's 'Second Nun's Tale.'" *Modern Philology* 87:337–61.

Rhodes, J. 1994. "The Dreamer Redeemed: Exile and the Kingdom in the Middle English *Pearl.*" *Studies in the Age of Chaucer* 16:119–42.

Richardson, H. G. 1936. "Heresy and the Lay Power under Richard II." *English Historical Review* 51:1–28.

————. 1960. "The Coronation in Medieval England: The Evolution of the Office and the Oath." *Traditio* 16:111–203.

Richardson, H. G., and G. O. Sayles. 1981. *The English Parliament in the Middle Ages.* London: Hambledon.

Ricoeur, P. 1984. *The Reality of the Historical Past.* Milwaukee: Marquette University Press.

Riddy, F. 1993. "'Women Talking About the Things of God': A Late Medieval Sub-Culture." In *Women and Literature in Britain, 1150–1500,* edited by C. M. Meale, 104–17. Cambridge: Cambridge University Press.

Ridley, F. H. 1987. "Explanatory Notes to *The Second Nun's Prologue and Tale.*" In *The Riverside Chaucer,* edited by L. D. Benson, general editor. Boston: Houghton Mifflin.

Riehle, W. 1981. *The Middle English Mystics*. Translated by B. Standring. London: Routledge and Kegan Paul.

Riley, D. 1988. *"Am I That Name?" Feminism and the Category of "Women" in History*. London: MacMillan.

Ringbom, S. 1965. *Icon to Narrative: The Rise of the Dramatic Close-Up in Fifteenth-Century Devotional Painting*. Abo: Abo Akademi.

Robertson, D. W., Jr. 1968. *Chaucer's London*. New York: John Wiley and Sons.

———. 1985. "The Probable Date and Purpose of Chaucer's *Troilus*." *Medievalia et Humanistica*, n.s., 13:143–71.

Robertson, E. 1993. "Medieval Medical Views of Women and Female Spirituality in the *Ancrene Wisse* and Julian of Norwich's *Showings*." In *Feminist Approaches to the Body in Medieval Literature*, edited by L. Lomperis and S. Stanbury, 142–67. Philadelphia: University of Pennsylvania Press.

Rosenberg, B. 1968. "The Contrary Tales of the Second Nun and the Canon's Yeoman." *Chaucer Review* 2:278–91.

Rosenthal, J. T. 1972. *The Purchase of Paradise: Gift Giving and the Aristocracy, 1307–1485*. London: Routledge and Kegan Paul.

Roskell, J. S. 1968. *The Commons and Their Speakers in English Parliaments, 1376–1523*. 2 vols. Manchester: Manchester University Press.

Rowland, B. 1971. *Blind Beasts: Chaucer's Animal World*. Kent: Kent State University Press.

Rubin, M. 1991. *Corpus Christi: The Eucharist in Late Medieval Culture*. Cambridge: Cambridge University Press.

———. 1992. "The Eucharist and the Construction of Medieval Identities." In *Culture and History, 1350–1600*, edited by D. Aers, chap. 2. Hemel Hempstead: Harvester Wheatsheaf.

———. 1994. "The Person in the Form: Medieval Challenges to Bodily 'Order.'" In *Framing Medieval Bodies*, edited by S. Kay and M. Rubin, chap. 5. Manchester: Manchester University Press.

Ruggiers, P. G. 1979. "Serious Chaucer: The *Tale of Melibeus* and the *Parson's Tale*." In *Chaucerian Problems and Perspectives: Essays Presented to Paul E. Beichner, C.S.C.*, edited by E.d Vasta and Z. P. Thundy, 83–94. Notre Dame: University of Notre Dame Press.

Ryan, M. 1982. *Marxism and Deconstruction*. Baltimore: Johns Hopkins University Press.

Salter, E. 1962a. *The Knight's Tale and the Clerk's Tale*. London: Edward Arnold.

———. 1962b. *Piers Plowman: An Introduction*. Oxford: Blackwell.

———. [as Zeeman]. 1969. "*Piers Plowman* and the Pilgrimage to Truth." In *Style and Substance in Piers Plowman*, edited by R. J. Blanch, chap. 6. Knoxville: University of Tennessee Press.

———. 1974. *Nicholas Love's "Myrrour of the Blessed Lyf of Jesu Christ."* Salzburg: Salzburg University Press.

———. 1983. *Fourteenth-Century English Poetry*. Oxford: Clarendon Press.

———. 1988. *English and International: Studies in the Literature, Art, and Patronage of Medieval England*. Cambridge: Cambridge University Press.

Scanlon, L. 1994. *Narrative, Authority, and Power: The Medieval Exemplum and the Chaucerian Tradition*. Cambridge: Cambridge University Press.

Scase, W. 1989. *"Piers Plowman" and the New Anticlericalism*. Cambridge: Cambridge University Press.

Scattergood, V. J. 1981. "Chaucer and the French War: *Sir Thopas* and *Melibee*." In *Court and Poet: Selected Proceedings of the Third Congress of the International Courtly Literature Society*, edited by G. S. Burgess, 287–96. Liverpool: Francis Cairns.

———. 1987. "Chaucer in the Suburbs." In *Medieval Literature and Antiquities": Studies in Honour of Basil Cottle*, edited by M. Stokes and T. L. Burton, 145–62. Cambridge: Brewer.

Schama, S. 1989. *Citizen: A Chronicle of the French Revolution*. New York: Knopf.

Schibanoff, Susan. 1988. "The New Reader and Female Textuality in Two Early Commentaries on Chaucer." *Studies in the Age of Chaucer* 10:71–108.

Schillebeeckx, E. 1979. *Jesus: An Experiment in Christology*. Translated by H. Hoskins. New York: Seabury.

———. 1987. *Jesus in Our Western Culture*. Translated by J. Bowden. London: SCM Press.

———. 1990. *Christ: The Experience of Jesus as Lord*. Translated by J. Bowden. New York: Crossroad.

Schiller, G. 1972. *Iconography and Christian Art*. Vol. 2, *The Passion of Jesus Christ*. London: Lund Humphries.

Schlauch, M. 1945. "Chaucer's Doctrine of Kings and Tyrants." *Speculum* 20:133–56.

Schramm, P. E. 1937. *A History of the English Coronation*. Oxford: Clarendon Press.

Schussler-Fiorenza, E. 1983. *In Memory of Her*. New York: Crossroads.

Schweitzer, E. C. 1986. "The Misdirected Kiss and the Lover's Malady in Chaucer's *Miller's Tale*." In *Chaucer in the Eighties*, edited by J. Wasserman and R. J. Blanch, 223–33. Syracuse: Syracuse University Press.

Scott, J. W. 1988. *Gender and the Politics of History*. New York: Columbia University Press.

———. 1992. "Experience." In *Feminists Theorize the Political*, edited by J. B. and J. W. Scott, 22–40. New York: Routledge.

Searle, E., and R. Burghart. 1972. "The Defense of England and the Peasants' Revolt." *Viator* 3:365–88.

Segundo, J. L. 1985. *Jesus of Nàzareth Yesterday and Today*. New York: Orbis.

Simpson, J. 1990a. "The Constraints of Satire in 'Piers Plowman' and 'Mum and the Sothsegger.'" In *Langland, the Mystics and the Medieval English Religious Tradition*, edited by H. Phillips, 11–30. Cambridge: Brewer.

———. 1990b. *Piers Plowman: An Introduction to the B-Text*. London: Longman.

Sinanoglou, L. 1973. "The Christ Child as Sacrifice: a Medieval Tradition and the Corpus Christi Plays." *Speculum* 48:491–509.

Skinner, Q. 1978. *The Foundations of Modern Political Thought*. 2 vols. Cambridge: Cambridge University Press.

————. 1988. *Meaning and Context: Quentin Skinner and his Critics.* Edited by J. Tully. Cambridge: Polity Press.

Smith, B. H. 1966. *Traditional Imagery of Charity in Piers Plowman.* The Hague: Mouton.

————. *Contingencies of Value.* Cambridge; Harvard University Press.

Southern, R. W. 1953. *The Making of the Middle Ages.* London: Hutchinson.

Spearing, A. C. 1985. *Medieval to Renaissance in English Poetry.* London: Cambridge University Press.

————. 1993. *The Medieval Poet as Voyeur: Looking and Listening in Medieval Love-Narratives.* Cambridge: Cambridge University Press.

Staley, L. *See also* Johnson, L. Staley.

Staley, L. 1994. *Margery Kempe's Dissenting Fictions.* University Park: Pennsylvania State University Press.

Stanbury, S. 1991. *Seeing the "Gawain"-Poet: Description and the Act of Perception.* Philadelphia: University of Pennsylvania Press.

Steinberg, L. 1984. *The Sexuality of Christ in Renaissance Art and in Modern Oblivion.* London: Faber.

Steinberg, T. L. 1991. *Piers Plowman and Prophecy: An Approach to the C-Text.* New York: Garland.

Stillwell, G. 1944. "The Political Meaning of Chaucer's *Tale of Melibee.*" *Speculum* 19:433–44.

Stock, B. 1983. *The Implications of Literacy: Written Language and Models of Interpretation in the Eleventh and Twelfth Century.* Princeton: Princeton University Press.

————. 1990. *Listening for the Text: On the Uses of the Past.* Baltimore: Johns Hopkins University Press.

Stokes, M. 1984. *Justice and Mercy in Piers Plowman.* Beckenham: Croom Helm.

Storey, R. L. 1971. "Liveries and Commissions of the Peace, 1388–90." In *The Reign of Richard II: Essays in Honour of May McKisack,* edited by F. R. H. DuBoulay and C. M. Barron, 131–52. London: Athlone.

Strauss, B. R. 1988. "The Subversive Discourse of the Wife of Bath: Phallocentric Discourse and the Imprisonment of Criticism." *ELH* 55:527–54.

Strohm, P. 1979. "Form and Social Statement in *Confessio Amantis* and *The Canterbury Tales.*" *Studies in the Age of Chaucer* 1:17–40.

————. 1989. *Social Chaucer.* Cambridge: Harvard University Press.

————. 1992. *Hochon's Arrow: The Social Imagination of Fourteenth-Century Texts.* Princeton: Princeton University Press.

Suggett, H. 1947. "A Letter Describing Richard II's Reconciliation with the City of London, 1392." *English Historical Review* 62:209–13.

Swanson, H. 1989. *Medieval Artisans.* Oxford: Blackwell.

Tanner, N. P. 1984. *The Church in Late Medieval Norwich, 1370–1532.* Toronto: Pontifical Institute of Mediaeval Studies.

Taylor, J. 1968. "The Manuscripts of the 'Modus Tenendi Parliamentum.'" *English Historical Review* 83:673–88.

————. 1971. "Richard II's Views on Kingship." *Leeds Philosophical and Literary Society: Proceedings* 14:189–205.

Tentler, T. N. 1977. *Sin and Confession on the Eve of the Reformation*. Princeton: Princeton University Press.

Thomson, J. A. F. 1965. *The Later Lollards, 1414–1520*. Oxford: Oxford University Press.

———. 1989. "Orthodox Religion and the Origins of Lollardy." *History* 74:39–55.

Thrupp, S. L. 1989. *The Merchant Class of Medieval London, 1300–1500*. Ann Arbor: University of Michigan Press. 1948, 1989.

Tout, T. F. 1970. "The English Parliament and Public Opinion, 1376–88." In *Historical Studies of the English Parliament*, edited by E. B. Fryde and E. Miller, 299–316. Cambridge; Cambridge University Press.

Tracy, D. 1981. *The Analogical Imagination: Christian Theology and the Culture of Pluralism*. London: SCM Press.

Travis, P. 1982. *Dramatic Design in the Chester Cycle*. Chicago: University of Chicago Press.

Tuck, A. 1973. *Richard II and the English Nobility*. London: Edward Arnold.

———. 1985. *Crown and Nobility, 1272–1461: Political Conflict in Late Medieval England*. Totowa, N.J.: Barnes and Noble.

Tuck, J. A. 1984a. "Carthusian Monks and Lollard Knights: Religious Attitudes at the Court of Richard II." *Studies in the Age of Chaucer. Proceedings* 1:149–61.

———. 1984b. "Nobles, Commons and the Great Revolt of 1381." In *The English Rising of 1381*, edited by R. H. Hilton and T. H. Aston, 194–212. Cambridge: Cambridge University Press.

Vauchez, A. 1981. *La Sainteté en Occident aux Derniers Siècles du Moyen Age*. Rome: Ecole Française de Rome.

Vitto, C. L. 1989. "The Virtuous Pagan in Middle English Literature." *Transactions of the American Philosophical Society* 79:60–89.

Volosinov, V. N. 1986. *Marxism and the Philosophy of Language*. London: Seminar Press, 1973; repr. Cambridge: Harvard University Press.

Waldron, R. A. 1986. "Langland's Originality: The Christ-Knight and the Harrowing of Hell." In *Medieval English Religious and Ethical Literature*, edited by G. Kratzman and J. Simpson, 66–81. Cambridge: Brewer.

Walker, S. 1990. *The Lancastrian Affinity, 1361–1399*. Oxford: Clarendon Press.

Wallace, D. 1990. "'When She Translated Was': A Chaucerian Critique of the Petrarchan Academy." In *Literary Practice and Social Change in Britain, 1380–1530*, edited by L. Patterson, 156–215. Berkeley and Los Angeles: University of California Press.

———. 1991. "Writing the Tyrant's Death: Chaucer, Bernabò Visconti and Richard II." In *Poetics: Theory and Practice in Medieval English Literature*, edited by P. Boitani and A. Torti, 117–30. Cambridge: Brewer.

———. 1992. "Chaucer and the Absent City." In *Chaucer's England: Literature in Historical Context*, edited by B. A. Hanawalt, 59–90. Minneapolis: University of Minnesota Press.

———. Forthcoming. *Chaucer and Polity*. Stanford: Stanford University Press.

[Ward], Sister Benedicta. 1988. "Julian the Solitary." In *Julian Reconsidered*, by K. Leech and Benedicta Ward, 11–35. Oxford: SLG Press.

Watson, N. 1991. *Richard Rolle and the Invention of Authority*. Cambridge: Cambridge University Press.

———. 1992. "The Trinitarian Hermeneutic in Julian of Norwich's *Revelation of Love*." In *The Medieval Mystical Tradition in England*, Exeter Symposium V, edited by M. Glasscoe, 79–100. Cambridge: Brewer.

———. 1993. "The Composition of Julian of Norwich's *Revelation of Divine Love*." *Speculum* 68:637–83.

———. 1995. "Censorship and Cultural Change in Late Medieval England: Vernacular Theology, the Oxford Translation Debate and Arundel's *Constitutions*." *Speculum* 70:822–65.

———. Forthcoming. "The Middle English Mystics." In *The Cambridge History of Medieval Literature*, edited by D. Wallace, Cambridge: Cambridge University Press.

Waugh, S. L. 1991. *England in the Reign of Edward III*. Cambridge: Cambridge University Press.

Weldon, J. F. G. 1989. "Gesture of Perception: The Pattern of Kneeling in *Piers Plowman*." *Yearbook of Langland Studies* 3:49–66.

Wetherbee, W. 1989a. *The Canterbury Tales*. Cambridge: Cambridge University Press.

———. 1989b. "Constance and the World in Chaucer and Gower." In *John Gower: Recent Readings*, edited by R. F. Yeager, 65–93. Kalamazoo: Western Michigan University.

Whatley, G. 1984. "The Uses of Hagiography: The Legend of Pope Gregory and the Emperor Trajan in the Middle Ages." *Viator* 15:25–63.

White, H. 1988. *Nature and Salvation in Piers Plowman*. Cambridge: Brewer.

Wickham, G. 1959. *Early English Stages, 1300 to 1576*. London: Routledge and Kegan Paul.

Wiethaus, U. 1991. "Sexuality, Gender and the Body in Late Medieval Women's Spirituality." *Journal of Feminist Studies in Religion* 7:35–52.

———. 1993. *Maps of Flesh and Light*. Syracuse: Syracuse University Press.

Wilks, M. 1962. "Chaucer and the Mystical Marriage in Medieval Political Thought." *Bulletin of the John Rylands Library* 44:489–530.

———. 1972. "*Reformatio Regni*: Wyclif and Hus as Leaders of Religious Protest Movements." *Studies in Church History* 9:109–30.

———. 1994. "Wyclif and the Great Persecution." In *Prophecy and Eschatology*, edited by M. Wilks, 39–64. Oxford: Basil Blackwell.

Williamson, J. B. 1985. "Philippe de Mézière's Book for Married Ladies: A Book from the Entourage of the Court of Charles VI." In *The Spirit of the Court*, edited by G. S. Burgess and R. A. Taylor, 393–408. Cambridge: Brewer.

Wilson, E. 1973. *A Descriptive Index of the English Lyrics in John of Grimestone's Preaching Book*. Medium Ævum Monographs, n.s., 11. Oxford: Basil Blackwell.

Windeatt, B. A. 1977. "Julian of Norwich and Her Audience." *Review of English Studies* 28:1–17.

Withington, R. 1918. *English Pageantry*. 2 vols. Cambridge: Harvard University Press.

Wittgenstein, L. 1958. *Philosophical Investigations.* 2d ed. Translated by G. E. M. Anscombe. Oxford: Blackwell.

Wittig, J. 1972. *"Piers Plowman B,* Passus IX–XII: Elements in the Design of the Inward Journey." *Traditio* 28:211–80.

Woolf, R. 1968. *English Religious Lyric in the Middle Ages.* Oxford: Clarendon Press.

Yeager, R. F. 1987. *"Pax Poetica:* On the Pacifism of Chaucer and Gower." *Studies in the Age of Chaucer* 9:97–122.

———. 1990. *John Gower's Poetic: The Search for a New Arion.* Woodbridge, Suffolk; Rochester, N.Y.: Brewer.

Yunck, J. A. 1963. *The Lineage of Lady Meed.* Notre Dame: University of Notre Dame Press.

Zeeman [Salter], E. 1958. "Piers Plowman and the Pilgrimage to Truth." *Essays and Studies* 11:1–16.

———. 1969. "Piers Plowman and the Pilgrimage to Truth." In *Style and Symbolism in Piers Plowman,* edited by R. J. Blanch, chap. 6. Knoxville: University of Tennessee Press. Reprint of Zeeman (1958).

Zika, C. 1988. "Hosts, Processions and Pilgrimages in Fifteenth-Century Germany." *Past and Present* 118:25–64.

Zizek, S. 1989. *The Sublime Object of Ideology.* London: Verso.

Index